INTRODUCTION TO
LOGIC

IRVING M. COPI

Associate Professor of Philosophy
University of Michigan

3259

THE MACMILLAN COMPANY, New York

INTRODUCTION TO LOGIC

THE MACMILLAN COMPANY
NEW YORK · CHICAGO
DALLAS · ATLANTA · SAN FRANCISCO

**THE MACMILLAN COMPANY
OF CANADA, LIMITED**
TORONTO

*This book is dedicated to
my mother and father*

Preface

(primarily for teachers)

The past few years have seen the publication of a considerable number of elementary textbooks of logic. Hence any writer who adds still another to that list can reasonably be expected to explain his action. The obvious motivation is to provide a more useful instrument for the teaching of his subject. Any explanation, then, must inevitably focus attention on those novel aspects of the new book which—it is hoped—make it more useful.

In Part One, which is devoted to language, a modern discussion of the different functions of language is presented and is used in explaining the misleading character of certain informal fallacies. The treatment of definition is more comprehensive than that usually included in an elementary text and has the advantage of being separated from the topic of classification, which is more fruitfully discussed in connection with inductive logic.

Part Two, which deals with deductive logic, begins with three chapters, along fairly traditional lines, on immediate inference, the categorical syllogism, enthymemes, sorites, and dilemmas. Besides a discussion of rules and fallacies, the Venn diagram technique for testing categorical syllogisms is presented. That technique is far superior to the Euler diagrams which still occur in some textbooks. A more systematic treatment than usual is given to the problem of translating categorical syllogisms from ordinary language into the standard forms to which the usual testing methods are applicable. This is in line with the writer's intention of stressing the *usefulness* of logic.

Part Two also contains three chapters on symbolic logic, in which its *use* in evaluating arguments is stressed. The material presented here includes not only truth tables and the method of formal proof by deduction, but also convenient methods of proving invalidity and enough theory of quantification to permit the symbolic treatment of categorical syllogisms and even some asyllogistic but non-relational arguments. The method of introducing material implication is one which the writer has found in actual teaching to succeed better than any other in avoiding the strangeness and artificiality which too often attach to that notion for the student.

Part Three, on inductive logic, begins with a more systematic treatment of argument by analogy than is usually accorded this frequently used and important type of inductive argument. Mill's Methods are explained and illustrated *before* being criticized, and they are defended as fundamental to the method of controlled experiment. In the separate chapter accorded to hypothesis as the method of science, the usually isolated topic of classification is incorporated as another example of the pervasive method of hypothesis. The final chapter on probability includes an elementary treatment of the important topic of expectation, which is too often omitted.

A considerable number of exercises are included to help the student acquire a *working knowledge* of the various topics covered. Since most elementary logic courses are scheduled for one semester only, it is expected that not all the topics of the present book will be covered in the average course. A judicious selection from among those topics, however, will adapt the book to almost any one-semester course which attempts to cover more than formal logic alone. Some teachers may prefer not to include any symbolic logic in their introductory course, and for their convenience an informal treatment of the dilemma is included along with enthymemes and sorites in Chapter Seven. Those who wish to cover some symbolic logic in addition to the more traditional material may find it profitable to delay assigning Section VI of Chapter Seven (The Dilemma) until after truth tables have been developed in Chapter Eight.

The writer wishes to thank many friends, both colleagues and former students, for many helpful suggestions. He is particularly indebted to Professor A. W. Burks, of the University of Michigan, and Professor A. Kaplan, of the University of California at Los Angeles, both of whom read early drafts and made very valuable criticisms and suggestions. Special thanks are also due to Mr. D. B. Terrell, of the University of Minnesota, who read and criticized an early portion of the manuscript, and Mr. R. Workman, of the University of Michigan, who read the final version. The writer's indebtedness to other writers, from whose books he has taught logic, on and off, since 1939, is too great and too pervasive to permit detailed acknowledgment.

Acknowledgments

The following authors and publishers have kindly allowed the use of quotations from the publications cited.

Allen and Unwin, Ltd.: *Sceptical Essays,* by Bertrand Russell.

Appleton-Century-Crofts, Inc.: *Smith's College Chemistry,* by James Kendall.

Jonathan Cape Limited: *Hunger Fighters,* by Paul de Kruif.

Doubleday and Company, Inc.: *Clarence Darrow for the Defense,* by Irving Stone.

Harcourt, Brace and Company, Inc.: *The Autobiography of Lincoln Steffens,* by Lincoln Steffens, *Microbe Hunters,* by Paul de Kruif, and *Hunger Fighters,* by Paul de Kruif.

Harper and Brothers, Publishers: *General College Physics,* by Randall, Williams, and Colby, and *The Proper Study of Mankind,* by Stuart Chase.

Paul Henle and W. K. Frankena: *Exercises in Elementary Logic.*

The editor of *The Journal of the American Medical Association:* Quotations from two articles.

The editor of *The Journal of Psychology:* Quotations from one article.

Alfred A. Knopf, Inc.: *Selected Prejudices,* by H. L. Mencken, and *Testament of a Critic,* by George Jean Nathan.

Little, Brown and Company: *Wigmore's Code of the Rules of Evidence in Trials at Law,* by John Wigmore.

Longmans, Green and Company, Inc.: *Pragmatism,* by William James.

The Macmillan Company: *Art of Cross Examination,* by F. L. Wellman.

McGraw-Hill Book Company, Inc.: *A Source Book in Physics,* by William Francis Magie, *The Elements of Astronomy,* by Edward Arthur Fath, and *Introduction to Modern Physics,* by F. K. Richtmyer.

The editor of *Nature:* Quotations from one article.

The editor of *The New Yorker:* Two quotations from one issue.

W. W. Norton and Company, Inc.: *Sceptical Essays,* by Bertrand Russell.

Oxford University Press: *An Introduction to Logic,* by H. W. B. Joseph.

W. B. Saunders Company: *Psychoanalysis: Its Theories and Practical Applications,* by Dr. A. A. Brill.

The editor of *Science:* Quotations from two articles.

The editor of *Science Digest:* Quotations from one article.

The editor of *Scientific American:* Quotations from six articles.

The editor of *The Scientific Monthly:* Quotations from one article.

Simon and Schuster, Inc.: *How to Think Straight,* by Robert H. Thouless, and *Outposts of Science,* by Bernard Jaffe.

The Viking Press, Inc.: *The Gift of Tongues,* by Margaret Schlauch.

John Wiley and Sons, Publishers: *Cybernetics,* by Norbert Wiener.

Direct quotations and use of the literary material from the works of Sir Arthur Conan Doyle have been made by special permission of the Estate of Sir Arthur Conan Doyle.

Full references to the sources of the quotations will be found in the places of their occurrence in the text.

Contents

PART TWO. DEDUCTION

Contents

PART ONE

Language

CHAPTER ONE

Introduction

I. WHAT IS LOGIC?

The words "logic" and "logical" are familiar to all of us. We often speak of "logical" behavior as contrasted with "illogical" behavior, a "logical" procedure as contrasted with an "illogical" one, a "logical" explanation, a "logical" mind, and the like. In all such cases the word "logical" is used in very much the same sense as "reasonable." A person with a "logical" mind is a "reasonable" person; an "unreasonable" procedure is one that is "illogical." All these uses can be regarded as deriving from a more technical use of the terms "logical" and "illogical" to characterize arguments. The connection will become increasingly clear as the student reads further and increases his knowledge of the subject.

Of course, really to understand what logic is, one must study logic. In a sense this entire book is an extended explanation of logic. But the student will be helped in his reading of it if he is given a preliminary explanation of what to expect. He must be warned, however, that only a rough and approximate explanation of logic will be attempted in the present chapter.

The study of logic is the study of the methods and principles used in distinguishing correct from incorrect argument. This definition is not intended to imply, of course, that one can argue correctly only if he has studied logic. To say so would be as much a mistake as to claim that one can run well only if he has studied the physics and physiology involved in describing that activity. Some excellent athletes are quite ignorant of the complex processes that go on inside themselves when they perform. And, needless to say, the somewhat elderly professors who know most about such things would perform very poorly were they to risk their dignity on the athletic field. Even given the same basic muscular and nervous apparatus, the person who knows might not surpass the "natural athlete."

But given the same native keenness of intellect, the person who has studied logic is more likely to argue correctly than one who has never considered the general principles involved in that activity. There are several reasons for this. First of all, the proper study of logic will approach it as an art as well as a science, and the student will do exercises in all parts of the theory being learned. Here, as anywhere else, practice will help to make perfect. In the second place, a traditional part of the study of logic has been the examination and analysis of incorrect methods of argument, or fallacies. Not only does this part of the subject give increased insight into the principles of argument in general, but an acquaintance with these pitfalls definitely helps us avoid falling into them. And finally, the study of logic will give the student certain techniques, certain easily applied methods for testing the correctness of all arguments, including his own. This knowledge is of value because when mistakes are easily detected they are less likely to be made.

Logic has frequently been defined as the science of the laws of thought. But this definition, although it gives a clue to the nature of logic, is not accurate. In the first place, thinking is one of the processes studied by psychologists. Logic cannot be "the" science of the laws of thought, because psychology is also a science which deals with the laws of thought (among other things) .

And logic is not a branch of psychology; it is a separate and distinct field of study.

In the second place, if "thought" is any mental process that occurs in people's minds, not all thought is an object of study for the logician. All reasoning is thinking, but not all thinking is reasoning. Thus one may "think" of a number between one and ten, as in a parlor game, without doing any "reasoning" about it. There are many mental processes or kinds of thought that are different from reasoning. One may remember something, or imagine it, or regret it, without doing any *reasoning* about it. Or one may let his thoughts "drift along" in a day-dream or reverie, building castles in the air, or following what psychologists call "free association," where one image is replaced by another in an order that is anything but logical. There is often great significance to the sequence of thoughts in such free association, and some psychiatric techniques are based upon that significance. One need not be a psychiatrist, of course, to gain insight into a person's character by observing the flow of his stream of consciousness. It is the basis of a very effective literary technique, pioneered by James Joyce in his novel *Ulysses*. Conversely, if a person's character is sufficiently well-known beforehand, the course of his stream of consciousness can be traced or even anticipated. We all remember how Sherlock Holmes used to break in on his friend Watson's silences, to answer the very question to which Dr. Watson had been "led" in his musings. There seem to be certain laws governing reverie, but they are not the sort that have traditionally been studied by logicians. They are more properly to be studied by psychologists; and the laws which describe the mind's progressions in reverie are psychological laws rather than logical principles. To define logic as the science of the laws of thought is to make it include too much.

Another common definition of logic is that it is the science of reasoning. This definition avoids the second objection, but it still will not do. Reasoning is a special kind of thinking, in which inference takes place or in which conclusions are drawn from premises. But it is still thought and therefore still part of the psychologist's subject matter. As psychologists examine the reasoning process they find it to be extremely complex, highly emotional, consisting of awkward trial and error procedures illuminated by sudden—and sometimes apparently irrelevant—flashes of insight. These are all of importance to psychology. But the logician is not in the least concerned with the dark ways by which the mind arrives at its conclusions during the actual processes of reasoning. He is concerned only with the *correctness* of the completed process. His question is always: does the conclusion reached *follow* from the premises used or assumed? If the conclusion does follow from the premises, that is, if the premises constitute grounds or good evidence for the conclusion, so that asserting the premises to be true warrants asserting the conclusion to be true also, then the reasoning is correct. Otherwise it is incorrect. The distinction between correct and incorrect reasoning is the central problem with which logic deals. The logician's methods and techniques have been developed primarily for the purpose of making this distinction clear. The logician is interested in all reasoning, regardless of its subject matter, but only from this special point of view.

II. SOME TECHNICAL TERMS

To clarify the explanation of logic proposed in the preceding section, it will help to set forth and discuss some of the special terms which the logician uses in his work. Inference has been characterized as a process in which one proposition is arrived at and affirmed on the basis of one or more other propositions, which were accepted as the starting point of the process. The logician is not concerned with the *process* of inference, but with the propositions which constitute the initial and end points of that process, and the relationships between them.

Propositions are either true or false, and in this they differ from questions, commands, and exclamations. Only propositions can be either affirmed or denied: questions may be *asked* and commands *given* and exclamations *uttered,* but none of them can be affirmed or denied, or judged to be either true or false. The formulations in language of propositions, questions, commands, and exclamations are divided by grammar into declarative, interrogative, imperative, and exclamatory sentences. These are familiar notions.

It is necessary to distinguish between declarative sentences and their meanings. Two declarative sentences, which are clearly two because they consist of different words differently arranged, may have the same meaning. For example:

> John loves Mary.
> Mary is loved by John.

are two different sentences, for the first contains three words, whereas the second contains five, the first begins with the word "John," whereas the second begins with the word "Mary," and so on. Yet the two sentences have exactly the same meaning. It is customary to use the word "proposition" to denote the *meaning* of a declarative sentence.

The difference between sentences and propositions is brought out by remarking that a declarative sentence is always a part of a language, the language in which it is enunciated, whereas propositions are not peculiar to any of the languages in which they may be formulated. The three statements:

> It is raining.
> Il pleut.
> Es regnet.

are certainly different, for the first is in English, the second in French, the third in German. Yet they have but a single meaning, and this common meaning is the *proposition* of which each of them is a different formulation. The logician is interested in propositions rather than in the sentences which formulate them.

Although the *process* of inference is not of interest to logicians, corresponding to every possible inference is an *argument*, and it is with these arguments that logic is chiefly concerned.

An argument, in this sense, is any group of propositions of which one is claimed to follow from the others, which are regarded as providing evidence for the truth of that one. Of course the word "argument" is often used to refer to the process itself, but in logic it has the technical sense explained. An argument is not a mere collection of propositions, but has a structure. In describing this structure, the terms "premiss" and "conclusion" are usually employed. The *conclusion* of an argument is that proposition which is affirmed on the basis of the other propositions of the argument, and these other propositions which are affirmed as providing evidence or reasons for accepting the conclusion are the *premisses* of that argument.

It should be noted that "premiss" and "conclusion" are relative terms: one and the same proposition can be a premiss of one argument and a conclusion in another. Consider, for example, the following argument:

No act performed involuntarily should be punished.
Some criminal acts are performed involuntarily.
Therefore some criminal acts should not be punished.

Here the proposition *some criminal acts should not be punished* is the conclusion, and the other two propositions are the premisses. But the first premiss in this argument, *no acts performed involuntarily should be punished,* is the conclusion in the following (different) argument:

No act beyond the control of the agent should be punished.
All involuntary acts are beyond the control of the agent.
Therefore no act performed involuntarily should be punished.

No proposition, taken all by itself, in isolation, is either a premiss or a conclusion. It is a premiss only when it occurs in an argument which assumes it for the sake of showing that some other proposition is thereby justified. And it is a conclusion only when it occurs in an argument which attempts to establish or prove it on the basis of other propositions which are assumed. This notion is common enough: it is like the fact that a man, taken by himself, is neither an employer nor an employee, but may be either in different contexts, employer to his gardener, employee of the firm for which he works.

Arguments are traditionally divided into two different types, *deductive* and *inductive*. While every argument involves the claim that its premisses provide evidence for the truth of its conclusion, only a *deductive* argument claims that its premisses provide *conclusive* evidence. In the case of deductive arguments the technical terms "valid" and "invalid" are used in place of "correct" and "incorrect." A deductive argument is *valid* when its premisses do provide conclusive evidence for its conclusion, that is, when premisses and conclusion are so related that it is absolutely impossible for the premisses to be true unless the conclusion is true also. Every deductive argument is either valid or invalid, and the task of deductive logic is to clarify the nature of the relationship which holds between premisses and conclusion in a valid argument, and thus to allow us to discriminate between valid and invalid arguments. The theory of deduction, including both traditional and symbolic logic, occupies Part Two of this book.

An inductive argument, on the other hand, does not claim that its premisses give conclusive evidence for the truth of its conclusion, but only that they provide *some* evidence for it. Inductive arguments are neither *valid* nor *invalid* in the sense in which those terms are applied to deductive arguments. Inductive arguments may, of course, be evaluated as better or worse, according to the degree of likelihood or probability which their premisses confer upon their conclusions. Our discussion of probability and the theory of induction is presented in Part Three.

Truth and falsehood may be predicated of propositions, but never of arguments. And the properties of validity and invalidity can belong only to deductive arguments, never to propositions. There is a connection between the validity or invalidity of an argument and the truth or falsehood of its premisses and conclusion, but this connection is by no means a simple one.

Some valid arguments contain only true propositions, as, for example:

> All whales are mammals.
> All mammals have lungs.
> Therefore all whales have lungs.

But an argument may contain false propositions exclusively, and be valid nevertheless, as, for example:

> All spiders have six legs.
> All six legged creatures have wings.
> Therefore all spiders have wings.

This argument is valid because *if* its premisses were true its conclusion would have to be true also, even though in fact they are all false. On the other hand, if we reflect upon the argument:

If I owned all the gold in Fort Knox, then I would be very wealthy.
I do not own all the gold in Fort Knox.
Therefore I am not very wealthy.

we see that although its premisses and conclusion are true, the argument is invalid. That the premisses *could* be true and the conclusion false, if not immediately apparent, may be made clear by considering that if I were to inherit a million dollars, the premisses would remain true while the conclusion would become false. This point is further illustrated by the following argument, which is of the same form as the preceding one:

If Rockefeller owned all the gold in Fort Knox, then Rockefeller would be very wealthy.
Rockefeller does not own all the gold in Fort Knox.
Therefore Rockefeller is not very wealthy.

The premisses of this argument are true, and its conclusion is false. Such an argument cannot be valid, because it is impossible for the premisses of a valid argument to be true while its conclusion is false.

The preceding examples show that there are valid arguments with false conclusions, as well as invalid arguments with true conclusions. Hence the truth or falsehood of its conclusion does not determine the validity or invalidity of an argument. Nor does the validity of an argument guarantee the truth of its conclusion. There are perfectly valid arguments which have false conclusions—but any such argument must have at least one false premiss. The term "sound" is introduced to characterize a valid argument all of whose premisses are true. Clearly the conclusion of a *sound* argument is true. A deductive argument fails to establish the truth of its conclusion if it is *unsound,* which means either that it is not *valid,* or that not all of its premisses are *true.* To test the truth or falsehood of premisses is the task of science in general, since premisses may deal with any subject matter at all. The logician is not so much interested in the truth or falsehood of propositions as in the logical relations between them, where by the "logical" relations between propositions we mean those which determine the correctness or incorrectness of arguments in which they may occur. Determining the correctness or incorrectness of arguments falls squarely within the province of logic. The logician is interested in the correctness even of arguments whose premisses might be false.

A question might be raised about the value of this last point. It might be suggested that we ought to confine ourselves to arguments which have true premisses, ignoring all others. But as a matter of fact we *are* interested in, and must often depend upon, the correctness of arguments whose premisses are not known to be true. Examples of such situations suggest themselves readily. When a scientist is interested in verifying his theories by deducing testable consequences from them, he does not know beforehand which are true. If he did, there would be no need for verification. In our everyday affairs, we are often confronted with alternative courses of action. Where these courses are genuine alternatives which cannot both be adopted, we may try to reason about which should be chosen. Such reasoning generally takes the form of figuring out the consequences of each of the different actions between which we must choose. One might argue: suppose I choose the first alternative, then such and such will be the case. On the other hand, assuming that I choose the second alternative, then something else will follow. In general, we are inclined to choose between alternative courses of action on the basis of which set of consequences we prefer to have realized. In each case, we are interested in arguing correctly, lest we deceive ourselves. Were we interested only in arguments which have true premisses, we should not know which line of argument to consider until we knew which of the alternative premisses was true. And if we knew which premiss was true, we should not be interested in the argument at all, because our purpose in considering the arguments was to help us decide *which* alternative premiss to *make* true. To confine our attention to arguments with true premisses alone would be self-defeating and stultifying.

So far we have been speaking only about propositions and the arguments which contain them as premisses and conclusion. As has been explained, these are not linguistic entities such as sentences, but rather the *meanings* of sentences. Whether the actual process of thinking or reasoning requires language or not is an open question. It may be that thinking requires the use of symbols of some sort, words or images or what not. We all feel a certain sympathy with the girl who was told to think before she spoke, and replied, "But how can I know what I think until I hear what I say?" Perhaps all thinking does require words or some other kind of symbols, but that is not a question that concerns us here. We know, however, that the *communication* of any proposition or any argument requires symbols, and can be accomplished only by the use of language.

The use of language, however, complicates our problem. Certain accidental or misleading features of their formulations in language may make more difficult the task of investigating the logical relations between propositions. It is part of the task of the logician, therefore, to examine language itself, primarily from the point of view of discovering and describing those aspects of it which tend to obscure the difference between correct and incorrect argument. It is for this reason that **Part One** of this book is devoted to language.

EXERCISES

Which of the following passages express arguments? If arguments are present, indicate the premises and conclusions.

1. There is now less flogging in our great schools than formerly
   —but then less is learned there; so that what the boys get at
   one end they lose at the other.

   (Boswell, *Life of Johnson*)

2. Ay, knave, because thou strikest as a knight,
   Being but knave, I hate thee all the more.

   (Tennyson, *Gareth and Lynette*)

3. For it must be noted, that men must either be caressed or else
   annihilated; they will revenge themselves for small injuries, but
   cannot do so for great ones; the injury therefore that we do to
   a man must be such that we need not fear his vengeance.

   (Machiavelli, *The Prince*)

4. And he looked up, and saw the rich men casting their gifts into
   the treasury.
   And he saw also a certain poor widow casting in thither two
   mites.
   And he said, Of a truth I say unto you, that this poor widow
   hath cast in more than they all:
   For all these have of their abundance cast in unto the offerings
   of God: but she of her penury hath cast in all the living that
   she had.

   (Luke 21: 1–4)

5. Forever, and forever, farewell, Cassius!
   If we do meet again, why, we shall smile;
   If not, why then this parting was well made.

   (Shakespeare, *Julius Caesar*)

6. He that hath wife and children hath given hostages to fortune;
   for they are the impediments to great enterprises, either of virtue
   or mischief.

   (Francis Bacon, "Of Marriage and Single Life")

7. If wishes were horses then beggars might ride.

8. In any circuit, the work done in carrying a unit quantity of electricity completely around the circuit is a measure of the resultant electromotive force in that circuit. Since potential difference is also defined as work per unit quantity of electricity, it is evident that electromotive force and potential difference have the same physical nature and are measured in terms of the same units. The name electromotive force is unfortunate, since it is not a force.*

9. Viola: Save thee, friend, and thy music: dost thou live by thy labor?
   Clown: No, sir, I live by the church.
   Viola: Art thou a churchman?
   Clown: No such matter, sir: I do live by the church; for I do live at my house, and my house doth stand by the church.
   (Shakespeare, *Twelfth Night*)

10. "Nothing of the sort. I *knew* you came from Afghanistan. From long habit the train of thoughts ran so swiftly through my mind that I arrived at the conclusion without being conscious of intermediate steps. There were such steps, however. The train of reasoning ran, 'Here is a gentleman of a medical type, but with the air of a military man. Clearly an army doctor, then. He has just come from the tropics, for his face is dark, and that is not the natural tint of his skin, for his wrists are fair. He has undergone hardship and sickness, as his haggard face says clearly. His left arm has been injured. He holds it in a stiff and unnatural manner. Where in the tropics could an English army doctor have seen much hardship and got his arm wounded? Clearly in Afghanistan.' The whole train of thought did not occupy a second. I then remarked that you came from Afghanistan, and you were astonished."
    (A. Conan Doyle, *A Study in Scarlet*)

11. "Who did you pass on the road?" the King went on, holding out his hand to the messenger for some hay.
    "Nobody," said the messenger.

* By permission from *General College Physics* by Harrison M. Randall, Neil H. Williams, and Walter F. Colby. Copyright, 1929, by Harper and Brothers.

"Quite right," said the King: "this young lady saw him too. So of course Nobody walks slower than you."

"I do my best," the messenger said in a sullen tone. "I'm sure nobody walks much faster than I do!"

"He can't do that," said the King, "or else he'd have been here first. However, now you've got your breath, you may tell us what's happened in the town."

(Lewis Carroll, Through the Looking-Glass)

12. Here lies our sovereign lord the king,
  Whose word no man relies on;
He never says a foolish thing,
  Nor ever does a wise one.

(Earl of Rochester on Charles II)

13. Socrates: A question which I think that you must often have heard persons ask:—How can you determine whether at this moment we are sleeping, and all our thoughts are a dream; or whether we are awake, and talking to one another in the waking state?

  Theaetetus: Indeed, Socrates, I do not know how to prove the one any more than the other, for in both cases the facts precisely correspond; and there is no difficulty in supposing that during all this discussion we have been talking to one another in a dream; and when in a dream we seem to be narrating dreams, the resemblance of the two states is quite astonishing.

  Socrates: You see, then, that a doubt about the reality of sense is easily raised, since there may even be a doubt whether we are awake or in a dream.

(Plato, Theaetetus)

14. If ifs and ans were pots and pans there'd be no need for tinkers.

15. The problem is, in a broad sense, political: given that the bulk of mankind are certain to commit fallacies, is it better that they should deduce false conclusions from true premises or true conclusions from false premises? A question of this sort is insoluble. The only true solution seems to be that ordinary men and women should be taught logic, so as to be able to refrain from drawing conclusions which only *seem* to follow. When it

is said, for example, that the French are "logical," what is meant is that, when they accept a premiss, they also accept everything that a person totally destitute of logical subtlety would erroneously suppose to follow from the premiss. This is a most undesirable quality, from which, on the whole, the English-speaking nations have, in the past, been more free than any others. But there are signs that, if they are to remain free in this respect, they will require more philosophy and logic than they have had in the past. Logic was, formerly, the art of drawing inferences; it has now become the art of abstaining from inferences, since it has appeared that the inferences we naturally feel inclined to make are hardly ever valid. I conclude, therefore, that logic ought to be taught in schools with a view to teaching people not to reason. For, if they reason, they will almost certainly reason wrongly.*

EXERCISE IN REASONING

The following problems require *reasoning* for their solution. To prove that an answer is correct, once it is achieved, requires an *argument* whose *premisses* are contained in the statement of the problem, and whose *conclusion* is the answer to it. If the answer is *correct,* a *valid* argument can be constructed. In working at these problems, the reader is urged to concern himself not merely with discovering the answers, but also with formulating *arguments* to *prove* those answers *correct.*

1. In a certain mythical community, politicians always lie, and non-politicians always tell the truth. A stranger meets three natives, and asks the first of them if he is a politician. The first native answers the question. The second native then reports that the first native denied being a politician. Then the third native asserts that the first native is really a politician.

   How many of these three natives are politicians?

2. Of three prisoners in a certain jail, one had normal vision, the second had only one eye, and the third was totally blind. All

* By permission from *Sceptical Essays* by Bertrand Russell. Copyright, 1928, by Bertrand Russell. Published by W. W. Norton and Company, Inc., and by George Allen and Unwin. Ltd.

were of at least average intelligence. The jailer told the prisoners that from three white hats and two red hats he would select three and put them on the prisoners' heads. Each was prevented from seeing what color hat was placed on his own head. They were brought together, and the jailer offered freedom to the prisoner with normal vision if he could tell what color hat was on his head. The prisoner confessed that he couldn't tell. Next the jailer offered freedom to the prisoner with only one eye if he could tell what color hat was on his head. The second prisoner confessed that he couldn't tell. The jailer did not bother making the offer to the blind prisoner, but agreed to extend the same terms to him when he made the request. The blind prisoner then smiled broadly and said:

> "I do not need to have my sight;
> From what my friends with eyes have said,
> I clearly see my hat is _____!"

3. On a certain train, the crew consists of three men, the brakeman, the fireman, and the engineer. Their names listed alphabetically are Jones, Robinson, and Smith. On the train are also three passengers with corresponding names, Mr. Jones, Mr. Robinson, and Mr. Smith. The following facts are known:
   (a) Mr. Robinson lives in Detroit.
   (b) The brakeman lives halfway between Detroit and Chicago.
   (c) Mr. Jones earns exactly $10,000 a year.
   (d) Smith once beat the fireman at billiards.
   (e) The brakeman's next-door neighbor, one of the three passengers mentioned, earns exactly three times as much as the brakeman.
   (f) The passenger living in Chicago has the same name as the brakeman.
   What was the engineer's name?

4. The members of a small loan company are Mr. Black, Mr. White, Mrs. Coffee, Miss Ambrose, Mr. Kelly, and Miss Earnshaw. The positions they occupy are manager, assistant manager, cashier, stenographer, teller, and clerk, though not necessarily in that order. The assistant manager is the manager's grandson; the cashier is the stenographer's son-in-law; Mr. Black is a

bachelor. Mr. White is 22 years old, Miss Ambrose is the teller's step-sister, and Mr. Kelly is the manager's neighbor.

Who holds each position?

5. Benno Torelli, genial host at Hamtramck's most exclusive night-club, was shot and killed by a racketeer gang because he fell behind in his protection payments. After considerable effort on the part of the police, five men were brought before the District Attorney, who asked them what they had to say for themselves. Each of the men made three statements, two true and one false. Their statements were:

Lefty: "I did not kill Torelli. I never owned a revolver. Spike did it."

Red: "I did not kill Torelli. I never owned a revolver. The other guys are all passing the buck."

Dopey: "I know nothing about the murder. I never saw Butch before. Spike is guilty."

Spike: "I am innocent. Butch is the guilty man. Lefty lied when he said I did it."

Butch: "I know nothing about the murder. Red is the guilty man. Dopey will vouch for me—he's known me for years."

Whodunnit?

6. Mrs. Adams, Mrs. Baker, Mrs. Catt, Mrs. Dodge, Mrs. Ennis, and that dowdy Mrs. Fisk all went shopping one morning at the Emporium. Each woman went directly to the floor carrying the article which she wanted to buy, and each woman bought only one article. They bought a book, a dress, a handbag, a necktie, a hat, and a lamp.

All the women, except Mrs. Adams, entered the elevator on the main floor. Two men also entered the elevator. Two women, Mrs. Catt and the one who bought the necktie, got off at the second floor. Dresses were sold on the third floor. The two men got off at the fourth floor. The woman who bought the lamp got off at the fifth floor, leaving that dowdy Mrs. Fisk all alone to get off at the sixth floor.

The next day Mrs. Baker, who received the handbag as a surprise gift from one of the women who got off at the second floor, met her husband returning the necktie which one of the other women had given him. If books are sold on the main floor, and Mrs. Ennis was the sixth person to get out of the elevator, what did each of these women buy?

7. Five men who were buddies in the late war are having a reunion. They are White, Brown, Peters, Harper, and Nash, who by occupation are printer, writer, barber, neurologist, and heating-contractor. By coincidence, they live in the cities of White Plains, Brownsville, Petersburg, Harper's Ferry, and Nashville, but no man lives in the city having a name similar to his, nor does the name of his occupation have the same initial as his name or the name of the city in which he lives.

   The barber doesn't live in Petersburg, and Brown is neither heating-contractor nor printer—nor does he live in Petersburg or Harper's Ferry. Mr. Harper lives in Nashville and is neither barber nor writer. White is not a resident of Brownsville, nor is Nash, who is not a barber, nor a heating-contractor.

   If you have only the information given above, can you determine the name of the city in which Nash resides?

8. Daniel Kilraine was killed on a lonely road, two miles from Pontiac, at 3:30 A.M., March 17, 1952. Otto, Curly, Slim, Mickey, and the Kid were arrested a week later in Detroit and questioned. Each of the five made four statements, three of which were true and one of which was false. One of these men killed Kilraine. Whodunnit? Their statements were:

   Otto said: "I was in Chicago when Kilraine was murdered. I never killed anyone. The Kid is the guilty man. Mickey and I are pals."

   Curly said: "I did not kill Kilraine. I never owned a revolver in my life. The Kid knows me. I was in Detroit the night of March 17th."

   Slim said: "Curly lied when he said he never owned a revolver. The murder was committed on St. Patrick's day. Otto was in Chicago at this time. One of us is guilty."

   Mickey said: "I did not kill Kilraine. The Kid has never been in Pontiac. I never saw Otto before.

Curly was in Detroit with me on the night of March 17th."

The Kid said: "I did not kill Kilraine. I have never been in Pontiac. I never saw Curly before. Otto lied when he said I am guilty."

9. A woman recently gave a tea party to which she invited five guests. The names of the six women who sat down at the circular table were Mrs. Abrams, Mrs. Banjo, Mrs. Clive, Mrs. Dumont, Mrs. Ekwall, and Mrs. Fish. One of them was deaf, one was very talkative, one was terribly fat, one simply hated Mrs. Dumont, one had a vitamin deficiency, and one was the hostess.

The woman who hated Mrs. Dumont sat directly opposite Mrs. Banjo. The deaf woman sat opposite Mrs. Clive, who sat between the woman who had a vitamin deficiency and the woman who hated Mrs. Dumont. The fat woman sat opposite Mrs. Abrams, next to the deaf woman and to the left of the woman who hated Mrs. Dumont. The woman who had a vitamin deficiency sat between Mrs. Clive and the woman who sat opposite the woman who hated Mrs. Dumont. Mrs. Fish, who was a good friend of everyone, sat next to the fat woman and opposite the hostess.

Can you identify each of these lovely women?

10. Five men are in a poker game: Brown, Perkins, Turner, Jones, and Reilly. Their brands of cigarettes are Luckies, Camels, Kools, Old Golds, and Chesterfields, but not necessarily in that order. At the beginning of the game, the number of cigarettes possessed by each of the players was 20, 15, 8, 6, and 3, but not necessarily in that order.

During the game, at a certain time when no one was smoking, the following conditions obtained:

(a) Perkins asked for three cards.

(b) Reilly had smoked half of his original supply, or one less than Turner smoked.

(c) The Chesterfield man originally had as many more, plus half as many more, plus 2½ more cigarettes than he now has.

(d) The man who was drawing to an inside straight had absent-mindedly lit the tipped end of his fifth cigarette, the last one he smoked. .

(e) The man who smokes Luckies had smoked at least two more than anyone else, including Perkins.

(f) Brown drew as many aces as he originally had cigarettes.

(g) No one had smoked all his cigarettes.

(h) The Camel man asks Jones to pass Brown's matches.

How many cigarettes did each man have to begin with, and of what brand?

CHAPTER TWO

The Uses of Language

I. THREE BASIC FUNCTIONS OF LANGUAGE

Language is so subtle and complicated an instrument that the multiplicity of its uses is often lost sight of. Here, as in many other situations, there is danger in our tendency to oversimplify things.

A not uncommon complaint of those who take too narrow a view of the legitimate uses of language concerns the way in which words are "wasted" at social functions. "So much talk, and so little said!" sums up this kind of criticism. And more than one person has been heard to remark, "So and so asked me how I felt. What a hypocrite! He doesn't care in the least how I feel!" Such remarks reveal a failure to understand the complex purposes for which language is used. It is shown also in the deplorable conduct of the bore, who, when asked how he feels, actually proceeds to tell about the state of his health —usually at great length and in much detail. But people do not usually talk at parties to instruct each other. And ordinarily the question "How are you?" is a friendly greeting, not a request for a medical report.

One very important use of language is to communicate information. Ordinarily this is accomplished by formulating and affirming (or denying) propositions. Language used to affirm or deny propositions, or to present arguments, is said to be serving the *informative function*. In this context we use the word "information" to include misinformation: false as well as true propositions, incorrect as well as correct arguments. Informative discourse is used to *describe* the world, and to reason about it. Whether the alleged facts that are being described are important or unimportant, general or particular, does not matter; in any case the language used to describe or report them is being used informatively.

We may distinguish two basic uses or functions of language in addition to the informative, and refer to them as the *expressive* and the *directive*. Just as science provides us with the clearest examples of informative discourse, so poetry furnishes us the best examples of language serving an *expressive* function. The following lines of Burns:

> O my Luve's like a red, red rose
> That's newly sprung in June:
> O my Luve's like the melodie
> That's sweetly play'd in tune!

are definitely not intended to inform us of any facts or theories concerning the world. The poet's purpose is to communicate not knowledge but feelings and attitudes. The passage was not written to report any information but to *express* certain emotions that the poet felt very keenly and to evoke feelings of a similar kind in the reader. Language serves the *expressive* function whenever it is used to vent or communicate feelings or emotions.

Not all expressive language is poetry, however. We express sorrow by saying "That's too bad," or "Oh my," and enthusiasm by shouting "Wow!" or "Oh boy!" The lover expresses his delicate passion by murmuring "Darling!" or "Oh baby!" The poet expresses his complex and concentrated emotions in a sonnet or some other verse form. A worshipper may express his feeling of wonder and awe at the vastness and mystery of the universe by reciting the Lord's Prayer or the twenty-third Psalm of David. All these are uses of language not to communicate information but to express emotions, feelings, or attitudes. Expressive discourse *as expressive* is neither true nor false. For a person to apply only the criteria of truth or falsehood, correctness or incorrectness, to expressive discourse like a poem is to miss its point and to lose much of its value. The student whose enjoyment of Keat's sonnet *On first looking into Chapman's Homer* is marred by his historical knowledge that Balboa rather than Cortez discovered the Pacific Ocean is a "poor reader" of poetry. The purpose of the poem is not to teach history, but something else entirely. This is not to say that poetry can have no literal significance. Some poems *do* have an informative content which may be an important ingredient in their total effect. Some poetry may well be "criticism of life," in the words of a great poet. But such poems are more than merely expressive, as we are using the term here. Such poetry may be said to have a "mixed usage," or to serve a multiple function. This notion will be explained further in the following section.

Expression may be analyzed into two components. When a man curses to himself when he is alone, or a poet writes poems which he shows to no one, or a man prays in solitude, his language functions to express or evince his own attitude but does not serve to evoke a similar attitude in anyone else. On the other hand, when an orator seeks to inspire his audience—not to action, but to share enthusiasm; when a lover courts his beloved in poetic language; when the crowd cheers its athletic team; the language used not only evinces the attitudes of the speakers but also is intended to evoke the same attitudes in the hearers. Expressive discourse, then, is used either to *evince* the speaker's feelings or to *evoke* certain feelings on the part of the auditor. Of course it may do both.

Language serves the *directive* function when it is used for the purpose of causing (or preventing) overt action. The clearest examples of directive discourse are commands and requests. When a mother tells her little boy to wash his hands before supper, she does not intend to communicate any information to him or to evince or evoke any particular emotion. Her language is intended to get results, to cause action of the indicated kind. When the same mother asks the grocer to deliver certain goods to her house, she is again using language directively, to motivate or effect *action*. To ask a question is ordinarily to request an answer, and is also to be classified as directive discourse. The difference between a command and a request is a rather subtle one, for almost any command can be translated into a request by adding the word "please," or by suitable changes in tone of voice or in facial expression.

In its nakedly imperative form, directive discourse is neither true nor false. A command such as "Close the window" cannot be either true or false in any literal sense. Whether the command is obeyed or disobeyed does not affect or determine its truth-value, for it has none. We may disagree about whether a command has been obeyed or not; we may disagree about whether a command should be obeyed or not; but we never disagree about whether a command is true or false, for it cannot be either. However, the reasonableness or propriety, the unreasonableness or impropriety of commands are properties somewhat analogous to the truth or falsehood of informative discourse. And questions of the propriety of given commands can be raised and resolved in ways that are strictly within the scope of logic.

II. DISCOURSE SERVING MULTIPLE FUNCTIONS

In the preceding section the examples presented were chemically pure specimens, so to speak, of the three basic kinds of communication. The threefold division proposed is illuminating and valuable, but it cannot be applied mechanically, because almost any ordinary communication will probably exemplify, to a greater or less extent, all three uses of language. Thus a poem, which is primarily expressive discourse, may have a moral and be in effect a command to the reader (or hearer) to lead a certain kind of life, and may also convey a certain amount of information. On the other hand, although a sermon is predominantly directive, seeking to cause certain appropriate action by members of the congregation (whether to abandon their evil ways, or to contribute money to the church, or what not), it may evince and evoke sentiments, thus serving the expressive function, and may also include some information, communicating some factual material. And a scientific treatise, essentially informative, may evince something of the writer's own enthusiasm, thus serving an expressive function, and may also, at least implicitly, serve some directive function or other, perhaps bidding the reader to verify independently the author's conclusion. Most ordinary uses of language are mixed.

It is not always the result of any confusion on the part of the speaker when his language serves mixed or multiple functions. It is rather the case that *effective* communication demands certain combinations of function. Few of us stand to each other in the relation of parent to child or employer to employee. And outside the context of such formal relationships as these, one cannot simply issue an order with any expectation of having it obeyed. Consequently a certain indirection must be employed: a bald command would arouse antagonism or resentment and be self-defeating. One cannot cause action by merely voicing an imperative; it is necessary to use a more subtle method of stimulating the desired action.

Action may be said to have very complex causes. Motivation is more properly to be discussed by a psychologist than a logician, but it is common knowledge that actions are usually caused by both desires and beliefs. A man who *desires* to eat food will not touch what is on his plate unless he *believes* it to be food; and even though he *believes* it to be food he will not touch it unless he *desires* to eat. This fact is relevant to our present discussion because desires are a special type of what we have been calling "attitudes."

Consequently actions may be caused by evoking appropriate

attitudes *and* communicating relevant information. Assuming your listeners to be benevolent, you may cause them to contribute to a given charity by informing them of its effectiveness in accomplishing benevolent results. In such a case your use of language is ultimately directive, since its purpose is to cause action. But a naked command would be far less effective in this situation than the informative discourse used. Suppose, on the other hand, that your listeners are already persuaded that the charity in question does accomplish benevolent results. Here again you cannot simply command with any great hope of being obeyed, but you may succeed in causing them to act in the desired fashion by somehow arousing a sufficiently benevolent feeling or emotion in them. The discourse you use to realize your end is expressive discourse; you must make a "moving appeal." Thus your language will have a mixed use, functioning both expressively and directively. Or finally, let us suppose that you are seeking a donation from people who have *neither* a benevolent attitude *nor* a belief that the charity serves a benevolent purpose. Here you must use *both* informative and expressive language. In such a case the language used serves all three functions, being directive, informative, and expressive all at once, not accidentally as a mere mixture that just happens to occur, but essentially, as necessary to successful communication.

Some writers on language have suggested that discourse serves more than these three distinct functions. It is possible, however, to understand any other function as a mixture or combination of two or possibly all three of the basic uses that have been distinguished here. The most important of these others has frequently been called the "ceremonial" use of language. Included within this category are many different kinds of phrases, ranging from relatively trivial words of greeting to the more portentous discourse of the marriage ceremony, phrasings of state documents, and the verbal rituals performed on holy days in houses of worship. But these can all be regarded as mixtures of expressive and directive discourse, rather than some altogether different and unique kind. For example, the usual ceremonial greetings and chit-chat at social gatherings serve the purpose of evincing and evoking goodwill and sociability. Perhaps for some speakers they are intended also to serve the directive purpose of causing their hearers to act in certain definite ways, to patronize the speaker's business, to offer him employment, or to invite him to dinner. At the other extreme, the impressive language of the marriage ceremony is intended to emphasize the solemnity of the occasion (its expressive function), and also to cause the bride and groom to perform in their new roles with heightened appreciation of the seriousness of the marriage contract (its directive function).

III. THE FORMS OF DISCOURSE

Textbooks of grammar commonly define a sentence as the unit of language that expresses a complete thought, and divide sentences into four categories, usually called declarative, interrogative, imperative, and exclamatory. These four categories are not identical with those of assertions, questions, commands, and exclamations. We may be tempted to identify form with function—to think that declarative sentences and informative discourse coincide, and that exclamatory sentences are suitable only for expressive discourse. Regarding questions as requests for answers, we may be led further to think that directive discourse consists exclusively of sentences in the interrogative and imperative moods. Were such identifications possible, it would immensely simplify the problem of communication, for then we should be able to tell the intended use or function of a passage by its form, which is open to direct inspection. Some people apparently do identify form with function, but these are not sensitive readers, for the identification often makes them misunderstand what is said, and they "miss the point" of much that is to be communicated.

It is a mistake to believe that everything in the form of a declarative sentence is informative discourse, to be valued if true and rejected if false. "I had a very nice time at your party," is a declarative sentence, but its function need not be informative at all, but rather ceremonial or expressive, evincing a feeling of friendliness and appreciation. Many poems and prayers are in the form of declarative sentences, despite the fact that their functions are not informative. To regard them as such and to attempt to evaluate them by the criteria of truth or falsehood is to shut oneself off from aesthetic and religious satisfactions. Again, many requests and commands are expressed indirectly—perhaps more gently—by means of declarative sentences. The declarative sentence, "I would like some coffee," should not be taken by a waitress to be a mere report of the psychological fact it apparently asserts about her customer, but as a command or request for action. Were we invariably to judge the truth or falsehood of declarative sentences such as "I'd appreciate some help with this," or "I hope you'll be able to meet me after class at the library," and do no more than register them as information received, we should soon be without friends. These examples should suffice to show that the declarative form is no certain indication of the informative function. Declarative sentences lend themselves to the formulation of every kind of discourse.

It is the same with other forms of sentences. The interrogative sentence, "Do you realize that we're almost late?" is not necessarily a request for information but may be a command to hurry. The interrogative sentence "Isn't it true that Russia and Germany signed a pact in 1939 which precipitated the Second World War?" may not be a question at all but either an oblique way of communicating information or an attempt to express and evoke a feeling of hostility towards Russia, functioning informatively in the first instance and expressively in the second. Even what is grammatically an imperative, as in official documents beginning, "Know all men by these presents that . . . ," may not be a command, but rather informative discourse in what it asserts and expressive discourse in its use of language to evoke the appropriate feelings of solemnity and respect. In spite of its close affinity to the expressive, an exclamatory sentence may serve a quite different function. The exclamation "Good Lord it's late!" may really communicate a command to hurry. And the exclamation, "What a beautiful ring!" uttered by a young lady to her gentleman friend as they pass a jeweler's window, may function ever so much more directively than expressively.

It should be remembered that some discourse is intended to serve two or possibly all three functions of language at once. In such cases each aspect or function of a given passage is subject to its own proper criteria. One having an informative function may have that aspect evaluated as true or false. The same passage as serving a directive function may have that aspect evaluated as proper or improper, right or wrong. And if there is also an expressive function served by the passage in question, that component of it may be evaluated as sincere or insincere, as valuable or otherwise. Properly to evaluate a given passage requires knowledge of the function or functions it is intended to serve.

Truth and falsehood, and the attendant notions of correctness and incorrectness of argument, are more important in the study of logic than the others mentioned. Yet the logician's criteria are to be applied only to informative discourse. Hence, as students of logic, we must be able to differentiate discourse that functions informatively from that which does not. And we must be able further to disentangle the informative function a given passage serves from whatever other functions it may also be serving. To do this "disentangling" we must know what different functions language can serve and be able to tell them apart. The grammatical structure of a passage often serves as a cue to its function, but there is no *necessary* connection between function and grammatical form. Nor is there any strict relation between the function and the *content*—in the sense of what might seem to be *asserted* by a passage. This is very clearly shown by an example of Bloomfield's in his chapter on *Meaning:* "A petulant child, at bed-time, says *I'm hungry,* and his mother, who is up to his tricks, answers by packing him off to bed. This is an example of displaced speech." * The child's speech here is neither expressive nor informative, but directive—even though it does not succeed in procuring the wanted diversion. By the function of a passage we mean the *intended* function. But this, unfortunately, is not always easy to determine.

When a passage is quoted in isolation, it is often difficult to say what language function it is primarily intended to serve. The reason for this difficulty is that *context* is extremely important in determining the answer to such a question. What is an imperative or a flat statement of fact, by itself, may in its proper context function expressively, as part of a larger whole whose poetic effect is derived from all its parts in their arrangement. For example, in isolation, the sentence:

Give me my sword.

is an imperative serving the directive function; and the sentence

The King comes here tonight.

is a declarative sentence serving an informative function. But both are from Shakespeare's *Macbeth*, and in that context contribute to the expressive function served by the larger whole.

It is important also to distinguish between the proposition which a sentence formulates and what the fact of its assertion evinces about the person who speaks or writes it. When a man remarks, "It is raining," the proposition which he asserts is about the weather, not about himself. Yet his assertion gives evidence that *he believes* it to be raining, and this is a fact about the speaker. It also may happen that a person makes a statement which is ostensibly about his beliefs, not for the sake of giving information about himself, but simply as a way of saying something else. To say "I believe that gold is valuable," is ordinarily not to be construed as a psychological or autobiographical report on the beliefs of the speaker, but simply his way of saying

* Reprinted from *Language* by Leonard Bloomfield. Copyright, 1933, by Henry Holt and Company, Inc.

that gold *is* valuable. Similarly, to voice a command usually evinces the desires of the speaker, and under appropriate circumstances to assert that one has such and such a desire is to give a command. To utter an exclamation of joy gives evidence that the speaker is joyful, although the speaker makes no assertion in the process. On the other hand, to present a psychological report which affirms that the speaker is joyful is to assert a proposition, something quite different from exclaiming joyously.

In subsequent chapters we shall develop certain logical techniques that can be applied quite mechanically to arguments for the purpose of testing their validity. But there is no mechanical test applicable to language in general for the purpose of distinguishing the informative and argumentative from other types of discourse. This requires thought and demands an awareness of and sensitivity to the flexibility of language and the multiplicity of its uses.

EXERCISES

I. What language functions are most probably intended to be served by each of the following passages?

1. But I say unto you, That ye resist not evil: but whosoever shall smite thee on thy right cheek, turn to him the other also.

   (Matthew: 5–39)

2. It is only the man whose intellect is clouded by his sexual impulses that could give the name of *the fair sex* to that undersized, narrow-shouldered, broad-hipped, and short-legged race: for the whole beauty of the sex is bound up with this impulse.

   (Schopenhauer, "On Women")

3. The Bourgeoisie has stripped of its halo every occupation hitherto honored and looked up to with reverent awe. It has converted the physician, the lawyer, the priest, the poet, the man of science, into its paid wage laborers.

   (Marx and Engels, *Communist Manifesto*)

4. There is no force however great
   Can stretch a cord however fine

Into a horizontal line
That shall be accurately straight.

(William Whewell, "Physics")

5. "He's the chief foreman of the Iron Dike Company. He's a hard citizen, an old colour sergeant of the war, all scars and grizzle. We've had two tries at him; but had no luck, and Jim Carnaway lost his life over it. Now it's for you to take it over. That's the house—all alone at the Iron Dike crossroad, same as you see here on the map—without another within earshot. It's no good by day. He's armed and shoots quick and straight, with no questions asked. But at night—well, there he is with his wife, three children, and a hired help. You can't pick or choose. It's all or none. If you could get a bag of blasting powder at the front door with a slow match to it—"

(A. Conan Doyle, *The Valley of Fear*)

6. When we run over libraries, persuaded of these principles, what havoc must we make? If we take in our hand any volume; of divinity or school metaphysics, for instance; let us ask; *Does it contain any abstract reasoning concerning quantity or number?* No. *Does it contain any experimental reasoning concerning matter of fact and existence?* No. Commit it then to the flames: for it can contain nothing but sophistry and illusion.

(David Hume, *An Enquiry Concerning Human Understanding*)

7. Thus demandeth my great love to the remotest ones: *be not considerate of thy neighbor!* Man is something that must be surpassed.

(Friedrich Nietzsche, *Thus Spake Zarathustra*)

8. "An unhappy alternative is before you, Elizabeth. From this day you must be a stranger to one of your parents. Your mother will never see you again if you do *not* marry Mr. Collins, and I will never see you again if you *do*."

(Jane Austen, *Pride and Prejudice*)

9. And they said unto Moses, Because there were no graves in Egypt, hast thou taken us away to die in the wilderness? wherefore hast thou dealt thus with us, to carry us forth out of Egypt?

(Exodus: 14–11)

10. A free man thinks of nothing less than of death, and his wisdom is not a meditation upon death but upon life.
(Spinoza, *Ethics,* Prop. LXVII Fourth Part)

11. I think, this coming summer, the King of Sicilia means to pay Bohemia the visitation which he justly owes him.
(Shakespeare, *The Winter's Tale* Act I, Scene I)

12. The nobler and more perfect a thing is, the later and slower it is in arriving at maturity. A man reaches the maturity of his reasoning powers and mental faculties hardly before the age of twenty-eight; a woman, at eighteen.
(Schopenhauer, "On Women")

II. For each of the following passages, indicate what proposition it may be intended to assert, if any, what overt action it may be intended to cause, if any, and what it evinces about the speaker, if anything.

1. Is life so dear or peace so sweet as to be purchased at the price of chains and slavery? Forbid it, Almighty God! I know not what course others may take, but as for me, give me liberty, or give me death!

2. I come not, friends, to steal away your hearts:
I am no orator, as Brutus is;
But, as you know me all, a plain blunt man.

3. What God hath joined together, let no man put asunder.

4. I never talk about myself.

5. It matter not how strait the gate,
How charged with punishments the scroll,
I am the master of my fate,
I am the captain of my soul.

6. I wish I were as sure of anything as Macaulay is of everything.

7. Jones is a man of sound political judgment; he always votes Republican.

8. England expects every man to do his duty.

9. He prayeth best who loveth best
All things both great and small.

10. What can they see in the longest kingly line in Europe, save that it runs back to a successful soldier?
11. Rock of Ages, cleft for me,
    Let me hide myself in thee.
12. We fail!
    But screw your courage to the sticking-place,
    And we'll not fail.
13. I deprecate redundancy of verbiage and desiderate compendious locutions exclusively.
14. Blow, blow, thou winter wind!
    Thou art not so unkind
        As man's ingratitude.
15. The God who gave us life, gave us liberty at the same time.
16. Am I my brother's keeper?
17. It is certain to rain tomorrow.
18. I believe that it will rain tomorrow.
19. He believes that it will rain tomorrow, but it won't.
20. I believe that it will rain tomorrow, but it won't.

III. Name the grammatical form and the (probable) linguistic function of each of the following sentences:

1. My advice to you is to put in more time on your homework.
2. Gather ye rosebuds while ye may,
       Old time is still a-flying.
3. Hand me that book, please.
4. Did you ever hear such a magnificent performance?
5. Do you know what happens to little boys who don't mind their parents?
6. Why is the prosecution so eager to railroad an innocent man like Mr. Doakes to the penitentiary?
7. The first native is either a politician or a non-politician.
8. Age cannot wither her, nor custom stale
   Her infinite variety.
9. How sharper than a serpent's tooth it is
   To have a thankless child!
10. Blow, winds, and crack your cheeks! rage! blow!
11. If you don't slow down you'll get a ticket.

12. Patriotism is the last refuge of the scoundrel.
13. I pray that our Heavenly Father may assuage the anguish of your bereavement and leave you only the cherished memory of the loved and lost, and the solemn pride that must be yours to have laid so costly a sacrifice upon the altar of freedom.
14. Beware of rashness, but with energy and sleepless vigilance go forward and give us victories.
15. Men are never so likely to settle a question rightly as when they discuss it freely.

IV. EMOTIVE WORDS

We have already observed that one and the same sentence can serve both an informative and an expressive function. For the sentence to formulate a proposition, its words must have literal or cognitive meaning, referring to objects or events and their properties. When it expresses an attitude or feeling, however, some of its words may also have an emotional suggestiveness or impact. A single word or phrase can have both a literal meaning and an emotional impact. It has become customary to speak of the latter as "emotive significance" or "emotive meaning." There is a high degree of independence between the literal and emotive meanings of a word. For example, the words "bureaucrat," "government official," and "public servant" have almost identical literal meanings. But their emotive meanings are quite different. The term "bureaucrat" definitely tends to express resentment and disapproval, while the term "public servant" is an honorific one which tends to express favor and approval. The phrase "government official" is more nearly neutral than either of the others.

It is important to realize that one and the same fact or referent can be described by words that have greatly different emotive impacts. It might be thought that the emotive impact of a word or phrase is always connected with the properties possessed by the referent of that word or phrase. But consider the poet's phrase: "A rose by any other name would smell as sweet." It is true that the actual fragrance of the rose would remain the same through any change of name we might assign it. But it is doubtful if our attitude of approval would remain unchanged if we continually referred to roses, say, as "skunk-weeds." The purveyors of canned horse-mackerel sell much more of their product now that they call it "Tuna Fish." It has been said that language has a life of its own independent of the facts it is used to describe. In our terminology, words can have exactly the same descriptive or literal meanings and yet be either moderately or completely opposite in their emotive suggestiveness or meaning. Certain physiological activities pertaining to reproduction and elimination can be unemotionally described, using a medical vocabulary, without offending the most squeamish taste; but all of these terms have certain four-letter synonyms whose usage shocks all but the most hardened interpreters. A writer has reported

. . . the illuminating story of a little girl who, having recently learned to read, was spelling out a political article in the newspaper. "Father," she asked, "what is Tammany Hall?" And her father replied in the voice usually reserved for the taboos of social communication, "You'll understand that when you grow up, my dear." Acceding to this adult whim of evasion, she desisted from her inquiries; but something in Daddy's tone had convinced her that Tammany Hall must be connected with illicit *amour,* and for many years she could not hear this political institution mentioned without experiencing a secret non-political thrill.*

The emotive meaning of a word may always be acquired by association, but these associations need not always be directly with the word's literal referent.

An illuminating joke based upon the contrast between literal and emotive meaning was made by the philosopher Bertrand Russell, when he "conjugated" an "irregular verb" as

> I am firm; you are obstinate;
> he is a pig-headed fool.

* By permission from *The Gift of Tongues,* by Margaret Schlauch. Copyright, 1942, by Margaret Schlauch. Published by the Viking Press, Inc.

The London *New Statesman and Nation* subsequently ran a contest soliciting such irregular conjugations and picked among the winners the following:

> I am righteously indignant; you are annoyed;
>   he is making a fuss about nothing.
> I am fastidious; you are fussy;
>   he is an old woman.
> I have reconsidered it; you have changed your mind;
>   he has gone back on his word.

In his lively book entitled *How to Think Straight,* Robert Thouless made an experiment designed to show the importance of emotively-colored words in poetry. There he examined two lines from Keats' "The Eve of St. Agnes":

> Full on this casement shone the wintry moon,
> And threw warm gules on Madeline's fair breast.

He proposed to show that their beauty arises primarily from the proper choice of emotionally-colored words, by showing how that beauty is lost completely if those words are replaced by *neutral* ones. Selecting the words "casement," "gules," "Madeline," "fair," and "breast," Mr. Thouless wrote:

Casement means simply a kind of window with emotional and romantic associations. *Gules* is the heraldic name for red, with the suggestion of romance which accompanies all heraldry. *Madeline* is simply a girl's name, but one calling out favorable emotions absent from a relatively plain and straightforward name. *Fair* simply means, in objective fact, that her skin was white or uncolored—a necessary condition for the colors of the window to show—but also *fair* implies warm emotional preference for an uncolored skin rather than one which is yellow, purple, black, or any of the other colors which skin might be. *Breast* also has similar emotional meanings, and the aim of scientific description might have been equally well attained if it had been replaced by such a neutral word as *chest.*

Let us now try the experiment of keeping these two lines in a metrical form, but replacing all the emotionally-colored words by neutral ones, while making as few other changes as possible. We may write:

> "Full on this window shone the wintry moon,
> Making red marks on Jane's uncolored chest."

No one will doubt that all of its poetic value has been knocked out of the passage by these changes. Yet the lines still mean the same in external fact; they still have the same objective meaning. It is only the emotional meaning which has been destroyed.*

EXERCISES

1. Give five original "conjugations of irregular verbs," where literally the same activity is given a laudatory description in the first person, a fairly neutral one in the second person, and a derogatory one in the third person.
2. Select two brief passages of poetry and perform Thouless' "experiment" on them.

V. KINDS OF AGREEMENT AND DISAGREEMENT

The irregular verb conjugations mentioned in the preceding section make one thing abundantly clear. The same state of affairs can be described in different words which express widely divergent attitudes. And to the extent that anything can be described by means of alternative phrases, one of which expresses an attitude of approval, another an attitude of disapproval, still another a more or less neutral attitude, there are different kinds of agreement and disagreement expressible with respect to any situation or activity.

Two people may disagree as to whether or not something has happened, and when they do they may be said to have *disagreement in belief.* On the other hand, they may agree that an event has actually occurred, thus agreeing *in belief,* and yet they may have strongly divergent or even opposite attitudes towards it. One who approves of it will describe it in language which expresses approval, the other may choose terms that express dis-

* Reprinted from *How to Think Straight* by Robert H. Thouless. Copyright, 1932, 1939, by Simon and Schuster, Inc.

approval. There is disagreement here, but it is not disagreement in belief as to what has occurred. The disagreement manifested is rather a difference in feeling about the matter, a *disagreement in attitude*.*

With respect to any matter, two persons may agree in belief and disagree in attitude, or they may agree in both belief and attitude. It is also possible for people to agree in attitude despite disagreeing in belief. One may believe that so-and-so has changed his mind, and praise him for "listening to the voice of reason," while the other may believe that he has *not* changed his mind and praise him for "refusing to be swayed by blandishment." This third kind of situation often occurs in politics; people may support the same candidate for different and even incompatible reasons. There is a fourth possibility also, in which the disagreement is complete. One speaker may strongly approve of so-and-so for having wisely reconsidered a certain matter, while the second may just as vigorously disapprove of him for being too pig-headed to admit his mistake. Here there is disagreement in belief and also disagreement in attitude.

If we are interested in the problem of resolving disagreements, it is important to realize that agreement and disagreement may relate not only to the facts in a given case, but to attitudes towards those facts. Different methods are applicable to the resolution of different kinds of disagreement, and if we are unclear as to what kind of disagreement exists we shall be unclear as to what methods should be utilized. If the disagreement is in belief, it can be resolved by ascertaining the facts. In the instance mentioned above, the factual question is whether so-and-so at one time held a certain view and at a later time held a different view, or whether at the later time he still maintained the earlier view. To decide the question—were it of sufficient importance—the usual techniques for verification

* I am indebted to my friend and colleague Professor Charles L. Stevenson for the terms agreement and disagreement "in belief" and agreement and disagreement "in attitude," and also for the notion of *persuasive definition,* which will be discussed in Chapter 4. Cf. his *Ethics and Language,* Yale University Press, 1944.

could be utilized: witnesses could be questioned, documents consulted, records examined, and so on. Theoretically, the facts could be established and the issue decided, and this would resolve the disagreement. The methods of scientific inquiry are available here, and it suffices to direct them squarely at the question of fact about which there is disagreement in belief.

On the other hand, if there is disagreement in attitude rather than disagreement in belief, the techniques appropriate to settling it are rather different, being more inclusive and less direct. To call witnesses, consult documents, or the like, to the end of establishing either that the man held two different views on two different occasions or held the same view on the two occasions, would be fruitless in the case of this type of disagreement. What may be regarded as the facts of the case are not at issue; the disagreement is not over what the facts *are* but over how these facts are to be *valued*. A serious attempt to resolve this disagreement in attitude may involve reference to many factual questions—but not the one mentioned so far. Instead, it may be fruitful to consider what implications or *consequences* are entailed by the action in question, and what would have been entailed by this or that alternative course of action. Questions of *motive* and of *intention* are of great importance here. These are all factual questions, to be sure, but none of them is identical with what would be the issue if the disagreement were in belief rather than in attitude. Still other methods are available which may resolve a disagreement in attitude. Persuasion may be attempted, with its extensive use of expressive discourse. Rhetoric may be of paramount utility in unifying the will of a group, in achieving unanimity of attitude. But of course it is wholly worthless in resolving a question of fact.

Where disagreement is in attitude rather than in belief, the most vigorous—and, of course, genuine—disagreement may be expressed in statements which are all of them literally true, at least as far as their informative content is concerned. An illuminating example of this is reported by Lincoln Steffens in his *Autobiography*. Shortly after the turn of the century, Steffens, in his capacity as a muckraker, went up to Milwaukee to prepare an exposé of "that demagogue," Robert La Follette, then Governor of Wisconsin. Steffens called first on a banker, who said that La Follette was "a crooked hypocrite who stirred up the people with socialist-anarchist ideas and hurt business." Steffens asked the banker for evidence, and described what ensued as follows:

. . . the banker set out to demonstrate . . . hypocrisy, socialism-anarchism, etc., and he was going fast and hot till I realized that my witness had more feeling than facts; or if he had facts, he could not handle them. He would start with some act of La Follette and blow up in a rage. He certainly hated the man, but I could not write rage.*

Steffens' conversation with the banker was interrupted by the arrival of an attorney, who was prepared to present the "evidence" against La Follette. Steffen's account proceeds:

When I told him how far we had got, the banker and I, and how I wanted first the proofs of the dishonesty alleged, he said: "Oh, no, no. You are getting off wrong. La Follette isn't dishonest. On the contrary, the man is dangerous precisely because he is so sincere. He's a fanatic."

We may remark that the third possibility mentioned above is perfectly exemplified in the present example. There was disagreement in belief between the banker and the lawyer on the question of La Follette's honesty. But this factual question was completely overshadowed by that of attitude. Here there was vigorous agreement. Both disapproved La Follette and his actions: curiously enough, the banker because the Governor was "a crook," the lawyer because the Governor was "so sincere." Then the lawyer got down to cases. His motive here was to achieve agreement with Steffens. The report continues:

The attorney, with the banker sitting by frowning, impatient, presented in good order the charges against La Follette, the measures

---

* By permission from *The Autobiography of Lincoln Steffens.* Copyright, 1931, by Harcourt, Brace and Company, Inc.

he had furthered, the legislation passed and proposed, his political methods. Horrified himself at the items on his list and alarmed over the policy and the power of this demagogue, he delivered the indictment with emotion, force, eloquence. The only hitch was that Bob La Follette's measures seemed fair to me, his methods democratic, his purposes right but moderate, and his fighting strength and spirit hopeful and heroic.

What happened here was that the lawyer's statement of the facts, which presumably Steffens agreed with the lawyer in believing, was not sufficient to produce the kind of agreement in attitude which the lawyer desired. Steffens' attitude towards those facts was altogether different from the lawyer's. Adducing more evidence that the facts were as described—literally—would not have brought the two men a hair's breadth nearer to agreement—*in attitude.* The lawyer's "emotion, force, eloquence" were relevant, but not sufficient. What the lawyer regarded as new-fangled innovations and radical departures from established order, Steffens tended to regard as progressive improvements and the elimination of antiquated prejudice. Both would agree on the fact that *change* was involved. But their evaluations were different. The reverse was the case with the lawyer and the banker. Their evaluations were the same, even though they disagreed on the factual question of whether La Follette was crooked or sincere.

The lesson we may draw from these considerations is simple but important. When two parties claim to disagree and express their divergent views in statements which are logically consistent with each other, both being perhaps *literally true,* it would be a mistake to say that the parties do not "really" disagree, or that their disagreement is "merely verbal." They are not merely "saying the same thing in different words." They may, of course, be using their words to affirm what is *literally* the same fact, but they may also be using their words to express conflicting attitudes towards that fact. In such a case, their disagreement, although not "literal," is nevertheless *genuine.* It is not "merely verbal" because words function expressively as well as informatively. And if we are interested in resolving disagreements, we must be clear about their nature, since the techniques appropriate to the resolution of one kind of disagreement may be hopelessly beside the point for another.

Knowledge of the different uses of language is an aid in discerning what kinds of disagreements may be involved and is thus an aid in resolving them. Drawing the indicated distinctions does not by itself solve the problem or resolve the disagreement, of course. But it clarifies the discussion and reveals the kind and locus of the disagreement. And if it is true that questions are more easily answered when they are better understood, then the study of the different uses of language is of considerable value.

EXERCISES

Identify the kinds of agreement or disagreement exhibited by the following pairs of statements:

1. a. Mrs. Smith's new dress is a vivid red.
   b. Mrs. Smith's new dress is a glaring red.

2. a. Mrs. Smith's new dress is a lovely red.
   b. Mrs. Smith's new dress is a beautiful orange.

3. a. Mrs. Smith's new dress is an ugly red.
   b. Mrs. Smith's new dress is a glaring orange.

4. a. Mrs. Brown served a delightful little lunch.
   b. Mrs. Brown served a magnificent banquet.

5. a. Mrs. Brown served a positively skimpy meal.
   b. Mrs. Brown really overdid it serving such vulgarly excessive portions at her dinner.

6. a. Mr. Jones donated almost a hundred dollars.
   b. Mr. Jones donated over a hundred dollars.

7. a. Mr. Jones donated almost a hundred dollars.
   b. Mr. Jones donated less than a hundred dollars.

8. a. The Republocrats are the party of progress.
   b. The Republocrats are committed to preserving all of our great American principles and practices.

9. a. The Republocrats are the party of progress.
   b. The Republocrats threaten to desert the tried and true principles of Americanism.

10. a. The Republocrats are reactionaries.
    b. The Republocrats are the true conservatives.

11. a. We spent the whole evening studying.
    b. We wasted the whole evening studying.

12. a. The Does live in a snug little cottage.
    b. The Does live in a magnificent mansion.

13. a. The Does live in a snug little cottage.
    b. The Does live in a wretched little hovel.

14. a. The Does live in a cosy little home.
    b. The Does live in a big barn of a house.

15. a. Communists sweep ahead in five mile advance.
    b. Reds stopped cold after five mile push.

VI. EMOTIVELY NEUTRAL LANGUAGE

In the preceding discussion it has been insisted that the expressive use of language is just as legitimate as the informative. There is nothing wrong with emotive language; and there is nothing wrong with language that is non-emotive, or neutral. Similarly, we can say that there is nothing wrong with pillows and nothing wrong with hammers. True enough, but it does not mean that we should be successful in attempting to drive nails with pillows or comfortable in trying to sleep with our heads resting on hammers. A great deal of value was lost in Thouless' translation of Keats' lines into neutral language—although the literal meaning was preserved. Here is a case in which emotively colored language is preferable to neutral language. Are there any circumstances in which neutral language is preferable to emotively colored language?

Clearly, when we are trying to "get at the facts," to follow an argument, or to learn the truth about something, anything which distracts us from that goal tends to frustrate us. It is a commonplace that the passions tend to cloud the reason, and this view is reflected in the usage of "dispassionate" and "objective" as near synonyms. It follows that when we are attempting to reason about facts in a cool and objective fashion, referring to them in strongly emotive language is a hindrance rather than a help. If we are interested in calculating, for example, what economic consequences in terms of productivity and efficiency would follow from various degrees of government economic control, we shall find our task made more difficult if we insist upon referring to the phenomena in question by words as emotionally charged as "freedom" and "bureaucratic interference," on the one hand, and "license" and "irresponsibility" on the other.

The use of such *stereotypes* is properly frowned upon, not merely because of their lack of literary value, but because of the way in which the hackneyed emotional reactions stirred by them get in the way of any objective appraisal of the facts they refer to. This danger is familiar to those who have studied public opinion polls, like Gallup's or Roper's. In seeking to discover people's views, interviewers must be careful not to prejudice the issue by phrasing their questions in such a way as to influence the answers. An interesting report on this problem is given by Stuart Chase in his recent book, *The Proper Study of Mankind:*

In 1946 Roper ran an interesting semantic test. He matched two groups of people so they were practically identical samples. He proved it by asking various questions and getting percentage results which were very close. He then asked each group a similar series of questions except that for one group a new and ugly word was introduced, the word "propaganda."

The general topic was the usefulness of foreign broadcasts by the State Department. Group A was asked to select from three alternative positions, one of which read: "Some people say it is better to explain our point of view as well as give the news." The answer came back "yes," 42.8 percent. Group B got the following wording, *and observe it is precisely the same question:* "Some people say it is better to include some propaganda as well as give the news."

The "yes" reaction was almost cut in half, to 24.7 percent! It would be hard to find a better example of what an emotion-stirring word will do to people's opinions! *

It may be doubted whether it *is* "precisely the same question" which was asked the two groups. As often used today, at least part of the *literal* meaning of the word "propaganda" concerns the use of non-rational methods to cause acceptance of a point of view. To propagandize is surely a different thing from simply explaining our point of view. Not all emotive differences between closely related words are independent of their descriptive meanings; some are directly derived from them. The differences in our attitudes toward *education* and *indoctrination*, for example, are based on real differences between the two activities, as well as on whatever emotive differences may attach to the two words.

The point, however, is this. If our purpose is to achieve and communicate information, that language is most useful which has the least emotive impact. In other words, if our interest is scientific, we shall do well to avoid expressive language and to cultivate as emotively neutral a set of terms as we can. This has been done most extensively in the physical sciences. Older and more emotively exciting terms such as "noble" and "base" for characterizing metals have either been displaced by a special jargon or have come through the passage of time to be completely divorced from their former honorific or derogatory associations. This has been a contributing factor to scientific progress.

Thus if we are concerned to investigate the literal truth or falsity of a view and to discover its logical implications, our task will be facilitated if we translate any highly emotive formulation concerning it into as nearly neutral a description as possible. Suppose, for example, we are interested in the question of national compulsory health insurance. In the course of our investigations we shall come across certain highly emotive

* By permission from *The Proper Study of Mankind* by Stuart Chase. Copyright, 1948, by Stuart Chase. Published by Harper and Brothers.

phraseology, as in the text of the statement by Dr. Elmer L. Henderson, Chairman of the Board of Trustees of the American Medical Association, on President Truman's proposed national compulsory health insurance program. Dr. Henderson states that:

There is a great deal of double talk in the President's message, but what he actually proposes is a national compulsory health insurance system which would regiment doctors and patients alike under a vast bureaucracy of political administrators, clerks, bookkeepers and lay committees.*

Now, can this passage be translated into more nearly neutral language without doing violence to the informative content? No more information is presented by Dr. Henderson in the passage cited than in the following:

There is some ambiguity in the President's message, but its intended meaning is the proposal to set up a national compulsory health insurance system in which contact between doctors and patients would be regulated by an administrative agency of large size, which would employ government officials, clerks and bookkeepers, and committees not composed exclusively of M.D.'s.

These are the facts as Dr. Henderson sees them, and his information may well be correct. But when it is formulated with such a liberal sprinkling of emotively-explosive words like "double talk," "regimentation," "vast bureaucracy," *"political* administrators," and when there is the hint that "doctors and patients alike" would be *under* clerks and bookkeepers (as though no doctor ever employed a clerk or bookkeeper to keep his own records straight), then it requires a disproportionate amount of effort to cut through to the actual information presented.

Emotive language is not in itself bad, but when it is information we are after, we shall do well to choose words whose emo-

* By permission from *The Journal of the American Medical Association*, Vol. 140, No. 1, May 7, 1949. Page 114.

tive meanings do not distract and hinder us from dealing successfully with what they describe. As students of logic, we are concerned not only to work out a more adequate terminology to use in connection with argument, but are also interested in examining critically the results of ignoring the above directive. The careless use of language in argument often results in fallacies, which will occupy our attention in the following chapter.

EXERCISE

Select a brief passage of highly emotive writing from some current periodical and translate it in such a way as to retain its informative content while reducing its expressive significance to a minimum.

CHAPTER THREE

Informal Fallacies

Although all textbooks of logic contain discussions of fallacies, their treatments are not the same. There is no universally accepted classification of fallacies. This situation is not surprising, for as De Morgan, an early modern logician, has aptly said, "There *is* no such thing as a classification of the ways in which men may arrive at an error: it is much to be doubted whether there ever *can be*."

The word "fallacy" is itself a rather vague term. One perfectly proper use of the word is to designate any mistaken idea or false belief, like the "fallacy" of believing that all men are honest. But logicians use the term in the narrow technical sense of an error in reasoning or in argument. A fallacy, as we shall use the term, is a type of incorrect argument. Since it is a type of incorrect argument, we can say of two different arguments that they contain or commit the *same* fallacy. Many arguments, of course, are so obviously incorrect as to deceive no one. It is customary in the study of logic to reserve the term "fallacy" for arguments which although incorrect are psychologically persuasive. We therefore define a fallacy as a form of argument that *seems* to be correct but which proves, upon examination, not to be so. It is profitable to study such arguments, for familiarity and understanding will help keep us from being misled by them. To be forewarned is to be forearmed.

Traditionally, fallacies are divided into two broad groups, formal and informal. Formal fallacies are most conveniently discussed in connection with certain patterns of valid inference to which they bear a superficial resemblance. We shall accordingly defer consideration of them to subsequent chapters. For the present, we shall be concerned with informal fallacies, errors in reasoning into which we may fall either because of carelessness and inattention to our subject matter or through being misled by some ambiguity in the language used to formulate our argument. We may divide informal fallacies into fallacies of *relevance* and fallacies of *ambiguity*. No attempt will be made at completeness; only fifteen informal fallacies will be considered, the most common and deceptive ones.

I. FALLACIES OF RELEVANCE

Common to all arguments which commit fallacies of relevance is the circumstance that their premises are *logically irrelevant* to the truth or falsehood of the conclusions which they purport to establish. The irrelevance here is logical rather than psychological, of course, for unless there were some psychological connection, there would be no persuasiveness or *seeming* correctness. How psychological relevance can be confused with logical relevance is most satisfactorily explained by reference to the fact that language is used directively and expressively as well as informatively. This is perhaps best shown in connection with some actual examples.

1. **Irrelevant Conclusion.** The fallacy of "irrelevant conclusion" is committed when an argument supposedly intended to establish a particular conclusion is directed to proving a different conclusion. For example, when a particular proposal for housing legislation is under consideration, a legislator may rise to speak in favor of the bill and argue only that decent housing for all the people is desirable. His remarks are then

logically irrelevant to the point at issue, for the question concerns the particular measure at hand. Presumably everyone agrees that decent housing for all the people is desirable (even those will pretend to agree who do not really think so). The question is: will this particular measure provide it, and if so, will it provide it better than any practical alternative? The speaker's argument is fallacious, committing the fallacy of *irrelevant conclusion*.

In a law court, in attempting to prove that the accused is guilty of murder, the prosecution may argue at length that murder is a horrible crime. He may even succeed in *proving* that conclusion. But when he infers from his remarks about the horribleness of murder that the defendant is guilty of it, he is committing the fallacy of *irrelevant conclusion*.

The question naturally arises, how do such arguments ever fool anybody? Once it is seen that the conclusion is logically irrelevant, why should the argument mislead anyone? In the first place, it is not always obvious that a given argument *is* an instance of *irrelevant conclusion*. During the course of an extended discussion, fatigue may lead to inattention and errors and irrelevancies may tend to pass unnoticed. That is only part of the answer, of course. The other part has to do with the fact that language may serve to evoke emotion as well as to communicate information.

Consider the first example of *irrelevant conclusion*. By urging that decent housing for all the people is desirable the speaker has succeeded in evoking an attitude of approval for himself and for what he says, and this attitude will tend to get transferred to his final conclusion, more by psychological association than by logical implication. The speaker may have succeeded in evoking such a positive sentiment for housing improvement that his hearers will vote more enthusiastically for the bill he supports than if he had really proved its passage to be in the public interest.

Again, in the second example, if the prosecution has given a sufficiently moving picture of the horribleness of murder, the jury may be so aroused, such horror and disapproval may have been evoked in them, that they will bring in a verdict of "guilty" more swiftly than if the prosecutor had "merely" proved that the defendant had *committed* the crime.

A number of particular types of irrelevant argument have traditionally been given Latin names. Some of these Latin names have become part of the English language, "ad homi-nem," for example. Others are less familiar. We shall consider only a few of these here, making no pretense to an exhaustive treatment. The theoretical explanation of how they succeed in being persuasive despite their logical incorrectness is in each case to be given in terms of their expressive function in evok-ing such attitudes as fear, pity, reverence, disapproval, or en-thusiasm.

2. **Argumentum ad Baculum (appeal to force).** The *argu-mentum ad baculum* is the fallacy committed when one appeals to force or the threat of force to cause acceptance of a conclu-sion. It is usually resorted to only when evidence or rational arguments fail. The *ad baculum* is epitomized in the saying "might makes right." The use and threat of "strong-arm" methods to coerce political opponents provide contemporary examples of this fallacy. Appeal to non-rational methods of in-timidation may of course be more subtle than the open use or threat of concentration camps or "goon squads." The lobbyist uses the *ad baculum* when he reminds a representative that he (the lobbyist) represents so many thousands of voters in the representative's constituency, or so many potential contributors to campaign funds. Logically these considerations have nothing to do with the merits of the legislation the lobbyist is attempt-ing to influence. But they may be, unfortunately, very per-suasive. On the international scale, the *argumentum ad baculum* means war or the threat of war. An amusing though at the same time frightening example of *ad baculum* reasoning at the in-ternational level is told in Harry Hopkins' account of the "Big Three" meeting at Yalta towards the end of World War II. Churchill is reported to have told the others that the Pope had

suggested that such and such a course of action should be followed. And Stalin is supposed to have indicated his disagreement by asking, "And how many divisions did you say the Pope had available for combat duty?"

3. **Argumentum ad Hominem (abusive).** The phrase *"argumentum ad hominem"* translates literally into "argument directed to the man." It is susceptible of two interpretations, whose interrelationship will be explained after the two are discussed separately. We may designate this fallacy on the first interpretation as the "abusive" variety. It is committed when instead of trying to *disprove the truth* of what is asserted one attacks the man who made the assertion. Thus it may be argued that Bacon's philosophy is untrustworthy because he was removed from his chancellorship for dishonesty. This argument is fallacious, because the personal character of a man is logically irrelevant to the truth or falsehood of what he says or the correctness or incorrectness of his argument. To argue that proposals are bad or assertions false because they are proposed or asserted by Communist (or by "economic royalists," or by Catholics, or by anti-Catholics, or by wife beaters) is to argue fallaciously and to be guilty of committing an *argumentum ad hominem,* (abusive). The way in which this irrelevant argument may sometimes persuade is through the psychological process of transference. Where an attitude of disapproval towards a person can be evoked, it may possibly tend to overflow the strictly emotional field and become disagreement with what that person says. But this connection is only psychological, not logical. Even the most wicked of men may sometimes tell the truth or argue correctly.

The classic example of this fallacy has to do with British law procedure. There the practice of law is divided between *solicitors,* who prepare the cases for trial, and *barristers,* who argue or "plead" the cases in court. Ordinarily their cooperation is admirable, but sometimes it leaves much to be desired. On one such latter occasion, the barrister ignored the case completely until the day it was to be presented at court, depending upon the solicitor to investigate the defendant's case and prepare the brief. He arrived at court just a moment before the trial was to begin and was handed his brief by the solicitor. Surprised at its thinness, he glanced inside to find written: "No case; abuse the plaintiff's attorney!"

4. **Argumentum ad Hominem (circumstantial).** The second interpretation of the fallacy of *argumentum ad hominem,* the "circumstantial" variety, can be explained as follows. Where two men are disputing, one may ignore the question of whether his own contention is *true* or *false* and seek instead to prove that his opponent ought to accept it because of his opponent's special circumstances. Thus if one's adversary is a clergyman, one may argue that a certain contention *must* be accepted because its denial is incompatible with the Scriptures. This is not to prove it *true* but to urge its acceptance by that particular individual because of his special circumstances, in this case his religious affiliation. Or if one's opponent is, say, a Republican, one may argue not that a certain proposition is *true* but that he ought to assent to it because it is implied by the tenets of his party. The classical example of this fallacy is the reply of the hunter when accused of barbarism in sacrificing unoffending animals to his own amusement. His reply is to ask his critic, "Why do *you* feed on the flesh of harmless cattle?" The sportsman here is guilty of an *argumentum ad hominem* because he does not try to prove that it is right to sacrifice animal life for human pleasure, but merely that it cannot consistently be decried by his critic because of the critic's own special circumstances, in this case his not being a vegetarian. Arguments such as these are not *correct;* they do not present good evidence for the *truth* of their conclusions but are only intended to win assent to the conclusion from one's opponent because of his special circumstances. This they frequently do; they are often very persuasive.

The connection between these two varieties of *argumentum ad hominem* is not difficult to see. The second may even be regarded as a special case of the first. For the second, the "circumstantial" kind, in effect charges the man who disputes your conclusion with inconsistency, either among his beliefs or between his preaching and his practice. And this *may* be regarded as a kind of reproach or abuse.

5. **Argumentum ad Ignorantiam (argument from ignorance).** The fallacy of *argumentum ad ignorantiam* is illustrated by the argument that there must be ghosts because no one has ever been able to prove that there aren't any. The *argumentum ad ignorantiam* is committed whenever it is argued that a proposition is true simply on the basis that it has not been proved false, or that it is false because it has not been proved true. But our ignorance of how to prove or disprove a proposition clearly does not establish either the truth or the falsehood of that proposition. This fallacy is most often connected with such matters as psychic phenomena, telepathy, and the like, where there is no clear-cut evidence either for or against. It is curious how many of the most enlightened people are prone to this fallacy, as witness the many students of science who affirm the falseness of spiritualist and telepathic claims simply on the grounds that their truth has not been established.

The *argumentum ad ignorantiam* is fallacious in every context but one. The exception is a court of law, where the guiding principle is that a person is presumed innocent until proven guilty. The defense can legitimately claim that if the prosecution has not proved guilt, this warrants a verdict of *not guilty*. But since this position is based upon the special legal principle mentioned, it does not refute the claim that the *argumentum ad ignorantiam* constitutes a fallacy in every other context.

It is sometimes claimed that the *argumentum ad hominem* (abusive), is not fallacious when used in a court of law in an attempt to impeach the testimony of a witness. True enough, doubt can be cast upon a witness's testimony if it can be shown that he is a chronic liar and perjurer. Where this can be shown, it certainly reduces the credibility of the testimony offered. But if one infers from this that the witness's testimony establishes the falsehood of that to which he testifies, instead of concluding merely that his testimony does not establish its truth, then his reasoning is fallacious, being an *argumentum ad ignorantiam*. Such errors are more common than one would think.

A qualification should be made at this point. In some circumstances it can safely be assumed that *if* a certain event had occurred, evidence of it could be discovered by qualified investigators. In such circumstances it is perfectly reasonable to take the absence of proof of its occurrence as positive proof of its non-occurrence. Of course, the proof here is not based on ignorance but on our *knowledge* that if it had occurred it would be known. For example, if a serious F.B.I. investigation fails to unearth any evidence that Mr. X is a communist, it would be wrong to conclude that their research has left them ignorant. It has rather established that Mr. X is *not* one. Failure to draw such conclusions is the other side of the bad coin of innuendo, as when one says of a man that there is "no proof" that he is a scoundrel. In some cases not to draw a conclusion is as much a breach of correct reasoning as it would be to draw a mistaken conclusion.

6. **Argumentum ad Misericordiam (appeal to pity).** The *argumentum ad misericordiam* is the fallacy committed when pity is appealed to for the sake of getting a conclusion accepted. This argument is frequently encountered in courts of law, when a defense attorney may disregard the facts of the case and seek to win his client's acquittal by arousing pity in the jurymen. Clarence Darrow, the celebrated trial lawyer, was a master at using this device. In defending Thomas I. Kidd, an officer of the Amalgamated Woodworkers Union, who was indicted on a charge of criminal conspiracy, Darrow spoke these words to the jury:

I appeal to you not for Thomas Kidd, but I appeal to you for the long line—the long, long, line reaching back through the ages and forward to the years to come—the long line of despoiled and downtrodden people of the earth. I appeal to you for those men who rise in the morning before daylight comes and who go home at night when the light has faded from the sky and given their life, their strength, their toil to make others rich and great. I appeal to you in the name of those women who are offering up their lives to this modern god of gold, and I appeal to you in the name of those little children, the living and the unborn.*

Is Thomas Kidd guilty as charged? Darrow's appeal was sufficiently moving to make the average juror want to throw questions of evidence and of law out the window. Yet however persuasive such a plea might be, from the point of view of logic that argument is fallacious which draws from "premisses" such as these the conclusion that the accused is innocent.

An older and considerably more subtle example of the *argumentum ad misericordiam* is reported by Plato in the *Apology,* which purports to be a record of Socrates' defense of himself during his trial.

Perhaps there may be some one who is offended at me, when he calls to mind how he himself on a similar, or even a less serious occasion, prayed and entreated the judges with many tears, and how he produced his children in court, which was a moving spectacle, together with a host of relations and friends; whereas I, who am probably in danger of my life, will do none of these things. The contrast may occur to his mind, and he may be set against me, and vote in anger because he is displeased at me on this account. Now if there be such a person among you,—mind, I do not say that there is,—to him I may fairly reply: My friend, I am a man, and like other men, a creature of flesh and blood, and not "of wood or stone," as Homer says; and I have a family, yes, and sons, O Athenians, three in number, one almost a man, and two others who are still young; and yet I will not bring any of them hither in order to petition you for acquittal.

The *argumentum ad misericordiam* is sometimes used with ludicrous effect, as in the case of the youth who was tried for a particularly brutal crime, the murder of his mother and father with an axe. Confronted with overwhelming evidence, he pleaded for leniency on the grounds that he was an orphan.

---

* As quoted in *Clarence Darrow for the Defense* by Irving Stone. Copyright, 1941, by Irving Stone. Published by Garden City Publishing Company, Inc. Garden City, N. Y.

7. **Argumentum ad Populum.** The *argumentum ad populum* is sometimes defined as the fallacy committed in directing an emotional appeal "to the people" or "to the gallery" to win their assent to a conclusion unsupported by valid argument. But this definition is so broad as to include the *ad misericordiam,* the *ad hominem* (abusive), and almost all of the other fallacies of relevance. We may define the *argumentum ad populum* fallacy a little more narrowly as the attempt to win popular assent to a conclusion by arousing the passions and enthusiasms of the multitude. This is a favorite device with the propagandist, the demagogue, and—the advertiser. Faced with the task of mobilizing public sentiment for or against a particular measure, the propagandist will avoid the laborious process of collecting and presenting evidence and rational argument by using the short cut methods of the *argumentum ad populum.* Where the proposal is for a change and he is against it, he will express suspicion of "newfangled innovations" and praise the wisdom of "the existing order." If he is for it, he will be for "progress" and opposed to "antiquated prejudice." Here we have the use of invidious terms with no rational attempt made to argue for them or to justify their application. This technique will be supplemented by displaying the flag, brass bands, and whatever else may serve to stimulate and excite the public. The demagogue's use of the *argumentum ad populum* is beautifully illustrated by Shakespeare's version of Marc Antony's funeral oration over the body of Julius Caesar.

It is to the huckster, the ballyhoo artist, the Twentieth-Century advertiser that we may look to see the *argumentum ad populum* elevated almost to the status of a fine art. Here every attempt is made to set up associations between the product being advertised and objects of which we can be expected to approve strongly. To eat a certain brand of processed cereal is proclaimed a patriotic duty. To bathe with a certain brand of soap is described as a thrilling experience. Strains of symphonic music precede and follow the mention of a certain dentifrice on the radio program sponsored by its manufacturer. In pictorial advertisements, the people portrayed as using the products advertised are always pictured as wearing the kind of clothing and living in the kind of houses calculated to arouse the approval and admiration of the average consumer. The young men pictured as delightedly using the products are clear-eyed and broad-shouldered, the older men are invariably "of distinction." The women are all slim and lovely, either very well dressed or hardly dressed at all. Whether you are interested in economical transportation or in high-speed driving, you will be assured by each automobile manufacturer that his product is "best," and he will "prove" his assertion by displaying his car surrounded by pretty girls in bathing suits. Advertisers "glamorize" their products and sell us daydreams and delusions of grandeur with every package of pink pills or garbage disposal unit.

Here, *if* they are trying to prove that their products adequately serve their ostensible functions, their procedures are glorified examples of the *argumentum ad populum*. Besides the "snob appeal" already referred to, we may include under this heading the familiar "bandwagon argument." The campaigning politician "argues" that he should receive our votes because "everybody" is voting that way. We are told that such and such a breakfast food, or cigarette, or motor car is "best" because it is America's largest seller. A certain belief "must be true" because "everyone knows it." But popular acceptance of a policy does not prove it to be wise; widespread use of certain products does not prove them to be satisfactory; general assent to a claim does not prove it to be true. To argue in this way is to commit the *ad populum* fallacy.

8. **Argumentum ad Verecundiam (appeal to authority).** The *argumentum ad verecundiam* is the appeal to authority, that is, to the feeling of respect people have for the famous, to win assent to a conclusion. This method of argument is not always strictly fallacious, for the reference to an admitted authority in the special field of his competence may carry great weight and constitute relevant evidence. If laymen are disputing over some

question of physical science and one appeals to the testimony of Einstein on the matter, that testimony is very relevant. Although it does not prove the point, it certainly tends to confirm it. This is a relative matter, however, for if experts rather than laymen are disputing over a question in the field in which they are experts, their appeal would be only to the facts and to reason, and any appeal to the authority of another expert would be completely without value as evidence.

But when an authority is appealed to for testimony in matters outside the province of his special field, the appeal commits the fallacy of *argumentum ad verecundiam*. If in an argument over religion one of the disputants appeals to the opinions of Darwin, a great authority in biology, the appeal is fallacious. Similarly an appeal to the opinions of a great physicist like Einstein to settle a political or economic argument would be fallacious. The claim might be made that a person brilliant enough to achieve the status of an authority in an advanced and difficult field like biology or physics must have correct opinions in fields other than his specialty. But the weakness of this claim is obvious when we realize that in this day of extreme specialization, to obtain thorough knowledge of one field requires such concentration as to restrict the possibility of achieving authoritative knowledge in others.

Advertising "testimonials" are frequent instances of this fallacy. We are urged to smoke this or that brand of cigarettes because a champion swimmer or midget auto racer affirms their superiority. And we are assured that such and such a cosmetic is better because it is preferred by opera singers or movie stars. Of course, such an advertisement may equally well be construed as snob appeal and listed as an example of an *argumentum ad populum*. But where a proposition is claimed to be literally *true* on the basis of its assertion by an "authority" whose competence lies in a different field, we have a fallacy of *argumentum ad verecundiam*.

9. **False Cause.** The fallacy which we call that of the "false cause" has been variously analyzed in the past and given alterna-

tive Latin names, such as *non causa pro causa* and *post hoc ergo propter hoc*. The first of these is more general, and means to mistake what is not the cause of a given effect for its real cause. The second is the inference that one event is the cause of another from the bare fact that the first occurs earlier than the second. We shall regard any argument that incorrectly attempts to establish a causal connection as an instance of the fallacy of *false cause*.

What actually constitutes a good or correct argument for causal connections is perhaps the central problem of inductive logic or scientific method and will be discussed in later chapters. It is easy to see, however, that the mere fact of coincidence or temporal succession does not establish any causal connection. Certainly we should reject the savage's claim that beating his drums is the cause of the sun's reappearance after an eclipse, even though he can offer as evidence the fact that every time drums have been beaten during an eclipse, the sun has reappeared! No one would be misled by this argument, but countless people are "suckers" for patent medicine testimonials which report that Mrs. X suffered from a head cold, drank three bottles of a "secret" herb decoction, and in two weeks lost her cold!

10. Complex Question.   The last fallacy of relevance to be considered is that of the *complex question*. We all know that there is something "funny" about questions like "Have you given up your evil ways?" or "Have you stopped beating your wife?" These are not simple questions to which a straightforward "yes" or "no" answer is possible. Such questions as these assume that a definite answer has already been given to a prior question that was not even asked. Thus the first assumes that the answer "yes" has been given to the unasked question "Have you in the past followed evil ways?" and the second assumes an affirmative answer to the unasked question "Have you ever beaten your wife?" In either case, if a simple "yes" or "no" answer to the "trick" question is given, it has the effect of ratifying or affirming the implied answer to the unasked question. A question of this sort does not admit of a simple "yes" or "no" answer because it is not a simple or single question but a complex question which consists of several questions rolled into one.

The fallacy of the *complex question* is committed when the plurality of questions is undetected and a single answer is demanded or returned to a complex question as if it were a simple one. This fallacy is not confined to obvious jokes like our first two examples. In cross-examination a lawyer may ask complex questions of a witness to confuse or even to incriminate him. He may ask: "Where did you hide the evidence?" "What did you do with the money you stole?" or the like. In propaganda, where a flat statement might be extremely difficult to prove or get accepted, the idea may be "put across" very persuasively by means of the *complex question*. A spokesman for utilities interests may propound the question: "Why is private development of resources so much more efficient than any public control?" A jingo may demand of his audience: "How long are we going to tolerate foreign interference with our national interests?"

In all such cases, the intelligent procedure is to treat the complex question not as a simple one, but to analyze it into its component parts. It may well be the case that when the implicit or implied prior question is correctly answered, the second or explicit one simply dissolves. If I did not hide any evidence, the question of where I hid it does not make sense. There are other varieties of the *complex question*. A mother may ask her youngster if he wants to be a good boy and go to bed? Here the matter is less deceptive. There are clearly two questions involved; one does not presuppose a particular answer to the other. The fallacy here lies in the implication that one and the same answer must be given to *both* of the questions. Are you "for" the Republicans and prosperity, or not? Answer "yes" or "no"! But here is a complex question, and it is at least conceivable that the two questions have different answers.

In parliamentary procedure, the motion "to divide the question" is a *privileged* motion. This rule acknowledges that questions may be complex and can therefore be considered more intelligently when separated. Our practice with respect to the

President's veto power is less enlightened. The President can veto a measure as a whole, but he cannot veto the part he disapproves and sign the remainder. The President cannot divide the question but must veto or approve, answer "yes" or "no," to any question no matter how complex. This restriction has led, as is well known, to the congressional practice of attaching, as "riders," to measures that the President is generally known to approve, certain additional—often completely irrelevant—clauses to which he is known to be opposed. When presented with such a bill, the President must either approve something of which he disapproves or veto something he approves.

Still another version of this fallacy is found in certain question-begging epithets, as when one asks "Is so and so a screwball radical?" or "an unthinking conservative?" or "Is this policy going to lead to ruinous deflation?" Here, as elsewhere, one must *divide* the complex question. The answers might be, "a radical, yes, but not a screwball," "a conservative, yes, but not unthinking," or "It will lead to deflation, yes; however, that will not be ruinous but a healthy readjustment."

EXERCISES

Classify and explain the various fallacies of relevance contained in the following:

1. It is uneconomical and unsound to ignore the sex of an employee and to give equal pay for equal work, for it is a fact that in some jobs requiring heavy lifting it is impossible for a woman to do as much work as a man.

2. The *Journal of the American Medical Association* for November 26, 1949, reports on page 933 that ". . . the chiropractors have failed entirely in their task to establish that their concepts have a scientific base . . ." Therefore the concepts of the chiropractors have no scientific base at all.

3. The question before us is simply this: when are we going to stop the hideous waste and corruption of the incumbent office-

holders? When we face that question squarely, our only answer can be *NOW!*

4. Let's get down to brass tacks.   None of us here is a Philadelphia lawyer, we're just plain folks trying to see our way clear. There's been a lot of high-falutin' talk about "economic implications" and such like, but the plain fact is that if they build that dam here it will cost us money we just don't have. I'm against it— we're all against it.

5. Boss, I think my work deserves more money. I've got a wife and family, and the wife's been sick a lot lately, and what with doctor bills and clothes for the kids, I don't know how we'll manage on what I'm making now.

6. Whatever Mr. Morgan has to say about the new tax bill can be ignored, for as a wealthy man he can be expected to oppose the levying of any additional taxes.

7. From a coffee advertisement:
   More coffee is consumed in the United States than anywhere else, and America has become the strongest nation. Protect your American heritage by continuing to use coffee!

8. Mr. Editor, I'm sure you will agree that this little escapade of my son has no real news value. Doesn't my firm buy thousands of dollars worth of advertising space in your paper each year?

9. Nietzsche argued that the moral law is a mere man-made convention. But Nietzsche was a sickly self-tormented disloyal little man who spent the last years of his life in an insane asylum. His conclusion is thus clearly seen to be false.

10. Attendance at Church or Sunday School is a valuable factor in the training of youth, for it is recommended strongly by all our leading industrialists and business men.

11. Gentlemen, how could we ever remove the enormous deficit that would be incurred if we adopted the proposed advertising campaign? There is no way; so I vote against undertaking the campaign.

12. That law is unfair to labor, Mr. Senator, and ought to be repealed. The unions have gone on record against it, and there are a quarter of a million union members in your constituency.

13. The Truman administration's policies were all wrong, for they have been condemned by General MacArthur, one of the greatest military geniuses of all time.

14. The theory of economic determinism in history is clearly false, since its only advocates are those Communists who would seek to subvert all morality to their own power-mad self-seeking interests.

15. Whatever testimony Reuther offers against the proposed legislation may be discounted, for as a labor union official he is bound to oppose any measures to control the labor movement.

16. There are more churches in New York City than in any other city in the nation, and more crimes are committed in New York than anywhere else. This makes it clear that to eliminate the criminal we must abolish the church.

17. A careful examination of the literary style and factual content of the plays attributed to Shakespeare reveals that they could not possibly all have been written by the same man. It follows that at least some of the plays attributed to Shakespeare were actually written by Bacon.

18. We have not the slightest shred of evidence that they will negotiate in good faith. So we can only believe that they will try to deceive us.

19. Professor, don't you think my examination is worth just a little higher grade? I'm working pretty long hours outside to put myself through school, and it's not always easy, just studying and waiting on tables while the other students are having a high old time!

20. The removal of rent controls would benefit the tenant as well as the landlord, for freedom of contract is part of the great American heritage which has made our nation the strongest in the world and all our citizens the most prosperous!

21. In reply to the gentleman's arguments, I need only say that two years ago he advocated the very measure which he now opposes.

22. The President's decision to veto the tax bill was a wise one. Never has a man taken office under such difficult conditions. The

nation's economy dislocated by a long and costly war, its nerves stretched to the snapping point by the threat of another, he is faced by a revolt within the ranks of his own party and has been subject to a continuous torrent of abuse from a hostile press.

23. The Slobovian government must be made to realize that they have no legitimate interest in the Danube area. Our airforce is still the strongest in the world, and our newest planes can fly non-stop clear around the world, carrying atomic bombs half the way.

24. If we adopt the board's proposal, we shall realize a modest profit at a very slight risk. The board's proposal is therefore better than any alternative plan.

25. It is wrong for America to belong to the United Nations Organization, for Washington, the Father of Our Country, specifically warned us against entangling alliances.

26. Salesman: "Will you want to pay cash and receive the special discount or would you care to avail yourself of our convenient credit terms? While you decide I can make arrangements for immediate delivery."

27. Scratchies are America's largest selling breakfast food. They must be good.

28. The governor advocates raising the corporation tax, but let me remind you that he came into office by the narrowest of pluralities after a scurrilous and lying campaign in which he demagogically appealed to the lowest passions of our people and promised everything to everybody, knowing full well that he could not keep those promises. The corporation tax should therefore not be raised.

29. Smith must be a scoundrel, for no one has a good word to say for him.

30. The following is quoted from *The Art of Cross Examination*, by F. L. Wellman. (The Macmillan Company, New York, 1946.) The conclusion here, it should be noted, is implied rather than explicitly drawn.

　　A very well-known doctor had given important testimony in

a case where his most intimate friend appeared as opposing counsel. These two men—doctor and lawyer—stood equally high in their respective professions, and had been close friends for many years and were frequent dinner companions at one another's homes, with their wives and children. In fact, they had practically grown up together. The lawyer knew that his friend had testified to his honest opinion, which no amount of cross-examination could weaken. He therefore confined himself to the following few interrogations; and, fearing that he could not keep a straight face while he put his questions, he avoided facing the witness at all, keeping his face turned toward a side window.

Q. "Doctor, you say you are a practicing physician. Have you practiced your profession in the City of Chicago for any length of time?"

A. "Yes, I have been in practice here in Chicago now for about forty years."

Q. "Well, doctor, during that time I presume you have had occasion to treat some of our most prominent citizens. Have you not?"

A. "Yes, I think I have."

Q. "By any chance, doctor, were you ever called as a family physician to prescribe for the elder Marshall Field?"

A. "Yes, I was his family physician for a number of years."

Q. "By the way, I haven't heard of him lately. Where is he now?" (Still looking out of the window.)

A. "He is dead."

Q. "Oh—I'm sorry. Were you ever the family physician to the elder Mr. McCormick?"

A. "Yes, also for many years."

Q. "Would you mind my asking where he is now?"

A. "He is dead."

Q. "Oh—I'm sorry."

Then he proceeded in the same vein to make inquiries about eight or ten of the leading Chicago citizens whom he knew his friend had attended, all of whom were dead, and having exhausted the list he sat down quietly amid the amused chuckles of the jurors with the comment: "I don't think it is necessary to ask you any more questions. Please step down."

II. FALLACIES OF AMBIGUITY

The second group of informal fallacies to be considered is traditionally called "fallacies of ambiguity" or "fallacies of clearness." These occur in arguments whose formulations contain ambiguous words or phrases, whose meanings shift and change more or less subtly in the course of the argument and thus render it fallacious. The following are all fallacies of ambiguity, but it is helpful to divide and classify them according to the different ways in which their ambiguities arise.

1. **Equivocation.** The first fallacy of ambiguity we shall consider is that which arises through simple *equivocation*. Most words have more than one literal meaning, as the word "hide" may denote either the process of concealing something or the skin of an animal. When we keep these different meanings apart, no difficulty arises. But when we confuse the different meanings a single word or phrase may have, using it in different senses in the same context without realizing it, we are using it *equivocally*. If the context happens to be an argument, we commit the fallacy of *equivocation*.

A traditional example of this fallacy is the following: "The end of a thing is its perfection; death is the end of life; hence, death is the perfection of life." This argument is fallacious because two different senses of the word "end" are confused in it. The word "end" may mean either "goal" or "last event." Both these meanings are of course legitimate. But what is illegitimate is to confuse the two, as in this argument. The premisses are only plausible when the word "end" is interpreted differently in each of them, as: "The *goal* of a thing is its perfection," and "Death is the *last event* of life." But the conclusion that "death is the perfection of life" does not even apparently follow from *these* premisses. Of course the *same* sense of "end" could be used in both premisses, but then the argument would lose all its plausibility, for it would have either the unplausible premiss "The *last event* of a thing is its perfection" or the patently false premiss "Death is the *goal* of life." Some examples of the fallacy of *equivocation,* so absurd as to fool no one, are a kind of joke. Such, for example, would be:

> Some dogs have fuzzy ears.
> My dog has fuzzy ears.
> Therefore my dog is some dog!

There is a special kind of equivocation that deserves special mention. This has to do with "relative" terms, which have different meanings in different contexts. For example, the word "tall" is a relative word; a *tall man* and a *tall building* are in quite different categories. A tall man is one who is taller than most men, a tall building is one which is taller than most buildings. Certain forms of argument which are valid for non-relative terms break down when relative terms are substituted for them. The argument "an elephant is an animal; therefore a gray elephant is a gray animal," is perfectly valid. The word "gray" is a non-relative term. But the argument "an elephant is an animal; therefore a small elephant is a small animal," is ridiculous. The point here is that "small" is a relative term: a small elephant is a very large animal. The fallacy is one of *equivocation* on the relative term "small." Not all equivocation on relative terms is so obvious, however. The word "good" is a relative term and is frequently equivocated on when it is argued, for example, that so and so would be a good President because he is a good general, or must be a good man because he is a good mathematician, or is a good teacher because he is a good scholar.

2. **Amphiboly.** The fallacy of *amphiboly* occurs in arguing from premises whose formulations are ambiguous because of their grammatical construction. A statement is *amphibolous* when its meaning is unclear because of the loose or awkward way in which its words are combined. An amphibolous statement may be true on one interpretation and false on another. When it is stated as premiss with the interpretation which makes it true, and a conclusion is drawn from it on the interpretation which makes it false, then the fallacy of *amphiboly* has been committed.

The classic example of *amphiboly* has to do with Croesus and the Oracle of Delphi. *Amphibolous* utterances were of course the chief stock in trade of the ancient oracles. Croesus, the king of Lydia, was contemplating war with the kingdom of Persia. Being a prudent man, he did not wish to war unless he were sure to win. He consulted Delphi on the matter and received the oracular reply that "If Croesus went to war with Persia, he would destroy a mighty kingdom." Delighted with this prediction, Croesus went to war and was speedily defeated by Cyrus, king of the Persian host. Afterwards, his life having been spared, Croesus wrote a bitterly complaining letter to the Oracle, presumably signing it "irate subscriber." His letter was answered by the priests of Delphi who claimed that the Oracle had been right. In going to war Croesus *had* destroyed a mighty kingdom —his own! Amphibolous statements make dangerous premises. They are, however, seldom encountered in serious discussion.

Some amphibolous sentences are not without their humorous aspects, as in posters urging us to "Save Soap and Waste Paper," or when anthropology is defined as "The science of man embracing woman." We should be mistaken if we inferred immodest dress on the woman described in a story: ". . . loosely wrapped in a newspaper, she carried three dresses." Amphiboly is often exhibited by newspaper headings and brief items, as in "The farmer blew out his brains after taking affectionate farewell of his family with a shotgun."

3. **Accent.** Like all fallacies of ambiguity, the fallacy of *accent* is committed in an argument whose deceptive but invalid nature depends upon a change or shift in meaning. The way in which the meaning shifts in the fallacy of *accent* depends upon what parts of it may be emphasized or accented. That some statements have quite different meanings when different words are stressed is clear. Consider the different meanings that are given according to which of the italicized words is stressed in the injunction:

We should not speak ill of our friends.

When read without any undue stresses, the injunction is perfectly sound. But if the conclusion is drawn that we should feel
free to speak ill of someone who is *not* our friend, then this conclusion follows *only* if the premiss has the meaning it acquires
when its last word is accented. But when its last word is accented, it is no longer acceptable as a moral law, it has a different meaning, and it is in fact a different premiss. The argument is a case of the fallacy of *accent*. So too would be the
argument which drew from the same premiss the conclusion that
we are free to *work* ill upon our friends if only we do it silently.
And similarly with the other fallacious inferences which suggest
themselves. In the same light vein, depending upon how it is
accented, the statement:

> Woman without her man would be lost.

would be perfectly acceptable to either sex. But to infer the
statement with one accent from the statement accented differently would be an instance of the fallacy of *accent*.

A more serious commission of this fallacy, in a slightly wider
sense of the term, can occur in making a quotation, where inserting or deleting italics may change the meaning. The same
fallacious accenting may be done without any variation in the
use of italics, when the passage quoted is torn from its context.
For often a passage can be correctly understood only in the light
of its context, which may make clear the *sense* in which the
passage is intended, or may contain explicit qualifications without which the passage has a quite different meaning. Therefore
a responsible writer who makes a direct quotation will indicate
whether or not any words italicized in his quotation were italicized in the original and will indicate any omission of words or
phrases by the use of dots.

A statement which is literally true but quite uninteresting
when read or written "normally" may be made quite exciting
when accented in certain ways. But this accenting may change
its meaning, and with its different meaning it may no longer be
true. Thus truth is sacrificed to sensationalism by means of the

fallacious inference produced by accenting (typographically) one half of a sentence more than the other. This technique is a deliberate policy of certain tabloid newspapers to make their headlines arresting. Such a paper may run as a headline in large boldface type the words,

REVOLUTION IN FRANCE

and then below, in considerably less prominent and smaller type, may be found the words "feared by authorities." The complete statement that "Revolution in France (is) feared by authorities" may be perfectly true. But as accented in the tabloid the assertion is given an exciting but utterly false significance. The same kind of misleading accenting is found in many advertisements. Where a presumably net price is quoted for a particular commodity, closer inspection of the announcement may reveal the words, invariably in much smaller print, "plus tax" or perhaps the phrase "and up." In advertisements directed towards a presumably less literate section of the public, this kind of accenting is often quite flagrant.

How even the literal truth can be a vehicle for falsehood when *accented* by being put in a misleading context is illustrated by the following sea story. At almost the very outset of a certain ship's voyage, there had been a falling-out between the captain and his first mate. The dissension was aggravated by the mate's tendency to drink, for the captain was a fanatic on temperance and seldom let an occasion go by without lecturing the mate on his failings. Needless to say, this nagging only made the mate drink more heavily. After repeated warnings, one day when the mate had imbibed even more than usual, the captain entered the fact in the ship's log book, writing, "The mate was drunk today." When next it was the mate's turn to keep the log he was horrified to find this official record of his misbehavior. The log would be read by the ship's owner, whose reaction would probably mean the mate's discharge, with a bad reference to boot. He pleaded with the captain to remove the entry, but the captain refused. The mate didn't know what to do, but he finally hit upon a method of revenge. At the end of the regular entries he made in the log book that day he added, "The captain was sober today."

4. **Composition.** The term "fallacy of composition," is applied to both of two closely related types of invalid argument. The first may be described as reasoning fallaciously from the properties of the parts of a whole to the properties of the whole itself. A particularly flagrant example would be to argue that since every part of a certain machine is light in weight, the machine "as a whole" is light in weight. The error here is manifest when we consider that a very heavy machine may consist of a very great number of lightweight parts. Not all examples of this kind of fallacious *composition* are so obvious, however. Some are misleading. I have heard it seriously argued that since each scene of a certain play was a model of artistic perfection, the play as a whole was artistically perfect. But this is as much a fallacy of *composition* as it would be to argue that since every player on a team is an outstanding athlete the team must be an outstanding team. This first type of *composition* fallacy is committed when one infers that a whole has a certain property from the premiss that every constituent part of that whole possesses the property in question.

The other type of *composition* fallacy is strictly parallel to that just described. Here the fallacious reasoning is from properties possessed by individual elements or members of a collection to properties possessed by the class or collection as such. This *may* be regarded as an equivocation on the verb "to be," for in connection with this fallacy we may distinguish between two senses of that verb. The statement "Men are mortal," means that each and every member of the class of men is mortal. Here we have the *distributive* sense of the verb, where a property is predicated of men taken *severally* as members of the class of men. The verb "to be" may also be used in the *collective* sense, as in the equally true statement "Men are numerous." Here we are clearly not predicating of each and every man the property of being numerous, for that would

simply not make sense. What is intended is to predicate numer-
ousness of men *collectively,* of the class or collection as a whole.
Similarly, in the statement "Rodents have four feet," we mean
to predicate the property four-footedness of rodents *distributively;* that is, we assert that each and every rodent has four feet.
But in the statement "Rodents are widely distributed over the
earth," we are speaking of rodents *collectively;* it is certainly
not intended to assert of each and every rodent that *it* is widely
distributed over the earth—whatever that might mean. This
second kind of *composition* fallacy may be defined as the invalid
inference that what may truly be predicated of a class *distributively* may also be truly predicated of the class *collectively.* Thus
the atomic bombs dropped during World War II did more
damage than the ordinary bombs dropped—but only distributively. The matter is exactly reversed when the two kinds of
bombs are considered *collectively,* because there were so many
more bombs of the conventional type dropped than atomic ones.
Ignoring this distinction in an argument would permit the
fallacy of *composition.*

These two varieties of *composition,* although parallel, are
really distinct, because of the difference between a mere collection of elements and a whole constructed out of those elements.
Thus a mere collection or class of parts is no machine; a mere
collection or class of bricks is neither a house nor a wall. A
whole like a machine, a house, or a wall has its parts organized
or arranged in certain definite ways. And since organized wholes
and mere classes or collections are distinct, so are the two versions of the *composition* fallacy, one proceeding to wholes from
their parts, the other to classes from their members or elements.
5. **Division.** The fallacy of *division* is simply the reverse of the
fallacy of *composition.* In it the same confusion is present but
the inference proceeds in the opposite direction. As in the case
of *composition,* two varieties of the fallacy of *division* may be
distinguished. The first kind of *division* consists in arguing that
what is true of a whole must also be true of each of its parts. To
argue that since a certain corporation is very important, and

Mr. Doe is an official of that corporation, therefore Mr. Doe is very important, is to commit the fallacy of *division*. This first variety of the *division* fallacy would be committed in any such argument, as in going from the premiss that a certain machine is heavy, or complicated, or valuable, to the conclusion that this or any other *part* of the machine must be heavy, or complicated, or valuable. To argue that so-and-so must be an outstanding athlete because he plays on an outstanding team would be still another instance of this first kind of *division*.

The second type of *division* fallacy is committed when one argues from the properties of a collection of elements to the properties of the elements themselves. To argue that since all the trees in the park make a thick shade, therefore every tree in the park makes a thick shade would be to commit the second kind of *division* fallacy. Clearly *each* tree might be skimpy and throw a meagre shadow, yet there might be so many that together they give a solid thick shade. Here it would be true that all trees in the park, *collectively,* make a thick shade but false that all trees in the park, *distributively,* do so. Instances of this variety of the fallacy of *division* often look like valid arguments, for what is true of a class *distributively* is certainly true of each and every member. Thus the argument:

> Small towns are quiet.
> College towns are small.
> _____
> Therefore college towns are quiet.

is perfectly valid (though it might not be sound, of course). On the other hand, although it closely resembles the foregoing, the argument:

> Small towns are numerous.
> College towns are small.
> _____
> Therefore college towns are numerous.

is invalid, committing the fallacy of division. Some instances of *division* are obviously jokes, as when the classical example of valid argumentation:

Men are mortal.
Socrates is a man.

Therefore Socrates is mortal.

is parodied by the fallacious:

American Indians are disappearing.
That man is an American Indian.

Therefore that man is disappearing.

The old riddle "Why do white sheep eat more than black ones?" turns on the confusion involved in the fallacy of *division*. For the answer, "Because there are more of them," treats *collectively* what seemed to be referred to *distributively* in the question.

EXERCISES

Classify and explain the various fallacies of ambiguity contained in the following:

1. . . . each person's happiness is a good to that person, and the general happiness, therefore, a good to the aggregate of all persons.

   John Stuart Mill, *Utilitarianism*, Chapter 4

2. Those men seem to be walking very carefully; so I needn't slow down for them. After all, I was only told to watch out for *careless* pedestrians.

3. I have decided to cut my son Hezekiah out of my will entirely, because of the disrespect he showed me in having engraved on my late wife's tombstone the words:

   Sacred to the Memory
   of
   Abigail Concord
   After living with her husband for fifty-two years,
   she departed in the hope of a better life.

4. He who is most hungry eats most. He who eats least is most hungry. Therefore he who eats least eats most.

5. Long-haired dachshunds are seldom found in the Middle West, so if you take yours with you on your trip you must be very careful not to lose him.

6. You say that it would be a mistake for us to request any more funds for our project. I agree with you completely: we must get someone else to request the additional funds for us.

7. You enjoy walking alone, and I enjoy walking alone; so I am sure we should like doing it together.

8. It is illegal to interfere with a man's business. To sell goods cheaper than another man certainly interferes with his business and must therefore be illegal.

9. A Cadillac is a very expensive car, so any spare parts for it must cost a good deal.

10.   DOG BITES GIRL, ASKS
            OWNER FOR $7,500 BALM
    —Headline in the San Rafael (Calif.) *Independent*.
    Our dog is the same way—wants to make something of every situation.

    (*New Yorker*, Feb. 17, 1951)

11. Since every man is mortal, there will come a time when no man will remain alive.

12. I know I shouldn't talk about Helen behind her back, but she's facing in our direction now so it's all right for me to tell you what Betty told me about her . . .

13. I know that I advertised that children of both sexes would be admitted free, but that doesn't mean that your little boys don't have to pay admission. They're boys, not girls, so they're not children of both sexes.

14. Physicians have practiced medicine for thousands of years. Since practice makes perfect, Dr. Malpractice must have achieved perfection in his field by now.

15. I have a right to criticize the present administration. I have an obligation to do what is right. Therefore I have an obligation to criticize the present administration.

III. THE AVOIDANCE OF FALLACIES

Fallacies are pitfalls into which any of us may tumble in our reasoning. Just as danger signals are erected to warn travelers away from dangerous places, so the labels for fallacies presented in this chapter may be regarded as so many danger signals posted to keep us away from the bogland of incorrect argument. Familiarity with these errors and the ability to name and analyze them may well keep us from being deceived by them.

There is no "royal road" for the avoidance of fallacies. To avoid the fallacies of relevance requires constant vigilance and awareness of the many ways in which irrelevance can intrude. Our study of the different uses of language is helpful in this connection. A realization of the flexibility of language and the multiplicity of its uses will keep us from mistaking an *exhortation* to *accept* and *approve* a conclusion for an *argument* designed to *prove* that conclusion *true*.

The fallacies of ambiguity are subtle things. Words are slippery, and most of them have a variety of different senses or meanings. Where these different meanings are confused in the formulation of an argument, the reasoning is fallacious. To avoid the various fallacies of ambiguity we must have and keep the meanings of our terms clearly in mind. One way to accomplish this is by defining the key terms that are used. Since shifts in the meanings of terms can make arguments fallacious, and since ambiguity can be avoided by careful definition of the terms involved, definition is an important matter for the student of logic. It is to the topic of definition that our next chapter is devoted.

EXERCISES

Classify and explain each of the various fallacies contained in the following:

1. Despite all the noise and protest generated, the labor and consumer groups have failed to prove that removing price controls

would lead to any sharp increases in the cost of living. It follows that no price increases would follow the removal of controls.

2. The arguments against raising our immigration quotas have all been presented by just those persons who stand to reap a personal profit by cutting off the flow of additional labor to our shores. It is clear from this that their arguments are without any objective merit.

3. Our immigration restrictions should be relaxed, for the only defenders of the present policy are the short-sighted stand-patters who cling to outmoded practices through cowardly fear of progress and selfish greed for the unfair advantages the outdated present policy gives them.

4. If you think it over, I am sure you will see that the proposed legislation is unsound. After all, my friends and I contributed over twenty thousand dollars for your campaign in the last election, and you are coming up for reelection next November.

5. Mrs. J. W. Ikerman, of the Ways and Means Committee, poured the tea over a lovely lace covered table.—Ravenna-Kent (Ohio) Evening *Record* and Daily *Courier-Tribune*.
   Butterfingers!
   (*New Yorker,* Feb. 17, 1951)

6. I hope the Smiths don't rent the house next door, because I don't like them at all, and we are supposed to love our neighbors.

7. Permitting increased immigration will actually strengthen this nation's economy. The unhappy peoples of other lands, the homeless of the world, children torn from their mothers' arms, should be given a chance to find a new life among us.

8. I am unalterably opposed to relaxing our immigration restrictions. Our fair countryside and gleaming cities must not be darkened and wasted by the cholera-ridden Asiatic hordes which constitute the Yellow Peril threatening our gentle Pacific slopes, nor by the scrapings of the European Ghettos whose scaly hands are clawing and clutching at our Eastern Seaboard.

9. These pills must be safe and effective for reducing, for they have been endorsed by Miss Betty Shapely, star of stage, screen, and television.

10. Barbers have been cutting hair for generations, so my barber is really an expert.

11. Jones was a very promising youth, but he has not fulfilled those promises. Only a liar does not keep his promises. Jones must therefore be a liar.

12. From the circumstances surrounding the bankruptcy we cannot tell whether Jones intended to defraud his creditors or his partners. From this it is clear, however, that there was an intent to defraud.

13. Robinson is the most widely traveled among all the applicants for the position. He has visited every country on the globe and will therefore make an excellent geography teacher.

14. Do you remember the bread lines and the Hoovervilles, the soup kitchens and the unemployed selling apples on every corner? These marked the last days of the Republican administration. So if you want to see those "good old days" again, go ahead and vote for the Republican candidate!

15. Every stockholder in the new corporation is an honest man and always pays his debts. Hence we may be confident that the new corporation will pay any debts it may incur.

16. It must be dangerous to belong to the Y.M.C.A. because the paper reports that last night the Reverend Smith gave a lecture to young men about their perils at the Y.M.C.A.

17. Dr. Cuttem advised an operation, but as a specialist in surgery he has a special interest in the matter; so his advice can safely be ignored.

18. Why has the Administration refused to avail itself of the help of Chiang's 800,000 well-trained fighters instead of playing into the Communists' hands by keeping them immobilized on Formosa? It is clear that the government's policy is incapable of bringing us victory in Korea!

19. It will really help your business, Mr. Brown, to join our protective association. All of your competitors have already joined

except Smith—you know, the Mr. Smith who had that peculiar traffic accident last Thursday. I'd hate to think of anything happening to Mrs. Brown or your children. I'm sure you can see that a membership in our association will improve your business . . .

20. Don't trust Monsieur Duval—after all, the French repudiated their war debt to us after the First World War.

21. The doctrine of free will must be true, for its acceptance is a necessary presupposition of every person who deliberates and decides what action he should take. Everyone accepts that doctrine in fact, consciously or unconsciously.

22. He is an accomplished pianist. Whatever is accomplished is all through. Hence he is all through as a pianist.

23. Diamonds have traditionally been used as mere baubles and playthings, as shiny toys for the idle rich to play with. It is obvious, therefore, that diamonds can be of no use in any serious undertaking.

24. During the present century, every Democratic administration has seen the advent of bitter and costly wars. During Wilson's regime it was the First World War, during Franklin Roosevelt's it was the Second World War, and during Truman's second term, the Korean conflict. If you wish our country to be continuously involved in an unending series of wars, be sure to vote Democratic!

25. No single member of the crowd would dare to attack the jail; so there is no danger that the crowd will attempt to enter.

26. Our immigration quotas should not be raised, for the advocates of raising those quotas are the radicals and troublemakers, the chronic malcontents who are always seeking to interfere with the accepted orderly arrangements of things.

27. If elected, Brown will give the citizens of this state an efficient and economical administration. He was wounded twice in the war, as a result of which his left leg had to be amputated. He is the sole support of an invalid mother and deserves all our votes.

28. I have never come across any argument for price controls that any sensible man could accept. Therefore price controls are obviously wrong.

29. We have been warned not to speak freely to each other in front of the natives, but I suppose it will be all right to speak freely to the natives themselves.

30. There must be something to psychical research, since such famous physicists and astronomers as Lodge and Jeans and Eddington took it seriously.

CHAPTER FOUR

Definition

I. THE PURPOSES OF DEFINITION

Language is a very complicated instrument. People learn to use it the same way that they learn the use of other tools, such as automobiles or kitchen equipment. A boy who does much riding with his father seldom needs to be given formal instruction in driving the family car; he acquires his knowledge by observing and imitating his father. A girl who spends much time in the kitchen with her mother learns the use of quite complicated kitchen apparatus by the same method. Similarly with language, certainly in childhood, and for many of us throughout our lives, we learn the proper use of language by observing and imitating the linguistic behavior of the people we meet and the books we read.

There are, however, limits to this sort of unconscious learning. The rising devastation of traffic accidents has made it desirable for drivers to have some formal training besides the learning by imitation that has traditionally sufficed. The need for girls to supplement their learning by imitation has long been recognized in the inclusion of courses in home economics in high school and even college curricula. The situation is similar in language study. There are occasions when the usual methods of observation and imitation do not suffice; then formal instruction, that is, deliberate explanation of the meanings of terms, is required. To explain the meaning of a term is to give a *definition* of it. To give a definition is not the primary method of educating people in the proper use and understanding of language; it is rather a supplementary device for filling the gaps left by the primary method.

In conversation or in reading, one often comes upon unfamiliar words whose meanings are not made clear by the context. To understand what is being said, it is necessary to find out what the words mean; here *definitions* are required. One purpose of definition, then, is to increase the vocabulary of the person for whom the definition is constructed.

Another purpose served by definition is the elimination of ambiguity. Perhaps most words have two or more distinct meanings or senses, but usually no trouble arises from this fact. In some contexts, however, it is not clear which sense of a given word is intended, and here its occurrence is said to be *ambiguous*. Fallacious arguments that result from the unwitting use of ambiguous terms have been discussed in the preceding chapter, where they were characterized as fallacies of equivocation. Such arguments are misleading only if the ambiguity passes unnoticed. When the ambiguity is resolved, the persuasiveness vanishes and the fallacy is exposed. But to resolve the ambiguity, we require definitions to explain the different meanings of the ambiguous word or phrase.

Ambiguous language can lead not only to fallacious argumentation but also to disputes which are merely verbal. Some apparent disagreements turn not on any genuine differences of opinion but merely upon different uses of a term. Where the ambiguity of a key term has led to a verbal dispute, we can often resolve the disagreement by pointing out the ambiguity. We do this by giving the two different definitions of the term, so the different meanings can be clearly distinguished and the

confusion dispelled. A now classic example of the method of resolving verbal disputes by defining the ambiguous terms involved is due to William James. In his second lecture on *Pragmatism,* James wrote:

> Some years ago, being with a camping party in the mountains,
> I returned from a solitary ramble to find every one engaged in
> a ferocious metaphysical dispute. The *corpus* of the dispute was a
> squirrel—a live squirrel supposed to be clinging to one side of a
> tree-trunk; while over against the tree's opposite side a human being
> was imagined to stand. This human witness tries to get sight of the
> squirrel by moving rapidly round the tree, but no matter how fast
> he goes, the squirrel moves as fast in the opposite direction, and
> always keeps the tree between himself and the man, so that never
> a glimpse of him is caught. The resultant metaphysical problem is
> this: *Does the man go round the squirrel or not?* He goes round
> the tree, sure enough, and the squirrel is on the tree; but does he
> go round the squirrel? In the unlimited leisure of the wilderness,
> discussion had been worn threadbare. Everyone had taken sides,
> and was obstinate; and the numbers on both sides were even. Each
> side, when I appeared, therefore appealed to me to make it a ma-
> jority. Mindful of the scholastic adage that whenever you meet a
> contradiction you must make a distinction, I immediately sought
> and found one, as follows: "Which party is right," I said, "depends
> on what you *practically mean* by 'going round' the squirrel. If you
> mean passing from the north of him to the east, then to the south,
> then to the west, and then to the north of him again, obviously
> the man does go round him, for he occupies these successive posi-
> tions. But if on the contrary you mean being first in front of him,
> then on the right of him, then behind him, then on his left, and
> finally in front again, it is quite obvious that the man fails to go
> round him, for by the compensating movements the squirrel makes,
> he keeps his belly turned towards the man all the time, and his
> back turned away. Make the distinction, and there is no occasion
> for any further dispute. You are both right and both wrong accord-
> ing as you conceive the verb 'go round' in one practical fashion or
> the other."

Although one or two of the hotter disputants called my speech
a shuffling evasion, saying they wanted no quibbling or scholastic

hair-splitting, but meant just plain honest English "round," the majority seemed to think that the distinction had assuaged the dispute.*

As James points out, no new "facts" were required to resolve the dispute; none could possibly have helped. What was needed was just what James supplied, a distinction between different meanings of the key term in the argument. This could be accomplished, of course, only by supplying alternative *definitions* of the term "go round." We can settle verbal disputes only by giving definitions of the ambiguous terms involved. The second purpose of definition, then, is to eliminate ambiguity, both for the sake of exposing fallacies of equivocation and resolving disputes which are merely verbal.

Another occasion we might have for defining a term is when we desire to use it but are not quite sure of the limits of its applicability, although *in a sense* we do know its meaning. This motive for wanting a term defined is different from the first one discussed. There the motive was to teach the meaning of an unfamiliar term. Here the motive is to *clarify* the meaning of a term already known. Where a term is in need of clarification, we say the term is *vague*. To clarify the term is to reduce its vagueness, and this is accomplished by giving a definition of the term which will permit a decision as to its applicability in a given situation. This is sometimes confused with the second motive discussed, because *vagueness* is sometimes confused with *ambiguity*. But vagueness and ambiguity are two quite different properties. A term is ambiguous in a given context when it has two distinct meanings and the context does not make clear which one is intended. On the other hand, a term is vague when there exist "borderline cases" such that it cannot be decided whether the term applies to them or not. Most words are vague in the sense indicated. Scientists have been unable to decide whether certain viruses are "living" or "non-living," not because they do not know whether or not the virus has the powers of locomo-

* By permission from *Pragmatism* by William James. Longmans, Green and Company, 1907.

tion, of reproduction, etc., but because the word "living" is so vague a term. Perhaps more familiar is the difficulty in deciding whether or not a certain country is a "democracy," or whether a given work of art is "obscene" or not.

These "difficulties" may seem trivial, but under certain circumstances they can assume great practical importance. Suppose, for example, that we had the task of administering a law which provided that financial aid be given only to countries with "democratic" governments. Here decisions on borderline cases would be fraught with the gravest moral, political, and possibly even military significance, in addition to financial implications involving millions of dollars.

The indecision attending such borderline cases may be resolved by giving a definition of the vague term which will make clear whether it is to be applied or not. Thus to decide whether a house trailer is to be taxed as a *vehicle* or as a *dwelling*, we must find out how the law defines these terms. And if the definitions on record are not sufficiently precise to determine a decision, then the court within whose jurisdiction the question arises must promulgate new definitions which will permit of clear application. Another purpose of giving definitions, then, is to reduce the vagueness of familiar terms, which is a different purpose from those previously mentioned.

Still another purpose we may have in defining a term is to formulate a theoretically adequate characterization of the objects to which it is applied. For example, physical scientists have defined the term "force" as the product of mass and acceleration. This definition is not given to increase anyone's vocabulary or to eliminate ambiguity, but to embody part of Newtonian mechanics into the very meaning of the term "force" itself. Such a definition might well reduce the vagueness of the term being defined, but its primary purpose is not that but something else instead. Another example of a *theoretical* definition is the chemist's definition of "acid" as meaning a substance which contains hydrogen as a positive radical. Everything which is correctly called an acid in ordinary usage is denoted by the term as defined by the chemist, but no pretense is made that the chemist's principle for distinguishing acids from other substances is actually applied by housewives or sheet metal workers in their use of the term. The chemist's definition is intended to attach to the word, as meaning, that property which in the context of his theory is most useful for understanding and predicting the behavior of those substances which the word denotes. When the scientist constructs such definitions as these, his purpose is theoretical.

In addition to the preceding, which are the most important reasons for defining terms, there is another motive, which leads to the formulation of rhetorical or *persuasive* "definitions." A person who gives a "persuasive definition" of a term is not attempting to explain the literal meaning of that term but rather to influence the attitude or to stir the emotions of his readers or hearers in certain definite ways. Thus a man may rise to the defense of a friend accused of tactlessness by praising his friend's *honesty,* offering the definition of "honesty" as always telling the truth regardless of circumstances. Here the speaker's purpose is not to give an explanation of the literal meaning of the word "honesty," but to cause his listeners to transfer to his friend's behavior the laudatory emotive value that attaches to the term "honesty." His language is not informative; it is functioning expressively. The emotive value to be transferred need not belong initially to the term being defined but can attach to a word *used* in stating the definition. For example, a proponent of socialism may define "socialism" to mean *democracy extended to the economic field.* Here the word "socialism" is not being defined for the purpose of explaining its literal or descriptive meaning, but rather to win for it some of the approval and enthusiasm usually aroused by the word "democracy." It may be questioned whether rhetorical devices like these should be called *definitions,* but the word is frequently used in this way, as in newspaper contests for the "best definitions" of various terms.

Now that we have seen how definitions can have an expressive as well as an informative function, it may be well to qualify somewhat our previous discussion of verbal issues. It is true, as was stated, that some disagreements are merely verbal, the result of confusing two different senses of an ambiguous term. James' example of the squirrel was clearly such a case. There the quarrel was simply over words. But such cases bear a superficial resemblance to other disputes which are really genuine.

Consider the prolonged disagreement between the United States and Soviet Russia following World War II. Among the points at issue have been such questions as whether or not this or that Eastern European nation should be accorded certain rights and privileges, such as admission to the United Nations Organization. Some newspaper commentators and editorialists stigmatized these disputes as being merely verbal. All that was needed, the critics seemed to imply, was a well turned definition of the key word "democratic." After all, both of the two great powers agreed that democratic countries should have all possible rights and privileges. But the situation might better have been characterized as a "merely verbal agreement." The two powers agreed upon the emotive meaning of the word "democratic," but any definition either might have offered would have been merely *persuasive*, for genuine and far reaching disagreement separated this country and Russia. Significant moral and political issues were at stake, and to suggest that they could be settled by redefining terms would be superstitious belief in the efficacy of "word magic." In the presence of real issues separating the two nations, their agreement on the emotive meaning of the word "democracy" served to prevent agreement on any descriptively adequate definition of the term. Such a definition could be reached only as a *result* of having resolved the moral and political disagreement, not as a *means* to such resolution. Of course, agreement on the literal meaning of the word "democracy" *could* have been reached while the nations stood opposed, but only on condition that one or the other repudiate the honorific emotive meaning of the term.

Some disagreements are merely verbal, but of course not all

of them are. And where there is genuine disagreement, it is not to be resolved by so simple a measure as framing new definitions of the terms involved. Attempts to do so result in "persuasive definitions," which are merely another kind of rhetorical device, which may or may not work, but cannot be depended upon to do so.

EXERCISES

Distinguish those of the following disputes which are merely verbal from those which only seem to be so. Resolve those which are merely verbal by defining the ambiguous terms which appear in them. In the case of those which only seem to be verbal, explain what basic non-verbal differences are involved.

1. Black: A tree falling in a wilderness, with nobody around to hear, will make no sound. There can be no sensation unless someone actually senses it.

   White: No, whether anyone is there to hear it or not, the crash of a falling tree will set up vibrations in the air and will therefore make a sound in any event.

2. Black: Socialism is impossible because it is absurd. Just try to imagine sharing your toothbrush and razor, or even your shirts and trousers, with millions of other men!

   White: Socialism is not impossible at all. When the government can tell the farmers what to raise, and goes into the power business more and more all the time, socialism is practically here already!

3. Black: Mr. Gray is a real Christian. He speaks well of everyone and is never too busy to give friendly help to anyone who asks.

   White: I wouldn't call Gray a Christian—he spends all his Sundays sleeping late and puttering around his yard, never showing his face in Church from one end of the year to the other!

4. Black: Slobovia is a real democracy at last. They have general elections every two years, in which every citizen over eighteen years old can vote.

White: I wouldn't call Slobovia a democracy at all. The government exercises a rigid political censorship over the press and the radio there, and only one political party is legal, the others all being outlawed by the party in power.

5. Black: It looks as if our friend Brown has moved into a very nice neighborhood. All of his new neighbors are very friendly and helpful.

   White: If you were to ask me, I'd say that it's a terrible neighborhood! The houses are all run down, and the factories near it have caused a terrific depreciation of property values there.

6. Black: I see by the financial pages that money is much more plentiful than it was six months ago.

   White: I don't understand how that can be. I read a government report just yesterday to the effect that more currency has been destroyed at the mint during the last half year than has been replaced. Money is therefore *less* plentiful, not more so.

7. Black: The inside of a watermelon cannot be red before it is cut open, because no one can see a color in the dark, and the rind effectively shuts off all light from the interior before it is cut.

   White: Of course the inside of a ripe watermelon is red before it is cut open. You don't think simply cutting the outside makes the inside change color, do you?

8. Black: Pride is a terrible vice. Nothing annoys me more than a man who has an exaggerated opinion of himself.

   White: I can't agree with you there. What I hate most is someone going around apologizing for himself all the time. A man ought to have a good opinion of himself, or else how can he expect anyone else to do so? Pride is really more of a virtue than otherwise.

9. Black: This country would be better off if we could get rid of all these politicians. They never take an honest stand

on any issue, but are always pussyfooting around on everything until they see which way the votes are going to be cast!

White: You can't mean that—*somebody* has to run the government! Politicians are necessary.

10. Black: This new labor bill is absolutely illegal. It is in direct conflict with the Bill of Rights!

White: It is a law passed by Congress and signed by the President. That makes it legal, doesn't it?

II. THE TYPES OF DEFINITION

Before distinguishing between different types of definition, it should be remarked that definitions are always of *symbols,* for only symbols have meanings for definitions to explain. We can define the word "chair," since it has a meaning; but although we can sit on it, paint it, burn it, or describe it, we cannot *define* a chair itself, for a chair is an article of furniture, not a symbol which has a meaning for us to explain. A definition can be expressed in either of two ways, by talking about the symbol to be defined, or by talking about its referent. Thus we can equally well say either:

The word "triangle" means a plane figure enclosed by three straight lines.

or

A triangle is (by definition) a plane figure enclosed by three straight lines.

Two technical terms used in the theory of definition may be introduced at this point. The symbol being defined is called the *definiendum,* and the symbol or set of symbols used to explain the meaning of the definiendum is called the *definiens.* For example, in the preceding definition the word "triangle" is the definiendum, and the phrase "a plane figure enclosed by three straight lines" is the definiens. The definiens is not the *meaning* of the definiendum, but another symbol or group of symbols which, according to the definition, *has the same mean-ing as* the definiendum.

The first type of definition to be discussed is that given a brand new term when it is first introduced. Anyone who intro-duces a new symbol has complete freedom to stipulate *what* meaning is to be given it. The assignment of meanings to new symbols is a matter of choice, and we may call the definitions which make the assignment *stipulative definitions*. Of course, the definiendum in a stipulative definition need not be a sound or mark or sequence of letters that is absolutely novel. It is sufficient that it be new in the context in which the defining takes place. Traditional discussions are not altogether clear, but it seems that what we are here calling *stipulative definitions* have sometimes been referred to as "nominal" or "verbal" definitions.

New terms may be introduced for a variety of reasons. For example, a commercial establishment with branches in foreign parts may compile a cable code in which single words are "short for" lengthy but routine messages. The advantages of intro-ducing such new terms may include the relative secrecy their use achieves and lower costs for transmitting cablegrams. If such a code is actually to be used for communication, its maker must explain the meanings of the new terms, and to do this he will give *definitions* of them.

New terms are frequently introduced into the sciences. There are many advantages to introducing a new and technical symbol defined to mean what would otherwise require a long sequence of familiar words for its expression. By doing so, the scientist economizes the space required for writing out his reports or theories, and also the time involved. More importantly, he re-duces the amount of attention or mental energy required, for when a sentence or equation grows too long its sense cannot easily be "taken in." Consider the economy on all counts achieved by the introduction of the exponent in mathematics. What is now written quite briefly as

$$A^{12} = B$$

would, prior to the adoption of the special symbol for exponentiation, have had to be expressed either by

$$A \times A \times A \times A \times A \times A \times A \times A \times A \times A \times A \times A = B$$

or by a sentence of ordinary language instead of a mathematical equation.

There is still another reason for the scientist's introduction of new symbols. The emotive suggestions of familiar words are often disturbing to one interested only in their literal or informative meanings. The introduction of new symbols, explicitly defined to have the same *literal* meanings as familiar ones, will free the investigator from the distraction of the latter's emotive associations. This advantage accounts for the presence of some curious words in contemporary psychology, such as Spearman's "*g* factor," for example, which is intended to convey the same descriptive meaning as the word "intelligence" but to share none of its emotional significance. And for the new terminology to be learned and used, the new symbols must have their meanings explained by *definitions*.

Since a symbol defined by a stipulative definition has had no prior meaning, the definition cannot be regarded as a statement or report that the definiendum and the definiens have the same meaning. They *will* have for anyone who accepts the definition, but that is something which *follows* the definition rather than a fact asserted by it. A stipulative definition is neither true nor false, but should be regarded as a *proposal* or *resolution* to use the definiendum to mean what is meant by the definiens, or as a *request* or *command*. In this sense a stipulative definition is directive rather than informative. Proposals may be rejected, resolutions violated, requests refused, commands disobeyed, and stipulations ignored, but none of them are on that account either true or false. So it is with stipulative definitions.

Of course, stipulative definitions may be evaluated on other grounds. Whether or not a new term serves the purpose for which it was introduced is a question of fact. The definition may be either very obscure or so complex as to be unusable. It is not the case that any stipulative definition is as "good" as any other, but the grounds for their comparison must clearly be other than truth or falsehood, for these terms simply do not apply. Stipulative definitions are arbitrary only in the sense specified. Whether they are clear or unclear, advantageous or disadvantageous, or the like, are factual questions.

Where the purpose of a definition is to eliminate ambiguity or to increase the vocabulary of the person for whom it is constructed, then if the term being defined is not new but has an established usage, the definition is *lexical* rather than stipulative. A lexical definition does not give its definiendum a meaning which it hitherto lacked, but reports the meaning it already has. It is clear that a lexical definition may be either true or false. Thus the definition:

The word "mountain" means a large mass of earth or rock rising to a considerable height above the surrounding country.

is true; it is a true report of how English speaking people use the word "mountain" (i.e. of what they use it to mean). On the other hand, the definition:

The word "mountain" means a plane figure enclosed by three straight lines.

is false, being a false report of how English speaking people use the word "mountain." Here is the important difference between stipulative and lexical definitions. Since a stipulative definition's definiendum has no meaning apart from or prior to the definition introducing it, that definition cannot be false (or true). But because the definiendum of a lexical definition does have a prior and independent meaning, its definition is either true or false, depending upon whether that meaning is correctly or incorrectly reported. Although traditional discussions are not altogether clear on this point, it seems that what we are calling lexical definitions have sometimes been referred to as "real" definitions.

One point should be made clear, however, concerning the

question of "existence." Whether a definition is stipulative or lexical has nothing to do with the question of whether the definiendum names any "real" or "existent" thing. The following definition:

The word "unicorn" means an animal like a horse but having a single straight horn projecting from its forehead.

is a "real" or lexical definition, and a true one, because the definiendum is a word with long established usage and means exactly what is meant by the definiens. Yet the definiendum does not name or denote any existent, since there are no unicorns.

A qualification must be made at this point, for in asserting that lexical definitions of the kind illustrated were true or false, we were oversimplifying a complex situation. The fact is that many words are used in different ways, not because they have a plurality of standard meanings, but through what we should call "error." Not all instances of erroneous word usage are as funny as those of Sheridan's Mrs. Malaprop when she gives the order to "illiterate him . . . from your memory," or uses the phrase "As headstrong as an allegory on the banks of the Nile." Some words are used by many people in ways that might be called "erroneous" or "mistaken," but which are better described as *unorthodox*. And any definition of a word which ignores the way in which it *is used* by any sizable group of speakers is not "true to" actual usage, and is, therefore, not quite true.

Word usage is a statistical matter, and any definition of a word whose usage is subject to this kind of variation must not be a simple statement of "the meaning" of the term, but a statistical description of "the meanings" of the term, as determined by the uses it has in actual speech. The need for lexical statistics cannot be evaded by reference to "correct" usage, for that too is a matter of degree, being measured by the number of "first-rate" authors whose usages of a given term are in agreement. Moreover, literary and academic vocabularies tend to lag behind the growth of living language on the lips of the man in the street. Unorthodox usages have a way of becoming catholic, so that definitions which report only the meanings countenanced by an academic aristocracy are likely to be very misleading. Of course, the notion of statistical definitions is utopian, but dictionaries approximate it more or less by indicating which meanings are "archaic" or "obsolete," and which are "colloquial" or "slang." With the foregoing as qualification, we may repeat that lexical definitions are true or false, in the sense of being "true to" actual usage or failing to be "true to" it.

Neither stipulative nor lexical definitions can serve to reduce the vagueness of a term. A vague term is one for which border-line cases may arise, such that it cannot be decided whether the term should be applied to them or not. Ordinary usage cannot be appealed to for a decision, because ordinary usage is not sufficiently clear on the matter. To reach a decision, then, ordinary usage must be transcended; a definition capable of helping to decide borderline cases must go beyond what is merely lexical. Such a definition may be called a *precising definition*.

A precising definition is different from a stipulative one, because its definiendum is not a new term but one with an established, although vague, usage. Consequently, the maker of a precising definition is not free to assign any meaning he chooses to the definiendum. He must remain "true to" the established usage so far as it goes.

Yet he must go beyond that established usage if the vagueness of the definiendum is to be resolved. Exactly how he goes beyond, just how he fills the gaps or resolves the conflicts of established usage, is in a sense a matter of stipulation, but not completely so. A great many legal decisions involve precising definitions in which certain statutory terms are clarified so that they will specifically cover or specifically exclude the case at issue. Jurists usually present arguments intended to justify their decisions in such cases, and this practice shows that they do not regard their precising definitions as mere stipulations even in those areas not covered by precedent or established usage. Instead they seek to be guided in part by the supposed *intentions* of the legislators who enacted the law, and in part by what the jurist conceives to be *in the public interest*. The terms "true" and "false" apply only in a partial fashion to precising definitions, their application signifying that the definition conforms or fails to conform to established usage so far as it goes. In evaluating the way in which a precising definition goes beyond established usage where the latter is unclear, truth and falsehood do not apply, and we must speak instead of its convenience or inconvenience, and (especially in a legal or quasi-legal context) of its wisdom or folly.

It is in connection with *theoretical definitions* that most "disputing over definitions" occurs. We have characterized a theoretical definition of a term as one which attempts to formulate a theoretically adequate characterization of the objects to which it is applied. To propose a theoretical definition is tantamount to proposing the acceptance of a *theory*, and, as the name implies, theories are notoriously debatable. Here one definition is replaced by another as our knowledge and theoretical understanding increase. At one time physicists defined "heat" to mean a subtle imponderable fluid, now they define it to mean the average kinetic energy of molecules in random motion. Precisely the same criteria apply to theoretical definitions which apply to theories themselves. We postpone our discussion of the latter to Part Three of this book.

Those who have some acquaintance with the writings of Plato will recognize that the definitions he represented Socrates as continually seeking were neither stipulative, lexical, nor precising, but *theoretical*. Socrates was not interested in any merely statistical account of how people use the term "justice" (or "courage," or "temperance," or "virtue"); but at the same time he insisted that any proposed definition be consonant with actual usage. Nor was he interested in giving precising definitions of these terms, for borderline cases were not emphasized. To define such terms as "good" and "true" and "beautiful" is the aim of many philosophers. That they dispute over each other's proposed definitions indicates that they are not seeking merely stipulative definitions. Nor are they after merely lexical definitions, or recourse to dictionaries or public opinion polls on word usage could settle the matter easily. That some philosophers can agree on the application of the term "good" in all circumstances, without being bothered by any borderline cases, and still disagree over how the term "good" ought to be defined, indicates that they are not seeking a precising definition of the term. Philosophers as well as scientists are most interested in the construction of *theoretical* definitions. Theoretical definitions are sometimes referred to as "analytical" definitions, although this latter term has another sense as well.

III. VARIOUS KINDS OF MEANING

Since a definition is an explanation of the *meaning* of a term, it is important for us to have clearly in mind the different senses of the word "meaning." This topic was discussed in Chapter Two and we need not repeat what was said there. However, a certain further distinction must be drawn in connection with what was there called descriptive or literal meaning, especially in connection with *general terms* or *class terms* applicable to more than a single object. A general term such as "planet" is applicable in the same sense equally to Mercury, Venus, Earth, Mars, etc. In a perfectly acceptable sense, these various objects to which the term "planet" is applied are *meant* by the word, or constitute its meaning. Thus, if I assert that all planets have elliptical orbits, part of what I may intend to assert is that Mars has an elliptical orbit, and another part, that Venus has an elliptical orbit, and so on. In *one* sense the meaning of a term consists of the objects to which the term may be applied. This sense of "meaning," its referential sense, has traditionally been called *extensional* or *denotative* meaning. A general or class term *denotes* the objects to which it may correctly be applied, and these objects constitute the *extension* or *denotation* of the term.

However, the foregoing is not the *only* sense of the word

"meaning." To understand a term is to know how to apply it correctly, but for this it is not necessary to know all of the objects to which it may be correctly applied. It is only required that we have a criterion for deciding of any given object whether it falls within the extension of that term or not. All objects in the extension of a given term have some common properties or characteristics which lead us to use the same term to denote them. The properties possessed by all of the objects in a term's extension are called the *intension* or *connotation* of that term. General or class terms have both an *intensional* or *connotative* meaning and an *extensional* or *denotative* one. Thus, the intension or connotation of the term "skyscraper" consists of the properties common and peculiar to all buildings over a certain height; while the extension or denotation of that term consists of the Empire State Building, the Chrysler Building, the Wrigley Tower, and so on.

The word "connotation" has other uses, in which it refers to the *total* significance of a word, emotive as well as descriptive, and sometimes to its emotive meaning alone. Thus one may say of a person that he is "not a *man*." Here the word "man" is used expressively, to communicate a certain attitude or feeling. This expressive function is sometimes equated with, sometimes included in, the "connotation" of a term. But logicians use the word in a narrower sense. In our usage, *connotation* and *intension* are part of the informative significance of a term.

Even with this restriction, various senses of "connotation" have yet to be distinguished. There are three different senses of the term "connotation," which have been called the *subjective,* the *objective,* and the *conventional.* The *subjective connotation* of a word for a particular interpreter is the set of all the properties that *he believes* to be possessed by the objects comprising that word's extension. It is clear that the *subjective connotation* of a term may vary from one individual to another. I have met New Yorkers for whom the word "skyscraper" had a *subjective connotation* which included the property of being located in New York City. The notion of subjective connotation is inconvenient for purposes of definition because it varies not merely from individual to individual but even from time to time for the same individual, as he acquires new beliefs or abandons old ones. We are more interested in the *public* meanings of words than in their private interpretations; so having mentioned *subjective connotations* we shall eliminate them from further consideration.

The *objective connotation* or *objective intension* of a term is the total set of characteristics common to all the objects which make up that term's extension. It does not vary at all from interpreter to interpreter, for if all planets do have the property of moving in elliptical orbits, for example, this will be part of the *objective connotation* of the word "planet" whether any user of the term knows it or not. But the concept of *objective connotation* is inconvenient for reasons of its own. Even in those rare cases where the complete extension of a term is known, it would require omniscience to know *all* of the characteristics shared by the objects in that extension. And since no one has that omniscience, the *objective connotation* of a term is not the public meaning in whose explanation we are interested.

Since we do communicate with each other and understand the terms we use, the intensional or connotative meanings involved are neither subjective nor objective in the senses explained above. Those who attach the same meaning to a term must use the same criterion for deciding of any object whether it is part of the term's extension or not. Thus we have agreed to use *the property of being a closed plane curve all points of which are equidistant from a point within called the center* as our criterion for deciding of any figure whether it is to be called a "circle" or not. This agreement establishes a convention, and so this meaning of a term is known as its *conventional connotation* or *conventional intension*. The *conventional connotation* of a term is its most important aspect for purposes of definition and communication, since it is both public and can be known by people who are not omniscient. For the sake of brevity we shall use the words "connotation" and "intension" to mean *conventional connotation* or *conventional intension* **unless** otherwise specified.

The extension or denotation of a term has been explained to be the collection of all those objects to which the term applies. There are no troublesome different senses of extension comparable to those found in the case of intension. However, the notion of *extension* is not without interest. For one thing, the extension of a term has been alleged to change from time to time in a way that the intension does not. The extension of the term "man" has been said to change almost continually as men die and babies are born. This varying extension does not belong to the term "man" conceived as denoting *all* men, the dead as well as the yet unborn, but rather to the term "living man." But the term "living man" has the sense of "man living *now,*" in which the word "now" refers to the fleeting present. Any term whose extension varies has an intension which also changes with the time. So in spite of the apparent difference, one is as constant as the other; when the intension of a term is fixed, the extension is fixed also.

Worth mentioning in this connection is the fact that extension is determined by intension, but not the other way around. Thus, the term "equilateral triangle" has for its intension or connotation the property of being a plane figure enclosed by three straight line segments of equal length. It has as its extension all objects and only those objects which have this property. The term "equiangular triangle" has a different intension, connoting the property of being a plane figure enclosed by three straight line segments which intersect each other to form equal angles. But the extension of the term "equiangular triangle" is exactly the same as the extension of the term "equilateral triangle." Thus terms may have different intensions but the same extension, although terms with different extensions cannot possibly have the same intension.

Consider the following sequence of terms, each of whose intensions is included within the intension of the terms following it: "man," "living man," "living man over twenty years old," "living man over twenty years old having red hair." The intension of each of these terms (except the first, of course) is greater than the intensions of those preceding it in the sequence; the terms are arranged, we may say, in order of *increasing intension*. But if we turn to the extensions of those terms, we find the reverse to be the case. The extension of the term "man" is greater than that of "living man," and so on. In other words, the terms are arranged in order of *decreasing extension*. Consideration of such sequences has led some logicians to formulate a "law of inverse variation," asserting that if a series of terms is arranged in order of increasing intension, their extensions will be in decreasing order; or in other words, that extension and intension vary inversely with each other. This alleged law may have a certain suggestive value, but it cannot be accepted without modification. This fact is shown by the following sequence of terms: "living man," "living man with a spinal column," "living man with a spinal column less than one thousand years old," "living man with a spinal column less than one thousand years old who has not read all the books in the Library of Congress." Here the terms are clearly in order of increasing intension, but the extension of all of them is the same, not decreasing at all. The law has been revised to accord with such cases as these, in its amended version asserting that if terms are arranged in order of increasing intension, their extensions will be in non-increasing order; that is, *if* the extensions vary at all, they will vary inversely with the intensions.

Finally, we turn to those terms which, although perfectly meaningful, do not denote anything at all. We use such terms whenever we deny the existence of things of a certain kind. When we say that there are no unicorns, we assert that the term "unicorn" does not denote, that it has no extension or denotation. Sometimes it is convenient to say that such terms have an "empty" or "null" extension, which comes to the same thing. Such terms show that "meaning" pertains more to intension than to extension. For although the term "unicorn" has a *null* extension, or no extension at all, this is not to say that the term "unicorn" is *meaningless*. It has no extension because there are no unicorns; but if the term "unicorn" were meaningless, so also would be the statement, "There are no unicorns." But far from being meaningless, the statement is in fact true.

Our distinction between intension and extension, and the recognition that extensions may be empty or null, can be used to resolve the ambiguity of some occurrences of the term "meaning." Thus we can refute the following fallacy of equivocation:

The word "God" is not meaningless and therefore has a meaning. But by definition the word "God" means a supremely good and omnipotent being. Therefore, that supremely good and omnipotent being, God, must exist.

The equivocation here is on the words "meaning" and "meaningless." The word "God" is not meaningless, and so there is an intension or connotation which is its meaning *in one sense*. But it does not follow simply from the fact that a term has connotation that it also has denotation, that is, a meaning in the (other) sense of an object to which the term applies. The distinction between intension and extension is an old one, but it is still valuable and important.

EXERCISES

I. Arrange each of the following groups of terms in order of increasing intension:

1. book, history textbook, modern American history textbook, modern history textbook, textbook.
2. even number, number, number divisible by 4, real number, whole number.
3. aircraft, airplane, bomber, jet bomber, vehicle.
4. European, German, human, Junker, Prussian.
5. animal, python, reptile, snake, vertebrate.

II. Divide the following list of terms into five groups of five terms each, arranged in order of increasing intension:

aquatic animal, beast of burden, beverage, brandy, cognac, colt, domestic animal, filly, fish, game fish, horse, instrument, liquid, liquor, musical instrument, muskellunge, parallelogram, pike, polygon, quadrilateral, rectangle, square, Stradivarius, string instrument, violin.

IV. TECHNIQUES FOR DEFINING

We may divide techniques for defining into two groups, the first centering more on denotation or extension, the second on connotation or intension. The obvious and easy way to instruct someone about the denotation of a term is to give examples of objects denoted by it. This technique is often used and is often very effective. It has certain limitations, however, which ought to be recognized.

An obvious but trivial limitation of the method of definition by example is that it cannot be used to define words which have no denotation, such as the words "unicorn" or "centaur." Having mentioned it, however, let us go on to more serious limitations.

It was observed in the preceding section that two terms with different meanings (intensions) may have identically the same extensions. If one such term is defined by giving even a complete enumeration of the objects denoted by it, this definition will fail to distinguish it from the other term which denotes the same objects, even though the two terms are not synonyms. This limitation of the method of definition by example is a consequence of the fact that although intension determines extension, extension does not determine intension.

The preceding is a very "academic" limitation, however, because only a very few terms can have their extensions completely enumerated. It is impossible to enumerate all of the infinitely many numbers denoted by the term "number," and it is *practically* impossible to enumerate the finite but literally astronomical number of objects denoted by the term "star." In cases like these we are restricted to giving a sample or partial enumeration of objects denoted, and this restriction involves a more serious limitation. Any given object has many, many properties and is therefore included in the extensions of many,

many different terms. Hence any example mentioned in the denotative definition of any one term will be just as appropriately mentioned in the denotative definitions of many other terms. A particular individual, John Doe, can be mentioned as an example in defining either "man" or "animal" or "husband" or "mammal" or "father." Therefore mentioning him will not help to distinguish between the meanings of any of these terms. The same is true also for two examples, or three, or for any number which falls short of the total. Thus, three obvious examples to use in defining the term "skyscraper," the Chrysler, Empire State, and Woolworth buildings, serve equally as examples of the denotation of the terms "building," "structures completed since 1911," "objects located in Manhattan," "expensive things," and so on. Yet each of these terms denotes objects not denoted by the others, so that definition by partial enumeration cannot serve even to distinguish terms which have *different* extensions. Of course, "negative instances" may be brought in to help specify the definiendum's meaning, as in adding to the above definition of "skyscraper" that the term does *not* denote such things as the Taj Mahal or the Pentagon Building or Central Park or the Hope diamond. But since the enumeration of these negative instances must itself be incomplete, the basic limitation remains. Definition by enumeration of examples, whether complete or partial, may have psychological reasons to recommend it, but it is logically inadequate to specify precisely the meanings of the terms being defined.

The foregoing remarks have been concerned with denotative definitions in which examples are named or enumerated one at a time. Perhaps a more efficient way to give examples is not to mention the individual members of the class which is the extension of the term being defined, but to mention instead whole groups of its members. Thus to define the word "metal" as meaning gold and iron and silver and tin and the like, is different from defining "skyscraper" as meaning the Chrysler and Empire State and Woolworth buildings and the like. This special kind of definition by example—definition by subclasses

—also permits of complete enumeration, as when "vertebrate" is defined to mean amphibians and birds and fishes and mammals and reptiles. In spite of the indicated difference, this second kind of denotative definition has the same advantages and limitations as those that have already been discussed.

A special kind of definition by example is called *ostensive* or *demonstrative* definition. Instead of naming or describing the objects denoted by the term being defined, as in the ordinary sort of denotative definition, an *ostensive* definition refers to the examples by means of pointing or some other gesture. An example of an ostensive or demonstrative definition would be: the word "desk" means *this,* accompanied by a gesture such as pointing a finger or nodding one's head in the direction of a desk.

It is clear that ostensive definitions have all of the limitations that have been mentioned in the preceding discussion. In addition, ostensive definitions have some limitations peculiar to themselves. Apart from the relatively trivial geographical limitation that one cannot ostensively define the word "skyscraper" in a village or the word "mountain" on the prairie, there is the essential ambiguity of gestures to consider. To point to a desk is also to point to a part of it, and to the color of the desk, the shape, the size, the material of the desk, and also, in fact, to everything that lies in the general direction of the desk, such as the wall behind it or the garden beyond. This ambiguity can be resolved only by adding some descriptive phrase to the definiens, which results in what may be called a quasi-ostensive definition, as, for example, "The word 'desk' means this *article of furniture*" (accompanied by an appropriate gesture).

This addition, however, defeats the purposes that ostensive definitions have been claimed to serve. Ostensive definitions have sometimes been alleged to be the "first" or "primary" definitions, in the sense that all other definitions must assume that some words (those used in the definiens) are already understood, and therefore cannot be used until those words have previously been defined. It has been suggested that this difficulty can be avoided by beginning with ostensive definitions. It is by means of ostensive definitions, some writers have claimed, that we learn to understand our first words. This claim is easily seen to be mistaken, for the meaning or significance of gestures themselves must be learned. If you point with your finger to the side of a baby's crib, the baby's attention, if attracted at all, is as likely to be directed towards your finger as in the direction pointed. And surely one is in the same difficulty concerning the definition of gestures by means of other gestures. To understand the definition of *any* sign, some signs must already be understood. This bears out our earlier remark that the primary way of learning to use language is by observation and imitation, rather than definition.

It should be acknowledged that these remarks about ostensive definitions are pertinent only for the particular interpretation placed on them here. Some writers on logic have understood the phrase "ostensive definition" to include the process of "frequently hearing the word when the object it denotes is present." But such a *process* would not be a definition at all, as we have been using the term in the present chapter. It would rather be the primary, pre-definitional way of learning to use language.

EXERCISES

I. Define the following terms by example, enumerating three for each term:

1. author	4. island	7. painting
2. bridge	5. mountain	8. poem
3. city	6. novel	9. river
		10. theatre

II. For each of the terms in exercise I, can you find a non-synonymous term that your examples serve equally well to illustrate?

Before turning to the topic of connotative definition proper, some mention should be made of the frequently used technique of defining a single word by giving another single word which has the same meaning. Two words which have the same meaning are called "synonyms"; so a definition of this type is called a *synonymous* definition. Many dictionaries, especially smaller ones, use this method extensively. Thus a pocket dictionary may define "adage" as meaning proverb, "bashful" as meaning shy, and so on. Synonymous definitions are almost always used in textbooks and dictionaries designed to explain the meanings of foreign words, where we have foreign words correlated in parallel columns with their English synonyms, as:

annonce	advertisement
boîte	box
chat	cat
Dieu	God
élève	pupil

The preceding is a good method of defining terms, easy and efficient. Its applicability is limited, however, by the fact that some words have no exact synonyms. And it cannot be used in the construction of *precising* or *theoretical* definitions.

Where a synonymous definition is unavailable or inappropriate, we can use a *definition by genus and difference*. This type of definition is also called "definition by division," "analytical definition," "definition *per genus et differentia*," or simply "connotative definition." It is regarded by many writers as the most important type of definition, and by some as the only "genuine" kind. There is scarcely any justification for the latter view, but there is a certain merit to the former, since it is more generally applicable than any other technique. The possibility of defining terms by genus and difference depends upon the fact that some properties are complex, in the sense of being analyzable into two or more other properties. This complexity and analyzability can best be explained in terms of classes.

Classes having members may have their memberships divided into subclasses. For example, the class of all triangles may be divided into three non-empty subclasses: scalene triangles, isosceles triangles, and equilateral triangles. The terms "genus" and "species" are often used in this connection: the class whose membership is divided into subclasses is the *genus*, the various subclasses are *species*. As used here, the words "genus" and "species" are *relative* terms, like "parent" and "offspring." Just as the same person may be a parent in relation to his children and an offspring in relation to his parents, so one and the same class may be a genus in relation to its own subclasses and a species in relation to some larger class of which it is a subclass. Thus the class of all triangles is a genus relative to the species *scalene triangle,* and a species relative to the genus *polygon.* The logician's use of the words "genus" and "species" as *relative* terms is different from the biologist's use of them as absolute terms, and the two should not be confused.

Since a class is a collection of entities having some common property, all the members of a given genus will have some property in common. Thus all members of the genus *polygon* share the property of being closed plane figures bounded by intersecting straight lines. This genus may be divided into different species or subclasses such that all the members of one subclass have some further property in common which is not shared by any member of any other subclass. The genus *polygon* is divided into *triangles, quadrilaterals, pentagons, hexagons,* and so on. These species of the genus *polygon* are different, and the *specific* difference between members of the subclass *triangle* and members of any other subclass is that only members of the subclass *triangle* have three sides. More generally, although all members of all species of a given genus have some property in common, the members of any one species share some further property which differentiates them from the members of any other. The characteristic that serves to distinguish them is called the *specific difference.* Thus having three sides is the *specific difference* between the species *triangle* and all other species of the genus *polygon.*

It is in this sense that the property of being a triangle may be said to be analyzable into the property of being a polygon and the property of having three sides. To someone who did not know the meaning of the word "triangle" or of any synonym of it, but who did know the meanings of the terms "polygon," "sides," and "three," the meaning of the word "triangle" could be explained by means of a *definition by genus and difference:*

The word "triangle" means polygon having three sides.

The ancient definition of the word "man" as meaning *rational animal* is another example of definition by genus and difference. Here the species *man* is subsumed under the genus *animal* and the difference between it and other species is said to be *rationality*. One defines a term by genus and difference by naming a genus of which the species designated by the definiendum is a subclass, and then naming the difference which distinguishes it from other species of that genus. Of course, in the definition of "man" just mentioned, we could regard *rational* as the genus and *animal* as the difference, as well as the other way round. The order is not absolute from the point of view of logic, although there may be other, perhaps metaphysical, reasons for considering one as genus rather than the other.

Two limitations of this technique for defining terms may be mentioned quite briefly. In the first place, the method is applicable only to words which connote *complex* properties. If there are any simple, unanalyzable properties, then the words connoting them are not susceptible of definition by genus and difference. Examples that have been suggested of such properties are the sensed qualities of specific shades of color. Whether there really are any such properties is an open question, but if there are, they limit the applicability of definition by genus and difference. Another limitation has to do with words connoting *universal* properties, if they may be called that, such as the words "being," "entity," "existent," "object," or the like. These cannot be defined by the method of genus and difference because the class of all *entities,* for example, is not a species of some broader genus; *entities* themselves constitute the very highest genus or "summum genus," as it is called. The same remark applies to words for ultimate metaphysical categories, such as "substance" or "property." These limitations, while worth mentioning, are of but little practical importance in appraising this method of definition.

EXERCISES

I. Give synonymous definitions for each of the following terms:

1. absurd	8. hasten	15. omen
2. buffoon	9. infant	16. panacea
3. cemetery	10. jeopardy	17. quack
4. dictator	11. kine	18. rostrum
5. egotism	12. labyrinth	19. scoundrel
6. feast	13. mendicant	20. tepee
7. garret	14. novice	

II. Construct definitions for the following terms by matching the definiendum with an appropriate genus and difference:

Definiendum	Definiens	
	(Genus)	*(Difference)*
1. Bachelor	1. Offspring	1. Female
2. Banquet	2. Horse	2. Male
3. Boy	3. Man	3. Married
4. Brother	4. Meal	4. Unmarried
5. Child	5. Parent	5. Very large
6. Colt	6. Sheep	6. Very small
7. Daughter	7. Sibling	7. Young
8. Ewe	8. Woman	
9. Father		
10. Giant		
11. Girl		
12. Husband		
13. Lamb		
14. Mare		
15. Midget		
16. Mother		
17. Pony		
18. Ram		
19. Sister		
20. Snack		
21. Son		
22. Spinster		
23. Stallion		
24. Wife		

Certain rules have traditionally been laid down for definition by genus and difference. They do not constitute a recipe which will enable us to construct good definitions without having to think, but they are valuable as criteria for evaluating definitions once they are proposed. There are five such rules, which are intended to apply primarily to *lexical* definitions.

Rule 1: A definition should state the essential attributes of the species.

As stated, this rule is somewhat cryptic, because *in itself,* a species has just those attributes that it has, and none is more "essential" than any other. But if we understand the rule properly, as dealing with *terms,* it becomes clear. We distinguished earlier between the *objective connotation* of a term and its *conventional connotation,* the latter being those properties the possession or lack of which constitute the conventional criterion by which we decide whether an object is denoted by the term or not. Thus it is part of the objective connotation of "circle" to enclose a greater area than any other plane closed figure of equal perimeter. But to define the word "circle" by this property would be to violate the spirit or the intention of our first rule, because it is not *the* property that people have agreed to mean by that word. The conventional connotation is the property of being a closed plane curve all points of which are equidistant from a given point called the center. To define it in these terms would be to state its "essence" and thus to conform to this first rule. In our present terminology, perhaps a better way to phrase the rule would be: "A definition should state the conventional connotation of the term being defined."

It should be kept in mind that the "conventional connotation" of a term need not be an intrinsic characteristic of the things denoted by it, but might well have to do with the origin of those things, the relations they have to other things, or the uses to which they are put. Thus the word "Stradivarius," which denotes a number of violins, need not connote any actual physical characteristic shared by all those violins and not

possessed by any other, but rather has the conventional connotation of being a violin which was made in the Cremona
workshop of Antonio Stradivari. Again, *governors* are not phys-
ically or mentally different from all other men, they simply are
related differently to their fellows. Finally, the word "shoe"
cannot be defined exclusively in terms of the shapes or materials
of the things denoted by it; its definition must include reference to the *use* to which those things are put, as outer cover-
ings for the foot.

Rule 2: A definition must not be circular.

It is obvious that if the definiendum itself appears in the
definiens, the definition will explain the meaning of the term
being defined only to those who already understand it. In other
words, if a definition is circular, it will fail in its purpose,
which is to explain the meaning of its definiendum. The rule
must be understood, when applied to definition by genus and
difference, not merely to rule out letting the definiendum appear in the definiens, but also to rule out using any synonym
of it. The reason for this interpretation is that if a synonym
is assumed to be understood, one might as well give a synonymous definition instead of using the more powerful but more
complicated technique of definition by genus and difference.

Rule 3: A definition must be neither too broad nor too narrow.

This rule asserts that the definiens should not denote more
things than are denoted by the definiendum, nor fewer things
either. It is clear that this consideration does not apply when
we are making a stipulative definition, for in such cases the
definiendum has no meaning apart from its definition, and
Rule 3 could not possibly be violated. Of course, if the first
rule is obeyed, the third one must be also, for if the definiens
really names the conventional connotation of the definiendum,
they are bound to be equivalent in denotation.

The story is told that Plato's successors in the Academy at
Athens spent much time and thought on the problem of defining the word "man." Finally they decided that it meant *feather-*

less biped. They were much pleased with this definition, until Diogenes plucked a chicken and threw it over the wall into the Academy. Here was a featherless biped, surely, but just as surely it was not a man. The definiens was too broad, for it denoted more than the definiendum. After additional thought, the Academics added the phrase "with broad nails" to their definiens. Rule 3 is a difficult one to follow.

A violation of this rule in the other direction would be committed by defining the word "shoe" as a leather covering for the human foot, for there are wooden shoes as well as leather ones. This definition of the word "shoe" is too narrow, since there are objects denoted by the definiendum that are not denoted by the definiens.

Rule 4: A definition must not be expressed in ambiguous, obscure, or figurative language.

Ambiguous terms should certainly be avoided in framing definitions, because if the definiens is itself ambiguous, the definition obviously fails to perform its function of explaining the definiendum. And since the purpose of definition is to clarify meaning, the use of obscure terms defeats this purpose. Of course, obscurity is a relative matter. Words that are obscure to children are reasonably clear to most adults, and terms that are obscure to laymen are perfectly familiar to specialists in some particular field. Consider the definition of the term "dynatron oscillator" as meaning *a circuit which employs a negative-resistance volt-ampere curve to produce an alternating current.* (*Fundamentals of Engineering Electronics*, by W. G. Dow. New York, 1937, p. 331.) To the layman this definition is terribly obscure. But it is perfectly intelligible to the students of electrical engineering for whom it was written. This definition is not obscure, but justifiably technical. On the other hand, in non-technical matters, to use obscure language is to attempt to explain the unknown by the still more unknown, a futile procedure. A good example of self-defeating obscurity is found in Herbert Spencer's definition of "evolution" as:

An integration of matter and concomitant dissipation of motion, during which the matter passes from an indefinite, incoherent homogeneity to a definite, coherent heterogeneity, and during which the retained motion undergoes a parallel transformation.

Another example of obscurity in definition often cited is Dr. Samuel Johnson's celebrated second definition of the word "net" as meaning any thing made with *interstitial vacuities.*

A definition which uses figurative or metaphorical language may give some feeling for the use of the term being defined, but it cannot succeed in giving a clear explanation of what the definiendum means. Thus to define "bread" as the staff of life gives very little explanation of the meaning of that word. Often figurative definitions are humorous, as in the definition of "wedding ring" as a matrimonial tourniquet designed to stop circulation, or the definition of "discretion" as something that comes to a person after he's too old for it to do him any good. Sometimes *persuasive* definitions are highly figurative, as in the liberal's definition of "prejudice" as being down on what you aren't up on. But any definition which contains figurative language, however entertaining or persuasive, cannot serve as a serious explanation of the precise meaning of the term to be defined.

Rule 5: A definition should not be negative where it can be affirmative.

The reason for this rule is that a definition is supposed to explain what a term means, not what it does not mean. It is important, because for the vast majority of terms there are far too many things that they do *not* mean for any negative definition possibly to cover. To define the word "couch" as meaning *not a bed and not a chair* is to fail miserably to explain the meaning of the word, for there are infinitely many other things that are *not* meant by the word "couch." On the other hand, there are many terms which are essentially negative in meaning and which *require* negative definition. The word "orphan" means a child who does *not* have parents living; the word "bald" means the state of *not* having hair on one's head; and so on. Often the choice between an affirmative and a negative definition is simply a matter of the choice of words. There is not much basis for preferring to define the word "drunkard" as meaning one who drinks excessively rather than as one who is *not* temperate in drink. It should be emphasized that even where a negative definition is permissible, the definiens must not be *wholly* negative, as in the ridiculous definition of "couch" mentioned above, but must have an "affirmative" mention of the genus and a negative characterization of the species by rejecting all other species of the genus mentioned. It is only in exceptional cases that there are few enough species of the given genus for them to be conveniently mentioned and rejected in a negative definition. Since there are only three species of triangle, when that genus is divided according to the relative lengths of the sides, a perfectly adequate definition of "scalene triangle" is that it means a triangle which is neither equilateral nor isosceles. But we cannot define the word "quadrilateral" as meaning a polygon which is neither a triangle nor a pentagon nor a hexagon nor . . .—because there are too many alternative species of the genus polygon to be excluded. In general affirmative definitions are preferred to negative ones.

EXERCISES

I. Construct a definition by genus and difference for each of the terms in Exercise I on page 113.

II. Criticize the following in terms of the rules for definition by genus and difference:

1. "Coed" means a young woman attending a college.

2. "Square" means a plane figure consisting of two isosceles right triangles having a common hypotenuse.

3. "Architecture" means frozen music.

4. "Ornament" means something not necessary for practical use.

5. "Fragrance" means any odor.

6. "Lie" means a locution deliberately antithetical to a verity apprehended by the intellect.

7. "Alimony" means when two people make a mistake and one of them continues to pay for it.

8. "Painting" means a picture drawn on canvas with a brush.

9. "Honesty" means the habitual absence of the intent to deceive.

10. "Cause" means something that produces an effect.

11. "Satisfaction" means the state of not having any unfulfilled desires.

12. "Eating" means the successive performances of the functions of mastication, humectation, and deglutination.

13. "Antidote" means a remedy to counteract the effects of arsenic.

14. "Poison" means anything that has a toxic effect.

15. "Research" means the process of finding out what we're going to do after we can't keep on doing what we're doing now.

16. "Etiquette" means doing little things that you don't want to.

17. "Bus" means a large automobile which carries passengers for hire from one city to another.

18. "Advertising" means something which makes one think he's longed all his life for something he never even heard of before.

19. "Sleep" means a dormant state of the organism.

20. "Explorer" means a bum with an excuse.

21. "Cynic" means one who knows the price of everything and the value of nothing.

22. "Diplomat" means a man who convinces his wife that a woman looks stout in a fur coat.

23. "Repartee" means clever conversation a man thinks up on his way home from a party.

24. "Monopolist" means a man who keeps an elbow on each arm of his theater chair.

25. "Conference" means a meeting of a group of men who singly can do nothing, but who collectively agree that nothing can be done.

PART TWO

Deduction

CHAPTER FIVE

Categorical Propositions

I. CATEGORICAL PROPOSITIONS AND CLASSES

The preceding chapters have dealt, for the most part, with the topic of language and its influence on argumentation. We turn now to that special kind of argument called deduction. A deductive argument is one whose premises are claimed to provide conclusive evidence for the truth of its conclusion. Every deductive argument is either valid or invalid: valid if it is impossible for its premises to be true without its conclusion being true also, invalid otherwise. The theory of deduction is intended to explain the relationship between premises and conclusion of a valid argument and to provide techniques for the appraisal of deductive arguments, that is, for discriminating between valid and invalid deductions.

Informal fallacies were discussed at length in Chapter Three. But even where no informal fallacy is involved, a deductive argument may be invalid rather than valid; so further techniques for appraising such arguments must be devised. The classical or Aristotelian study of deduction centered on arguments involving propositions of a special kind called "categorical propositions." In the argument:

> No athletes are vegetarians.
> All football players are athletes.
> Therefore no football players are vegetarians.

both premises and conclusion are *categorical* propositions. Propositions of this kind are usually regarded as assertions about classes, affirming or denying that one class is included in another, either in whole or in part. The premises and conclusion of the argument stated above are assertions about the class of *athletes,* the class of *vegetarians,* and the class of *football players.*

Classes were mentioned briefly in the preceding chapter, where a *class* was explained to be the collection of all objects which have some specified characteristic in common. There are various ways in which classes may be related to each other. If every member of one class is also a member of a second class, then the first class is said to be *included* or *contained* in the second. If only some members of one class are members of another, then the first may be said to be *partially* contained in the second. Of course, there are pairs of classes having no members in common, such as the class of all triangles and the class of all circles. These various different relationships between classes are affirmed or denied by *categorical propositions.*

There are four different *standard forms* of categorical propositions, which are illustrated by the four following propositions:

> 1. All politicians are liars.
> 2. No politicians are liars.
> 3. Some politicians are liars.
> 4. Some politicians are not liars.

The first is a *universal affirmative* proposition. It is an assertion about two classes, the class of all politicians and the class of all liars, saying that the first class is *included* or *contained* in the second, which means that every member of the first class is also a member of the second class. In the present example, the *subject term* "politicians" designates the class of all politicians, and the *predicate term* "liars" designates the class of all liars. Any universal affirmative proposition may be written schematically as:

All *S* is *P*.

where the letters *"S"* and *"P"* represent the subject and predicate terms, respectively. The name "universal affirmative" is appropriate because the proposition *affirms* that the relationship of class inclusion holds between the two classes, and that the inclusion is complete or *universal,* all members of *S* being said to be members of *P* also.

The second example:

No politicians are liars.

is a *universal negative* proposition. It denies of politicians universally that they are liars. Making an assertion about two classes, it says that the first class is *excluded* from the second— wholly excluded—which is to say that there is no member of the first class which is also a member of the second. Any universal negative proposition may be written schematically as:

No *S* is *P*.

where, again, the letters *"S"* and *"P"* represent the subject and predicate terms. The name "universal negative" is appropriate because the proposition *denies* that the relation of class inclusion holds between the two classes, and denies it *universally,* no members at all of *S* being members of *P*.

The third example:

Some politicians are liars.

is a *particular affirmative* proposition. Clearly what the present example affirms is that some members of the class of all politicians are (also) members of the class of all liars. But it does not affirm this of politicians universally: not all politicians uni-

versally are said to be liars, but rather some particular politician or politicians. This proposition neither affirms nor denies
that *all* politicians are liars; it makes no pronouncement on the
matter. It does not literally assert that some politicians are *not*
liars, although in some special circumstances it might be interpreted as implying it. The literal, minimal interpretation of
the present proposition is that the class of politicians and the
class of liars have some member or members in common. For
definiteness, we shall adopt that minimal interpretation here.

The word "some" has a certain indefiniteness. Does it mean
"at least one," or "at least two," or "at least a hundred"? Or
how many? For the sake of greater precision, although this may
depart from ordinary usage, it is customary to regard the word
"some" as meaning *at least one*. Thus a particular affirmative
proposition, written schematically as:

Some *S* is *P*.

is interpreted as asserting that at least one member of the class
designated by the subject term *"S"* is also a member of the class
designated by the predicate term *"P."* The name "particular
affirmative" is appropriate because the proposition *affirms* that
the relationship of class inclusion holds, but does not affirm it
of the first class universally, but only partially, of some *particular* member or members of the first class.

The fourth example:

Some politicians are not liars.

is a *particular negative* proposition. This example, like the
preceding, is particular in that it does not refer to politicians
universally but only to some particular member or members of
that class. But unlike the former, it does not affirm that the particular members of the first class referred to are included in the
second class: this is precisely what is *denied*. A particular negative proposition, schematically written as:

Some *S* is not *P*.

asserts that at least one member of the class designated by the subject term "*S*" is excluded from the whole of the class designated by the predicate term "*P*."

It was traditionally held that all deductive arguments were analyzable in terms of these four standard forms of categorical propositions, and a considerable amount of theory was built up around them. Not all standard form categorical propositions are as simple and straightforward as the examples considered thus far. Although the subject and predicate terms of a standard form categorical proposition must designate classes, they may be quite complicated expressions instead of single words. For example, the proposition:

All candidates for the position are men of honor and integrity.

has as its subject and predicate terms, respectively, the phrases "candidates for the position" and "men of honor and integrity."

EXERCISES

Identify the subject and predicate terms, and name the form of each of the following propositions:

1. All substances which have the power to turn blue litmus paper red are acids.

2. Some plays written over two thousand years ago are smash hits on Broadway today.

3. Some men who never worked a day in their lives are successful heads of large labor unions.

4. No philosophers that ever lived were wiser men than the authors of the Constitution.

5. All veterans are members or former members of the Army or Navy who saw active service during the war.

6. Some very wealthy men are members of the United States Senate.

7. Some cracked and shabby articles of furniture for which even dealers are willing to pay large sums of money are not genuine antiques.

8. No acids other than sulphuric are liquids capable of dissolving gold.

9. Some almost priceless works of art are paintings that were sold by their creators for only a few pennies.

10. Some extremely successful and widely read leaders in government and industry are not college graduates.

II. QUALITY, QUANTITY, AND DISTRIBUTION

Every standard form categorical proposition is said to have both a "quality" and a "quantity." The *quality* of a proposition is *affirmative* or *negative* according to whether class inclusion is affirmed or denied by the proposition. Thus both universal affirmative and particular affirmative propositions are *affirmative* in quality, while universal negative and particular negative propositions are both *negative*. It is customary to use the letters *"A," "E," "I,"* and *"O"* as names for the four standard forms of categorical propositions, universal affirmative, universal negative, particular affirmative, and particular negative, respectively. The letter names are presumed to come from the Latin words *"AffIrmo"* and *"nEgO,"* which mean *I affirm* and *I deny,* respectively.

The quantity of a proposition is *universal* or *particular* according to whether the proposition refers to all members or only to some members of the class designated by its subject term. Thus the *A* and *E* propositions are universal in quantity, while the *I* and *O* propositions are particular in quantity. We observe that the names "universal affirmative," "universal negative," "particular affirmative," and "particular negative" uniquely describe each of the four standard forms by mentioning first its quantity and then its quality.

Every standard form categorical proposition begins with one of the words "all," "no," or "some." These words indicate the *quantity* of the proposition, and are called the "quantifiers." The first two indicate that the proposition is universal, the third that it is particular. In addition to expressing the universal quantity, the quantifier "no" serves to indicate the negative quality of the **E** proposition.

Between the subject and predicate terms of every standard form categorical proposition occurs some form of the verb "to be" (accompanied by the word "not" in the case of the **O** proposition.) This serves to *connect* the subject and predicate terms, and is called the "copula." In the schematic formulations given in the preceding section, only "is" and "is not" appear, but depending upon how the proposition is worded otherwise, some other form of the verb "to be" may be more appropriate. For example, in the propositions:

> Some Roman Emperors were monsters.
> All communists are fanatics.
> Some soldiers will not be heroes.

the symbols "were," "are," and "will not be" serve as copulas. The general skeleton or schema of a standard form categorical proposition consists of four parts: first the quantifier, then the subject term, next the copula, and finally the predicate term. This schema may be written as:

> Quantifier (subject term) copula (predicate term).

On the class interpretation, the subject and predicate terms of a standard form categorical proposition designate classes of objects, and the proposition is regarded as being *about* these classes. Propositions may refer to classes in different ways, of course. A proposition may refer to *all* members of a class, or it may refer to only *some* members of that class. Thus the proposition:

> All congressmen are citizens.

refers to or is about *all* congressmen, but does not refer to all citizens. It asserts that each and every member of the class of congressmen is a citizen, but it makes no assertion about all citizens. It does not affirm that each and every citizen is a congressman, but it does not deny this either. Any *A* proposition, of this form:

All *S* is *P*.

is thus seen to refer to *all* members of the class designated by its subject term "*S*," but does not refer to all members of the class designated by its predicate term "*P*."

The technical term "distribution" is introduced to characterize the ways in which terms can occur in categorical propositions. A proposition *distributes* a term if it refers to all members of the class designated by the term. As we have seen, the subject term of an *A* proposition is *distributed in* (or *by*) that proposition, while its predicate term is *undistributed in* (or *by*) it. Let us examine the other standard form categorical propositions to see which terms are distributed or undistributed in them.

An *E* proposition, such as:

No athletes are vegetarians.

asserts of each and every athlete that he (or she) is not a vegetarian. The whole of the class of athletes is said to be excluded from the class of vegetarians. All members of the class designated by its subject term are referred to by an *E* proposition, which is therefore said to *distribute* its subject term. On the other hand, in asserting that the whole class of athletes is excluded from the class of vegetarians, it is also asserted that the whole class of vegetarians is excluded from the class of athletes. The given proposition clearly asserts of each and every vegetarian that he (or she) is not an athlete. An *E* proposition, therefore, refers to all members of the class designated by its predicate term, and is said to distribute its predicate term also. *E* propositions distribute *both* their subject and predicate terms.

The situation is different with respect to *I* propositions. Thus:

Some soldiers are cowards.

makes no assertion about *all* soldiers and makes no assertion about all cowards either. It says nothing about each and every soldier, nor about each and every coward. Neither class is said to be either wholly included or wholly excluded from all or even part of the other. Both subject and predicate terms are *undistributed* in any particular affirmative proposition.

The particular negative or **O** proposition is similar in that it too does not distribute its subject term. Thus the proposition:

Some horses are not thoroughbreds.

says nothing about *all* horses but refers to *some* members of the class designated by the subject term. It says of this part of the class of all horses that it is excluded from the class of all thoroughbreds, that is, from the *whole* of the latter class. Given the particular horses referred to, it says that each and every member of the class of thoroughbreds is *not* one of those particular horses. When something is said to be excluded from a class, the whole of the class is referred to, as when a man is excluded from a country all parts of that country are forbidden him. The particular negative proposition *does* distribute its predicate term, but not its subject term.

We may summarize these remarks on distribution as follows. Universal propositions, both affirmative and negative, distribute their subject terms, while particular propositions, whether affirmative or negative, do not distribute their subject terms. Thus the *quantity* of any standard form categorical proposition determines whether its *subject* term is distributed or undistributed. Affirmative propositions, whether universal or particular, do not distribute their predicate terms; while negative propositions, both universal and particular, do distribute their predicate terms. Thus the *quality* of any standard form categorical proposition determines whether its *predicate* term is distributed or undistributed.

The diagram at the top of the following page summarizes the above information, and may be useful in helping the student to remember which propositions distribute which of their terms.

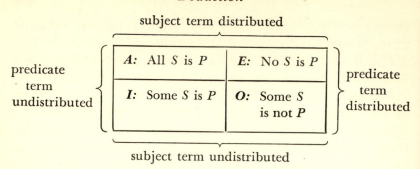

subject term distributed

predicate term undistributed

| A: All S is P | E: No S is P |
| I: Some S is P | O: Some S is not P |

predicate term distributed

subject term undistributed

Name the quality and quantity of each proposition in the exercise set on pages 127–128, and state whether their subject and predicate terms are distributed or undistributed.

III. THE TRADITIONAL SQUARE OF OPPOSITION

Standard form categorical propositions having the same subject and predicate terms may differ from each other in quality or in quantity or in both. This kind of differing was given the technical name "opposition" by older logicians, and certain important truth relations were correlated with the various kinds of opposition. Two propositions are *contradictories* if one is the denial of the other, that is, if they cannot both be true *and* they cannot both be false. It is clear that two standard form categorical propositions having the same subject and predicate terms but differing from each other *both* in quantity and in quality are contradictories. Thus the *A* and *O* propositions:

All judges are lawyers.

and

Some judges are not lawyers.

which are opposed both in quantity and in quality, are obviously contradictories. At least one is true, and at least one is false. Similarly, the *E* and *I* propositions:

No politicians are idealists.

and

Some politicians are idealists.

are opposed both in quantity and quality, and are contradictories. Schematically we may say that the contradictory of *All S is P* is *Some S is not P*, and the contradictory of *No S is P* is *Some S is P; A* and *O* are contradictories, as are *E* and *I*.

Two propositions are said to be *contraries* if they cannot both be true, though they might both be false. The traditional or Aristotelian account of categorical propositions held that universal propositions having the same subject and predicate terms but differing in quality were contraries.* Thus, it was urged, *A* and *E* propositions such as:

> All poets are idlers.

and

> No poets are idlers.

cannot both be true, athough both might be false, and are therefore to be regarded as contraries.

Two propositions are said to be *subcontraries* if they cannot both be false, though they might both be true. The same traditional account held that particular propositions having the same subject and predicate terms but differing in quality were subcontraries. It was affirmed that *I* and *O* propositions such as:

> Some diamonds are precious stones.

and

> Some diamonds are not precious stones.

could both be true, but could not both be false, and must therefore be regarded as subcontraries.

Thus far the examples of opposition between propositions have been such as to suggest disagreement. But "opposition" in the present context is a technical term and applies even where disagreement in the ordinary sense is not present. Thus where two propositions, again having the same subject and predicate terms, agree in quality and differ only in quantity, there is *opposition* even though there is no disagreement implied.   In

---

* This traditional view will be examined critically in Section V below.

such cases the truth of the particular proposition was asserted to follow from or to be implied by the truth of the universal. Thus from the truth of an *A* proposition, such as:

All spiders are eight-legged animals.

the truth of the corresponding *I* proposition:

Some spiders are eight-legged animals.

was supposed to follow. And from the truth of an *E* proposition, such as:

No spiders are insects.

the truth of the corresponding *O* proposition:

Some spiders are not insects.

was supposed to follow. The opposition between a universal proposition and its corresponding particular (that is, the particular proposition having the same subject and predicate terms and the same quality as the universal) was named *"subalternation."* In this situation the universal proposition is called the *"subalternant,"* or *"superaltern,"* and the particular is referred to either as the *"subalternate"* or simply as the *"subaltern."* In subalternation, it was held, the *subalternant* implies the *subalternate*. The implication does not hold from subalternate to subalternant, for such subalternates as:

Some animals are cats.

and

Some animals are not cats.

are both true while their subalternants are clearly both false.

These various kinds of opposition were represented by a diagram called *The Square of Opposition,* which is reproduced on the following page.

The relationships diagrammed by this Square of Opposition were believed to provide a logical basis for validating certain rather elementary forms of argument. In this connection it is customary to distinguish between *mediate* and *immediate* inference. Any inference is the drawing of a conclusion from one or more premisses. Where there is more than one premiss in-

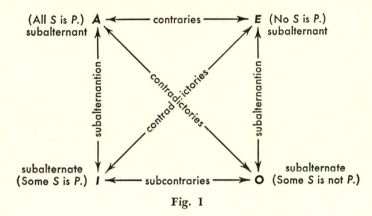

Fig. 1

volved, as in a syllogism, which has two premisses, the inference is said to be *"mediate"*—presumably because the conclusion is supposed to be drawn from the first premiss through the *mediation* of the second. Where a conclusion is drawn from only one premiss, the inference is said to be *"immediate."* The information embodied in the traditional Square of Opposition clearly provides a basis for a number of immediate inferences. Thus if an *A* proposition is taken as premiss, then according to the Square of Opposition one can validly infer that the corresponding *O* proposition (that is, the *O* proposition having the same subject and predicate terms as the *A*) is false. And from the same premiss one can immediately infer that the corresponding *I* proposition is true. Of course, from the truth of an *I* proposition the truth of its corresponding *A* proposition does not follow, but the falsehood of the corresponding *E* proposition does. The traditional Square of Opposition provides the basis for a considerable number of such immediate inferences. Given the truth or falsehood of any one of the four standard form categorical propositions, the truth or falsehood of some or all of the others can be inferred immediately. These immediate inferences based on the traditional Square of Opposition may be listed as follows:

A being given as true: *E* is false, *I* is true, *O* is false.
E being given as true: *A* is false, *I* is false, *O* is true.
I being given as true: *E* is false, while *A* and *O* are undetermined.
O being given as true: *A* is false, while *E* and *I* are undetermined.

A being given as false: *O* is true, while *E* and *I* are undetermined.
E being given as false: *I* is true, while *A* and *O* are undetermined.
I being given as false: *A* is false, *E* is true, *O* is true.
O being given as false: *A* is true, *E* is false, *I* is true.

EXERCISES

What can be inferred about the truth or falsehood of the remaining propositions in each of the following sets if we assume the first to be true? If we assume it to be false?

1. (a) All amino acids are organic compounds.
    (b) No amino acids are organic compounds.
    (c) Some amino acids are organic compounds.
    (d) Some amino acids are not organic compounds.

2. (a) No reptiles are warm blooded animals.
    (b) Some reptiles are warm blooded animals.
    (c) Some reptiles are not warm blooded animals.
    (d) All reptiles are warm blooded animals.

3. (a) Some former college presidents have been successful candidates for the Presidency of the United States.
    (b) Some former college presidents have not been successful candidates for the Presidency of the United States.
    (c) All former college presidents have been successful candidates for the Presidency of the United States.
    (d) No former college presidents have been successful candidates for the Presidency of the United States.

4. (a) Some radium compounds are not radioactive substances.
    (b) All radium compounds are radioactive substances.
    (c) No radium compounds are radioactive substances.
    (d) Some radium compounds are radioactive substances.

IV. FURTHER IMMEDIATE INFERENCES

There are other kinds of immediate inference in addition to those associated with the traditional Square of Opposition. In this section we shall present three of these other types. The most obvious kind of immediate inference proceeds by simply interchanging the subject and predicate terms of a proposition. This is called "conversion" and is perfectly valid in the case of *E* and *I* propositions. Clearly, "No men are angels" makes the same assertion as "No angels are men," and either can be validly inferred from the other by the immediate inference called *conversion*. Just as clearly, "Some writers are women" and "Some women are writers" are logically equivalent, so that each can validly be inferred from the other by *conversion*. One standard form categorical proposition is said to be the "converse" of another when it is formed by simply interchanging its subject and predicate terms. Thus "No idealists are politicians" is the converse of "No politicians are idealists," and each can validly be inferred from the other by *conversion*.

But the converse of an *A* proposition does not follow validly from that *A* proposition. Thus if our original proposition is "All dogs are animals," its converse "All animals are dogs" does not follow from the original proposition at all, the original being true while its converse is false. Traditional logic recognized this fact, of course, but asserted that something very much *like* conversion was valid for *A* propositions. This was named "conversion by limitation" (or *per accidens*). It proceeds by interchanging subject and predicate terms *and* changing the quantity of the proposition from universal to particular. Thus it was claimed that from the premiss "All dogs are animals" the conclusion "Some animals are dogs" could validly be inferred, the inference being a *conversion by limitation*. This type of conversion will be considered further in the next section.

Finally, it should be observed that an *O* proposition cannot validly be converted at all. For the true *O* proposition "Some animals are not dogs" would have as its converse the false proposition "Some dogs are not animals." It is customary to express this fact by saying that an **O** proposition "has no converse"— meaning by this only that conversion is not a valid form of inference when applied to **O** propositions.

The term "convertend" is used to refer to the premiss of an immediate inference by conversion, and the conclusion is called the "converse." The following table was traditionally held to give a complete picture of valid conversions:

Conversions

Convertend	Converse
A: All *S* is *P*	**I:** Some *P* is *S* (by limitation)
E: No *S* is *P*	**E:** No *P* is *S*
I: Some *S* is *P*	**I:** Some *P* is *S*
O: Some *S* is not *P*	(no converse)

The converse of a given proposition contains exactly the same terms as the given proposition (their order being reversed), and has the same *quality*.

The next type of immediate inference to be discussed is called "obversion." Before explaining it, we shall find it helpful to return briefly to the notion of a "class" and to introduce some new ideas which enable us to discuss obversion more easily. A class is the collection of all objects having a certain common property, which we refer to as the "class-defining characteristic." Thus the class of all humans is the collection of all things which have the property of being human, and its *class-defining characteristic* is the property humanity. The *class-defining characteristic* need not be a "simple" property in any sense, for *any* property determines a class. Thus the complex property of being left-handed and red-headed and a student determines a class—the class of all left-handed red-headed students.

Every class has associated with it a *complementary class*, or *complement*, which is the collection of all things which do *not* belong to the original class. Thus the *complement* of the class of all men is the class of all things which are *not* men. The class-defining characteristic of the complementary class is the (negative) property of *not being a man*. The complement of the class of all men contains no men, but contains everything else: shoes and ships and sealing wax, and cabbages—but no kings, since kings are men. It is sometimes convenient to speak of the complement of the class of all men as "the class of all non-men." The complement of the class designated by the term "*S*" is then designated by the term "non-*S*," and we may speak of the term "non-*S*" as being the *complement* of the term "*S*." We are using the word "complement" in two senses: one the sense of class complement, the other the sense of the complement of a term. The two senses, although different, are very closely connected. One term is the (term) complement of another where the first term designates the (class) complement of the class designated by the second term. It should be noted that just as a class is the (class) complement of its own complement, a term is the (term) complement of its own complement. A sort of "double negative" rule is involved here, so that we need not have strings of "non's" prefixed to a term. Thus we should write the complement of the term "voter" as "non-voter," but we should write the complement of the latter term simply as "voter" rather than "non-non-voter." One must be careful not to mistake *contrary* terms for complementary terms, as in identifying "cowards" and "non-heroes." Those terms are contraries in that no person can be both a coward and a hero, but not everyone—and certainly not everything—need be either one or the other. Thus the complement of the term "winner" is not "loser," but "non-winner," for although not everything—or even everyone—is either a winner or a loser, absolutely everything is either a winner or a non-winner.

Now that we understand what is meant by the complement of a term, the process of *obversion* is easy to describe. In *obversion,* the subject term remains unchanged, and so does the quantity of the proposition being obverted. In obverting a proposition we change the quality of the proposition and replace the predicate term by its complement. Thus the *A* proposition:

> All residents are voters.

has as its *obverse* the *E* proposition:

> No residents are non-voters.

These two propositions, it is clear, are logically equivalent, so that either one can validly be inferred from the other. Obversion is a valid immediate inference when applied to *any* standard form categorical proposition. Thus the *E* proposition:

> No umpires are partisans.

has as its obverse the logically equivalent *A* proposition:

> All umpires are non-partisans.

Similarly, the obverse of the *I* proposition:

> Some metals are conductors.

is the *O* proposition:

> Some metals are not non-conductors.

And finally the *O* proposition:

> Some nations were not belligerents.

has as its obverse the *I* proposition:

> Some nations were non-belligerents.

All four standard form categorical propositions have obverses, and the immediate inference known as obversion is valid for all of them. In any inference of this type, the premiss is called the "obvertend" and the conclusion is called the "obverse." Every standard form categorical proposition is logically equivalent to its obverse. To obtain the obverse of a proposition, we leave the quantity and the subject term unchanged, change the quality of the proposition, and replace the predicate term by its complement. The following table gives a complete picture of all valid obversions:

Obversions

Obvertend	Obverse
A: All S is P	**E:** No S is non-P
E: No S is P	**A:** All S is non-P
I: Some S is P	**O:** Some S is not non-P
O: Some S is not P	**I:** Some S is non-P

The third variety of immediate inference to be discussed introduces no new principles, for it can be reduced, in a sense, to the first two. To form the *contrapositive* of a given proposition we replace its subject term by the complement of its predicate term *and* replace its predicate term by the complement of its subject term. Thus the *contrapositive* of the *A* proposition:

> All members are voters.

is the *A* proposition:

> All non-voters are non-members.

That these two are logically equivalent will be evident upon a moment's reflection, and from this it is clear that *contraposition* is a valid form of immediate inference when applied to *A* propositions.

It introduces nothing new for we can get from any *A* proposition to its contrapositive by first obverting it, next applying conversion, and then obversion again. Thus, beginning with *All S is P* we obvert it to obtain *No S is non-P* which converts to *No non-P is S* whose obverse is *All non-P is non-S*. Thus the contrapositive of any *A* proposition is the obverse of the converse of the obverse of that proposition.

Contraposition is most useful in working with *A* propositions, but it is a valid form of immediate inference when applied to *O* propositions also. Thus the contrapositive of the *O* proposition:

> Some students are not idealists.

is the somewhat cumbersome *O* proposition:

> Some non-idealists are not non-students.

which is logically equivalent to the first. That logical equivalence can be shown by deriving the contrapositive a step at a time through obverting, converting, and then obverting again, as in the following schematic derivation: *Some S is not P* obverts to *Some S is non-P* converts to *Some non-P is S* obverts to *Some non-P is not non-S* (the contrapositive) .

Contraposition is not valid for *I* propositions. This can be seen by noting that the true *I* proposition:

> Some citizens are non-congressmen.

has as its contrapositive the *false* proposition:

> Some congressmen are non-citizens.

Why contraposition is invalid when applied to *I* propositions can be seen when we attempt to derive the contrapositive of an *I* proposition by successively obverting, converting, and obverting. The obverse of the *I* proposition *Some S is P* is the *O* proposition *Some S is not non-P,* which has no converse—by which we mean that conversion of an *O* proposition is invalid.

The contrapositive of the *E* proposition *No S is P* is *No non-P is non-S,* and this does not follow validly from the original, as can be seen by observing that the *E* proposition:

> No wrestlers are weaklings.

which is true, has as its contrapositive the false proposition:

> No non-weaklings are non-wrestlers.

If we attempt to derive the contrapositive of an *E* proposition by successive obversion, conversion, and obversion, we find the reason for this invalidity. The obverse of the *E* proposition *No S is P* is the *A* proposition *All S is non-P,* and this cannot validly be converted except *by limitation.* If we do convert it by limitation to obtain *Some non-P is S,* then the latter can be obverted to obtain *Some non-P is not non-S,* which we may call the "contrapositive by limitation."

Thus we see that contraposition is a valid form of immediate inference only when applied to *A* and *O* propositions. Contraposition is not valid at all for *I* propositions, and for *E* propositions only *by limitation*. This may also be presented in the form of a table:

Contraposition

Premiss		Contrapositive
A: All *S* is *P*	*A:*	All non-*P* is non-*S*
E: No *S* is *P*	*O:*	Some non-*P* is not non-*S* (by limitation)
I: Some *S* is *P*		Invalid
O: Some *S* is not *P*	*O:*	Some non-*P* is not non-*S*

There are many other types of immediate inference which have been classified and given special names, but since they involve no new principles we shall not discuss them here.

EXERCISES

I. State the converses of the following propositions:

1. Some men who were completely ignorant of mathematics have been great inventors.

2. No visitors who overstay their leaves are welcome guests.

3. All elections in which equal opportunities to present their views and programs are extended to all candidates for office are contests whose results faithfully represent the will of the electorate.

4. No men who are indifferent to the well-being of their fellows are persons who can safely be entrusted with positions of leadership.

5. Some books which have become best sellers are works of only indifferent literary merit.

II. State the obverses of the following propositions:

1. No Quakers were combatants.

2. Some beverages are intoxicants.

3. All acids are corrosives.

4. Some educators are not teachers.

5. No objects suitable for door stops are objects which weigh less than twenty pounds.

III. State the contrapositives of the following propositions:

1. All historians are optimists.

2. All elements are non-compounds.

3. Some suspects were not criminals.

4. All non-worshippers are atheists.

5. All things over five feet tall are objects weighing at least fifty pounds.

IV. If *all scientists are philosophers* is true, what may be inferred about the truth or falsehood of the following propositions?

1. No non-philosophers are scientists.

2. Some non-philosophers are not non-scientists.

3. All non-scientists are non-philosophers.

4. No scientists are non-philosophers.

5. No non-scientists are non-philosophers.

6. All philosophers are scientists.

7. Some non-philosophers are scientists.

8. All non-philosophers are non-scientists.

9. Some scientists are not philosophers.

10. No philosophers are non-scientists.

V. EXISTENTIAL IMPORT

A proposition is said to have "existential import" when it asserts the existence of objects of some specified kind. For example, the proposition *there are books on my desk* has existential import, while the proposition *there are no unicorns* does not. Which, if any, of the four standard form categorical propositions have existential import, and which, if any, do not? It seems clear that both affirmative and negative *particular* propositions have existential import. The *I* proposition, *some writers are women,* definitely asserts that there exists at least one writer who is a woman. And the *O* proposition, *some writers are not women,* asserts that there exists at least one writer who is not a woman.

There are some apparent exceptions which must be briefly noted. Such statements as "Some ghosts appear in Shakespeare's plays," and "Some Greek Gods are described in the *Iliad,*" are true despite the fact that there are neither ghosts nor Greek Gods. A little thought will reveal that these apparent exceptions are formulated in a misleading fashion. These statements do not assert the existence of ghosts or Greek Gods; what they really assert is that certain *other* propositions are asserted or implied in Shakespeare's plays and the *Iliad.* Shakespeare's and Homer's propositions are false, but it is nevertheless true *that they asserted them.* And this is all that the apparent exceptions assert. Outside these fairly uncommon literary or mythological contexts, *I* and *O* propositions do have existential import. Both particular propositions assert that the classes designated by their subject terms are not empty or null, that is, that they do have members.

Ordinary English usage varies in the case of *A* and *E* propositions. When a mother (mistakenly) warns her child that "All dogs are dangerous animals" she clearly intends to assert not merely that any member of the class of dogs is also a member of the class of dangerous animals, but that *there are members* of these classes. On the other hand, the statement, "All trespassers will be prosecuted," far from asserting that the class of trespassers has members, is ordinarily understood as a threat intended to insure that the class remain empty. We cannot look to ordinary usage to decide the question of existential import for universal propositions, because that usage varies. Depending upon the situation and the intention of the speaker, the *A* proposition *All S is P* means either that any member that *S* may have is also a member of *P or* that *S* has members *and* all of them are members of *P*.

Now what bearing do these remarks about existential import have on our preceding discussion of the traditional Square of Opposition and other immediate inferences? When we admit that *I* and *O* propositions both have existential import, we must admit that corresponding particular propositions which differ in quality can both be false. Since there are no ghosts of any kind, there are no ghosts which are millionaires and there are no ghosts which are not millionaires. Consequently the *I* proposition *Some ghosts are millionaires* and the *O* proposition *Some ghosts are not millionaires* are both false. For either of them to be true, there would have to exist at least one ghost; but there are no ghosts at all. Since *subcontraries* are propositions which can both be true but cannot both be false, it follows that *I* and *O* propositions are not really subcontraries, and this means that part of the traditional Square of Opposition must be rejected.

The traditional Square of Opposition breaks down further whether we understand universal propositions to have existential import or not. If we interpret *A* and *E* propositions as having existential import, then they can be true only if the classes designated by their subject terms have members. Since there are no ghosts, the corresponding *A* and *E* propositions *All ghosts are millionaires* and *No ghosts are millionaires* are false along with the *I* and *O* propositions mentioned in the preceding paragraph. Since *contradictories* are propositions which cannot both be true and cannot both be false, it follows that *A* and *O* propositions are not really contradictories, and that *E* and *I* propositions are not contradictories either. On the assumption that *A* and *E* propositions have existential import, the two diagonals of the traditional Square of Opposition must be rejected.

On the other hand, if we take universal propositions *not* to have existential import, then the immediate inferences based on subalternation become invalid. It is clear that a proposition which asserts existence cannot validly be inferred from a proposition which makes no such claim. If we interpret *All unicorns are quadrupeds* as a true proposition which does not assert the existence of unicorns, and *Some unicorns are quadrupeds* as a false proposition which does assert the existence of unicorns, then it is clear that any inference from the former to the latter must be invalid. More than the Square of Opposition is invalidated by this interpretation. Conversion by limitation must be rejected also, for by it the false proposition *Some quadrupeds are unicorns* would follow from the same true premiss. And since what we have called "contraposition by limitation" depends upon or involves conversion by limitation, it too must be rejected as an invalid form of inference.

Considerations such as these have led some writers to reject the traditional or Aristotelian logic as unsatisfactory. The traditional Square of Opposition and other suspect forms of immediate inference can be saved, however, if we lay down the general assumption or presupposition that all of the classes which we permit ourselves to discuss do have members. When this is presupposed, any existential import carried by standard form categorical propositions is automatically satisfied. Within the scope of this assumption, *A* and *E* propositions *are* contraries, *I* and *O* propositions *are* subcontraries, and *A* and *O* propositions *are* contradictories, as are *E* and *I*. And on the presupposition mentioned, not only the immediate inferences based on subalternation but also conversion by limitation and contraposition by limitation are perfectly valid. This existential presupposition, moreover, is faithful to ordinary English usage in the vast majority of cases. Suppose, for example, someone asserts that *All of the apples in the barrel are Jonathans,* and we look in the barrel and find it empty. Ordinarily we should not take this as making the proposition true, *nor* as making it false. We would feel more inclined to point out that there are no apples in the barrel, indicating that in this particular case the existential presupposition was mistaken. The existential presupposition necessary and sufficient for the correctness of the traditional Aristotelian logic is in close accord with ordinary usage. That tradition is not to be rejected out of hand.

It must be insisted, of course, that some classes do *not* have members. And it is important to realize that we do not always know whether a class has members or not. At the moment I do not know whether or not the class of *children on my porch at home* is null, and no one on earth knows (as yet) whether the class of *inhabitants of Mars* is null or has members. For this reason modern logicians have proposed to depart from the traditional view by not committing themselves to this blanket existential assumption. Where it is necessary for valid inference, the assumption of existence can be stated as an explicit additional premiss. In contrast to the traditional or Aristotelian interpretation, the modern treatment of standard form categorical propositions is called "Boolean," after the English mathematician and logician George Boole (1815–1864), one of the founders of modern symbolic logic.

On the Boolean interpretation, *I* and *O* propositions have existential import, so where the class *S* is null, the propositions *Some S is P* and *Some S is not P* are both false. The universal propositions *A* and *E* are still taken to be the contradictories of the *O* and *I* propositions, respectively. Where *S* is a null class, both particular propositions are false, and their contradictories *All S is P* and *No S is P* are both true. On the Boolean interpretation, universal propositions are understood as having no existential import. However, a universal proposition formulated in ordinary English which is intended to assert existence *can be represented* in Boolean terms. This is accomplished by using two propositions, the Boolean non-existential universal *and* the corresponding existential particular.

We shall adopt the Boolean interpretation in all that follows. This means that *A* and *E* propositions can both be true and are therefore not contraries, and that *I* and *O* propositions can both be false and are therefore not subcontraries. Moreover, since *A* and *E* can be true while *I* and *O* are false, inferences based on subalternation fail; and this means that the diagonal (contradictory) relations are all that remain of the traditional Square of Opposition. Obversion remains valid when applied to any proposition, but conversion (and contraposition) by limitation are rejected as not valid. Conversion remains valid for *E* and *I* propositions, and contraposition remains valid for *A* and *O* propositions.

EXERCISES

Analyze each of the following arguments in terms of the preceding discussion of existential import:

I.   (1) No mathematician is one who has squared the circle;

therefore, (2) No one who has squared the circle is a mathematician;

therefore, (3) All who have squared the circle are non-mathematicians;

therefore, (4) Some non-mathematician is one who has squared the circle.

II.   (1) No citizen is one who has succeeded in accomplishing the impossible;

therefore, (2) No one who has succeeded in accomplishing the impossible is a citizen;

therefore, (3) All who have succeeded in accomplishing the impossible are non-citizens;

therefore, (4) Some who have succeeded in accomplishing the impossible are non-citizens;

therefore, (5) Some non-citizen is one who has succeeded in accomplishing the impossible;

III.   (1) No acrobat is one who can lift himself by his own bootstraps;

therefore, (2) No one who can lift himself by his own bootstraps is an acrobat;

therefore, (3) Some one who can lift himself by his own bootstraps is not an acrobat. (From which it follows that there is at least one being who can lift himself by his own bootstraps.)

IV.   (1) It is true that: *No unicorns are animals found in the Bronx Zoo;*

therefore, (2) It is false that: *All unicorns are animals found in the Bronx Zoo;*

therefore, (3) It is true that: *Some unicorns are not animals found in the Bronx Zoo.* (From which it follows that there exists at least one unicorn.)

V.   (1) It is false that: *Some mermaids are members of college sororities;*

therefore, (2) It is true that: *Some mermaids are not members of college sororities.* (From which it follows that there exists at least one mermaid.)

VI. SYMBOLISM AND DIAGRAMS FOR CATEGORICAL PROPOSITIONS

Since the Boolean interpretation of categorical propositions depends heavily upon the notion of a null class, it is convenient to have a special symbol to represent it. The zero symbol *"O"* is used for this purpose. To assert that the class designated by the term *"S"* has no members, we write an equals sign between *"S"* and *"O."* Thus the equation *"S = O"* asserts that there are no *S*'s, or that *S* has no members.

To assert that the class designated by *"S" does* have members is to deny that *S* is empty. To assert that there are *S*'s is to deny the proposition symbolized by *"S = O."* We symbolize that denial by drawing a slanting line through the equality sign. Thus the inequality *"S ≠ O"* asserts that there are *S*'s, by denying that *S* is null.

Standard form categorical propositions refer to *two* classes; so the equations which represent them are somewhat more complicated. Where each of two classes is already designated by a symbol, the class of all things which belong to both of them can be represented by juxtaposing the symbols for the two original classes. For example, if the letter "*S*" designates the class of all satires and the letter "*P*" designates the class of all poems, then the class of all things which are both satires and poems is represented by the symbol "*SP*," which thus designates the class of all satiric poems (or poetic satires). The common part or common membership of two classes is called the "product" or "intersection" of the two classes. The *product* of two classes is the class of all things which belong to both of them. The product of the class of all Americans and the class of all sailors is the class of all American sailors.

This new notation permits us to symbolize **E** and **I** propositions as equations and inequalities. The **E** proposition *No S is P* asserts that no members of the class *S* are members of the class *P*, that is, there are no things which belong to both classes. This can be rephrased by saying that the *product* of the two classes is empty, and this is symbolized by the equation "$SP = O$." The **I** proposition *Some S is P* asserts that at least one member of *S* is also a member of *P*. This means that the product of the classes *S* and *P* is not empty, and this is symbolized by the inequality "$SP \neq O$."

To symbolize **A** and **O** propositions, it is convenient to introduce a new method of representing class complements. The complement of the class of all soldiers is the class of all things which are not soldiers, the class of all non-soldiers. Where the letter "*S*" symbolizes the class of all soldiers, we symbolize the class of all non-soldiers by "$\overline{S}$" (read "*S* bar"), the symbol for the original class with a bar above it. The **A** proposition *All S is P* asserts that all members of the class *S* are also members of the class *P*, that is, that there are no members of the class *S* which are not members of *P*, or (by obversion) that *No S is non-P*. This, like any other **E** proposition, asserts that the product of the classes designated by its subject and predicate terms is empty. It is symbolized by the equation "$S\overline{P} = O$." The **O** proposition *Some S is not P* obverts to the logically equivalent **I** proposition *Some S is non-P*, which is symbolized by the inequality "$S\overline{P} \neq O$."

In their symbolic formulations, the interrelations among the four standard form categorical propositions appear very clearly. It is obvious that the *A* and *O* propositions are contradictories when they are symbolized as "$S\bar{P} = O$" and "$S\bar{P} \neq O$," and it is equally obvious that the *E* and *I* propositions, "$SP = O$" and "$SP \neq O$" are contradictories. The Boolean "Square of Opposition" may be represented thus:

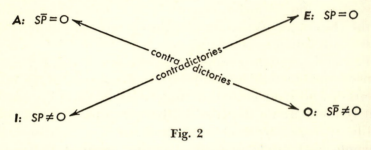

A: $S\bar{P} = O$ E: $SP = O$

contradictories

contradictories

I: $SP \neq O$ O: $S\bar{P} \neq O$

Fig. 2

Propositions can be expressed diagrammatically through diagramming the classes to which they refer. We represent a class as a circle labeled with the term which designates that class. Thus the class *S* is diagrammed as in Figure 3.

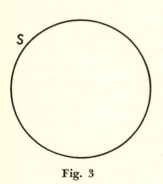

Fig. 3

This diagram is of a class, not a proposition. It merely represents the class *S*, but makes no assertion about it. To diagram the proposition which asserts that *S* has no members, or that there are no *S*'s, we shade all of the interior of the circle representing *S*—indicating in this way that it contains nothing, but is empty. To diagram the proposition asserting that there are *S*'s, which we interpret as saying that there is *at least one* member of *S*, we place an "*x*" in the interior of the circle representing *S*—indicating in this way that there *is* something inside it, that it is not empty. Thus the two propositions *there are no S's* and *there are S's* are represented by the two following diagrams, respectively:

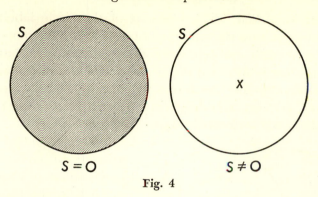

Fig. 4

It should be noted in passing that the circle which diagrams the class S will also, in effect, diagram the class $\bar{S}$, for just as the interior of the circle represents all members of S, so the exterior of the circle represents all members of $\bar{S}$.

To diagram a standard form categorical proposition, not one but two circles are required. The skeleton or framework for diagramming any standard form proposition whose subject and predicate terms are abbreviated by "S" and "P" is constructed by drawing two intersecting circles, as in Figure 5.

This figure diagrams the two classes S and P, but diagrams no proposition concerning them. It does not assert that either or both have members, nor does it deny that they have. As a matter of fact, there are more than two classes diagrammed by the two intersecting circles. The part of the circle labeled "S"

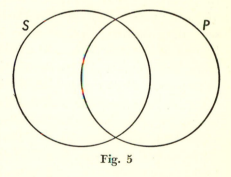

Fig. 5

which does *not* overlap the circle labeled "P" diagrams all S's which are not P's, and can be thought of as representing the product of the classes S and $\bar{P}$. We may label it "$S\bar{P}$." The overlapping part of the two circles represents the product of the classes S and P, and diagrams all things belonging to both of them. It is labeled "*SP*." The part of the circle labeled "*P*" which does *not* overlap the circle labeled "*S*" diagrams all *P*'s which are not *S*'s, and represents the product of the class $\bar{S}$ and *P*. It is labeled "$\bar{S}P$." Finally, that part of the diagram which is external to both circles represents all things which are not in *S* and not in *P* either; it diagrams the fourth class $\bar{S}\bar{P}$, so labeled. With these labels inserted, Figure 5 becomes Figure 6:

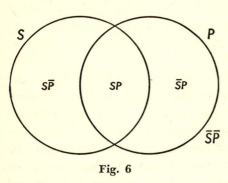

Fig. 6

This diagram can be interpreted in terms of the various different classes determined by the class of all Spaniards (*S*) and the class of all painters (*P*) . *SP* is the product of these two classes, containing all those things and only those things which belong to both of them. Every member of *SP* must be a member of both *S* and *P*; every member must be both a Spaniard and a painter. This product class *SP* is the class of all Spanish painters, which contains, among others, Velasquez and Goya. $S\bar{P}$ is the product of the first class and the complement of the second, containing all those things and only those things which belong to the class *S* but not to the class *P*. It is the class of all Spaniards who are not painters, all Spanish non-painters, and it will contain neither Velasquez nor Goya, but it will include both the novelist Cervantes and the dictator Franco, among many others. $\bar{S}P$ is the product of the second class and the complement of the first, and is the class of all painters who are not Spaniards. This class $\bar{S}P$ of all non-Spanish painters includes, among others, both the Dutch painter Rembrandt and the French painter Cézanne. Finally, $\bar{S}\bar{P}$ is the product of the complements of the two original classes. It contains all those things and only those things which are neither Spaniards nor painters. It is a very large class indeed, containing not merely English Admirals and Swiss mountain climbers, but such things as the Mississippi River and

Mount Everest. All of these classes are diagrammed in Figure 6, where the letters "*S*" and "*P*" are interpreted as in the present paragraph.

By shading or inserting "*x*'s" in various parts of this picture we can diagram any one of the four standard form categorical propositions. To diagram the **A** proposition *All S is P*, symbolized as "$S\bar{P} = O$," we simply shade off that part of the diagram which represents the class $S\bar{P}$, thus indicating that it has no members, or is null. To diagram the **E** proposition *No S is P*, symbolized as "$SP = O$," we shade off that part of the diagram which represents the class *SP*, to indicate that it is empty. To diagram the **I** proposition *Some S is P*, symbolized "$SP \neq O$," we insert an "*x*" into that part of the diagram which represents the class *SP*. This insertion indicates that the class product is not empty but has at least one member. Finally for the **O** proposition *Some S is not P*, symbolized "$S\bar{P} \neq O$," we insert an "*x*" into that part of the diagram which represents the class $S\bar{P}$, to indicate that it is not null but has at least one member. Placed side by side, the diagrams for the four standard form categorical propositions display their different meanings very clearly:

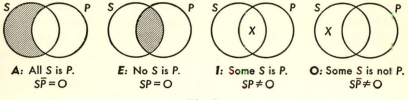

| **A:** All S is P. | **E:** No S is P. | **I:** Some S is P. | **O:** Some S is not P. |
| $S\bar{P} = O$ | $SP = O$ | $SP \neq O$ | $S\bar{P} \neq O$ |

Fig. 7

One aspect of these Venn Diagrams (named for the nineteenth century English mathematician and logician John Venn, who first introduced them) must be emphasized. The bare two-circle diagram, labeled but not otherwise marked, represents classes but expresses no proposition. That a space is left blank signifies nothing—neither that there are nor that there are not members of the class represented by that space. A proposition is expressed only by a diagram in which a part has been shaded out or in which an "*x*" has been inserted.

We have constructed diagrammatic representations for *No S is P* and *Some S is P,* and since these are logically equivalent to their converses *No P is S* and *Some P is S,* the diagrams for the latter have already been shown. To diagram the *A* proposition *All P is S,* symbolized as "$P\overline{S} = O$," within the same framework, we must shade out that part of the diagram which represents the class $P\overline{S}$. It should be obvious that the class $P\overline{S}$ is the same as the class $\overline{S}P$, if not immediately, then by considering the fact that every object which belongs both to the class of all painters and the class of all non-Spaniards must (also) belong to the class of all non-Spaniards and the class of all painters—all painting non-Spaniards are non-Spanish painters, and *vice versa.* And to diagram the *O* proposition *Some P is not S,* symbolized by "$P\overline{S} \neq O$," we insert an "*x*" into that part of the diagram which represents the class $P\overline{S}$ ($= SP$). The diagrams for these propositions then appear:

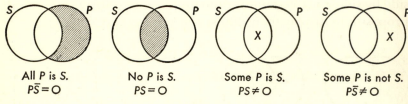

| All P is S. | No P is S. | Some P is S. | Some P is not S. |
| $P\overline{S} = O$ | $PS = O$ | $PS \neq O$ | $P\overline{S} \neq O$ |

Fig. 8

This further adequacy of the two-circle diagrams is mentioned because in the following chapter it will be important to be able to use a given pair of overlapping circles with given labels, say, "*S*" and "*M*," to diagram any standard form categorical proposition containing "*S*" and "*M*" as its terms, regardless of the order in which they occur in it.

The Venn Diagrams constitute an *iconic* representation of the standard form categorical propositions, in which spatial inclusions and exclusions correspond to the non-spatial inclusions and exclusions of classes. They not only provide an exceptionally clear method of notation, but also are the basis of the simplest and most direct method of testing the validity of categorical syllogisms, as will be explained in the following chapter.

EXERCISES

Express each of the following propositions as equations or inequalities, representing each class by the first letter of the English term designating it, and symbolize them by means of Venn Diagrams:

1. No spinsters are pretty girls.

2. All sailors who have sailed the seven seas are men of considerable experience.

3. Some masters of the art of short story writing are poor novelists.

4. No materialistic philosophies of life are satisfactory guides to successful living.

5. Some pirates were not scoundrels.

6. Some political leaders are not men of sound judgment.

7. All silver compounds are pretty good conductors of electricity.

8. Some mixtures containing arsenic are not poisons.

9. No manufacturers of munitions are sincere opponents of war.

10. Some portrait painters of the late eighteenth century were mercenary souls who did not scruple to paint what was expected of them rather than what they actually saw.

CHAPTER SIX

Categorical Syllogisms

I. STANDARD FORM CATEGORICAL SYLLOGISMS

A categorical syllogism is an argument having two premisses and a conclusion, all of which are categorical propositions. In this chapter we shall confine our attention to standard form categorical syllogisms, which are explained as follows. In the first place, a standard form categorical syllogism contains only standard form categorical propositions. In the second place, a standard form categorical syllogism contains exactly three *terms*, or class names, each of which occurs in exactly two of its constituent propositions. The final defining characteristic of a standard form categorical syllogism has to do with the order of its premisses and conclusion. Before this can be stated, certain special names for the terms and premisses of categorical syllogisms must be explained.

The conclusion of a standard form categorical syllogism will be a standard form categorical proposition which contains two of the syllogism's three terms. The predicate term of the conclusion is called the "major term" of the syllogism, and the subject term of the conclusion is called the "minor term" of the syllogism. Thus in the standard form categorical syllogism:

> No heroes are cowards.
> Some soldiers are cowards.
> ——————————————————————
> Therefore some soldiers are not heroes.

the term "soldiers" is the *minor term* and the term "heroes" is the *major term*. The third term of the syllogism, which does not occur in the conclusion, appearing instead in both premisses, is called the "middle term." In our example, the term "coward" is the *middle term*.

The major and minor terms of a standard form syllogism each occurs in a different one of the premisses. The premiss containing the major term is called the "major premiss," and the premiss containing the minor term is called the "minor premiss." In the syllogism stated above, the major premiss is *No heroes are cowards,* and the minor premiss is *Some soldiers are cowards.*

Now the final defining characteristic of a standard form categorical syllogism can be enunciated. It is that the major premiss is stated first, the minor premiss second, and the conclusion last. It should be emphasized that the major premiss is not *defined* in terms of its position, but as that premiss which contains the major term (which is by definition the predicate term of the conclusion). And the minor premiss is not defined in terms of its position, but is that premiss which contains the minor term (which is defined as the subject term of the conclusion).

The *mood* of a standard form categorical syllogism is determined by the kinds of standard form categorical propositions it contains. It is represented by three letters, the first of which names the form of the syllogism's major premiss, the second that of the minor premiss, and the third that of the conclusion. For example, in the case of the preceding syllogism, since its major premiss is an *E* proposition, its minor premiss an *I* proposition, and its conclusion an *O* proposition, the *mood* of the syllogism is *EIO*.

But the *mood* of a standard form categorical syllogism does

not completely characterize its form. Consider the two following syllogisms:

> All great scientists are college graduates.
> Some professional athletes are college graduates.
> ———————————————
> Therefore some professional athletes are great scientists.

and

> All artists are egotists.
> Some artists are paupers.
> ———————————————
> Therefore some paupers are egotists.

Both are of mood *AII,* but they are of different forms. We can
bring out the difference in their forms most clearly by displaying their logical "skeletons," abbreviating the minor terms by
"*S*," the major terms by "*P*," and the middle terms by "*M*." The
forms or "skeletons" of these two syllogisms are:

All *P* is *M*.	All *M* is *P*.
Some *S* is *M*.	Some *M* is *S*.
∴ Some *S* is *P*.	∴ Some *S* is *P*.

In the first, the middle term is the predicate term of both premisses, while in the second, the middle term is the subject term
of both premisses. These examples show that although the form
of a syllogism is partially described by stating its mood, syllogisms having the same mood may differ in their forms depending upon the relative positions of their middle terms.

The form of a categorical syllogism may be *completely* described, however, by stating its mood *and figure,* where the
figure indicates the position of the middle term in the premisses.
It is clear that there are four possible different *figures* that syllogisms may have. The middle term may be the subject term
of the major premiss and the predicate term of the minor premiss, or it may be the predicate term in both premisses, or it may
be the subject term of both premisses, or it may be the predicate
term of the major premiss and the subject term of the minor
premiss. These different possible positions of the middle term

constitute the First, Second, Third, and Fourth figures, respectively. They are schematized below, where only the relative
positions of the terms are shown, and any reference to mood is
suppressed by not representing either quantifiers or copulas.

$M - P$	$P - M$	$M - P$	$P - M$
$S - M$	$S - M$	$M - S$	$M - S$
$\therefore S - P$	$\therefore S - P$	$\therefore S - P$	$\therefore S - P$
FIRST	SECOND	THIRD	FOURTH
FIGURE	FIGURE	FIGURE	FIGURE

We give a complete description of the form of any standard
form categorical syllogism by naming its *mood and figure*. Thus
any syllogism of mood **AOO** in the Second Figure (named more
briefly as **AOO**–2) will have the form:

All P is M.
Some S is not M.
$\therefore$ Some S is not P.

Abstracting from the infinite variety of their possible subject
matters, there are many different forms that syllogistic arguments may assume. Were the reader to list all possible different
moods, beginning with **AAA, AAE, AAI, AAO; AEA, AEE,
AEI, AEO; AIA**, . . . , and continuing through, by the time he
reached **OOO** sixty-four different moods would have been
enumerated. And since each *mood* can occur with each of the
four different *figures*, there must be two hundred fifty-six distinct forms which standard form categorical syllogisms may
assume. Of these, only some are valid, of course.

EXERCISES

Rewrite each of the following syllogisms in standard form, and name
its mood and figure:

1. Since all northern industrialists are Republicans, and no Republicans are supporters of states' rights, no northern industrialists
are supporters of states' rights.

2. No Eastern European countries are democracies, so no Russian satellites are democracies, since all Eastern European countries are Russian satellites.

3. All evergreens are trees, and some evergreens are objects of worship, so some trees are objects of worship.

4. Some persons with poor judgment are intellectuals, because all Communist sympathizers are persons with poor judgment and some intellectuals are Communist sympathizers.

5. No sulphur compounds are water soluble substances, so, since some strong acids are sulphur compounds, some water soluble substances are not strong acids.

6. All barbiturates are narcotics, so some narcotics are not habit forming drugs since some barbiturates are not habit forming drugs.

7. All anarchists are advocates of force and violence, so all militarists are anarchists, since all militarists are advocates of force and violence.

8. No atheists are men who trust in the Lord, but all men who trust in the Lord are wise men, so no atheists are wise men.

9. No unskilful actors are good liars, but all good poker players are good liars, so no unskilful actors are good poker players.

10. Some evergreens are not elms, because all elms are shade trees and some shade trees are not evergreens.

II. THE FORMAL NATURE OF SYLLOGISTIC ARGUMENT

The form of a syllogistic argument is, from the point of view of logic, its most important aspect. The validity or invalidity of a categorical syllogism depends exclusively upon its form and is completely independent of its specific content or subject matter. Thus any syllogism of form **AAA**–1:

All M is P.

All S is M.

∴ All S is P.

is a *valid* argument, *regardless of its subject matter*. That is, no matter which terms are substituted in this form or "skeleton" for the letters *"S," "P,"* and *"M,"* the resulting argument will be valid. If we substitute the terms "Athenians," "men," and "Greeks" for those letters, we obtain the valid argument:

> All Greeks are men.
> All Athenians are Greeks.
> _____
> Therefore all Athenians are men.

And if we substitute the terms "soaps," "water-soluble substances," and "sodium salts" for the letters *"S," "P,"* and *"M"* in the same form we obtain:

> All sodium salts are water-soluble substances.
> All soaps are sodium salts.
> _____
> Therefore all soaps are water-soluble substances.

which is also valid.

A valid categorical syllogism is a formally valid argument, valid by virtue of its form alone. This implies that if a given syllogism is valid, *any other syllogism of the same form will also be valid.* And if a syllogism is invalid, *any other syllogism of the same form will also be invalid.* The common recognition of this fact is attested by the frequent use of "logical analogies" in argumentation. Suppose we were presented with the argument:

All Communists are proponents of socialized medicine.
Some members of the administration are proponents of socialized medicine.
_____
Therefore some members of the administration are Communists.

and felt (justifiably) that regardless of the truth or falsehood of its constituent propositions, the argument was invalid. By far the best way of exposing its fallacious character would be to construct another argument having *exactly the same form* but whose invalidity was immediately apparent. We might seek to expose the given argument by replying: "You might as well argue that:

> All rabbits are very fast runners.
> Some horses are very fast runners.
> _____
> Therefore some horses are rabbits.

And you cannot seriously defend this argument," we might continue, "because here there is no question about the facts. The premises are known to be true and the conclusion is known to be false. Your argument is of the same pattern as this analogous one about horses and rabbits. It is invalid—so *your* argument is invalid." Here is an excellent method of arguing; the logical analogy is one of the most powerful weapons that can be used in debate.

Underlying the method of logical analogy is the fact that the validity or invalidity of such arguments as the categorical syllogism is a purely formal matter. Any fallacious argument can be proved invalid by finding a second argument which has exactly the same form and is known to be invalid by the fact that its premises are known to be true while its conclusion is known to be false. (It should be remembered that an invalid argument may very well have a true conclusion—that an argument is invalid simply means that its conclusion is not logically implied or necessitated by its premises.)

However, this method of testing the validity of arguments has serious limitations. Sometimes a logical analogy is difficult to "think up" on the spur of the moment. And there are far too many invalid forms of argument for us to prepare and try to remember refuting analogies for each of them in advance. Moreover, although being able to think of a logical analogy with true premises and false conclusion proves its form to be invalid, *not* being able to think of one does *not* prove the form valid, for it may only reflect the limitations of our thinking. There may be an invalidating analogy even though we are not able to think of it. A more effective method of establishing the formal validity or invalidity of categorical syllogisms is required. It is to the explanation of effective methods of testing syllogisms that the remaining sections of this chapter are devoted.

EXERCISES

Refute any of the following arguments which are invalid by the method of constructing logical analogies:

1. No employers are advocates of pro-labor legislation, but all advocates of pro-labor legislation are true friends of labor, so no employers are true friends of labor.

2. All drinks containing alcohol are intoxicants, and all drinks containing alcohol are stimulants, therefore some intoxicants are stimulants.

3. Some societies which had taboos against incest were not cultures dominated by a priestly caste, so some ancient civilizations were not societies which had taboos against incest, since some ancient civilizations were not cultures dominated by a priestly caste.

4. All successful labor organizers are union officials, so some union officials are subversives since some subversives are successful labor organizers.

5. No outspoken radicals are State Department executives, so some State Department executives are subversives, since some subversives are not outspoken radicals.

6. No strangers are welcome visitors in the Ozarks, because no revenue agents are welcome visitors in the Ozarks and some strangers are revenue agents.

7. No responsible legislators are hysterical fanatics, so some Senators are not hysterical fanatics since some Senators are responsible legislators.

8. All war veterans are supporters of bonus legislation, for all supporters of bonus legislation are members of this organization and all members of this organization are war veterans.

9. All boats which carry a crew of less than three are yachts, so some yachts are not ocean going vessels since no ocean going vessels are boats which carry a crew of less than three.

10. All alkaloids are tonics, so some foul tasting stuffs are tonics since some alkaloids are foul tasting stuffs.

III. VENN DIAGRAM TECHNIQUE FOR TESTING SYLLOGISMS

In the preceding chapter the use of two-circle Venn Diagrams for expressing standard form categorical propositions was presented and explained. To test a syllogism by the method of Venn Diagrams it is necessary to represent both of its premisses in one diagram. Here we are required to draw *three* overlapping circles, for the two premisses of a standard form syllogism contain three different terms, minor term, major term, and middle term, which we abbreviate as "*S*," "*P*," and "*M*," respectively. We first draw two circles just as for the diagramming of a single proposition, and then draw a third circle beneath overlapping both of the first two. We label the three circles "*S*," "*P*," and "*M*," in that order. Just as one circle labelled "*S*" diagrammed both the class *S* and the class $\bar{S}$; and as two overlapping circles labelled "*S*" and "*P*" diagrammed four classes: $S\bar{P}$, SP, $\bar{S}P$, and $\bar{S}\bar{P}$; so three overlapping circles labelled "*S*," "*P*," and "*M*" diagram *eight* classes: $S\bar{P}\bar{M}$, $SP\bar{M}$, $\bar{S}P\bar{M}$, $S\bar{P}M$, SPM, $\bar{S}PM$, $\bar{S}\bar{P}M$, and $\bar{S}\bar{P}\bar{M}$. These are represented by the eight parts into which the three circles divide the plane:

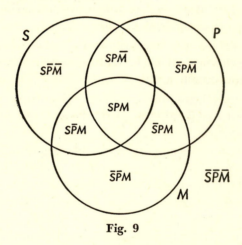

Fig. 9

This can be interpreted in terms of the various different classes determined by the class of all Scots (*S*), the class of all peasants (*P*), and the class of all maidens (*M*). *SPM* is the product of these three classes, which is the class of all Scottish peasant maidens. $SP\bar{M}$ is the product of the first two and the complement of the third, which is the class of all Scottish peasants who are not maidens. $S\bar{P}M$ is the product of the first and third and the complement of the second: the class of all Scottish maidens who are not peasants. $S\bar{P}\bar{M}$ is the product of the first

and the complements of the other two: the class of all Scots
who are neither peasants nor maidens. $\overline{S}PM$ is the product of
the second and third classes with the complement of the first: the
class of all peasant maidens who are not Scottish. $\overline{S}P\overline{M}$ is the
product of the second class with the complements of the other
two: the class of all peasants who are neither Scots nor maidens.
$\overline{S}\overline{P}M$ is the product of the third class and the complements of
the first two: the class of all maidens who are neither Scottish
nor peasants. Finally, $\overline{S}\overline{P}\overline{M}$ is the product of the complements
of the three original classes: the class of all things which are
neither Scots nor peasants nor maidens.

If we focus our attention on just the two circles labelled *"P"*
and *"M,"* it is clear that by shading out or inserting an *"x"* we
can diagram any standard form categorical proposition whose
two terms are *"P"* and *"M,"* regardless of which is the subject
term and which the predicate. Thus to diagram the proposition
"All *M* is *P,"* ($M\overline{P} = O$) we shade out all of *M* that is not contained in (or overlapped by) *P*. This area, it is seen, includes
both the portion labelled *"S\overline{P}M"* and *"\overline{S}\overline{P}M."* The diagram will
appear as:

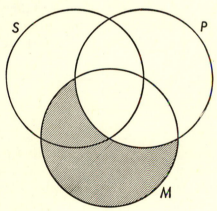

Fig. 10

And if we focus our attention on just the two circles *"S"* and
"M," by shading out or inserting an *"x"* we can diagram any
standard form categorical proposition whose two terms are *"S"*

and "*M*," regardless of the order in which they appear in it. To diagram the proposition *All S is M* $(S\overline{M} = O)$ we shade out all of *S* that is not contained in (or overlapped by) *M*. This area, it is seen, includes both the portion labelled "$S\overline{P}\overline{M}$" and "$SP\overline{M}$." The diagram for this proposition will appear as:

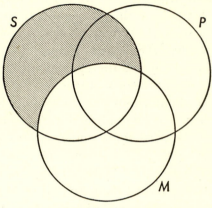

Fig. 11

Now the advantage of having three circles overlapping is that it allows us to diagram two propositions together—on condition of course, that only three different terms occur in them. Thus diagramming both *All M is P* and *All S is M* at the same time gives us:

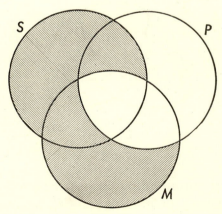

Fig. 12

This is the diagram for *both* premises of the syllogism *AAA*–1:

All *M* is *P*.

All *S* is *M*.

∴ All *S* is *P*.

Now the syllogism is *valid* if and only if the two premises imply or entail the conclusion—that is, if they jointly assert what is asserted by the conclusion. Consequently, *diagramming the premises of a valid argument should suffice to diagram its conclusion also, with no further marking of the circles needed.* To diagram the conclusion *All S is P* is to shade out both the portion labeled "$S\bar{P}\bar{M}$" and the portion labeled "$S\bar{P}M$." Inspecting the diagram which represents the two premises, we see that it *does* diagram the conclusion also. And from this fact we can conclude that *AAA*–1 is a valid syllogism.

Let us now apply the Venn Diagram test to an obviously invalid syllogism:

All dogs are mammals.

All cats are mammals.

Therefore all cats are dogs.

Diagramming both premises gives us:

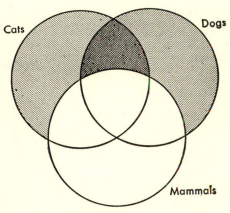

Fig. 13

In this diagram, where "*S*" designates the class of all cats, "*P*" the class of all dogs, and "*M*" the class of all mammals, the por-

tions $S\bar{P}\bar{M}$, $SP\bar{M}$, and $\bar{S}P\bar{M}$ have been shaded out. But the conclusion has not been diagrammed, because the part $S\bar{P}M$ has
been left unshaded, and to diagram the conclusion *both* $S\bar{P}\bar{M}$
and $S\bar{P}M$ must be shaded out. Thus we see that diagramming
the premisses of a syllogism of form AAA–2 does *not* suffice to
diagram its conclusion, which proves that the premisses do not
assert as much as the conclusion—that is, they do not imply the
conclusion. But an argument whose premisses do not imply its
conclusion is invalid, and so our diagram proves that the given
syllogism is *invalid*. (It proves, in fact, that *any* syllogism of the
form AAA–2 is *invalid*.)

When we use a Venn Diagram to test a syllogism with one
universal premiss and one particular premiss, it is advisable to
diagram the universal premiss first. Thus in testing the AII–3
syllogism:

> All artists are egotists.
> Some artists are paupers.
> _____
> Therefore some paupers are egotists.

we should diagram the universal premiss *All artists are egotists*
before inserting an "*x*" to diagram the particular premiss *Some
artists are paupers*. Properly diagrammed, the premisses appear
as:

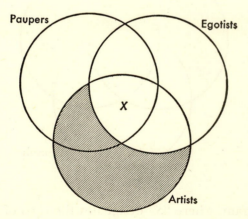

Fig. 14

Had we tried to diagram the particular premiss first, before the region $S\overline{P}M$ was shaded out along with $\overline{S}\overline{P}M$ in diagramming the universal premiss, we should not have known whether to insert an "x" in SPM or in $S\overline{P}M$ or in both. And had we put it in $S\overline{P}M$ or on the line separating it from SPM, the subsequent shading of $S\overline{P}M$ would have obscured the information the diagram was intended to contain. Now that the information contained in the premisses has been inserted into the diagram, we examine it to see whether the conclusion has already been diagrammed. For the conclusion *Some paupers are egotists* to be diagrammed, an "x" must appear in the overlapping part of the circles labeled "paupers" and "egotists." This overlapping part consists of both of the regions $SP\overline{M}$ and SPM, which together constitute SP. There is an "x" in the region SPM, so there *is* an "x" in the overlapping part SP. The conclusion of the syllogism is diagrammed by the diagramming of its premisses; therefore the syllogism is *valid*.

Let us consider still another example, the discussion of which will bring out a further important point about the use of Venn Diagrams. In testing the argument:

All great scientists are college graduates.
Some professional athletes are college graduates.

Therefore some professional athletes are great scientists.

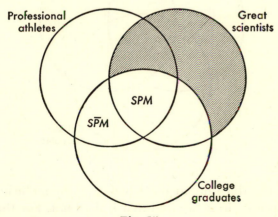

Fig. 15

after diagramming the universal premiss first by shading out both regions $SP\overline{M}$ and $\overline{S}P\overline{M}$, we may still be puzzled about where to put the *"x"* required to diagram the particular premiss. That premiss is *Some professional athletes are college graduates,* so an *"x"* must be inserted in the overlapping part of the two circles labeled "professional athletes" and "college graduates." That overlapping part, however, contains two regions: SPM and $S\overline{P}M$. In which of these should the *"x"* be placed? The premisses do not tell us, and if we made an arbitrary decision to place it in one rather than the other, we should be inserting more information into the diagram than the premisses warrant—and this would spoil the diagram's use as a test for validity. Placing an *"x"* in each of them would also go beyond what the premisses assert. By placing the *"x"* *on the line* which divides the overlapping region SM into the two parts SPM and $S\overline{P}M$ we can diagram exactly what the second premiss asserts without adding anything to it. Placing an *"x"* on the line between two regions indicates that there is something which belongs in one of them, *but does not indicate which one.* The completed diagram of both premisses should be:

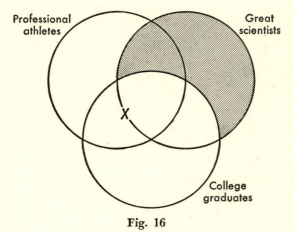

Fig. 16

Inspecting the diagram to see whether the conclusion of the syllogism appears in it, we find that it does not. For the conclu-

sion *Some professional athletes are great scientists* to be diagrammed, an *"x"* would have to occur in the overlapping part of
the two upper circles, either in $SP\overline{M}$ or in SPM. The first of
these is shaded out and certainly contains no *"x."* The diagram
does not show an *"x"* in SPM either. True, there must be a
member of either SPM or $S\overline{P}M$, but the diagram does not tell
us that it is in the former rather than the latter, and so *for all
the premisses tell us, the conclusion may be false.* We do not
know that the conclusion *is* false, but only that it is not asserted
or implied by the premisses. The latter is enough, however, to
let us know that the argument is *invalid.* The diagram suffices
to show not merely that the given syllogism is invalid, but that
all syllogisms of the form *AII*–2 are invalid.

The general technique of using Venn Diagrams to test the
validity of any standard form categorical syllogism may be sum-
marily described as follows. First, label the circles of a three
circle Venn Diagram with the syllogism's three terms. Next,
diagram both premisses, diagramming the universal one first
if these is one universal and one particular, being careful in
diagramming a particular proposition to put the *"x" on a line*
if the premisses do not determine on which side of the line it
should go. Finally, inspect the diagram to see whether or not the
diagram of the premisses contains the diagram of the conclusion:
if it does, the syllogism is valid, if it does not, the syllogism is
invalid.

What is the theoretical basis or explanation of the efficacy
of Venn Diagrams in distinguishing between valid and invalid
categorical syllogisms? The answer to this question divides into
two parts. The first has to do with the formal nature of syllogistic argument as explained in Section II. It was there shown
that one legitimate test of the validity or invalidity of a given
syllogism is to establish the validity or invalidity of a *different*
syllogism having exactly the same form. This technique is basic
to the use of Venn Diagrams. The explanation of how they serve
this purpose constitutes the second part of the answer to our
question.

Ordinarily a syllogism will be about classes of objects which are not all present, such as the class of all men, or great scientists, or sodium salts, or the like. The relationships of inclusion or exclusion among such classes may be reasoned about and may be empirically discoverable in the course of scientific investigation. But they are certainly not open to direct inspection, since not all members of the classes involved are ever present at one time to be inspected. We can, however, create situations of our own in which the only classes concerned will contain by their very definitions only things which are present and directly open to examination. And we can argue syllogistically about such situations of our own making. Venn Diagrams are devices for expressing standard form categorical propositions, but they are also situations of our own making, patterns of graphite or ink on papers or mounds of chalk raised on blackboards. And the propositions they express can be interpreted as referring to the diagrams themselves. An example can help make this clear. Suppose we have a particular syllogism:

All successful men are men who are keenly interested in their work.
No man who is keenly interested in his work is a person whose attention is easily distracted when he is working.

Therefore no person whose attention is easily distracted when he is working is a successful man.

Its form is *AEE*–4, and may be schematized as:

All P is M.
No M is S.
∴ No S is P.

We may test it by constructing the following Venn Diagram, with its regions $SP\overline{M}$ and $\overline{S}P\overline{M}$ shaded out to express the first premiss, and $S\overline{P}M$ and SPM shaded out to express the second premiss.

Examining the diagram, we find that SP (which consists of the regions SPM and $SP\overline{M}$) has been shaded out so that the syllogism's conclusion has already been diagrammed. Now how does

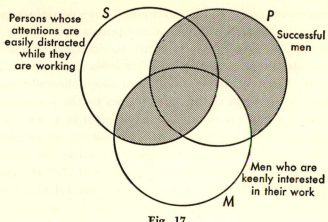

Fig. 17

this tell us that the syllogism is valid? That syllogism concerns large classes of remote objects: there are many persons whose attentions are easily distracted while they are working, and they are scattered far and wide. However, we can construct a syllogism of the same form dealing with objects which are immediately present and directly available for our inspection. These objects are the points within the unshaded portions of the circles labeled "*S*," "*P*," and "*M*" in our Venn Diagram. Here is the new syllogism:

All points within the unshaded part of the circle labeled "*P*" are points within the unshaded part of the circle labeled "*M*."
No points within the unshaded part of the circle labeled "*M*" are points within the unshaded part of the circle labeled "*S*."

Therefore no points within the unshaded part of the circle labeled "*S*" are points within the unshaded part of the circle labeled "*P*."

This new syllogism refers to nothing remote but is about the parts of a situation we ourselves have created—the Venn Diagram we have drawn. All the parts and all the possibilities of inclusion and exclusion among these classes are immediately present to us and directly open to inspection. We can literally *see* all the possibilities here and *know* that since all the points of

P are also points of *M,* and since *M* and *S* have no points in common, *S* and *P* cannot possibly have any points in common. Since it refers only to classes of points in the diagram, the new syllogism is literally *seen* to be valid by *looking* at the things it talks about. Since the original syllogism about classes of men has exactly the same form as this second one, by the formal nature of syllogistic argument the original syllogism is also seen to be valid. The explanation is exactly the same for Venn Diagram proofs of the invalidity of invalid syllogisms—there too we test the original syllogism indirectly by directly testing a second syllogism having exactly the same form but referring to the actual diagram which expresses that form.

EXERCISES

Put each of the following arguments into standard form, name its mood and figure, and test its validity by means of a Venn Diagram:

1. No politicians are martyrs, for no politicians are idealists and all martyrs are idealists.

2. No men of action are mere philosophers, and all soldiers are men of action, therefore no mere philosophers are soldiers.

3. Some ideas are explosive things, for some ideas are weapons and some weapons are explosive things.

4. No criminals are church members, all criminals are parasites, hence no church members are parasites.

5. No submarines are pleasure vessels, for all submarines are warships and no pleasure vessels are warships.

6. All criminals are unsavory persons, so no unsavory persons were pioneers since no pioneers were criminals.

7. Some musicians are not baseball fans, but all citizens are baseball fans, so some musicians are not citizens.

8. Some Methodists are not Catholics, for no Protestants are Catholic and all Methodists are Protestants.

9. Some active politicians are great liberals, so some labor leaders are active politicians, since all labor leaders are great liberals.

10. Some great liberals are wealthy men, so some labor leaders are wealthy men, since all great liberals are labor leaders.

IV. RULES AND FALLACIES

There are many ways in which a categorical syllogism may fail to establish its conclusion. Just as travel is facilitated by the mapping of highways, and the labeling of otherwise tempting roads as "Dead Ends," so validity of argument is made easier to attain by setting forth certain *rules* which enable the reasoner to avoid fallacies. The advantage of having a clearly stated set of easily applied rules is manifest. Any given standard form syllogism can be evaluated by observing whether the rules are violated or not. In the present section a set of six rules for standard form categorical syllogisms will be presented and explained.

Rule 1: A valid categorical syllogism must contain exactly three terms each of which is used in the same sense throughout the argument.

The conclusion of a categorical syllogism asserts that a certain relation holds between two terms. It is clear that the conclusion is justified only if the premises assert the relationship of each of the conclusion's terms to the same third term. Were this not asserted by the premises, no connection between the two terms of the conclusion would be established and the conclusion would not be implied by the premises. Three terms must be involved in every valid categorical syllogism; no more and no less. Any categorical syllogism which contains more than three terms is invalid, and is said to commit the *Fallacy of Four Terms* (in Latin, *Quaternio Terminorum*).*

If a term is used in different senses in the argument, it is being used equivocally, and the fallacy committed is that of *equivoca-*

---

* Even where it contains as many as five or six different terms, the same name is applied to the fallacy.

tion. An example of this was the Japanese argument circulated during the latter thirties, defending the "pacification" of China. It may be paraphrased as:

All attempts to end hostilities are efforts which should be approved by all nations.
All of Japan's present activities in China are attempts to end hostilities.

Therefore all of Japan's present activities in China are efforts which should be approved by all nations.

This syllogism appears to have only three terms, but there are really four, since one of them, the middle term, is used in different senses in the two premisses. Only if the term "attempts to end hostilities" is interpreted as designating such activities as proposing an armistice and negotiating a treaty in good faith, can the first premiss be accepted as true. But for the second premiss to be true, the phrase "attempts to end hostilities" must have its meaning shifted to include the vigorous prosecution of war. When the term in question is interpreted in the same sense throughout the argument, one or the other premiss becomes patently false.

Arguments of this sort are more common than one might suspect. It is generally the middle term whose meaning is shifted —in one direction to connect it with the minor term, in a different direction to relate it to the major term. But this connects the two terms of the conclusion with two *different* terms, so that the relationship asserted by the conclusion is not established. Although it is sometimes called "the fallacy of the ambiguous middle," that name is not generally applicable, since one of the other terms may have its meaning shifted instead, which would involve the same error.

The next two rules deal with distribution. As was explained in Section II of the preceding chapter, a term is distributed in a proposition when the proposition refers to all members of the class designated by that term; otherwise the term is said to be undistributed in (or by) that proposition.

Rule 2: In a valid categorical syllogism, the middle term must be distributed in at least one premiss.

Consider the following standard form categorical syllogism:

> All dogs are mammals.
> All cats are mammals.
> _____
> Therefore all cats are dogs.

The middle term "mammals" is not distributed in either premiss, and this violates Rule 2. Any syllogism which violates Rule 2 is said to commit the *Fallacy of the Undistributed Middle*. It should be clear that any syllogism which violates this rule is invalid, by the following considerations. The conclusion of any categorical syllogism asserts a connection between two terms. The premisses justify asserting such a connection only if they assert that each of the two terms is connected with a third term in such a way that the first two are appropriately connected with each other *through* or *by means of* the third. For the two terms of the conclusion really to be connected through the third, at least one of them must be related to the *whole* of the class designated by the third or middle term. Otherwise each may be connected with *different parts* of that class, and not necessarily connected with each other at all. This is obviously what occurs in the example. Dogs are included in *part* of the class of mammals, and cats are also included in *part* of the class of mammals. But different *parts* of that class may be (and, in this case, are) involved, so that the middle term does not connect the syllogism's major and minor terms. For it to connect them, *all* of the class designated by it must be referred to in at least one premiss, and this is what is meant by saying that in a valid syllogism the middle term must be *distributed* in at least one premiss.

Rule 3: In a valid categorical syllogism no term can be distributed in the conclusion which is not distributed in the premisses.

A valid argument is one whose premisses logically imply or entail its conclusion. The conclusion of a valid argument does not go beyond or assert any more than is (implicitly) contained in the premisses. If the conclusion does illegitimately "go beyond" what is asserted by the premisses, the argument is invalid. It is an "illicit process" for the conclusion to say more about its terms than the premisses do. A proposition which *distributes* one of its terms says more about the class designated by that term than it would if the term were *undistributed* by it. To refer to *all* members of a class is to say more about it (apart from questions of existence) than is said when only some of its members are referred to. Therefore when the conclusion of a syllogism distributes a term which was undistributed in the premisses, it says more about it than the premisses warrant, and the syllogism is invalid. Such an illicit process can occur in the case of either the major or the minor term. There are, then, two different ways in which Rule 3 may be violated. Special names have been given to the two fallacies involved.

When a syllogism contains its major term undistributed in the major premiss but distributed in the conclusion, the argument is said to commit the fallacy of *Illicit Process of the Major Term* (or, more briefly, the *Illicit Major*). An example of this fallacy is:

> All dogs are mammals.
> No cats are dogs.
> ———————————————
> Therefore no cats are mammals.

The conclusion makes an assertion about *all* mammals, saying that all of them are excluded from the class of cats. But the premisses make no assertion about *all* mammals; so the conclusion illicitly goes beyond what the premisses assert. Since "mammals" is the major term, the fallacy here is an *Illicit Major*.

When a syllogism contains its minor term undistributed in its minor premiss but distributed in its conclusion, the argument commits the fallacy of *Illicit Process of the Minor Term* (more briefly called the *Illicit Minor*). An example of this fallacy is:

All Communists are subversive elements.
All Communists are critics of the present administration.

Therefore all critics of the present administration are subversive elements.

The conclusion here makes an assertion about *all* critics of the present administration. But the premisses make no assertion about *all* such critics; so the conclusion illicitly goes beyond what the premisses warrant. Since it goes beyond the premisses in what it says about the minor term, the fallacy is an *Illicit Minor*.

The next two rules are called "Rules of Quality" because they refer to the ways in which the negative quality of one or both premisses restricts the kinds of conclusions which may validly be inferred.

Rule 4: No categorical syllogism is valid which has two negative premisses.

That this rule must be followed is seen when it is recalled what negative propositions assert. Any negative proposition (*E* or *O*) denies class inclusion, asserting that all or some of one class is excluded from the whole of the other. Where "*S*," "*P*," and "*M*" are the minor, major, and middle terms, respectively, two negative premisses can only assert that *S* is wholly or partially excluded from all or part of *M,* and that *P* is wholly or partially excluded from all or part of *M*. But these conditions may very well obtain no matter how *S* and *P* are related, whether by inclusion or exclusion, partial or complete. Therefore from two negative premisses, no relationship whatever between *S* and *P* can validly be inferred. Any syllogism which violates Rule 4 is said to commit the fallacy of *Exclusive Premisses*.

Rule 5: If either premiss of a valid categorical syllogism is negative, the conclusion must be negative.

An affirmative conclusion asserts that one class is either wholly or partly contained in a second. This can be "justified" only by premisses which assert that there is a third class which contains the first and is itself contained in the second. In other words, to entail an affirmative conclusion, both premises must assert class inclusion. But class inclusion can be expressed only by affirmative propositions. So an affirmative conclusion logically follows only from two affirmative premises. Hence if either premiss is negative, the conclusion cannot be affirmative but must be negative also. Arguments violating this rule are so implausible that they are very seldom encountered in serious discussions. Any syllogism which violates Rule 5 may be said to commit the fallacy of *Drawing an Affirmative Conclusion from a Negative Premiss.*

Our sixth and final rule concerns existential import. It is:

Rule 6: No valid categorical syllogism with a particular conclusion can have two universal premisses.

To violate this rule is to go from premises which have no existential import to a conclusion which does. A particular proposition asserts the existence of objects of a specified kind, and to infer this from two universal premisses, which do not assert the existence of anything at all, is clearly to go beyond what is warranted by the premisses. An example of a syllogism which violates this rule is:

All radioactive substances are commercially valuable materials.
No argon compounds are commercially valuable materials.

Therefore some argon compounds are not radioactive substances.

On the traditional interpretation, which did attribute existential import to universal propositions, such arguments were said to have "weakened conclusions," because the "stronger" conclusion, *No argon compounds are radioactive substances,* might equally well have been inferred. But the latter is not *stronger,* it is simply *different.* The syllogism with the same premises and the universal conclusion is perfectly valid. But the given syllogism is *invalid,* because its conclusion asserts that there are argon compounds (a false proposition), while its premises do not assert the existence of argon compounds (or of anything at all). Being universal propositions, they are without existential import. The conclusion would follow validly if to the two universal premisses were added the additional premiss *There are argon compounds*. But the resulting argument, although perfectly valid, would have *three premisses* and would therefore *not* be a *syllogism*.

The six rules here presented are intended to apply *only* to *standard form categorical syllogisms*. Within this area they provide an adequate test for the validity of any argument. If a standard form categorical syllogism violates any of these rules, it is invalid; whereas if it conforms to all of them it is valid.

EXERCISES

I. Name the fallacies committed by any of the following syllogisms which are invalid:

1. All textbooks are books intended for careful study.
   No sensational novels are textbooks.

   Therefore no sensational novels are books intended for careful study.

2. No poisonous things are nourishing foods.
   Some berries are not nourishing foods.

   Therefore some berries are poisonous things.

3. No pets are pests.
   Some pets are parrots.

   Therefore some parrots are not pests.

4. All departures from law are punishable offences.
   All things which happen by chance are departures from law.

   Therefore all things which happen by chance are punishable offences.

5. Some carbon compounds are exceedingly hard substances.
   All diamonds are carbon compounds.

   Therefore some diamonds are exceedingly hard substances.

6. No dogs of mixed breed are good hunters.
   Some dogs are good hunters.

   Therefore some dogs are not mongrels.

7. All women with infinite patience are women who would make excellent teachers.
   All women who would make excellent teachers are women who would make fine parents.

   Therefore some women who would make fine parents are women with infinite patience.

8. All chocolate eclairs are pastries.
   Some fattening foods are not pastries.

   Therefore all chocolate eclairs are fattening foods.

9. Some snakes are not warm-blooded animals.
   All snakes are reptiles.

   Therefore no reptiles are warm-blooded animals.

10. No dictators are timid men.
    Some extroverts are not timid men.

    Therefore some extroverts are not dictators.

II. Name the fallacies committed by any of the following syllogisms which are invalid:

1. All men who see new patterns in familiar things are inventors; so all inventors are eccentrics, since all men who see new patterns in familiar things are eccentrics.

2. No person who likes to talk is a diplomat, and no person who likes to talk is a fluent writer; hence no diplomats are fluent writers.

3. Some elephants are natives of Australia, because all elephants which are natives of Australia are elephants, and all elephants which are natives of Australia are natives of Australia.

4. All projects which create an abundance of work are things which make for prosperity; therefore all acts of arson on a large scale are things which make for prosperity, since all acts of arson on a large scale are projects which create an abundance of work.

5. All attics are places which are hot in summer and cold in winter, but no comfortable lodgings are places which are cold in winter and hot in summer; so no garrets are comfortable lodgings.

6. All those who urge their fellow men to mend their ways are moralists; so all preachers are moralists since all preachers are those who urge their fellow men to mend their ways.

7. Some professional wrestlers are not very highly skilled performers, but all good actors are very highly skilled performers; so some professional wrestlers are good actors.

8. All lubricants are oily substances, but some corrosives are not oily substances; so some lubricants are not corrosives.

9. No dwelling which dates back to the Civil War period is a house with modern plumbing; so the old Thompson place is a dwelling which dates back to the Civil War period, since the old Thompson place is not a house with modern plumbing.

10. All Plymouths are automobiles, but some automobiles are not General Motors products; so some Plymouths are not General Motors products.

III. Answer the following questions by appealing to the six rules. (Make sure you consider all possible cases.)

1. Can any standard form categorical syllogism be valid which contains exactly three terms each of which is distributed in both of its occurrences?

2. In what mood or moods, if any, can a first figure standard form categorical syllogism with a particular conclusion be valid?

3. In what figure or figures, if any, can the premises of a valid standard form categorical syllogism distribute both major and minor terms?

4. In what figure or figures, if any, can a valid standard form categorical syllogism have two particular premises?

5. In what figure or figures, if any, can a valid standard form categorical syllogism have only one term distributed, and that one only once?

6. In what mood or moods, if any, can a valid standard form categorical syllogism have just two terms distributed, each one twice?

7. In what mood or moods, if any, can a valid standard form categorical syllogism have two affirmative premisses and a negative conclusion?

8. In what figure or figures, if any, can a valid standard form categorical syllogism have a particular premiss and a universal conclusion?

9. In what mood or moods, if any, can a second figure standard form categorical syllogism with a universal conclusion be valid?

10. In what figure or figures, if any, can a valid standard form categorical syllogism have its middle term distributed in both premisses?

CHAPTER SEVEN

Arguments in Ordinary Language

I. REDUCING THE NUMBER OF TERMS IN A CATEGORICAL SYLLOGISM

In the preceding chapter two different tests were presented for distinguishing valid from invalid categorical syllogisms. These tests are applicable only to categorical syllogisms which are in *standard form*. A standard form categorical syllogism may be thought of as being "chemically pure," free from all obscurities and irrelevancies. Needless to say, of course, syllogisms do not always occur thus refined in a "state of nature." The categorical syllogism is not an uncommon kind of argument, but it usually appears in a guise far different from the stilted and artificial *standard form* to which the tests of the preceding chapter can be applied. It takes on such varied shapes that to devise special logical tests for all of them would require a hopelessly complicated logical apparatus. The combined interests of logical simplicity *and* adequacy to arguments formulated in ordinary language require that we do two things. First, easily applicable tests must be devised by which we can distinguish valid from invalid *standard form* categorical syllogisms. This has already been done. And second, the techniques of translating categorical syllogisms of *any* form into *standard form* must be understood and mastered. When these are both accomplished, *any* categorical syllogism may be easily tested: first, by translating it into *standard form,* and second, by applying to its *standard form* equivalent one of the tests described in the preceding chapter.

Apart from the relatively minor question of the order in which its premises and conclusion happen to be stated, a categorical syllogism may deviate from *standard form* in either or both of two ways. Its component propositions may not all be standard form categorical propositions. Or its component propositions may be standard form categorical propositions which *apparently* involve more than three terms. In the latter case, the syllogism is not to be rejected out of hand as invalid through committing the *Fallacy of Four Terms.* It is frequently possible to translate such an argument into a logically equivalent standard form syllogism which contains only three terms and is perfectly valid.

Consider the following argument, all of whose propositions are standard form categorical propositions:

> All mammals are warm-blooded animals.
> No lizards are warm-blooded animals.
> ───────────────────────────────
> Therefore all lizards are non-mammals.

Were we to apply to this syllogism the six Rules explained in Chapter Six, we should judge it to be invalid on more than one count. For one thing, it contains four terms: "mammals," "warm-blooded animals," "lizards," and "non-mammals." And for another, it has an affirmative conclusion drawn from a negative premiss. But it is nevertheless perfectly valid, as the reader can no doubt see intuitively for himself. Because it has four terms, it is not a standard form categorical syllogism, and the Rules are simply not applicable to it. To test it by means of the Syllogistic Rules presented in the preceding chapter, we must first translate it into standard form. In the case of the present example, this involves reducing the number of its terms to three, which is easily accomplished by simply *obverting* the conclusion. Performing this obversion we obtain the *standard form translation* of the original argument:

> All mammals are warm-blooded animals.
> No lizards are warm-blooded animals.
> _____
> Therefore no lizards are mammals.

which is logically equivalent to it, having identically the same premisses and a logically equivalent conclusion. This standard form translation conforms to all the Syllogistic Rules, and is thus known to be *valid*.

The latter is not the only standard form translation of the given syllogism, although it is the most easily obtainable. A different (but logically equivalent) standard form translation can be obtained by taking the contrapositive of the first premiss and obverting the second, leaving the conclusion unchanged. This would yield:

> All non-(warm-blooded animals) are non-mammals.
> All lizards are non-(warm-blooded animals).
> _____
> Therefore all lizards are non-mammals.

which is also valid by the Rules. There is no *unique* standard form translation of a given syllogism, but if any one is valid, all of the others must be also.

Any categorical syllogism containing four terms can be reduced to standard form or translated into a logically equivalent standard form syllogism, *if* one of its four terms is the complement of one of the other three. And any containing five (or six) terms can be reduced to standard form *if* two (or three) of its terms are the complements of two (or three) of the others. These reductions are all effected by means of the immediate inferences: conversion, obversion, and contraposition.

Categorical syllogisms whose constituent propositions are all in standard form may contain up to half-a-dozen different terms, and may require the drawing of more than one immediate inference for their reduction to standard form. An example of a six-term categorical syllogism which is perfectly valid is the following:

> No non-residents are citizens.
> All non-citizens are non-voters.
> _____
> Therefore all voters are residents.

There are alternative ways of reducing this argument to a standard form syllogism. One method, perhaps the most natural and obvious, requires the use of all three types of immediate inference. Converting the first premiss and then obverting, and taking the contrapositive of the second premiss yields the standard form categorical syllogism:

> All citizens are residents.
> All voters are citizens.
> _____
> Therefore all voters are residents.

which is easily proved valid by either of the methods set forth in the preceding chapter.

EXERCISES

Translate the following syllogisms into standard form, and test their validity by one of the methods of Chapter Six:

1. No mortals are perfect beings. No men are immortals. Therefore no men are perfect beings.

2. All copper alloys are metals, but no metals are non-conductors, so all copper alloys are conductors.

3. Some highways are dangerous things, since all straight roads are things that are safe, and some highways are not straight roads.

4. All things that are soiled are useless; so some textbooks are clean things since some textbooks are useful things.

5. All household pets are things which weigh less than fifty pounds, for all objects weighing fifty pounds or more are difficult things to lift, while all household pets are easy things to lift.

6. All members are city dwellers, but some eligible persons are those who live outside the city; so some eligible persons are non-members.

7. No ordinary objects are things which cost over ten thousand dollars. All passenger cars are things which cost no more than ten thousand dollars. Therefore no passenger cars are extraordinary things.

8. No damaged items were those which remained dry; so all those which were inside were those which were in perfect condition, for all those which got wet were those which were outside.

9. All inexpensive things are copies, since all expensive things are difficult things to obtain while no originals are things which are easy to obtain.

10. All who are excluded are those who are neither members nor guests of members. All who are included are conformists. Therefore no non-conformists are either members or guests of members.

II. TRANSLATING CATEGORICAL PROPOSITIONS INTO STANDARD FORM

The somewhat stilted *A, E, I,* and *O* forms are not the only ones in which categorical propositions may be expressed. Many categorical syllogisms contain non-standard form propositions. To reduce these arguments to standard form requires that their component propositions be translated into standard form. Some of the methods of translating non-standard form propositions into standard form will now be described.

We ought first to mention *singular* propositions, such as "Socrates is a man," and "This table is not an antique." These do not affirm or deny the inclusion of one class in another, but rather affirm or deny that a specified individual or object belongs to a class. It is customary to take singular propositions as being already in standard form, treating affirmative singular propositions as universal affirmative, and negative singular propositions as universal negative. That this interpretation preserves the adequacy of the tests described in the preceding chapter can be seen when it is realized that "Socrates is a man" is logically equivalent to the *A* proposition *All members of the class which contains only Socrates are men.* No *translations* are needed for singular propositions; they are classified as *A* or *E* propositions as they stand.

The first group of categorical propositions which require translation into standard form are those which have adjectives or adjectival phrases as predicates rather than substantives or class *terms.* For example, "Some flowers are beautiful," and "No warships are available for active duty," deviate from standard form only in that their predicates "beautiful" and "available for active duty" refer to properties rather than to classes. But every property *determines* a class, the class of things having that property; so to every such proposition corresponds a logically equivalent proposition which is in standard form. To the two examples cited correspond the *I* and *E* propositions *Some flowers are beauties* and *No warships are things available for active duty.* Where a categorical proposition is in standard form *except* that it has an adjectival predicate instead of a predicate *term,* the translation into standard form is made by replacing the adjectival predicate with a term designating the class of all objects of which the adjective may truly be predicated.

Next we turn to formulations of categorical propositions whose main verbs are other than the standard form copula *to be.* Examples of this type are "All men desire recognition," and "Some men drink." The usual method of translating such a statement into standard form is to regard all of it except the subject term and quantifier as naming a class-defining characteristic, and replace it by a standard copula and a term designating the class determined by that class-defining characteristic. Thus the two examples cited translate into the standard form categorical propositions *All men are desirers of recognition* and *Some men are drinkers.*

Another type of statement which is easily put into standard form is that in which· the standard form ingredients are all present but not arranged in standard form order. Two examples of this kind are: "Racehorses are all thoroughbreds," and "All is well that ends well." In such cases we must decide which is the subject term and then rearrange the words so as to express a standard form categorical proposition. It is clear that the proceding two statements translate into the *A* propositions *All racehorses are thoroughbreds* and *All things that end well are things that are well.*

Many categorical propositions have their quantities indicated by words other than the standard form quantifiers "all," "no," and "some." Statements involving the words "every" and "any" are very easily translated. The propositions "Every dog has his day," and "Any contribution will be appreciated," reduce to *All dogs are creatures which have their days* and *All contributions are things which are appreciated.* Similar to "every" and "any" are "everything" and "anything," and paralleling these, but pretty clearly restricted to classes of *persons* are "everyone," "anyone," "whoever," "whoso," "who," "he that," and the like. These should occasion no difficulty. The grammatical particles "a," "an," and "the" can also serve to indicate quantity. The first two sometimes mean *all* and in other contexts mean *some.* Thus "A bat is not a bird," and "An elephant is a pachyderm" are most reasonably interpreted as meaning *All bats are non-birds* (or *No bats are birds*) and *All elephants are pachyderms.* But "A bat flew in the window," and "An elephant escaped," pretty clearly do not refer to *all* bats or *all* elephants, but are more properly reduced to *Some bats are creatures which flew in the window* and *Some elephants are creatures which escaped.* The word "the" may be used to refer either to a particular individual or to all the members of a class. But there is little or no danger of ambiguity here, for such a statement as "The whale is a mammal" translates in almost any context into the *A* proposition *All whales are mammals,* while the singular proposition *The first President was a military hero* is already in standard form as an *A* proposition.

Categorical propositions involving the words "only" or "none but" are often called "exclusive" propositions, because in general they assert that the predicate applies *exclusively* to the subject named. Examples of such usages are "Only citizens can vote," and "None but the brave deserve the fair." These translate into the standard form categorical propositions *All those who can vote are citizens* and *All those who deserve the fair are those who are brave*. So-called *exclusive* propositions, beginning with "only" or "none but," translate into *A* propositions whose subject and predicate terms are the same, respectively, as the predicate and subject terms of the exclusive proposition. There are *contexts* in which "Only *S* is *P*" or "None but *S*'s are *P*'s" are intended to express not merely that *All P is S* but *also* either that *All S is P* or that *Some S is P*. This is not *always* the case, however. Where context helps to determine meaning, attention must be paid to it, of course. But in the absence of such additional information, the suggested translations are adequate.

Some categorical propositions contain no words at all to indicate quantity, e.g. "Dogs are carnivorous," and "Children are present." Where there is no quantifier, what the sentence is intended to express may be doubtful and we can determine its meaning only by examining the context in which it occurs. The two examples cited are reasonably clear, however. In the first it is probable that *all* dogs are referred to, while in the second it is more likely that only *some* children are intended. Their standard form translations are *All dogs are carnivores* and *Some children are beings who are present*.

Next we may consider briefly some propositions which do not resemble standard form categorical propositions at all, but which *can* be translated into standard form. Some examples are: "Not all children believe in Santa Claus," "There are white elephants," "There are no pink elephants," and "Nothing is both round and square." A moment's thought about the propositions expressed suffices to show that they are logically equivalent to, and therefore translate into, the following standard form propositions: *Some children are not believers in Santa Claus, Some elephants are white things, No elephants are pink things,* and *No round objects are square objects.*

It must be recognized that many propositions mention "quantity" more specifically than standard form propositions do. This specification is accomplished by the use of numerical or quasi-numerical quantifiers such as "one," "two," "three," . . . , "many," "a few," "most," "almost all," and so on. But arguments which depend for their validity upon numerical or quasi-numerical information are *asyllogistic,* and require a more penetrating analysis than is given in the simple theory of the categorical syllogism. Any *categorical syllogism* which contains such numerical or quasi-numerical propositions will have its validity or invalidity remain unchanged when those propositions are translated into standard form in a way which simply throws out and forgets about their numerical or quasi-numerical aspects. So for our purposes in connection with the categorical syllogism we may translate "One student was at the dance," "Two students were at the dance," etc., and "A few students were at the dance," "Many students were at the dance," and "Most students were at the dance," all indifferently as *Some students are those who were at the dance.*

Some quasi-numerical quantifiers are not so simply translated, however. These include: "almost all," "not quite all," "all but a few," "almost everyone." Propositions in which these phrases appear as quantifiers are "exceptive" propositions, which make *two* assertions rather than one. They are of the same type as explicitly *exceptive* propositions like: "All except employees are eligible," "All but employees are eligible," and "Employees alone are not eligible." Each of these logically equivalent propositions asserts not merely that *all non-employees are eligible,* but also that *no employees are eligible.* Where "employees" is abbreviated by *"S"* and "eligible persons" by *"P,"* these two propositions can be written as *All non-S is P* and *No S is P.* These are clearly independent and together assert that *S* and *P* are complementary classes.

Each of these exceptive propositions is compound, and therefore cannot be translated into a single standard form categorical proposition, but rather into an explicit conjunction of *two* standard form categoricals. Thus the three propositions about eligibility translate identically into *All non-employees are eligible persons **and** no employees are eligible persons*. Also compound are the following exceptive propositions with quasi-numerical quantifiers: "Almost all students were at the dance," "Not quite all students were at the dance," "All but a few students were at the dance," and "Only some students were at the dance." Each of these affirms that *some students were at the dance* and denies that *all students were at the dance*. The quasi-numerical information they present is irrelevant from the point of view of syllogistic inference, and all are translated indifferently as *Some students are persons who were at the dance **and** some students are not persons who were at the dance*.

Exceptive propositions can and do occur in syllogistic arguments in ordinary language. How should a categorical syllogism which contains an exceptive proposition be tested? It depends upon the exceptive proposition's position in the argument. If it is a premiss, then the argument may have to be given two separate tests. For example, consider the argument: "Everyone who saw the game was at the dance; not quite all the students were at the dance; so some students didn't see the game." Its first premiss and its conclusion are categorical propositions, which are easily translated into standard form. But its second premiss, being an exceptive proposition, is not simple but compound. To discover whether or not its premisses imply its conclusion, one first tests the syllogism composed of the first premiss of the given argument, the first half of its second premiss, and its conclusion. In standard form, we have:

All persons who saw the game are persons who were at the dance.
Some students are persons who were at the dance.
_____
Therefore some students are not persons who saw the game.

This standard form categorical syllogism is of form **AIO**–2 and violates Rule 2, committing the fallacy of the Undistributed Middle. But the original argument is not yet proved to be invalid, because the syllogism just tested contains only *part* of the premisses of the original argument. One now has the task of testing the categorical syllogism composed of the first premiss and the conclusion of the original argument together with the second half of the second premiss. In standard form we have:

All persons who saw the game are persons who were at the dance.
Some students are not persons who were at the dance.
───
Therefore some students are not persons who saw the game.

This standard form categorical syllogism is of a different form, **AOO**–2, and is easily shown to be *valid*. Hence the original argument is valid, for the conclusion is the same, and the premisses of the original argument *include* the premisses of this valid standard form syllogism. Thus to test a non-standard form syllogism one of whose premisses is an exceptive proposition may require the testing of two different standard form categorical syllogisms. If the premisses of an argument are both categorical propositions and its conclusion is exceptive, then we know it to be invalid, for although the two categorical premisses may imply one or the other half of the compound conclusion, they cannot imply them both. Finally, if an argument contains exceptive propositions as both premisses and conclusion, all possible syllogisms constructable out of the original argument may have to be tested in order to determine its validity. Enough has been explained to enable the student to cope with such situations.

It is important to acquire facility at translating non-standard form propositions into standard form, for the tests of validity that we have developed can be applied only to standard form categorical syllogisms.

EXERCISES

Translate each of the following into standard form categorical propositions:

1. Lions are carnivorous.

2. Sheep are not carnivorous.

3. Many brave hearts are asleep in the deep.

4. Nothing is both easy and important.

5. To know her is to love her.

6. Nothing worth having can be obtained easily.

7. If a house be divided against itself, that house cannot stand.

8. He that is not with me is against me.

9. A soft answer turneth away wrath.

10. Blessed is he that considereth the poor.

11. Only students may use the side door.

12. Students may use only the side door.

13. Most candidates have no chance at all for election.

14. Only members are admitted.

15. All that glitters is not gold.

16. He is no wise man that will quit a certainty for an uncertainty.

17. All that is human must retrograde if it does not advance.

18. Facts are stubborn.

19. He jests at scars that never felt a wound.

20. Few men have ever scaled Mt. Everest.

21. An envious man is not easily satisfied.

22. Nothing is secret which shall not be made manifest.

23. Every man shall bear his own burden.

24. Whatsoever a man soweth, that shall he also reap.

25. At least one witness told the truth.

III. UNIFORM TRANSLATION

For a categorical syllogism to be tested it must be expressed in propositions which contain exactly three terms. Sometimes this aim is difficult to accomplish and requires a more subtle approach than that suggested in the preceding sections. Consider the proposition "The poor always ye have with you." It clearly does not assert that *all* the poor are with you, or even that *some* (particular) poor are *always* with you. There are alternative methods of reducing this proposition to standard form, but one perfectly natural route is by way of the key word "always." This word means "at all times" and suggests the standard form categorical proposition *All times are times when ye have the poor with you.* The word "times," which appears in both the subject and predicate terms, may be regarded as a *parameter,* that is, an auxiliary symbol which is of aid in expressing the original assertion in standard form.

Care should be taken not to introduce and use parameters in a mechanical, unthinking fashion. One must always be guided by an understanding of the proposition to be translated. Thus the proposition "Smith always wins at billiards," pretty clearly does not assert that Smith is incessantly, *at all times,* winning at billiards! It is more reasonable to interpret it as meaning that Smith wins at billiards *whenever he plays.* And so interpreted, it translates directly into *All times when Smith plays billiards are times when Smith wins at billiards.* Not all parameters need be *temporal.* To translate some propositions into standard form the words "places" and "cases" can be introduced as parameters. Thus "Where there is no vision the people perish," and "Jones loses a sale whenever he is late," translate into *All places where there is no vision are places where the people perish* and *All cases in which Jones is late are cases in which Jones loses a sale.*

The introduction of parameters is often necessary for the *uniform translation* of all three constituent propositions of a syllogism into standard form. Since the validity of a categorical syllogism depends upon the presence of common terms in its premises and conclusion, it is necessary for its testing to have all its constituent propositions expressed in such a way that their common terms appear clearly. Thus it is advisable to eliminate all synonyms which occur in an argument before attempting to test its validity. Before attempting to apply Venn Diagrams or the Syllogistic Rules to the argument:

> No unnecessary clothing should be purchased.
> A waistcoat is an unnecessary garment.
> _____
> Therefore no vests should be bought.

we should eliminate the synonymous terms occurring in it. When this is done, the argument translates into:

No unnecessary garments are articles which should be purchased.
All waistcoats are unnecessary garments.
_____
Therefore no waistcoats are articles which should be purchased.

In this standard form *EAE*–1, the argument is easily seen to be valid.

There are other non-standard form syllogisms which cannot have the number of their terms reduced to three by the simple device of eliminating synonyms. Here uniform translation requires the introduction of a parameter—the *same* parameter —into all three of the component propositions. Consider the following argument:

Soiled paper plates are scattered only where careless people have picnicked.
There are soiled paper plates scattered about here.
_____
Therefore careless people must have been picnicking here.

This argument is perfectly valid, but before it can be proved valid by our diagrams or Rules, its premisses and conclusion must be translated into standard form categorical propositions which involve only three terms. The second premiss and the conclusion might be translated most naturally into: "Some soiled paper plates are things which are scattered about here," and "Some careless people are those who have been picnicking here." But these two statements appear to contain *four* different terms. To reduce the given argument to standard form we begin with the first premiss, which requires a parameter for its standard form expression, and then *use the same parameter* in translating the second premiss and the conclusion into standard form. The word "where" in the first premiss suggests that the parameter "places" can be used. If this parameter is used to obtain uniform standard form translations of all three proposi- tions, the argument translates into:

All places where soiled paper plates are scattered are places where careless people have picnicked.
This place is a place where soiled paper plates are scattered.

Therefore this place is a place where careless people have picnicked.

This standard form categorical syllogism has mood and figure *AAA*–1, and has already been proved valid.

The notion of standardizing expressions through the use of a parameter is not an altogether easy one to grasp, but some non-standard form arguments cannot be translated into standard form categorical syllogisms by any other method. Another ex- ample may help to make clear the technique involved. Let us take the argument:

The hounds bay wherever a fox has passed; so the fox must have taken another path, since the hounds are quiet.

First of all, we must understand what is asserted in the given argument. We may take the statement that the hounds are quiet as asserting that the hounds are not baying here and now. This step is part of the necessary process of eliminating synonyms, since the first assertion makes explicit reference to the baying of hounds. And in the same manner we may under- stand the conclusion that the fox must have taken another path as asserting that the fox did not pass *here*. The word "wherever" in the first assertion should suggest that the param- eter "places" can be used in its translation. The standard form translation thus arrived at is:

All places where a fox has passed are places where the hounds bay.
This place is not a place where the hounds bay.

Therefore this place is not a place where a fox has passed.

This standard form categorical syllogism has mood and figure *AEE*–2, and its validity is easy to establish.

EXERCISES

I. Translate the following propositions into standard form, using parameters where necessary:

1. Error of opinion may be tolerated where reason is left free to combat it.

2. The wicked flee when no man pursueth.

3. Ill fares the land, to hastening ills a prey,
   Where wealth accumulates, and men decay.

4. Men are never so likely to settle a question rightly as when they discuss it freely.

5. He never opens his mouth without putting his foot into it.

6. No matter where he might be, if he grew sleepy he would begin to nod.

7. Kings will be tyrants from policy, when subjects are rebels from principle.

8. You cannot both eat your cake and have it too.

9. If we do meet again, why, we shall smile.

10. Except I be by Sylvia in the night,
    There is no music in the nightingale.

II. Translate each of the following arguments into standard form, name the mood and figure of its standard form translation, test its validity by a Venn Diagram, and if it is invalid, name the fallacy which it commits:

1. No teachers are bigots, since no teachers are prejudiced and only bigots are prejudiced.

2. There are no insincere reformers; therefore no reformers are hypocrites since none but the insincere are hypocrites.

3. Some ideas are harmless; so not all weapons are harmful, since ideas are weapons.

4. Our neighbor must be away; for the blinds are closed, and the blinds are always closed when he is away.

5. There must be a strike at the factory; for there is a picket line there, and pickets are only present at strikes.

6. Only those who ignore the facts are likely to be mistaken. No one who is truly objective in his approach is likely to be mistaken. Hence no one who ignores the facts is truly objective in his approach.

7. Not all who have jobs are temperate in their drinking. Only debtors drink to excess. So not all the unemployed are in debt.

8. Any argument worthy of logical recognition must be such as would occur in ordinary discourse. Now it will be found that no argument occurring in ordinary discourse is in the fourth figure. Hence, no argument in the fourth figure is worthy of logical recognition.

9. All valid syllogisms distribute their middle terms in at least one premiss; so this syllogism must be valid for it distributes its middle term in at least one premiss.

10. This syllogism is valid, for all invalid syllogisms commit an illicit process, and this syllogism commits no illicit process.

11. All invalid syllogisms commit an illicit process of their major terms, but this syllogism is valid; so this syllogism does not commit an illicit process of its major term.

12. No valid syllogisms have two negative premisses. No syllogisms on this page are invalid. Therefore no syllogisms on this page have two negative premisses.

13. All syllogisms having two negative premisses are invalid. Some valid syllogisms are sound. Therefore some unsound arguments are syllogisms having two negative premisses.

14. There are plants growing here, and since vegetation requires water, water must be present.

15. No one present is out of work. No members are absent. Therefore all members are employed.

16. The competition is stiff, for there is a great deal of money involved and there is never easy competition where much money is at stake.

17. All who were penniless were convicted. Some of the guilty were acquitted. Therefore some who had money were not innocent.

18. Although he complains whenever he is sick, his health is excellent; so he won't complain.

19. There are handsome men, but only man is vile; so it is false that nothing is both vile and handsome.

20. The express train alone does not stop at this station, and as the last train did not stop it must have been the express train.

21. It must have rained lately, because the fish are not biting and fish never bite after a rain.

22. All buildings over three hundred feet tall are skyscrapers, but not all examples of modern architecture are buildings over three hundred feet tall, since skyscrapers are not the only examples of modern architecture.

23. It will be a good game tomorrow, for the conference title is at stake, and no title contest is ever dull.

24. Any two men who contradict each other cannot both be lying. Hence the first and third natives cannot both be lying since they contradict each other.

25. Not all is gold that glitters, for some base metals glitter and gold is not a base metal.

IV. ENTHYMEMES.

Categorical syllogisms are often used, but it is the exception rather than the rule for conclusion and both premisses to be stated explicitly. More often than not, only part of the argument is expressed, the rest being "understood." Thus one may justify the conclusion that "Jones is a citizen" by mentioning only the one premiss: "Jones is a native-born American." As stated, the argument is incomplete, but the missing premiss is easily supplied, being a well known proposition of the Constitution of the United States. Were the missing premiss to be stated, the completed argument would appear as:

All native-born Americans are citizens.
Jones is a native-born American.
_____
Therefore Jones is a citizen.

Fully stated, the argument is a categorical syllogism of form *AAA*–1, and perfectly valid. An argument which is stated incompletely, part being "understood" or only "in the mind," is called an "enthymeme." An incompletely stated argument is characterized as *enthymematic*.

In everyday discourse, and even in science, most inferences are expressed enthymematically. The reason is easy to understand. In most discussions, a large body of propositions can be presumed to be common knowledge. The majority of speakers and writers save themselves trouble by not repeating well known and perhaps trivially true propositions which their hearers or readers can perfectly well be expected to supply for themselves. Moreover, it is not at all unusual for an argument to be *rhetorically* more powerful and persuasive when stated enthymematically than when enunciated in complete detail. With this rhetorical aspect, however, the logician is not concerned.

Because it is incomplete, an enthymeme must have its suppressed parts taken into account when the problem arises of testing its validity. Where a necessary premiss is missing, without that premiss the inference is invalid. But where the unexpressed premiss is easily supplied, in all fairness it ought to be included as part of the argument in evaluating it. In such a case one assumes that the maker of the argument did have more "in mind" then he stated explicitly. In most cases there is no difficulty in supplying the tacit premiss that the speaker intended but did not express. A cardinal principle in supplying suppressed premisses is that the proposition must be one which the speaker can safely presume his hearers to accept as true. Thus it would be foolish to suggest taking the conclusion itself as a suppressed premiss, for if the arguer could have expected his auditors to accept that proposition as a premiss, without proof, it would have been idle for him to attempt to establish it as conclusion of an argument.

Enthymemes have traditionally been divided into different "orders," according to which part of the syllogism is left unexpressed. A *first order* enthymeme is one in which the syllogism's major premiss is not stated. The preceding example is of the first order. A *second order* enthymeme is one in which only the major premiss and the conclusion are stated, the minor premiss being suppressed. An example of this type is: "All students are opposed to the new regulations; so all coeds are opposed to them." Here the minor premiss is easily supplied, being the obviously true proposition *All coeds are students.* A *third order* enthymeme is one in which both premisses are stated, but the conclusion is left unexpressed. An example of this type is the argument: "No true Christian is vain, but some church goers are vain." If the context is such that the intended conclusion is "Some church goers are not true Christians," then the argument is valid. But if the speaker was intending to establish the conclusion that "Some true Christians are not church goers," then his enthymeme is invalid, committing the fallacy of Illicit Progress of the Major Term. Here the context is decisive. But in other cases, a third order enthymeme may be invalid regardless of context. Where both premisses are negative, or where both premisses are particular propositions, or where their middle term is undistributed, no syllogistic conclusion follows validly, and so such enthymemes are invalid in any context.

In testing an enthymeme for validity, two steps are involved. The first is to supply the missing parts of the argument; the second is to test the resulting syllogism. If one of the premisses is missing, it may be that only the addition of an implausible proposition as premiss will make the argument valid, while with any plausible proposition added the argument is invalid. Pointing this out is a legitimate criticism of an enthymematic argument. Of course, an even more crushing objection is to show that *no* additional premiss, no matter how implausible, can turn the enthymeme into a valid categorical syllogism.

It should be observed that no new logical principles need be introduced in dealing with enthymemes. They are ultimately tested by the same methods that apply to syllogisms. The difference between enthymemes and categorical syllogisms is rhetorical rather than logical.

EXERCISES

Name the order and discuss the correctness of each of the following enthymemes:

1. All physicians are college graduates, so all members of the American Medical Association must be college graduates.

2. It must have rained lately, because the fish just aren't biting.

3. Yond Cassius has a lean and hungry look . . . such men are dangerous.

4. Henry is interested only in making money, but you cannot serve both God and Mammon!

5. Adamson can't have a telephone, because his name isn't listed in the phone book.

6. No enthymemes are complete, so this argument is incomplete.

7. He would not take the crown
   Therefore 'tis certain he was not ambitious.

8. Any reader who completes this argument is a good student, for it is difficult.

9. He knows his own child, for he is a wise father.

10. Familiarity breeds contempt, so you cannot be contemptuous of Helen.

V. SORITES

There are occasions when a single categorical syllogism will not suffice for drawing a desired conclusion from a group of premisses. Thus from the premisses:

> All diplomats are tactful.
> Some government officials are diplomats.
> All government officials are men in public life.

one cannot draw the conclusion:

> Some men in public life are tactful.

by a single syllogistic inference. Yet the indicated conclusion is entailed by the stated premisses. To derive it requires two syllogisms rather than one. A stepwise process of argumentation must be resorted to, where each step is a separate syllogism. When stated explicitly, the required argument will be:

> All diplomats are tactful individuals.
> Some government officials are diplomats.
> _____
> Therefore some government officials are tactful individuals.
> All government officials are men in public life.
> _____
> Therefore some men in public life are tactful individuals.

The present argument is not a syllogism but a *chain* of categorical syllogisms, connected by the conclusion of the first, which is a premiss of the second. This chain has only two links, but more extended arguments may consist of a greater number. Since a chain is no stronger than its weakest link, an argument of this type is valid if and only if all of its constituent syllogisms are valid.

Where such an argument is expressed enthymematically, with only the premisses and the final conclusion stated, it is called a "sorites." Sorites may have three, four, or *any* number of premisses. Some are very lengthy indeed. The following example is due to the philosopher Leibnitz:

The human soul is a thing whose activity is thinking. A thing whose activity is thinking is one whose activity is immediately apprehended, and without any representation of parts therein. A thing whose activity is immediately apprehended without any representation of parts therein is a thing whose activity does not contain parts. A thing whose activity does not contain parts is one whose activity is not motion. A thing whose activity is not motion is not a body. What is not a body is not in space. What is not in space is insusceptible of motion. What is insusceptible of motion is indissoluble (for dissolution is a movement of parts). What is indissoluble is incorruptible. What is incorruptible is immortal. Therefore the human soul is immortal.*

This sorites contains no less than ten premises. Any sorites may be tested by making its intermediate conclusions or steps explicit and testing separately the various categorical syllogisms thus obtained. If we ignore the possibility that an equivocation is present, then the validity of Leibnitz's sorites is easily verified.

It will be convenient, in connection with the exercises provided below, to say that a sorites is in *standard form* when all of its propositions are in standard form, when it contains exactly one more term than it has premises, and when every proposition (except the last) has a term in common with the proposition which immediately follows it. Thus one standard form translation of Lewis Carroll's sorites:

    (1)   Every one who is sane can do Logic.
    (2)   No lunatics are fit to serve on a jury.
    (3)   None of *your* sons can do Logic.

    Therefore none of *your* sons is fit to serve on a jury.

is

    (2′) All persons fit to serve on a jury are sane persons.
    (1′) All sane persons are persons who can do Logic.
    (3′) No sons of yours are persons who can do Logic.

    Therefore no sons of yours are persons fit to serve on a jury.

It can be tested by stating the suppressed sub-conclusions explicitly, and then testing the resulting categorical syllogisms.

* From *An Introduction to Logic,* by H. W. B. Joseph. Oxford University Press, 1906, 1916.

EXERCISES *

I. Translate each of the following sorites into standard form, and test its validity:

1. (1) Babies are illogical.
   (2) Nobody is despised who can manage a crocodile.
   (3) Illogical persons are despised.

   Therefore babies cannot manage crocodiles.

2. (1) No experienced person is incompetent.
   (2) Jenkins is always blundering.
   (3) No competent person is always blundering.

   Therefore Jenkins is inexperienced.

3. (1) The only books in this library, that I do *not* recommend for reading, are unhealthy in tone.
   (2) The bound books are all well-written.
   (3) All the romances are healthy in tone.
   (4) I do not recommend you to read any of the unbound books.

   Therefore all the romances in this library are well-written.

4. (1) Only profound scholars can be dons at Oxford.
   (2) No insensitive souls are great lovers of music.
   (3) No one whose soul is not sensitive can be a Don Juan.
   (4) There are no profound scholars who are not great lovers of music.

   Therefore all Oxford dons are Don Juans.

5. (1) No interesting poems are unpopular among people of real taste.
   (2) No modern poetry is free from affectation.
   (3) All *your* poems are on the subject of soap bubbles.
   (4) No affected poetry is popular among people of real taste.
   (5) Only a modern poem would be on the subject of soap-bubbles.

   Therefore all *your* poems are uninteresting.

* Practically all of the following exercises are taken, with little or no modification, from Lewis Carroll's *Symbolic Logic.*

II. Each of the following sets of propositions can serve as premisses for a valid sorites. For each, find the conclusion and establish the argument as valid:

1. (1) No one takes in the *Times,* unless he is well-educated.
   (2) No hedge-hogs can read.
   (3) Those who cannot read are not well-educated.

2. (1) All puddings are nice.
   (2) This dish is a pudding.
   (3) No nice things are wholesome.

3. (1) The only articles of food, that my doctor allows me, are such as are not very rich.
   (2) Nothing that agrees with me is unsuitable for supper.
   (3) Wedding-cake is always very rich.
   (4) My doctor allows me all articles of food that are suitable for supper.

4. (1) All my sons are slim.
   (2) No child of mine is healthy who takes no exercise.
   (3) All gluttons, who are children of mine, are fat.
   (4) No daughter of mine takes any exercise.

5. (1) When I work a Logic-example without grumbling, you may be sure it is one that I can understand.
   (2) These Sorites are not arranged in regular order, like the examples I am used to.
   (3) No easy example ever makes my head ache.
   (4) I can't understand examples that are not arranged in regular order, like those I am used to.
   (5) I never grumble at an example, unless it gives me a headache.

VI. THE DILEMMA

The dilemma is a legacy from older times when logic and rhetoric were more closely connected than they are today. From the strictly logical point of view, the dilemma is not of much interest or importance. But rhetorically, the dilemma is perhaps the most powerful instrument of persuasion ever devised. It is a devastating weapon in controversy.

Today one says somewhat loosely that a person is in a dilemma when he must choose between two alternatives, both of which are bad or unpleasant. More picturesquely such a person is described as being "impaled on the horns of a dilemma." Traditionally, a dilemma is an argument intended to put one's opponent in just that kind of position. In debate, one uses a dilemma to offer alternative positions to one's adversary, from which he must choose, and then to prove that no matter which choice he makes, he is committed to a conclusion that is distasteful to him. Thus in a debate on a proposed protective tariff bill, an opponent of the measure may argue as follows:

If the proposed tariff produces scarcity, it will be injurious; and if it does not produce scarcity, it will be useless. It will either produce scarcity or else it won't. Therefore the proposed tariff will either be injurious or useless.

Such an argument is designed to push the opponent (in this case the sponsor of the bill) into a corner and there annihilate him. The second premiss, which offers the alternatives, is called a "disjunction." The first premiss, which asserts that *both* of the alternatives have certain undesirable consequences, is called a "conjunction." The conclusion of a dilemma may be another *disjunction,* offering alternatives, or it may be a categorical proposition. In the former case the dilemma is said to be "complex," in the latter case "simple." A dilemma need not have an unpleasant conclusion. An example of one with a happy conclusion is provided by the following *simple* dilemma:

If the blest in heaven have no desires, they will be perfectly content; so they will, if their desires are fully gratified; but either they will have no desires, or have them fully gratified; therefore, they will be perfectly content.

Because of its importance in debate, a number of ways of evading or refuting the conclusion of a dilemma have been given special names. They are all picturesque, relating to the fact that a dilemma has two (or more) "horns." The three ways of defeating or refuting a dilemma are known as "going (or escaping) between the horns," "taking (or grasping) it by the horns," and "rebutting it by means of a counter-dilemma." It should be borne in mind that these are not ways to prove the dilemma invalid, but are rather ways of avoiding its conclusion without challenging the formal validity of the argument.

One escapes between the horns of a dilemma by rejecting its disjunctive premiss. This method is often the easiest way to evade the conclusion of a dilemma, for unless one half of the disjunction is the explicit contradictory of the other, the disjunction may very well be false. One justification sometimes offered for giving grades to students is that recognizing good work will stimulate the student to study harder. A student may criticize this theory, using the following dilemma:

If a student is fond of learning he needs no stimulus, and if he dislikes learning no stimulus will be of any avail. But any student is either fond of learning or dislikes it. Therefore a stimulus is either needless or of no avail.

This argument is formally valid, but we can evade its conclusion by *going between the horns*. The disjunctive premiss is false, for students have all kinds of attitudes towards learning: some may be fond of it, many dislike it, but a vast majority are indifferent. And for that vast majority a stimulus may be both needed and of some avail. It should be remembered that going between the horns does not prove the conclusion to be false but shows merely that the argument does not constitute adequate grounds for accepting that conclusion.

Where the disjunctive premiss is unassailable, which it is when the alternatives exhaust the possibilities, it is impossible to escape between the horns. Another method of evading the conclusion must be sought. One such method is to *grasp the dilemma by the horns,* which involves rejecting the premiss which is a conjunction. To deny a conjunction we need only deny one of its parts. When we grasp the dilemma by the horns, we attempt to show that the conclusion is not really a consequence of the alternative from which it has been claimed to follow. Consider again the dilemma attacking the protective tariff. The proponent of the tariff bill might grasp the dilemma by the horns and argue that even if the proposed tariff were to produce scarcity, it would not be injurious. After all, a scarcity would stimulate domestic production, thus giving the country increased employment and more developed industry. Were any scarcity produced, he might argue, it would be only temporary, and, far from being injurious, would be highly beneficial. Of course there may be more to be said, but the original dilemma has been grasped firmly by the horns.

Rebutting a dilemma by means of a counter-dilemma is the most entertaining and ingenious method of all; but it is seldom sound, for reasons that will be explained presently. To rebut a given dilemma, one constructs another dilemma whose conclusion is *opposed* to the conclusion of the original. *Any* counter-dilemma may be used in rebuttal, but ideally the counter-dilemma should be built up out of the same ingredients (categorical propositions) that the original dilemma contained.

A classical example of this elegant kind of rebuttal concerns the following argument of an Athenian mother attempting to persuade her son not to enter politics:

If you say what is just, men will hate you; and if you say what is unjust the gods will hate you; but you must either say the one or the other; therefore you will be hated.

Her son rebutted the dilemma with the following one:

If I say what is just, the gods will love me; and if I say what is unjust, men will love me. I must say either the one or the other. Therefore I shall be loved!

In public discussion, where the dilemma is the strongest of controversial weapons, a rebuttal like this, which derives an opposite conclusion from almost the same premises, marks the absolute zenith of rhetorical skill. But if we examine the dilemma and rebutting counter-dilemma more closely, we see that their conclusions are not so "opposite" as might at first appear.

The conclusion of the first dilemma is that *the son will be hated* (*by men or by the gods*), while that of the rebutting dilemma is that *the son will be loved* (*by the gods or by men*). But these two conclusions are perfectly compatible. The rebutting counter-dilemma serves merely to establish a conclusion *different* from that of the original. Both conclusions may very well be true together, so no refutation has been accomplished. But in the heat of controversy analysis is unwelcome; and if such a rebuttal occurred in a public debate, the average audience would overwhelmingly agree that the rebuttal completely demolished the original argument.

That this sort of rebuttal does not refute, but only directs attention to a different aspect of the same matter, is perhaps more clearly shown in the case of the following little dilemma, advanced by an "optimist."

If I work I earn money, and if I am idle I enjoy myself. Either I work or I am idle. Therefore either I earn money or I enjoy myself.

A "pessimist" might offer the following counter-dilemma:

If I work, I don't enjoy myself; and if I am idle, I don't earn money. Either I work or I am idle. Therefore either I don't earn money or I don't enjoy myself.

These conclusions represent merely different ways of viewing the same facts; they do not constitute a disagreement over what the facts are.

No discussion of dilemmas would be complete unless it mentioned the celebrated lawsuit between Protagoras and Eulathus. Protagoras was a teacher who lived in Greece during the fifth century, B.C. He taught many subjects but specialized in the art of pleading before juries. Eulathus wanted to become a lawyer, but, not being able to pay the required tuition, he made an arrangement according to which Protagoras would teach him but not receive payment until Eulathus won his first case. When Eulathus finished his course of study, he delayed going into practice. Tired of waiting for his money, Protagoras brought suit against his former pupil for the tuition money that was owed. Unmindful of the adage that the lawyer who tries his own case has a fool for a client, Eulathus decided to plead his own case in court. When the trial began, Protagoras presented his side of the case in a crushing dilemma:

If Eulathus loses this case, then he must pay me (by the judgment of the court) ; if he wins this case, then he must pay me (by the terms of the contract). He must either lose or win this case. Therefore Eulathus must pay me.

The situation looked bad for Eulathus, but he had learned well the art of rhetoric. He offered the court the following counter-dilemma in rebuttal:

If I win this case, I shall not have to pay Protagoras (by the judgment of the court) ; if I lose this case, I shall not have to pay Protagoras (by the terms of the contract, for then I shall not yet have won my first case). I must either win or lose this case. Therefore I do not have to pay Protagoras!

Had you been the judge, how would you have decided?

It is to be noted that the conclusion of Eulathus' rebutting dilemma is *not* compatible with the conclusion of Protagoras' original dilemma. One conclusion is the explicit *denial* of the other. But it is a rare case in which a rebuttal stands in this relation to the dilemma against which it is directed. When it does so, the premisses involved are themselves inconsistent, and it is this implicit contradiction that the two dilemmas serve to make explicit.

EXERCISES

Discuss the various arguments which might be offered to refute each of the following dilemmas:

1. If we interfere with the publication of false and harmful doctrines we shall be guilty of suppressing the liberties of others, while if we do not interfere with the publication of such doctrines we run the risk of losing our own liberties. We must either

interfere or not interfere with the publication of false and harmful doctrines. Hence we must either be guilty of suppressing the liberties of others or else run the risk of losing our own liberties.

2. If we are to have peace we must not encourage the competitive spirit, while if we are to make progress we must encourage the competitive spirit. We must either encourage or not encourage the competitive spirit. Therefore we shall either have no peace or make no progress.

3. If you tell me what I already understand, you do not enlarge my understanding; while if you tell me something which I do not understand then your remarks are unintelligible to me. Whatever you tell me must be either something I already understand or something which I do not understand. Hence whatever you say either does not enlarge my understanding or else is unintelligible to me.

4. If what you say does not enlarge my understanding then what you say is without value to me, and if what you say is unintelligible to me then it is without value to me. Whatever you say either does not enlarge my understanding or else is unintelligible to me. Therefore nothing you say is of any value to me.

5. If the conclusion of a deductive argument goes beyond the premises then the argument is invalid; while if the conclusion of a deductive argument does not go beyond the premises then the argument brings nothing new to light. The conclusion of a deductive argument must either go beyond the premises or not go beyond them. Therefore deductive arguments are either invalid or else they bring nothing new to light.

6. If a deductive argument is invalid it is without value, while a deductive argument which brings nothing new to light is also without value. Deductive arguments are either invalid or else they bring nothing new to light. Therefore deductive arguments are without value.

7. If the general was loyal he would have obeyed his orders, and if he was intelligent he would have understood them. The general either disobeyed his orders or else he did not understand them.

Therefore the general must have been either disloyal or unintelligent.

8. If he was disloyal then his dismissal was justified, and if he was unintelligent then his dismissal was justified. He was either disloyal or unintelligent. Therefore his dismissal was justified.

9. If the several nations keep the peace, the United Nations Organization is unnecessary; while if the several nations go to war, the United Nations Organization will have been unsuccessful in its purpose of preventing war. Now either the several nations keep the peace or they go to war. Hence the United Nations Organization is unnecessary or unsuccessful.

10. If men are good, laws are not needed to prevent wrong doing; while if men are bad, laws will not succeed in preventing wrong doing. Men are either good or bad. Therefore either laws are not needed to prevent wrong doing or laws will not succeed in preventing wrong doing.

CHAPTER EIGHT

Symbolic Logic

> . . . the woof and warp of all thought and all
> research is symbols, and the life of thought and
> science is the life inherent in symbols; so it is
> wrong to say that a good language is *important* to
> good thought, merely; for it is the essence of it.
>
> —CHARLES SANDERS PEIRCE

I. THE VALUE OF SPECIAL SYMBOLS

Arguments formulated in English or any other natural language are often difficult to evaluate because of the vague and
equivocal nature of the words used, the amphiboly of their construction, the misleading idioms they may contain, their possibly
confusing metaphorical style, and the distraction that is due
to whatever emotive significance may attach to them. These
topics were discussed at length in Part One. Even when these
difficulties are resolved, the problem of deciding the validity
or invalidity of the argument remains. To avoid these peripheral
difficulties, it is convenient to set up an *artificial symbolic
language,* free from these defects, into which statements and
arguments from natural language can be translated.

219

Some of the advantages of a technical vocabulary for a science have already been mentioned in the early part of Chapter Four. The use of a special logical notation is not peculiar to modern logic. Aristotle, the ancient founder of the subject, made use of certain abbreviations to facilitate his own work. Although the difference between modern and classical logic is not one of kind but of degree, the difference in degree is tremendous. The greater extent to which modern logic has developed its own special technical language has made it immeasurably more powerful a tool for analysis and deduction. The special symbols of modern logic help us to exhibit with greater clarity the logical structures of propositions and arguments whose forms may tend to be obscured by the unwieldiness of ordinary language.

A further value of the logician's special symbols is the aid they give in the actual use and manipulation of statements and arguments. The situation here is comparable to that which led to the replacement of Roman numerals by the Arabic notation. We all know that Arabic numerals are clearer and more easily comprehended than the older Roman numerals which they displaced. But the real superiority of Arabic numerals is revealed only in computation. Any schoolboy can easily multiply 113 by 9. But to multiply CXIII by IX is a more difficult task, and the difficulty increases as larger and larger numbers are considered. Similarly, the drawing of inferences and the evaluation of arguments is greatly facilitated by the adoption of a special logical notation. To quote Alfred North Whitehead, one of the great contributors to the advance of symbolic logic:

. . . by the aid of symbolism, we can make transitions in reasoning almost mechanically by the eye, which otherwise would call into play the higher faculties of the brain.*

From this point of view, paradoxically enough, logic is not concerned with developing our powers of thought but with developing techniques that enable us to get along without thinking!

* *An Introduction to Mathematics* by A. N. Whitehead. Oxford University Press, 1911.

II. THE SYMBOLS FOR CONJUNCTION, NEGATION, AND DISJUNCTION

In this chapter we shall be concerned with relatively simple arguments such as:

The blind man has a red hat or the blind man has a white hat.
The blind man does not have a red hat.
Therefore the blind man has a white hat.

and

If Mr. Robinson is the brakeman's next-door neighbor, then Mr. Robinson lives halfway between Detroit and Chicago.
Mr. Robinson does not live halfway between Detroit and Chicago.
Therefore Mr. Robinson is not the brakeman's next-door neighbor.

Every argument of this general type contains at least one *compound statement*. It is customary in studying such arguments to divide all statements into two general categories, *simple* and *compound*. A *simple statement* is one which does not contain any other statement as a constituent part. For example, "Charlie's neat" is a simple statement. A *compound statement* is one which does contain another statement as a constituent part. For example, "Charlie's neat and Charlie's sweet" is a compound statement, for it contains two simple statements as constituent parts. Of course the constituent parts of a compound statement may themselves be compound.

The first type of compound statement to be considered is the *conjunction*. Where two statements are combined by the word "and," the resulting compound statement is a *conjunction*, and the two statements so combined are called *conjuncts*. Thus the compound statement "Charlie's neat and Charlie's sweet" is a conjunction, whose first conjunct is "Charlie's neat" and whose second conjunct is "Charlie's sweet."

The word "and" is a short and convenient word, but it has other uses besides that of connecting statements. For example, the statement "Lincoln and Grant were contemporaries" is *not* a conjunction but a simple statement expressing a relationship. To have a unique symbol whose only function is to connect statements conjunctively, we introduce the dot ("·") as our symbol for conjunction. Thus the previous conjunction can be written as "Charlie's neat · Charlie's sweet." More generally, where p and q are any two statements whatever, their conjunction is written $p \cdot q$.

The dot symbol is a *truth-functional* connective, which means that the truth or falsehood of any conjunction $p \cdot q$ is completely determined by (is a function of) the truth or falsehood of its constituent statements or conjuncts p and q. A conjunction is true only if both conjuncts are true; it is false otherwise. Given two statements, p and q, there are only four possible sets of truth values they can have—where the *truth value* of a true statement is *true* and the *truth value* of a false statement is *false*. These four possible cases, and the truth value of the conjunction in each, can be displayed as follows:

where p is true and q is true, $p \cdot q$ is true;
where p is true and q is false, $p \cdot q$ is false;
where p is false and q is true, $p \cdot q$ is false;
where p is false and q is false, $p \cdot q$ is false.

If we represent the truth values *"true"* and *"false"* by the capital letters *"T"* and *"F,"* the determination of the truth value of a conjunction by the truth values of its conjuncts can be represented more briefly by means of a *truth table* as:

p	q	$p \cdot q$
T	T	T
T	F	F
F	T	F
F	F	F

This truth table can be taken as *defining* the dot symbol, since it explains what truth values are assumed by $p \cdot q$ in every possible case. It should be remarked that the English words "but," "yet," "although," "however," "nevertheless," "still," etc. also serve to conjoin two statements into a single compound statement, and *in their conjunctive sense* they all can be represented by the dot symbol.

The *negation* (or contradictory or denial) of a statement in English is often formed by inserting a "not" into the original statement. It is also possible to express the negation of a statement in English by prefixing to it the phrase "it is false that" or "it is not the case that." It is customary to use the symbol "∼" (called a *curl* or, less frequently, a *tilde*) to express the negation of a statement. Thus where M symbolizes the statement "All men are mortal," the various statements "Not all men are mortal," "Some men are not mortal," "It is false that all men are mortal," "It is not the case that all men are mortal," are all indifferently symbolized as ∼ M. More generally, where p is any statement whatever, its negation is written ∼ p. It is obvious that the curl is a truth-functional operator. The negation of any true statement is false, and the negation of any false statement is true. This fact can be expressed by means of a truth table very simply:

p	$\sim p$
T	F
F	T

This truth table may be regarded as the *definition* of the negation symbol "∼."

The *disjunction* of two statements is formed in English by inserting the word "or" between them. The two constituent statements so combined are called *disjuncts*. The English word "or" is ambiguous, having two related but distinguishable meanings. One of them is exemplified in the statement, "Premiums will be waived in the event of sickness or unemployment," for the intention here is obviously that premiums are waived not only for sick persons and for unemployed persons, but also for persons who are *both* sick *and* unemployed. This sense of the word "or" is called *weak* or *inclusive*. An inclusive disjunction is true in case one or the other or both disjuncts are true; only if both disjuncts are false is their inclusive disjunction false. The inclusive "or" has the sense of "either, possibly both." Where precision is at a premium, as in contracts and other legal documents, this sense is made explicit by use of the phrase "and/or."

The word "or" is also used in a *strong* or *exclusive* sense, in which the meaning is not *at least one* but *at least one and at most one*. Where a restaurant lists "salad or dessert" on its table d'hôte menu, it is clearly meant that for the stated price of the meal, the diner may have one or the other *but not both*. When a mother succumbs to her child's teasing and gives permission to take "a cookie or a piece of cake," it would be a backward or disobedient child who helped himself to *both*. Where precision is at a premium and the exclusive sense of "or" is intended, the phrase "but not both" is usually added.

We interpret the inclusive disjunction of two statements as asserting that *at least one of the statements is true,* and their exclusive disjunction as asserting that *at least one of the statements is true and at least one of the statements is false*. We observe here that the two kinds of disjunction have a part of their meanings in common. This *partial common meaning,* that at least one of the disjuncts is true, is the *whole* meaning of the inclusive "or" and a *part* of the meaning of the exclusive "or."

Although disjunctions are expressed ambiguously in English, they are unambiguous in Latin. The Latin language has two different words corresponding to the two different senses of the English word "or." The Latin word *"vel"* expresses weak or inclusive disjunction, while the Latin word *"aut"* corresponds to the word "or" in its strong or exclusive sense. It is customary to use the initial letter of the word *"vel"* to stand for "or" in its weak, inclusive sense. Where p and q are any two statements whatever, their weak or inclusive disjunction is written $p \vee q$. Our symbol for inclusive disjunction (called a *wedge,* or, less frequently, a *vee*) is also a truth-functional connective. A weak disjunction is false only in case both of its disjuncts are false.

We may regard the wedge as being *defined* by the following truth table:

p	q	$p \lor q$
T	T	T
T	F	T
F	T	T
F	F	F

The first specimen argument presented in this section was a *Disjunctive Syllogism:*

The blind man has a red hat or the blind man has a white hat.
The blind man does not have a red hat.
Therefore the blind man has a white hat.

Its form is completely characterized by saying that its first premiss is a disjunction, its second premiss is the negation of the first disjunct of the first premiss, and its conclusion is the same as the second disjunct of the first premiss. It is evident that the Disjunctive Syllogism is valid on *either* interpretation of the word "or," that is, regardless of whether an inclusive or exclusive disjunction is asserted by the first premiss. Since all of the valid arguments involving disjunctions with which we shall be concerned in the present chapter are, like the Disjunctive Syllogism, valid on *either* interpretation of the word "or," a simplification may be effected by translating the English word "or" into our logical symbol "v"—*regardless of which meaning of the English word "or" is intended*. In general, only a close examination of the context or an explicit questioning of the speaker or writer can reveal which sense of "or" is *intended*. This problem, at best difficult and often impossible to resolve, can be avoided if we agree to treat *any* occurrence of the word "or" as inclusive. Where it is explicitly stated that the disjunction is intended to be exclusive, by means of the added phrase "but not both," for example, we have the symbolic machinery for expressing that additional sense, as will be shown directly.

In English, punctuation is absolutely required to make clear the meanings of statements, especially complicated ones. A great many different punctuation marks are used, without which many sentences would be highly ambiguous. For example, quite different meanings attach to "The teacher says John is a fool," when it is given different punctuations. Other sentences require punctuation for their very intelligibility, as, for example, "John where James had had had had had had had had had had the teacher's approval." Punctuation is equally necessary in mathematics. No number is uniquely denoted by the expression "$2 \times 3 + 5$," although when it is made clear how its constituents are to be grouped, it denotes either 11 or 16: the first when punctuated "$(2 \times 3) + 5$," the second when punctuated "$2 \times (3 + 5)$." Punctuation is needed in both arithmetic and English for ambiguity to be avoided and meaning made clear.

Punctuation is also required in the language of symbolic logic, for compound statements may themselves be compounded together into more complicated ones. The expression $p \vee q \cdot r$ is ambiguous: it might mean the disjunction of p with the conjunction of q and r, or it might mean the conjunction whose first conjunct is the disjunction of p with q and whose second conjunct is r. We distinguish between these two different senses by punctuating the given expression either as $p \vee (q \cdot r)$ or as $(p \vee q) \cdot r$. In symbolic logic parentheses, brackets, and braces are used as punctuation marks. That the different methods of punctuating the original expression do make a difference can be seen by considering the case in which p is true and q and r are both false. In this case the first punctuated expression is true (since its first disjunct is true) while the second one is false (since its second conjunct is false). Here the difference in punctuation makes all the difference between truth and falsehood, for different punctuations assign different truth values to the ambiguous expression $p \vee q \cdot r$.

Given a set of punctuation marks for our symbolic language, it is possible to formulate not merely conjunctions, negations, and *weak* disjunctions in it, but exclusive disjunctions as well.

The exclusive disjunction of p and q asserts that at least one of them is true *and* at least one of them is false. This is expressed quite simply as $(p \text{ v } q) \cdot (\sim p \text{ v } \sim q)$. In the interest of brevity, that is, to decrease the number of parentheses required, it is convenient to establish the convention that in any formula the negation symbol will be understood to apply to the smallest statement which the punctuation permits. Without this convention the formula $\sim p \text{ v } q$ is ambiguous, meaning either $(\sim p) \text{ v } q$ or $\sim (p \text{ v } q)$. But by our convention we take it to mean the first of these alternatives, for the curl *can* (and therefore by our convention *does*) apply to the first constituent, p, rather than to the larger expression $p \text{ v } q$.

Any compound statement which is built up out of simple statements by repeated use of the truth-functional connectives dot, curl, and wedge, will have its truth value completely determined by the truth or falsehood of its constituent simple statements. If we know the truth values of its simple constituent statements the truth value of any truth-functional compound of them is easily discovered. In doing so we always begin with the inmost constituents and work outward. For example, if A and B are true and X and Y are false statements, we discover the truth value of the compound statement $\sim [\sim (A \cdot X) \cdot (Y \text{ v } \sim B)]$ as follows. Since X is false, the conjunction $A \cdot X$ is false, and so its negation $\sim (A \cdot X)$ is true. B is true; so its negation $\sim B$ is false, and since Y is false also, the disjunction of Y with $\sim B$, $Y \text{ v } \sim B$ is false. The square bracketed expression $[\sim (A \cdot X) \cdot (Y \text{ v } \sim B)]$ is the conjunction of a true with a false statement and is therefore false. Hence its negation, which is the entire expression, is true. Such a stepwise procedure always enables us to determine the truth value of a compound statement from the truth values of its constituents.

EXERCISES

I. Which of the following statements are true?

1. Washington was assassinated v Lincoln was assassinated
2. $\sim$ (Washington was assassinated $\cdot$ Lincoln was assassinated)

3. ∼ Washington was assassinated · Lincoln was assassinated
4. Washington was assassinated · ∼ Lincoln was assassinated
5. (Washington was assassinated v Lincoln was assassinated) · (∼ Washington was assassinated v ∼ Lincoln was assassinated)
6. (Washington was assassinated · Lincoln was assassinated) v (∼ Washington was assassinated · ∼ Lincoln was assassinated)
7. Washington was assassinated v (∼ Washington was assassinated · ∼ Lincoln was assassinated)
8. ∼ Washington was assassinated v ∼ (∼ Washington was assassinated · ∼ Lincoln was assassinated)
9. ∼ Washington was assassinated · ∼ (∼ Washington was assassinated · ∼ Lincoln was assassinated)
10. ∼ (Washington was assassinated v Lincoln was assassinated)
11. ∼ [∼ (Washington was assassinated · Lincoln was assassinated)]
12. ∼ (∼ Washington was assassinated · Lincoln was assassinated)
13. ∼ [(Washington was assassinated · Lincoln was assassinated) v (∼ Washington was assassinated · ∼ Lincoln was assassinated)]
14. (∼ Washington was assassinated · Lincoln was assassinated) · New York is the largest city in America
15. ∼ Washington was assassinated v ∼ (Lincoln was assassinated · New York is the largest city in America)
16. Lincoln was assassinated · (Washington was assassinated v New York is the largest city in America)
17. (Lincoln was assassinated · Washington was assassinated) v (Lincoln was assassinated · New York is the largest city in America)
18. (Lincoln was assassinated · Washington was assassinated) · ∼ (Lincoln was assassinated · New York is the largest city in America)
19. Lincoln was assassinated · (Washington was assassinated v ∼ Washington was assassinated)
20. ∼ [(Washington was assassinated · ∼ Lincoln was assassinated) v Washington was assassinated] v Washington was assassinated

II. If *A, B,* and *C* are true statements, and *X, Y,* and *Z* are false statements, which of the following are true?

1. $(A \cdot X) \vee (B \cdot Y)$
2. $(A \vee X) \cdot (B \vee Y)$
3. $\sim (A \cdot X) \vee \sim (B \cdot Y)$
4. $\sim (A \vee X) \cdot \sim (B \vee Y)$
5. $\sim A \vee B$
6. $\sim A \vee Z$

7. $\sim X \vee Y$

8. $\sim X \vee C$

9. $(\sim A \vee B) \vee (\sim B \vee A)$

10. $(\sim A \vee X) \vee (\sim X \vee A)$

11. $\sim (A \cdot \sim B) \vee (X \cdot \sim Y)$

12. $\sim (A \cdot \sim B) \vee \sim (X \cdot \sim Y)$

13. $\sim [(A \cdot \sim B) \vee A] \vee A$

14. $\sim [(X \cdot \sim B) \vee X] \vee X$

15. $\sim [(X \cdot \sim Y) \vee X] \vee X$

16. $\sim [(Z \cdot \sim C) \vee Z] \vee Z$

17. $[A \cdot (B \vee C)] \vee \sim [(A \cdot B) \vee (A \cdot C)]$

18. $[X \cdot (Y \vee Z)] \vee \sim [(X \cdot Y) \vee (X \cdot Z)]$

19. $\sim \{[A \vee (B \cdot C)] \cdot \sim [(A \vee B) \cdot (A \vee C)]\}$

20. $\sim \{[X \vee (Y \cdot Z)] \cdot \sim [(X \vee Y) \cdot (X \vee Z)]\}$

III. IMPLICATIONS AND MATERIAL IMPLICATION

Where two statements are combined by placing the word "if" before the first and inserting the word "then" between them, the resulting compound statement is a *hypothetical* (also called a *conditional*, an *implication*, or an *implicative statement*). In a hypothetical, the constituent statement between the "if" and the "then" is called the *antecedent* (or the *implicans* or—rarely—the *protasis*), and the constituent statement which follows the "then" is the *consequent* (or the *implicate* or—rarely—the *apodosis*). For example, "If Mr. Jones is the brakeman's next-door neighbor then Mr. Jones earns exactly three times as much as the brakeman" is a hypothetical statement in which "Mr. Jones is the brakeman's next-door neighbor" is the antecedent, and "Mr. Jones earns exactly three times as much as the brakeman" is the consequent.

What a hypothetical statement asserts is that its antecedent *implies* its consequent. It does not assert that its antecedent is true, but only that *if* its antecedent is true then its consequent is true also. It does not assert that its consequent is true, but only that its consequent is true *if* its antecedent is true. The essential meaning of a hypothetical statement is the relation of *implication* that is asserted to hold between its antecedent and consequent, in that order. To understand the meaning of a hypothetical statement, then, we must understand what implication is.

The possibility suggests itself that perhaps "implication" has more than one meaning. We found it necessary to distinguish different senses of the word "or" before introducing a special logical symbol to correspond exactly to a single one of the meanings of the English word. Had we not done so, the ambiguity of the English would have infected our logical symbolism and prevented it from achieving the clarity and precision aimed at. It will be equally valuable to distinguish the different senses of "implies" or "if-then" before introducing a special logical symbol in this connection.

Let us begin by listing a number of different hypothetical statements, each of which seems to assert a different type of implication, and to each of which corresponds a different sense of "if-then."

A. If all men are mortal and Socrates is a man, then Socrates is mortal.

B. If Mr. Black is a bachelor than Mr. Black is unmarried.

C. If blue litmus paper is placed in acid, then the litmus paper will turn red.

D. If State loses the Homecoming Game then I'll eat my hat.

Even a casual inspection of these four hypothetical statements reveals that they are of quite different types. The consequent of *A* follows *logically* from its antecedent, while the consequent of *B* follows from its antecedent by the very *definition* of the term "bachelor," which means unmarried man. The consequent of *C* does not follow from its antecedent either by logic alone or by the definition of its terms; the connection must be discovered empirically, for the implication stated here is *causal*. Finally, the consequent of *D* does not follow from its antecedent either by logic or by definition, nor is there any causal law involved —— in the usual sense of the term. Most causal laws, those discovered in physics and chemistry, for example, describe what happens in the world *regardless of the hopes or desires of men*. There is no such law connected with statement *D*, of course. That statement reports a *decision* of the speaker to behave in a certain way under certain circumstances.

The four hypothetical statements examined in the preceding

paragraph are different, in that each asserts a different type of implication between its antecedent and consequent. But they are not *completely* different; all assert types of *implication*. Is there any identifiable common meaning, any partial meaning that is *common* to these admittedly different types of implication, although perhaps not the *whole* or *complete* meaning of any one of them?

The search for a common partial meaning takes on an added significance when we recall our procedure in working out a symbolic representation for the English word "or." In that case we proceeded as follows. First: we emphasized the difference between the two senses of that word, contrasting inclusive with exclusive disjunctions. The inclusive disjunction of two statements was observed to mean that *at least one of the statements is true,* and the exclusive disjunction of two statements was observed to mean that *at least one of the statements is true and at least one is false.* Second: we noted that these two types of disjunction had a common *partial* meaning. This *partial common meaning,* that *at least one of the disjuncts is true,* was seen to be the *whole* meaning of the weak, inclusive "or," and a *part* of the meaning of the strong, exclusive "or." We then introduced the special symbol "v" to represent this common partial meaning (which was the entire meaning of "or" in its inclusive sense). Third: we noted that the symbol representing the common partial meaning was an adequate translation of either sense of the word "or" for the purpose of retaining the Disjunctive Syllogism as a valid form of argument. It was admitted that translating an exclusive "or" into the symbol "v" ignored and lost part of the word's meaning. But the part of its meaning that is preserved by this translation is *all that is needed* for the Disjunctive Syllogism to remain a valid form of argument. Since the Disjunctive Syllogism is the basic kind of argument involving disjunction with which we are concerned in this part of our work, this partial translation of the word "or," which may abstract from its "full" or "complete" meaning in some cases, is wholly adequate for our present purposes.

Now we are concerned to follow out the same pattern again, this time in connection with the English phrase "if-then." The first part is already accomplished: we have already emphasized the differences between some four senses of the "if-then" phrase, corresponding to four different types of implication. We are now ready for the second step, which is to discover a sense that is at least a part of the meaning of all four different types of implication.

One way of approaching this problem is to ask what circumstances would suffice to establish the falsehood of a given hypothetical statement. Let us consider another example. Under what circumstances should we agree that the hypothetical statement:

If blue litmus paper is placed in this solution, then the litmus paper will turn red.

is false? There are, of course, many ways of investigating the truth of such a statement, and not all of them involve actually placing blue litmus paper in the solution. Some other chemical indicator might be used, and if it showed the solution to be acid, this would confirm the given hypothetical as true, since we know that blue litmus paper always turns red in acid. On the other hand, if it showed the solution to be alkaline, this would tend to show that the given hypothetical was false. It is important to realize that this hypothetical does not assert that any blue litmus paper is actually placed in the solution, or that any litmus paper actually turns red. It asserts merely that *if* blue litmus paper is placed in the solution, *then* the litmus paper will turn red. It is proved false in case blue litmus paper is actually placed in the solution and *does not turn red*. The acid test, so to speak, of the falsehood of a hypothetical statement is available when its antecedent is true, for if its consequent is false while its antecedent is true, the hypothetical itself is thereby proved false.

Any hypothetical statement *If p then q* is known to be false in case the conjunction $p \cdot \sim q$ is known to be true, that is, in case its antecedent is true and its consequent is false. For a hypothetical to be true, then, the indicated conjunction must be false, that is, its negation $\sim (p \cdot \sim q)$ must be true. In other words, for any hypothetical *If p then q* to be true, $\sim (p \cdot \sim q)$, the negation of the conjunction of its antecedent with the negation of its consequent, must also be true. We may, then, regard $\sim (p \cdot \sim q)$ as a *part* of the meaning of *If p then q*.

Every hypothetical statement means to deny that its antecedent is true and its consequent false, but this need not be the whole of its meaning. A hypothetical such as *A* above also asserts a logical connection between its antecedent and consequent, one like *B* asserts a definitional connection, *C* a causal connection, *D* a decisional connection. But no matter what type of implication is asserted by a hypothetical statement, part of its meaning is the negation of the conjunction of its antecedent with the negation of its consequent.

We now introduce a special symbol to represent this common partial meaning of the "if-then" phrase. We define the new symbol "$\supset$" (called a *horseshoe*) by taking "$p \supset q$" as an abbreviation of "$\sim (p \cdot \sim q)$." The exact significance of the "$\supset$" symbol can be indicated by means of a truth table:

p	q	$\sim q$	$p \cdot \sim q$	$\sim (p \cdot \sim q)$	$p \supset q$
T	T	F	F	T	T
T	F	T	T	F	F
F	T	F	F	T	T
F	F	T	F	T	T

Here the first two columns are the guide columns, the third is filled in by reference to the second, the fourth by reference to the first and third, the fifth by reference to the fourth, and the sixth is identically the same as the fifth *by definition*.

The symbol "$\supset$" is not to be regarded as denoting *the* meaning of "if-then," or standing for *the* relation of implication. It would be impossible, for there is no single meaning of "if-then"; there are several meanings. There is no *unique* relation of implication to be thus represented; there are several different implication relations. Nor is the symbol "⊃" to be regarded as somehow standing for *all* the meanings of "if-then." These are all different, and any attempt to abbreviate all of them by a single logical symbol would render that symbol multiply ambiguous—as ambiguous as the English phrase "if-then" or the English word "implication." The symbol "⊃" is completely unambiguous. What "$p \supset q$" abbreviates is "$\sim (p \cdot \sim q)$," whose meaning is included in the meanings of each of the various kinds of implications considered, but which does not constitute the entire meaning of any of them.

We can consider the symbol "⊃" as representing *another* kind of implication, and it will be expedient to do so, since convenient ways to read "$p \supset q$" are "if p then q" or "p implies q." But it is not the same kind of implication as any of those mentioned earlier. It is called *material implication* by logicians, who in giving it a special name admit that it is a special notion, not to be confused with other, more usual, types of implication.

Not all hypothetical statements in English need assert one of the four types of implication previously considered. Material implication constitutes a fifth type that may be asserted in ordinary discourse. Consider the remark: "If Hitler was a military genius then I'm a monkey's uncle." It is quite clear that it asserts neither logical, definitional, nor causal implication. It should also be apparent that it cannot represent a decisional implication, since it scarcely lies in the speaker's power to *make* the consequent true. No "real connection," either logical, definitional, or causal obtains between antecedent and consequent here. A hypothetical of this sort is often used as an emphatic or humorous method of denying its antecedent. The consequent of such a hypothetical is usually a statement which is obviously or ludicrously *false*. And since no true hypothetical can have both its antecedent true and its consequent false, to affirm such a hypothetical amounts to denying that its antecedent is true. The full meaning of the present hypothetical seems to be the denial that "Hitler was a military genius" is true when "I'm a monkey's uncle" is false. And since the latter is so obviously false, the former cannot be true.

No "real connection" between antecedent and consequent is suggested by a *material implication*. All that is asserted is that *as a matter of fact* it is not the case that the antecedent is true when the consequent is false. It should be noted that the material implication symbol is a truth-functional connective, just like the symbols for conjunction and disjunction. As such, it is *defined* by the truth table:

p	q	$p \supset q$
T	T	T
T	F	F
F	T	T
F	F	T

Now we propose to translate any occurrence of the "if-then" phrase into our logical symbol "$\supset$." This proposal means that in translating hypothetical statements into our symbolism we treat them all as merely material implications. Of course many, if not most English hypothetical statements assert *more* than a merely material implication to hold between their antecedents and consequents. So our proposal amounts to suggesting that we ignore, or throw away, or "abstract from" part of the meaning of the English hypothetical statement when we translate it into our symbolic language. How can this proposal be justified?

The previous proposal to translate both inclusive and exclusive disjunctions by means of the "v" symbol was justified on the grounds that the validity of the Disjunctive Syllogism was preserved even if the additional meaning which attaches to the exclusive "or" was ignored. Our present proposal to translate all hypothetical statements into the merely material implications symbolized by "$\supset$" is to be justified in exactly the same way. Many arguments contain hypothetical statements of various different kinds, but the validity of all valid arguments of the general type with which we will be concerned is *preserved* even if the additional meanings of their hypothetical statements are ignored. This remains to be proved, of course, and will occupy our attention in the next section.

EXERCISES

If *A*, *B*, and *C* are true statements and *X*, *Y*, *Z* are false statements, which of the following are true:

1. $(A \supset B) \supset C$
2. $(X \supset Y) \supset Z$
3. $(A \supset X) \supset B$
4. $A \supset (X \supset B)$
5. $(A \supset B) \supset (B \supset A)$
6. $(A \supset X) \supset (X \supset A)$
7. $(X \supset A) \supset (A \supset X)$
8. $(A \supset B) \supset (\sim B \supset \sim A)$
9. $(A \supset X) \supset (\sim X \supset \sim A)$
10. $(X \supset Y) \supset (\sim Y \supset \sim X)$
11. $[(A \supset B) \supset A] \supset A$
12. $[(A \supset X) \supset A] \supset A$
13. $[(X \supset B) \supset X] \supset X$
14. $[(X \supset Y) \supset X] \supset X$
15. $[A \supset (B \supset C)] \supset [(A \cdot B) \supset C]$
16. $[X \supset (Y \supset Z)] \supset [(X \cdot Y) \supset Z]$
17. $[A \supset (X \supset Y)] \supset [(A \cdot X) \supset Y]$
18. $[A \supset (X \supset Y)] \supset [X \supset (A \supset Y)]$
19. $[(A \supset X) \supset Y] \supset [A \supset (X \supset Y)]$
20. $[A \supset (X \supset Y)] \supset [(A \supset X) \supset Y]$

IV. ARGUMENT FORMS AND ARGUMENTS

In this section we wish to specify more precisely what is meant by the term "valid." We can relate our formal definition to more familiar and intuitive notions by considering the method of *refutation by logical analogy*.* If we are confronted with the argument:

If Bacon wrote the plays attributed to Shakespeare then Bacon was a great writer.

* Just as in discussing the categorical syllogism in Chapter Six, Section II.

Bacon was a great writer.
Therefore Bacon wrote the plays attributed to Shakespeare.

we may agree with the premises but disagree with the conclusion, judging the argument to be *invalid*. One way of proving its invalidity is by the method of logical analogy. "You might as well argue," we could retort, "that

If Washington was assassinated then Washington is dead.
Washington is dead.
Therefore Washington was assassinated.

And you cannot seriously defend this argument," we should continue, "because here the premises are known to be true and the conclusion known to be false. This argument is obviously invalid; your argument is of the *same form;* so yours is invalid also." This type of refutation is very effective.

Let us examine more closely the technique of refutation by logical analogy, for it points the way to an excellent general method of testing arguments. To prove the invalidity of any argument it suffices to formulate another argument which: (a) has the same form as the first, and (b) has true premises and a false conclusion. This method is based upon the fact that validity and invalidity are purely *formal* characteristics of arguments, which is to say that any two arguments having the same form are either both valid or both invalid, regardless of any differences in the subject matter with which they are concerned.

A given argument exhibits its form most clearly when the simple statements which appear in it are symbolized by capital letters. Thus we may symbolize the statements "Bacon wrote the plays attributed to Shakespeare," "Bacon was a great writer," "Washington was assassinated," and "Washington is dead" by the letters *"B," "G," "A,"* and *"D,"* respectively, and formulate the two preceding arguments as:

$$B \supset G \qquad\qquad A \supset D$$
$$\underline{G} \qquad \text{and} \qquad \underline{D}$$
$$\therefore B \qquad\qquad\qquad \therefore A$$

So written, their common form is easily seen.

If we are interested in discussing the forms of arguments rather than particular arguments having those forms, we need some method of symbolizing the forms themselves. To achieve such a method we introduce the notion of a *variable*. In the preceding sections we used *capital* letters to symbolize particular simple statements. To avoid confusion, we use *small* or *lower-case* letters from the middle part of the alphabet, "*p*," "*q*," "*r*," "*s*," . . . as *statement variables*. A statement variable, as we shall use the term, is simply a letter for which, or in place of which, a statement may be substituted. Compound statements as well as simple statements may be substituted for statement variables.

We define an *argument form* as any sequence of symbols containing statement variables but no statements, such that when the statement variables are replaced by statements—the same statement replacing the same statement variable throughout—the result is an argument. Thus the expression

$$p \supset q$$
$$q$$
$$\therefore p$$

is an argument form, for when the statement variables p and q are replaced by the statements B and G, respectively, the result is the first argument of this section. If the variables p and q are replaced by the statements A and D, the result is the second argument. Any argument which results from the substitution of statements for statement variables in an argument form is called a *substitution instance* of that argument form. It is clear that any substitution instance of an argument form may be said to *have* that form, and that any argument which has a certain form is a substitution instance of that form.

The form of a given argument is that argument form from which the argument results by replacing each distinct statement variable by a different simple statement. Thus the argument form above is *the* form of the two preceding arguments. Although both of those arguments are also substitution instances of the argument form

$$p$$
$$q$$
$$\overline{\therefore r}$$

from which they result by replacing the statement variables
p, q, and *r* by the statements *B ⊃ G, G,* and *B,* respectively, and
by *A ⊃ D, D,* and *A,* respectively, this latter form is not *the*
form of either of the two arguments because the substitutions
required to obtain them involve replacing a statement variable
by a *compound* statement. For a given argument, there is a
unique argument form which is *the* form of that argument.

The technique of refutation by logical analogy can now be
described more precisely. If *the* form of a given argument has
any substitution instance whose premises are true and whose
conclusion is false, then the given argument is invalid. We may
define the term "invalid" as applied to argument forms as follows: an argument form is *invalid* if and only if it has a substitution instance with true premises and a false conclusion.
Refutation by logical analogy is based on the fact that any argument of which *the* form is an *invalid argument form* is an
invalid argument. Any argument form which is not invalid
must be valid. An argument form is valid if and only if it has *no*
substitution instances with true premises and a false conclusion. And since validity is a formal notion, an argument is
valid if and only if *the* form of that argument is a valid argument form.

A given argument is proved invalid if a refuting analogy
for it can be found, but "thinking up" such refuting analogies
may not always be easy. Happily, it is not necessary, because for
arguments of this type there is a simpler, purely mechanical test
based upon the same principle. Given any argument, we test
the *form* of that argument, for its validity or invalidity determines the validity or invalidity of the argument.

To test an argument form we examine all possible substitution instances of it to see if any of them have true premises and
false conclusions. Of course any argument form has infinitely
many substitution instances, but we need not worry about hav-

ing to examine them one at a time. Since we are interested only in the truth or falsehood of their premises and conclusions, we need only consider the truth values involved. The arguments with which we are concerned here contain only simple state- ments and compound statements which are built up out of simple statements by means of the truth-functional connectives symbolized by the dot, curl, wedge, and horseshoe. Hence we obtain all possible substitution instances whose premises and conclusions have different truth values by examining all pos- sible different arrangements of truth values for the statements which can be substituted for the distinct statement variables in the argument form to be tested.

Where an argument form contains just two different state- ment variables p and q, all of its substitution instances are the result of either substituting true statements for both p and q, or a true statement for p and a false one for q, or a false one for p and a true one for q, or false statements for both p and q. These different cases are assembled most conveniently in the form of a truth table. To decide the validity of the argument form $p \supset q, q \therefore p$ we construct the following truth table:

p	q	$p \supset q$
T	T	T
T	F	F
F	T	T
F	F	T

Each row of this table represents a whole class of substitution in- stances. The T's and F's in the two initial or guide columns represent the truth values of the statements substituted for the variables p and q in the argument form. We fill in the third column by referring back to the initial or guide columns and the definition of the horseshoe symbol. The third column head- ing is the first "premiss" of the argument form, the second column is the second "premiss," and the first column is the "conclusion." In examining this truth table we find that in the third row there are T's under both premises and an F under the conclusion, which means that there is at least one substitution instance of this argument form which has true premises and a false conclusion. And this row suffices to show that the argument form is invalid. Any argument of this form is said to commit the *Fallacy of Affirming the Consequent,* since its second premise affirms the consequent of its hypothetical first premiss.

To show the validity of the Disjunctive Syllogism form $p \vee q$, $\sim p \therefore q$ we construct the following different truth table:

p	q	$p \vee q$	$\sim p$
T	T	T	F
T	F	T	F
F	T	T	T
F	F	F	T

Here too the initial or guide columns have written under them all possible different truth values of statements which may be substituted for the variables p and q. We fill in the third column by referring back to the first two, and the fourth by reference to the first alone. Now the third row is the only one in which a T appears under both premises (the third and fourth columns) and there a T appears under the conclusion also (the second column). The truth table thus shows that the argument form has no substitution instance having true premises and a false conclusion, and thereby proves the validity of the argument form being tested.

The truth table technique provides a completely mechanical method for testing the validity of any argument of the general type here considered. We are now in a position to justify our proposal to translate any occurrence of the "if-then" phrase into our material implication symbol "⊃". In the preceding section the claim was made that all valid arguments involving "if-then" statements remain valid when those statements are interpreted as expressing merely material implications. Truth tables can be used to substantiate this claim, and will justify our translation of "if-then" into the horseshoe symbol.

The simplest type of intuitively valid argument involving a hypothetical statement is illustrated by the argument:

If the second native told the truth then only one native is a politician.
The second native told the truth.
Therefore only one native is a politician.

The form of this argument, known as *modus ponens,* is $p \supset q,$ $p \therefore q$ and is proved valid by the following truth table:

p	q	$p \supset q$
T	T	T
T	F	F
F	T	T
F	F	T

Here the two premisses are represented by the third and first columns, and the conclusion represented by the second. Only the first row represents substitution instances in which both premisses are true, and the T in the second column shows that in these arguments the conclusion is true also. This truth table establishes the validity of any argument of form *modus ponens.*

Another common type of intuitively valid argument contains hypothetical statements exclusively and is called a Hypothetical Syllogism. An example is:

If the first native is a politician then he lies.
If he lies then he denies being a politician.
Therefore if the first native is a politician then he denies being a politician.

The form of this argument is $p \supset q,$ $q \supset r \therefore p \supset r.$ Since it contains three distinct statement variables, the truth table here must have three initial or guide columns and will require *eight* rows for the listing of all possible substitution instances. Besides the initial columns, three additional columns are required, two for the premisses, the third for the conclusion. The table appears as

p	q	r	$p \supset q$	$q \supset r$	$p \supset r$
T	T	T	T	T	T
T	T	F	T	F	F
T	F	T	F	T	T
T	F	F	F	T	F
F	T	T	T	T	T
F	T	F	T	F	T
F	F	T	T	T	T
F	F	F	T	T	T

In constructing it, we fill in the fourth column by referring back to the first and second, the fifth by reference to the second and third, and the sixth by reference to the first and third. Examining the completed table we observe that the premisses are true only in the first, fifth, seventh and eighth rows, and that in all of these the conclusion is true also. This truth table establishes the validity of the argument form, and proves that the Hypothetical Syllogism also remains valid when its hypothetical statements are translated by means of the horseshoe symbol.

Enough examples have been provided to illustrate the proper use of the truth table technique for testing arguments. And perhaps enough have been given to show that the validity of any valid argument involving hypothetical statements is preserved when its hypotheticals are translated into merely material implications. Any doubts that remain can be allayed by the reader's providing, translating, and testing his own examples.

As more complicated argument forms are considered, larger truth tables are required to test them, for a separate initial or guide column is required for each different statement variable in the argument form. Only two are required for a form with just two variables, and that table will have four rows. But three initial columns are required for a form with three variables, as for the Hypothetical Syllogism, and such truth tables will have eight rows. To test the validity of an argument form such as that of the Constructive Dilemma, $(p \supset q) \cdot (r \supset s)$, $p \lor r \therefore q \lor s$, which contains four distinct statement variables, a truth table with four initial columns and sixteen rows is required. In general, to test an argument form containing n distinct statement variables requires a truth table with n initial columns and 2^n rows.

The first argument form which we proved invalid, $p \supset q$, $q \therefore p$, bears a superficial resemblance to the valid argument form *modus ponens*. It has been called the *Fallacy of Affirming the Consequent*. Another invalid form which has been given a special name is $p \supset q$, $\sim p \therefore \sim q$, which is the *Fallacy of Denying the Antecedent*, and whose invalidity is readily established by means of truth tables. The latter fallacy bears a superficial resemblance to the valid argument form $p \supset q$, $\sim q \therefore \sim p$, called *modus tollens*.

EXERCISES

I. Use truth tables to prove the validity or invalidity of the following argument forms:

1. $p \supset q \therefore \sim q \supset \sim p$
2. $p \supset q, p \supset r \therefore q \supset r$
3. $(p \supset q) \cdot (r \supset q), \sim q \therefore \sim p \vee \sim r$
4. $(p \supset q) \cdot (p \supset r), \sim p \therefore \sim q \vee \sim r$
5. $(p \supset q) \cdot (r \supset s), p \vee r \therefore q \vee s$ (Constructive Dilemma)
6. $(p \supset q) \cdot (r \supset s), \sim q \vee \sim s \therefore \sim p \vee \sim r$ (Destructive Dilemma)
7. $p \vee (q \cdot r) \therefore (p \vee q) \cdot (p \vee r)$
8. $(p \cdot q) \vee (p \cdot r) \therefore p \cdot (q \vee r)$
9. $p \supset (q \cdot r), (r \vee s) \supset t \therefore p \supset t$
10. $p \supset (q \vee r), (r \cdot s) \supset t \therefore p \supset t$

II. Use truth tables to determine the validity or invalidity of each of the following arguments:

1. If you tell the truth then men will hate you, and if you tell lies then God will hate you. You will tell the truth or you will tell lies. Therefore men will hate you or God will hate you.
2. If Smith got the wire then (either) he took the plane or he chose to disregard our request. Smith did not take the plane. Therefore if Smith got the wire then he chose to disregard our request.

3. If Smith got the wire, then he took the plane and he will be here by noon. Smith did not take the plane. Therefore Smith did not get the wire.

4. If Smith got the wire, then (either) he took the plane or he chose to disregard our request. Smith took the plane. Therefore if Smith got the wire then he did not choose to disregard our request.

5. If Jones took the Limited then he was in the accident, and if he was in the accident then he missed the meeting. Jones took the Limited or he missed the meeting. Therefore Jones was in the accident.

6. If Jones receives the message then if he wants to keep his job then he will make the deposit. Jones wants to keep his job. Therefore if Jones received the message then he will make the deposit.

7. If Jones received the message then if he wants to keep his job then he will make the deposit. Jones will make the deposit. Therefore if Jones received the message then he wants to keep his job.

8. If Jones received the message then (either) he will attend the meeting or he will offer his resignation. Jones will not offer his resignation. Therefore if Jones did not receive the message then Jones will not attend the meeting.

9. If Jones received the message then (either) he will attend the meeting or he will offer his resignation. Jones will not offer his resignation. Therefore if Jones does not attend the meeting then Jones did not receive the message.

10. Either Brown has enemies in the administration or if he exceeds his quota then he will receive a promotion. Brown will not receive a promotion. Therefore Brown has enemies in the administration or he will not exceed his quota.

V. STATEMENT FORMS AND STATEMENTS

We have now to make explicit a notion that was tacitly assumed in the preceding section. It is the notion of a *statement form*. There is an exact parallel between the relation of argument to argument form, on the one hand, and the relation of statement to statement form, on the other. The definition of statement form makes this evident: a *statement form* is any sequence of symbols containing statement variables but no statements, such that when the statement variables are replaced by statements—the same statement replacing the same statement variable throughout—the result is a statement. Thus $p \vee q$ is a statement form, since when the variables p and q are replaced by statements a statement results. Since the resulting statement is a disjunction, $p \vee q$ is a *disjunctive statement form.* Analogously, $p \cdot q$ and $p \supset q$ are *conjunctive* and *hypothetical statement forms,* and $\sim p$ is a *negation form* or *denial form.* Just as any argument of a certain form is said to be a substitution instance of that argument form, so any statement of a certain form is said to be a substitution instance of that statement form. And just as we distinguished *the* form of a given argument, so we distinguish *the* form of a given statement as that statement form from which the statement results by replacing each distinct statement variable by a different simple statement. Thus $p \vee q$ is *the* form of the statement, "The blind man has a red hat or the blind man has a white hat."

It is perfectly natural to feel that although the statements "Lincoln was assassinated" (symbolized as L) and "Either Lincoln was assassinated or else he wasn't" (symbolized as $L \vee \sim L$) are both *true,* they are true "in different ways," or have "different kinds" of truth. Similarly, it is perfectly natural to feel that although the statements "Washington was assassinated" (symbolized as W) and "Washington was both assassinated and not assassinated" (symbolized as $W \cdot \sim W$) are both *false,* they are false "in different ways," or have "different kinds" of falsehood. While not pretending to give any kind of psychological explanation of these "feelings," we can nevertheless point out certain logical differences to which they are probably appropriate.

The statement L is true and the statement W is false; these are historical facts. There is no logical necessity about them. Events might have occurred differently, and the truth values of such statements as L and W must be discovered by an empirical study of history. But the statement L v $\sim L$, although true, is not a truth of history. There is a logical necessity here, events could not have been such as to make it false, and its truth can be known independently of any empirical investigation. The statement L v $\sim L$ is a formal truth, true in virtue of its form alone. It is a substitution instance of a statement form *all* of whose substitution instances are true statements.

A statement form which has only true substitution instances is a *tautologous* statement form, or a *tautology*. To show that the statement form p v $\sim p$ is a tautology we construct the following truth table:

p	$\sim p$	p v $\sim p$
T	F	T
F	T	T

There is only one initial or guide column to this truth table, since the form being examined contains only one statement variable. Consequently, there are only two rows, which represent all possible substitution instances. There are only T's in the column under the statement form in question, and this fact shows that all of its substitution instances are true. Any statement which is a substitution instance of a tautologous statement form is true in virtue of its form and is itself said to be tautologous, or a tautology.

A statement form which has only false substitution instances is said to be *self-contradictory*, or a *contradiction*. The statement form $p \cdot \sim p$ is self-contradictory, for in its truth table only F's occur under it, signifying that all of its substitution instances are false. Any statement, such as $W \cdot \sim W$, which is a substitution instance of a self-contradictory statement form is false in virtue of its form, and is itself said to be self-contradictory, or a contradiction.

Statement forms which have both true and false statements among their substitution instances are called *contingent* statement forms. Any statement whose form is contingent is called a contingent statement. Thus p, $\sim p$, $p \cdot q$, p v q, and $p \supset q$ are all contingent statement forms. And such statements as *L, W,* ~ *L, L · W,* and *L* v *W* are contingent statements, since their truth values are dependent or contingent on their contents rather than their forms.

Not all statement forms are so obviously tautological or self-contradictory or contingent as the simple examples cited above. For example, the statement form [(*p* ⊃ *q*) ⊃ *p*] ⊃ *p* is not at all obvious, though its truth table will demonstrate it to be a tautology. It even has a special name, being known as "Peirce's Law."

Two statements are said to be *materially equivalent,* or *equivalent in truth value,* when they are either both true or both false. This notion is expressed by the symbol "≡". Material equivalence is a truth function, and can be defined by the following truth table:

p	*q*	*p* ≡ *q*
T	*T*	*T*
T	*F*	*F*
F	*T*	*F*
F	*F*	*T*

Whenever two statements are materially equivalent they materially imply each other. This is easily verified by a truth table. Hence the symbol "≡" may be read either "is materially equivalent to" or "if and only if." Two statements are said to be *logically equivalent* when the statement of their equivalence is a tautology. Thus the "principle of double negation," expressed as *p* ≡ ~ ~ *p* is proved to be tautologous by the following truth table

p	~ *p*	~ ~ *p*	*p* ≡ ~ ~ *p*
T	*F*	*T*	*T*
F	*T*	*F*	*T*

There are two logical equivalences of some intrinsic interest and importance which formulate the interrelations between conjunction, disjunction, and negation. Since the disjunction *p* v *q* asserts merely that *at least one* of its two disjuncts is *true,* it is not contradicted by asserting that *at least one is false,* but only by asserting that *both* are false. Thus asserting the negation of the disjunction p v q is logically equivalent to asserting the conjunction of the negations of p and q. In symbols this is written $\sim (p \text{ v } q) \equiv (\sim p \cdot \sim q)$ and its logical truth is established by the following truth table:

p	q	p v q	$\sim (p \text{ v } q)$	$\sim p$	$\sim q$	$\sim p \cdot \sim q$	$\sim (p \text{ v } q) \equiv (\sim \text{p} \cdot \sim q)$
T T	*T*	*F*	*F*	*F*	*F*	*T*
T F	*T*	*F*	*F*	*T*	*F*	*T*
F T	*T*	*F*	*T*	*F*	*F*	*T*
F F	*F*	*T*	*T*	*T*	*T*	*T*

Similarly, since the conjunction of p and q asserts that *both* are *true,* to contradict it we need merely assert that *at least one* is *false.* Thus asserting the negation of the conjunction $p \cdot q$ is logically equivalent to asserting the disjunction of the negations of p and q. In symbols this is written $\sim (p \cdot q) \equiv (\sim p \text{ v } \sim q)$ and is easily proved to be a tautology. These two equivalences are known as De Morgan's Theorems, having been stated by the mathematician and logician Augustus De Morgan (1806–1871). De Morgan's Theorems can be given a combined formulation in English as: the negation of the
$\begin{Bmatrix} \text{disjunction} \\ \text{conjunction} \end{Bmatrix}$ of two statements is logically equivalent to the
$\begin{Bmatrix} \text{conjunction} \\ \text{disjunction} \end{Bmatrix}$ of the negations of the two statements.

Two statement forms are *logically equivalent* if no matter what statements are substituted for their statement variables—the same statements replacing the same statement variables in both statement forms—the resulting pairs of statements are equivalent. Since $\sim (p \cdot \sim q)$ and $\sim p \text{ v } q$ are logically equivalent (by De Morgan's Theorem and the principle of double negation), there is no logical reason for defining $p \supset q$ as $\sim (p \cdot \sim q)$ rather than $\sim p \text{ v } q$. And the latter is the more usual definition of the horseshoe symbol.

There is an important relationship between tautologies and valid arguments. To every argument there corresponds a hypothetical statement whose antecedent is the conjunction of the argument's premisses and whose consequent is the argument's conclusion. Thus to any argument of the form $p \supset q$, $p \therefore q$ corresponds a hypothetical statement of the form $[(p \supset q) \cdot p] \supset q$. It is clear that a truth table which proves an argument form valid will also show its corresponding hypothetical statement form to be tautologous. An argument form is valid if and only if its truth table has a T under the conclusion in every row in which there are T's under all of its premisses. But an F can occur in the column headed by the corresponding hypothetical statement form only where there are T's under all the premisses and an F under the conclusion. Hence only T's will occur under a hypothetical which corresponds to a valid argument. Thus for every valid argument, the statement that its premisses imply its conclusion is a tautology.

EXERCISES

I. Use truth tables to characterize the following statement forms as tautologous, self-contradictory, or contingent:

1. $(\sim p \cdot q) \cdot (p \supset q)$
2. $(\sim q \cdot p) \cdot (p \supset q)$
3. $(\sim p \cdot \sim q) \supset (p \supset q)$
4. $(p \cdot \sim p) \supset q$
5. $p \supset (q \vee \sim q)$
6. $\sim p \supset [q \equiv (p \vee q)]$
7. $\sim p \supset [p \equiv (q \vee p)]$
8. $\{[(p \supset q) \cdot (r \supset s)] \cdot [p \vee r]\} \supset (q \vee s)$
9. $\{[(p \supset q) \cdot (\sim r \supset p)] \cdot [r \supset p]\} \cdot (p \supset \sim q)$
10. $\{[(p \supset q) \cdot (p \supset \sim r)] \cdot [r \supset p]\} \cdot (\sim p \supset q)$

II. Use truth tables to decide which of the following pairs of statement forms are equivalent:

1. p and $p \cdot (p \vee q)$
2. p and $p \vee (p \cdot q)$
3. $p \supset q$ and $\sim q \supset \sim p$
4. $p \supset q$ and $\sim p \supset \sim q$

5. p v $(q \cdot r)$ and $(p$ v $q) \cdot (p$ v $r)$ 6. $(p \cdot q) \supset r$ and $p \supset (q \supset r)$
7. $p \cdot q$ and $(p$ v $\sim q) \cdot q$ 8. p v q and $(p \cdot \sim q)$ v q
9. p and $q \equiv (p \supset q)$ 10. $p \supset q$ and $(p$ v $q) \equiv q$

VI. THE PARADOXES OF MATERIAL IMPLICATION

There are two forms of statements, $p \supset (q \supset p)$ and $\sim p \supset (p \supset q)$, which are easily proved to be tautologies. Trivial as these statement forms may be in their symbolic formulation, when expressed in ordinary English they seem surprising and even paradoxical. The first may be expressed as "A true statement is implied by any statement whatever." Since it is true that the earth is round, it follows that "The moon is made of green cheese implies that the earth is round"; and this is very curious indeed, especially since it also follows that "The moon is *not* made of green cheese implies that the earth is round." The second tautology may be expressed as "A false statement implies any statement whatever." Since it is false that the moon is made of green cheese, it follows that "The moon is made of green cheese implies that the earth is round"; and this is all the more curious when it is realized that it also follows that "The moon is made of green cheese implies that the earth is *not* round."

These seem paradoxical because we believe that the shape of the earth and the matter of the moon are utterly irrelevant to each other, and we believe further that no statement, true or false, can *really* imply any other statement, false or true, to which it is utterly irrelevant. And yet truth tables establish that a false statement implies any statement, and that a true statement is implied by any statement. This paradox is easily resolved, however, when we acknowledge the ambiguity of the word "implies." In several senses of the word "implies" it is perfectly true that no contingent statement can imply any other contingent statement with unrelated subject matter. It is true in the case of *logical* implication, and *definitional,* and *causal* implications. It may even be true of *decisional* implications, although here the notion of *relevance* may have to be construed more broadly.

But subject matter or *meaning* is strictly irrelevant to *material implication,* which is a truth function. Only truth and falsehood are relevant here. There is nothing paradoxical in stating that any disjunction is true which contains at least one true disjunct, and this fact is all that is asserted by statements of the forms $p \supset (\sim q \vee p)$ and $\sim p \supset (\sim p \vee q)$, which are logically equivalent to the "paradoxical" ones. We have already given a justification of treating material implication as *a* sense of "if-then," and of the logical expediency of translating *every* occurrence of "if-then" into the "$\supset$" notation. That justification was the fact that translating "if-then" into the "$\supset$" preserves the validity of all valid arguments of the type with which we are concerned in this part of our logical studies. There are other proposed symbolizations, adequate to other types of implication, but they belong to the more advanced parts of logic and are beyond the scope of the present book.

VII. THE THREE "LAWS OF THOUGHT"

Those who have defined Logic as the science of the laws of thought have often gone on to assert that there are exactly three fundamental or basic laws of thought necessary and sufficient for thinking to follow if it is to be "correct." These have traditionally been called the "Principle of Identity," the "Principle of Contradiction" (sometimes the "Principle of Non-Contradiction"), and the "Principle of Excluded Middle." There are alternative formulations of these "Principles," appropriate to different contexts. The formulations appropriate here are the following:

The "Principle of Identity" asserts that *if any statement is true, then it is true.*
The "Principle of Contradiction" asserts that *no statement can be both true and false.*
The "Principle of Excluded Middle" asserts that *any statement is either true or false.*

In the terminology of the present chapter, we may rephrase them as follows. The "Principle of Identity" asserts that every statement of the form $p \supset p$ is true; that is, that every such statement is a tautology. The "Principle of Contradiction" asserts that every statement of the form $p \cdot \sim p$ is false; that is, that every such statement is self-contradictory. The "Principle of Excluded Middle" asserts that every statement of the form $p \vee \sim p$ is true; that is, that every such statement is a tautology.

Objections have been made to these "Principles" from time to time, but for the most part the objections seem to be based upon misunderstandings. The "Principle of Identity" has been objected to on the grounds that things change, for what was true, say, of the United States when it consisted of the thirteen original tiny states, is no longer true of the United States today. In one sense of the word "statement" this observation is correct; but that sense is not the one with which logic is concerned. Those "statements" whose truth values change with time are *elliptical* or incomplete expressions of propositions which do not change, and it is the latter with which logic deals. Thus the statement, "There are only thirteen states in the U.S.A." may be regarded as an *elliptical* or partial expression of "There were only thirteen states in the U.S.A. *in 1790,*" which is just as true in 1953 as it was in 1790. When we confine our attention to *complete* or *non-elliptical* statements, the "Principle of Identity" is perfectly true and unobjectionable.

The "Principle of Contradiction" has been objected to, especially by Hegelians, "General Semanticists," and Marxists, on the grounds that there *are* contradictions, or situations in which contradictory or conflicting forces are at work. That there are situations containing conflicting forces must be admitted: this is as true in the realm of mechanics as in the social and economic spheres. But it is a loose and inconvenient terminology to call these conflicting forces "contradictory." The heat applied to a contained gas, which tends to make it expand, and the container, which tends to keep it from expanding, may be described as conflicting with each other, but neither is the *negation* or *denial* or *contradictory* of the other. The private owner of a large factory, which requires thousands of laborers working together for its operation, may oppose and be opposed by the labor union which could never have been organized if its members had not been brought together to work in that factory; but neither owner nor union is the *negation* or *denial* or *contradictory* of the other. When understood in the sense in which it is intended, the "Principle of Contradiction" is unobjectionable and perfectly true.

The "Principle of Excluded Middle" has been the object of more attacks than either of the other "Principles." It has been urged that its acceptance leads to a "two-valued orientation" which implies, among other things, that everything is either *white* or *black,* with any middle ground "excluded." But although the statement "this is black" cannot be jointly true along with the statement "this is white" (where the word "this" refers to exactly the same thing in both statements), one is not the *denial* or *contradictory* of the other. Admittedly they cannot both be true, but they *can* both be false. They are contrary, but not contradictory. The negation or contradictory of "this is white," is "∼ this is white," and one of *these* two statements *must* be true—if the word "white" is used in precisely the same sense in both statements. When restricted to statements containing completely unambiguous and perfectly precise terms, the "Principle of Excluded Middle" also is perfectly true.

While the three "Principles" are true, it may be doubted whether they have the privileged and fundamental status traditionally assigned them. The first and third are not the only forms of tautologies, and the explicit contradiction $p \cdot \sim p$ is not the only contradictory form of statement. Yet the three "Laws of Thought" *can* be regarded as having a certain fundamental status in relation to truth tables. As we fill in subsequent columns by referring back to the initial columns, we are guided by the "Principle of Identity": when a T has been placed under a symbol in a certain row, in filling in all other columns under expressions containing that symbol, when we come to that row we consider that symbol still to be assigned a T. In filling out the initial columns, in each row we put either a T or an F, being guided by the "Principle of Excluded Middle"; and no-where do we put both a *T* and *F* together, being guided by the "Principle of Contradiction." The three "Laws of Thought" *can* be regarded as the basic principles governing the construction of truth tables.

Still, it should be remarked that when one attempts to set up logic *as a system,* the three "laws" are not merely no more "important" or "fruitful" than any others, but there are other tautologies which are *more* fruitful for purposes of deduction—and hence more important—than the three "Principles" discussed. A treatment of this point, however, lies beyond the scope of the present book.

Evaluating Extended

Arguments

I. FORMAL PROOF OF VALIDITY

Although in theory truth tables are adequate to test the validity of any argument of the general type here considered, in practice they grow unwieldy as the number of constituent statements increases. A more efficient method of establishing the validity of an extended argument is to *deduce* its conclusion from its premises by a sequence of elementary arguments each of which is known to be valid. This technique accords fairly well with ordinary methods of argumentation.

Consider, for example, the following argument:

If Anderson was nominated then he went to Boston.
If he went to Boston then he campaigned there.
If he campaigned there he met Douglas.
Anderson did not meet Douglas.
Either Anderson was nominated or someone more eligible was selected.

Therefore someone more eligible was selected.

Its validity is intuitively obvious, but let us consider the matter of *proof*. The discussion will be facilitated by translating the argument into our symbolism as:

$$A \supset B$$
$$B \supset C$$
$$C \supset D$$
$$\sim D$$
$$\underline{A \vee E}$$
$$\therefore E$$

To establish the validity of this argument by means of a truth table would require one with thirty-two rows, since there are five different simple statements involved. But we can *prove* the given argument valid by deducing its conclusion from its premisses by a sequence of four elementary valid arguments. From the first two premisses $A \supset B$ and $B \supset C$ we validly infer $A \supset C$ by a Hypothetical Syllogism. From $A \supset C$ and the third premiss $C \supset D$ we validly infer $A \supset D$ by another Hypothetical Syllogism. From $A \supset D$ and the fourth premiss $\sim D$ we validly infer $\sim A$ by *modus tollens*. And from $\sim A$ and the fifth premiss $A \vee E$ we validly infer E, the conclusion of the original argument, by a Disjunctive Syllogism. That the conclusion can be deduced from the five premisses of the original argument by four elementary valid arguments *proves* the original argument to be valid. Although the preceding discussion establishes the validity of the given argument, it has the defect of being extremely informal.

A more formal proof of validity is given by writing the premisses and the statements which follow from them in a single column, and setting off in another column, to the right of each statement, its "justification," or the reason we can give for including it in the proof. It is convenient to list all the premisses first, and to set down the conclusion slightly to one side, separated by a diagonal line from the premisses. The diagonal line automatically labels all statements above it as *premisses*. The formal proof is written as:

1. $A \supset B$
2. $B \supset C$
3. $C \supset D$
4. $\sim D$
5. $A \lor E /\therefore E$
6. $A \supset C$ from 1,2 by a Hypothetical Syllogism
7. $A \supset D$ from 6,3 by a Hypothetical Syllogism
8. $\sim A$ from 7,4 by *modus tollens*
9. E from 5,8 by a Disjunctive Syllogism.

A *formal proof* that a given argument is valid is a sequence of statements each of which is either a premiss of that argument or follows from preceding statements by an *elementary* valid argument, and such that the last statement in the sequence is the conclusion of the argument whose validity is being proved.

We define an *elementary valid argument* to be any argument which is a substitution instance of an elementary valid argument form. One matter to be emphasized is that *any* substitution instance of an elementary valid argument form is an elementary valid argument. Thus the argument

$$(A \cdot B) \supset [C \equiv (D \lor E)]$$
$$A \cdot B$$
$$\therefore C \equiv (D \lor E)$$

is an elementary valid argument since it is a substitution instance of the elementary valid argument form *modus ponens*. Since it results from $p \supset q, p \therefore q$ by substituting $A \cdot B$ for p and $C \equiv (D \lor E)$ for q, it is of that form even though *modus ponens* is not *the* form of the given argument.

Modus ponens is a very elementary valid argument form indeed, but what *other* valid argument forms are to be counted as "elementary"? Rather than attempt to give any sort of general theoretical definition of "elementary valid argument form," we shall define that term by *complete* enumeration, giving a list of all such forms. Any argument is an elementary valid argument if it is a substitution instance of one of the argument forms in the following list:

ELEMENTARY VALID ARGUMENT FORMS

1. *Modus Ponens* (M.P.): $p \supset q, p \therefore q.$
2. *Modus Tollens* (M.T.): $p \supset q, \sim q \therefore \sim p.$
3. Hypothetical Syllogism (H.S.): $p \supset q, q \supset r \therefore p \supset r.$
4. Disjunctive Syllogism (D.S.): $p \vee q, \sim p \therefore q.$
5. Constructive Dilemma (C.D.): $(p \supset q) \cdot (r \supset s), p \vee r \therefore q \vee s.$
6. Destructive Dilemma (D.D.): $(p \supset q) \cdot (r \supset s), \sim q \vee \sim s$
   $\therefore \sim p \vee \sim r.$
7. Simplification (Simp.): $p \cdot q \therefore p.$
8. Conjunction (Conj.): $p, q \therefore p \cdot q.$
9. Addition (Add.): $p \therefore p \vee q.$

Logically equivalent expressions may be substituted for each other wherever they occur.

10. De Morgan's Theorems
    (De M): $\sim (p \cdot q) \equiv (\sim p \vee \sim q).$
    $\sim (p \vee q) \equiv (\sim p \cdot \sim q).$
11. Commutation (Com.): $(p \vee q) \equiv (q \vee p).$
    $(p \cdot q) \equiv (q \cdot p).$
12. Association (Assoc.): $[p \vee (q \vee r)] \equiv [(p \vee q) \vee r].$
    $[p \cdot (q \cdot r)] \equiv [(p \cdot q) \cdot r].$
13. Distribution (Dist.): $[p \cdot (q \vee r)] \equiv [(p \cdot q) \vee (p \cdot r)].$
    $[p \vee (q \cdot r)] \equiv [(p \vee q) \cdot (p \vee r)].$
14. Double Negation (D.N.): $p \equiv \sim \sim p.$
15. Transposition (Trans.): $(p \supset q) \equiv (\sim q \supset \sim p).$
16. Definition of Material
    Implication (Impl.): $(p \supset q) \equiv (\sim p \vee q).$
17. Definitions of Material $(p \equiv q) \equiv [(p \supset q) \cdot (q \supset p)].$
    Equivalence (Equiv.): $(p \equiv q) \equiv [(p \cdot q) \vee (\sim p \cdot \sim q)].$
18. Exportation (Exp.): $[(p \cdot q) \supset r] \equiv [p \supset (q \supset r)].$
19. Tautology (Taut.): $p \equiv (p \vee p).$

The nineteen elementary valid argument forms listed are for the most part obvious. The first nine of them are argument forms which may be proved valid by means of truth tables. They occur frequently in ordinary discourse, and we shall make considerable use of them in evaluating extended arguments. The remainder are all instances of what may be called the Principle of Substitution. We may accept it here as intuitively valid on the grounds that we are dealing exclusively with truth functional expressions, so that if any part is replaced by another *of the same truth value,* the truth value of the entire expression will remain unchanged. The equivalences listed are all either tautologies or definitions—and that the alternative definitions of $p \equiv q$ are logically equivalent is readily established by the truth table method.

The names listed are for the most part standard. The abbreviations following the names should be used in referring to the elementary valid argument forms which justify the various steps of a formal proof, and are introduced for the purpose of allowing formal proofs to be set down with a minimum of writing. Some of the names are borrowed from corresponding or parallel equivalences within mathematics.

The nineteen valid forms listed are somewhat redundant, in the sense that they do not constitute a bare minimum which would be sufficient for our purpose, which is to construct formal proofs of validity for extended arguments. For example, *modus tollens* could be dropped from the list without any real weakening of our proof apparatus, for any step depending upon *modus tollens* can be justified by appealing to other forms in the list instead. Thus in the preceding formal proof step 8, $\sim A$, was deduced from steps 4 and 7, $\sim D$ and $A \supset D$, by *modus tollens,* but if *modus tollens* were eliminated as a reference form, we could still deduce $\sim A$ from $A \supset D$ and $\sim D$. This could be done by inserting the intermediate step $\sim D \supset \sim A$, which follows from $A \supset D$ by the Principle of Transposition (Trans.), and then obtaining $\sim A$ from $\sim D \supset \sim A$ and $\sim D$ by *modus ponens* (M.P.). But *modus tollens* is such a commonly used and intuitively obvious valid argument form that it has been included anyway. Others of the nineteen are also redundant in this same sense.

The list of nineteen elementary valid argument forms is characterized not only by redundancy, but also by a certain sort of deficiency. For example, although the argument $A \vee B$,

$\sim B \therefore A$ is intuitively valid, its form $p \lor q, \sim q \therefore p$ is not included in our list of elementary valid argument forms. The conclusion A does not follow from the premises $A \lor B$ and $\sim B$ by any single elementary valid argument form, although it can be deduced from them by *two* elementary valid arguments. A formal proof of validity for the given argument can be written as:

1. $A \lor B$
2. $\sim B \; / \therefore A$
3. $B \lor A$ 1, Com.
4. A 3,2, D.S.

We could eliminate the indicated deficiency by adding the valid argument form $p \lor q, \sim q \therefore p$ to our list, but if we made additions for all such cases we should end up with a list which was too long and therefore unmanageable.

The notion of *formal proof* is an *effective* notion. What this statement means is that it can be decided quite mechanically, in a finite number of steps, whether or not a given sequence of statements constitutes a formal proof (with reference to a given list of elementary valid argument forms). No *thinking* is required, either in the sense of thinking about what the statements in the sequence "mean," or in the sense of using logical intuition to check any step's validity. Only two things are required, of which the first is the ability to see that a statement occurring in one place is identically the same as a statement occurring in another, for we must be able to check that some statements in the proof are premises of the argument being proved valid, and that the last statement in the proof is the conclusion of that argument. The second thing required is the ability to see whether a given statement has a certain pattern or not, that is, to see if it is a substitution instance of a given statement form.

Thus any question about whether or not the preceding sequence of statements is a formal proof of validity can be settled in a completely mechanical fashion. That steps 1 and 2 are the premisses, and step 4 is the conclusion of the given argument is obvious on inspection. That 3 follows from preceding steps by one of the given elementary valid argument forms can be decided in a finite number of steps—even where the notation "1, Com." is not written at the side. The explanatory notation in the second column is a help and should always be included, but it is not, strictly speaking, part of the proof itself. At every step, there are only a finite number of preceding steps and only a finite number of reference forms to be consulted. Although time-consuming, it can be verified by inspection and comparison of shapes that 3 does not follow from 1 and 2 by *modus ponens,* or by *modus tollens,* or by a Hypothetical Syllogism, . . . And so on, until in following this procedure we come to the question of whether or not 3 follows from 1 by the Principle of Commutation, and there we see, simply by looking at the forms, that it *does.* In the same way the legitimacy of any statement can be tested in a finite number of steps, none of which involves anything more than comparing forms or shapes. It is to preserve this property of effectiveness that we lay down the rule that only one step should be taken at a time. One might be tempted to shorten a proof by combining steps, but the space and time saved are negligible. More important is the effectiveness we achieve by taking each step by means of one single elementary valid argument at a time.

Although a formal proof of validity is effective in the sense that it can be mechanically decided of any presented sequence whether or not it is a proof, *constructing* such a formal proof is *not* an effective procedure. In this respect formal proofs differ from truth tables. The use of truth tables is *completely* mechanical: given any argument of the sort with which we are now concerned, we can always construct a truth table to test its validity by following the simple rules of procedure set forth in the preceding chapter. But we have no effective or mechanical rules for the construction of formal proofs. Here one must *think* or "figure out" where to begin and how to proceed. Nevertheless, proving an argument valid by means of a formal proof is frequently much easier than the purely mechanical construction of a truth table with perhaps hundreds or even thousands of rows.

Although we have no purely mechanical rules for constructing formal proofs, some rough-and-ready rules of thumb or hints on procedure may be suggested. The first is simply to begin deducing conclusions from the given premisses by elementary valid arguments. As more and more of these sub-conclusions become available as premisses for further deductions the greater the likelihood of being able to find a way of deducing the conclusion of the argument to be proved valid. Another method is to work backward from the conclusion by looking for some statement or statements from which it can be deduced, and then trying to deduce those intermediate statements from the premisses. There is, however, no substitute for practice as a method of acquiring facility in constructing formal proofs of validity.

EXERCISES

I. Each of the following is a formal proof of validity for the indicated argument. State the "justification" for each step which is not a premiss:

1.
   1. $A \supset B$
   2. $A \cdot C / \therefore B$
   3. A
   4. B

2.
   1. $\sim (D \lor E)$
   2. $F \supset D / \therefore \sim F$
   3. $\sim D \cdot \sim E$
   4. $\sim D$
   5. $\sim F$

3.
   1. $G \lor (H \supset I)$
   2. $\sim G \cdot \sim I / \therefore \sim H$
   3. $\sim G$
   4. $H \supset I$
   5. $\sim I \cdot \sim G$
   6. $\sim I$
   7. $\sim H$

4.
   1. $J \supset K$
   2. $(K \cdot L) \supset M /$
      $\therefore L \supset (J \supset M)$
   3. $K \supset (L \supset M)$
   4. $J \supset (L \supset M)$
   5. $(J \cdot L) \supset M$
   6. $(L \cdot J) \supset M$
   7. $L \supset (J \supset M)$

5. 1. $(P \supset Q) \supset (\sim R \supset S)$
    2. $\sim Q \supset S$
    3. $P \supset \sim S /\therefore R \vee S$
    4. $\sim \sim S \supset \sim P$
    5. $S \supset \sim P$
    6. $\sim Q \supset \sim P$
    7. $P \supset Q$
    8. $\sim R \supset S$
    9. $\sim \sim R \vee S$
    10. $R \vee S$

6. 1. $N \supset O$
    2. $P \supset Q$
    3. $\sim N \supset (\sim P \supset R)$
    4. $\sim R /\therefore O \vee Q$
    5. $(\sim N \cdot \sim P) \supset R$
    6. $\sim (\sim N \cdot \sim P)$
    7. $\sim \sim N \vee \sim \sim P$
    8. $N \vee \sim \sim P$
    9. $N \vee P$
    10. $(N \supset O) \cdot (P \supset Q)$
    11. $O \vee Q$

7. 1. $(A \cdot B) \supset (C \cdot D)$
    2. $(E \supset A) \cdot (F \supset G)$
    3. $(F \supset B) \cdot (D \supset G)$
    4. $\sim C /\therefore E \supset \sim F$
    5. $\sim C \vee \sim D$
    6. $\sim (C \cdot D)$
    7. $\sim (A \cdot B)$
    8. $\sim A \vee \sim B$
    9. $E \supset A$
    10. $F \supset B$
    11. $(E \supset A) \cdot (F \supset B)$
    12. $\sim E \vee \sim F$
    13. $E \supset \sim F$

8. 1. $A \vee (B \cdot C)$
    2. $\sim B \vee (C \cdot A) /\therefore A$
    3. $(A \vee B) \cdot (A \vee C)$
    4. $A \vee B$
    5. $\sim \sim A \vee B$
    6. $\sim A \supset B$
    7. $(\sim B \vee C) \cdot (\sim B \vee A)$
    8. $(\sim B \vee A) \cdot (\sim B \vee C)$
    9. $\sim B \vee A$
    10. $B \supset A$
    11. $\sim A \supset A$
    12. $\sim \sim A \vee A$
    13. $A \vee A$
    14. A

9. 1. $(A \supset B) \cdot (B \supset C)$
    2. $(D \supset A) \cdot (C \supset D) /\therefore (\sim A \vee \sim C) \supset (\sim A \cdot \sim C)$
    3. $A \supset B$
    4. $(B \supset C) \cdot (A \supset B)$
    5. $B \supset C$
    6. $A \supset C$
    7. $D \supset A$
    8. $(C \supset D) \cdot (D \supset A)$
    9. $C \supset D$
    10. $C \supset A$
    11. $(A \supset C) \cdot (C \supset A)$
    12. $A \equiv C$
    13. $(A \cdot C) \vee (\sim A \cdot \sim C)$

14. $\sim \sim (A \cdot C) \text{ v } (\sim A \cdot \sim C)$
15. $\sim (A \cdot C) \supset (\sim A \cdot \sim C)$
16. $(\sim A \text{ v} \sim C) \supset (\sim A \cdot \sim C)$

10.
1. $A \cdot (B \cdot C)$
2. $(A \cdot B) \cdot (E \text{ v } F)$
3. $A \supset (F \supset \sim B)$
4. $(\sim G \text{ v} \sim B) \text{ v} \sim E / \therefore \sim G$
5. $[(A \cdot B) \cdot E] \text{ v } [(A \cdot B) \cdot F]$
6. $A \supset (\sim \sim B \supset \sim F)$
7. $A \supset (B \supset \sim F)$
8. $(A \cdot B) \supset \sim F$
9. $\sim (A \cdot B) \text{ v} \sim F$
10. $\sim [(A \cdot B) \cdot F]$

11. $[(A \cdot B) \cdot F] \text{ v } [(A \cdot B) \cdot E]$
12. $(A \cdot B) \cdot E$
13. $A \cdot (B \cdot E)$
14. $(B \cdot E) \cdot A$
15. $B \cdot E$
16. $\sim G \text{ v } (\sim B \text{ v} \sim E)$
17. $\sim \sim (B \cdot E)$
18. $\sim (\sim B \text{ v} \sim E)$
19. $G \supset (\sim B \text{ v} \sim E)$
20. $\sim G$

II. Construct a formal proof of validity for each of the following arguments, in each case using the suggested notation:

1. Either the manager didn't notice the change, or else he approves of it. He noticed it all right. So he must approve of it. (*N, A*)
2. The oxygen in the tube either combined with the filament to form an oxide, or else it vanished completely. The oxygen in the tube could not have vanished completely. Therefore the oxygen in the tube combined with the filament to form an oxide. (*C, V*)
3. If a statesman who sees his former opinions to be wrong does not alter his course he is guilty of deceit; and if he does alter his course he is open to a charge of inconsistency. He either alters his course or he doesn't. Therefore, he is either guilty of deceit or else he is open to a charge of inconsistency. (*A, D, I*)
4. It is not the case that he either forgot or wasn't able to finish. Therefore, he was able to finish. (*F, A*)
5. If the litmus paper turns red then the solution is acid. Hence if the litmus paper turns red then either the solution is acid or something is wrong somewhere. (*R, A, W*)
6. He can have many friends only if he respects them as individuals. If he respects them as individuals then he cannot expect them all to behave alike. He does have many friends. Therefore, he does not expect them all to behave alike. (*F, R, E*)
7. If the victim had money in his pockets, then robbery wasn't the motive for the crime. But robbery or vengeance was the motive

for the crime. The victim had money in his pockets. Therefore, vengeance must have been the motive for the crime. (*M, R, V*)

8. Napoleon is to be condemned if he usurped power that was not rightfully his own. Either Napoleon was a legitimate monarch or else he usurped power that was not rightfully his own. Napoleon was not a legitimate monarch. So Napoleon is to be condemned. (*C, U, L*)

9. If we extend further credit on the Wilkins account they will have a moral obligation to accept our bid on their next project. We can figure a more generous margin of profit in preparing our estimates if they have a moral obligation to accept our bid on their next project. Figuring a more generous margin of profit in preparing our estimates will cause our general financial condition to improve considerably. Hence a considerable improvement in our general financial condition will follow from our extension of further credit on the Wilkins account. (*C, M, P, I*)

10. If the laws are good and their enforcement is strict, then crime will diminish. If strict enforcement of law will make crime diminish, then our problem is a practical one. The laws are good. Therefore, our problem is a practical one. (*G, S, D, P*)

11. Had Roman citizenship guaranteed civil liberties, then Roman citizens would have enjoyed religious freedom. Had Roman citizens enjoyed religious freedom, there would have been no persecution of the early Christians. But the early Christians were persecuted. Hence Roman citizenship could not have guaranteed civil liberties. (*G, F, P*)

12. If the first disjunct of a disjunction is true, the disjunction as a whole is true. Therefore, if both the first and second disjuncts of the disjunction are true, then the disjunction as a whole is true. (*F, W, S*)

13. If the new courthouse is to be conveniently located, it will have to be situated in the heart of the city; and if it is to be adequate to its function, it will have to be built large enough to house all the city offices. If the new courthouse is situated in the heart of the city and is built large enough to house all the city offices, then its cost will run to over a million dollars. Its cost cannot exceed a million dollars. Therefore, either the new courthouse will have an inconvenient location or it will be inadequate to its function. (*C, H, A, L, O*)

14. Jones will come if he gets the message, provided that he is still interested. Although he didn't come he is still interested. Therefore, he didn't get the message. (*C, M, I*)

15. If the Mosaic account of the cosmogony is strictly correct, the sun was not created till the fourth day. And if the sun was not created till the fourth day, it could not have been the cause of the alternation of day and night for the first three days. But either the word "day" is used in Scripture in a different sense from that in which it is commonly accepted now, or else the sun must have been the cause of the alternation of day and night for the first three days. Hence it follows that either the Mosaic account of the cosmogony is not strictly correct, or else the word "day" is used in Scripture in a different sense from that in which it is commonly accepted now. (*M, C, A, D*)

16. If the teller or the cashier had pushed the alarm button, the vault would have locked automatically and the police would have arrived within three minutes. Had the police arrived within three minutes, the robbers' car would have been overtaken. But the robbers' car was not overtaken. Therefore, the teller did not push the alarm button. (*T, C, V, P, O*)

17. If a man is always guided by his sense of duty, he must forego the enjoyments of many pleasures; and if he is always guided by his desire for pleasure, he must often neglect his duty. A man is either always guided by his sense of duty or always guided by his desire for pleasure. If a man is always guided by his sense of duty, he does not often neglect his duty, and if he is always guided by his desire for pleasure, he does not forego the enjoyment of many pleasures. Therefore, a man must forego the enjoyment of many pleasures if and only if he does not often neglect his duty. (*D, F, P, N*)

18. The husband is wealthy, and his bride is poor but honest. If a bride is poor and her husband is wealthy, then either she has made a good match, or else they will be childless or will have family trouble. She did not make a good match, yet they are neither quarrelsome nor have they any family trouble. Therefore, they are childless. (*W, P, H, G, C, F, Q*)

19. Either the robber came in the door, or else the crime was an inside one and one of the servants is implicated. The robber could come in the door only if the latch had been raised from

the inside; but one of the servants is surely implicated if the latch was raised from the inside. Therefore, one of the servants is implicated. (*D, I, S, L*)

20. If I pay the tailor I won't have any money left. I can take my girl to the dance only if I have money. She'll be unhappy unless I take her to the dance. But if I don't pay the tailor he won't let me have my suit, and without the suit I certainly can't take my girl to the dance. I must either pay the tailor or not pay him. So my girl is bound to be unhappy! (*P, M, D, U, S*)

II. PROOF OF INVALIDITY

For an invalid argument there is of course no formal proof of validity. But if we fail to discover a formal proof of validity for a given argument, this failure does not prove that the argument is invalid and that no such proof can be constructed. It *may* mean only that we have not tried hard enough. Our inability to find a proof of validity *may* be caused by the fact that the argument is not valid, but it may be caused instead by our own lack of ingenuity—as a consequence of the non-effective character of the process of proof construction. Not being able to construct a formal proof of its validity does *not* prove an argument to be invalid. What does constitute a proof that a given argument is invalid?

The method about to be described is closely related to the truth table method, although it is a great deal shorter. It will be helpful to recall how an invalid argument is proved invalid by a truth table. If a single case (row) can be found in which truth values are assigned to the statement variables in such a way that the premises are made true and the conclusion false, then the argument is invalid. If we can somehow make an assignment of truth values to the simple constituent statements of an argument which will make its premises true and its conclusion false, making that assignment will suffice to prove the argument invalid. To make such an assignment is, in effect, what the truth table does. But if we can make such an assignment of truth values without actually constructing the whole truth table, a certain amount of work will be eliminated.

Consider the argument:

If the governor favors public housing, then he is in favor of restricting the scope of private enterprise.

If the governor were a communist, then he would be in favor of restricting the scope of private enterprise.

Therefore if the governor favors public housing then he is a communist.

This is symbolized as:

$$P \supset R$$
$$C \supset R$$
$$\therefore P \supset C$$

and we can prove it invalid without having to construct a complete truth table. First we ask: what assignment of truth values is required to make the conclusion false? It is clear that a hypothetical is false only when its antecedent is true and its consequent false. Hence assigning the truth value "true" to P and "false" to C will make the conclusion $P \supset C$ false. Now if the truth value "true" is assigned to R, both premises are made true, since a (material) hypothetical is always true when its consequent is true. We can say, then, that if the truth value "true" is assigned to P and to R, and the truth value "false" is assigned to C, the argument will have true premises and a false conclusion and is thus proved to be invalid.

This method of proving invalidity is an alternative to the truth table method of proof. The two methods are closely related, however, and the essential connection between them should be realized. In effect, what we did when we made the indicated assignment of truth values was to construct *one row* of the given argument's truth table. The relationship can perhaps be seen more clearly when the truth value assignments are written out horizontally, as

P	R	C	$P \supset R$	$C \supset R$	$P \supset C$
true	true	false	true	true	false

in which form they constitute one row of the truth table for the given argument. An argument is proved invalid if there is at least one row of its truth table in which all its premises are true but its conclusion is false. Consequently we need not examine *all* rows of its truth table to discover an argument's invalidity: the discovery of a single row in which its premises are all true and its conclusion false will suffice. The present method of proving invalidity is a method of constructing such a row without having to construct the entire truth table.

The present method is shorter than writing out a truth table, and the amount of time and work saved is proportionally greater for arguments involving a greater number of constituent simple statements. For arguments with a considerable number of premises, or with premises of considerable complexity, the relevant assignment of truth values may not be so easy to make. A certain amount of trial and error may be necessary. But it will be shorter and easier than writing out a complete truth table.

EXERCISES

Prove the invalidity of each of the following by the method of assigning truth values:

1. $A \supset B$
   $C \supset D$
   $A \lor C$
   $\therefore B \cdot D$

2. $E \lor \sim F$
   $\sim (\sim H \cdot G)$
   $\sim (\sim E \cdot \sim G)$
   $\therefore F \lor H$

3. $I \supset (J \lor K)$
   $(K \cdot L) \supset M$
   $\sim M$
   $\therefore \sim I$

4. $N \supset (O \lor P)$
   $O \supset (Q \lor R)$
   $P \supset (Q \lor S)$
   $R \supset [(Q \cdot S) \supset \sim R]$
   $\therefore \sim N$

5. $T \supset (U \lor V)$
   $U \supset (W \cdot X)$
   $W \supset (X \supset Y)$
   $\sim (T \cdot Y)$
   $\therefore T \equiv V$

6. $W \equiv (X \lor Y)$
   $X \equiv (Z \cdot T)$
   $Z \equiv (T \equiv V)$
   $\sim (W \equiv V)$
   $\therefore \sim W$

7. $K \supset (L \lor M)$
   $(M \supset N) \cdot (\sim L \supset \sim N)$
   $N \supset (O \lor P)$
   $\sim O \supset (Q \supset P)$
   Q
   $\therefore K \supset (N \lor P)$

8. $F \supset (G \cdot H)$
   $(\sim G \lor I) \lor \sim H$
   $J \lor (K \lor \sim I)$
   $(\sim K \lor \sim L) \cdot L$
   $(N \lor \sim J) \lor \sim M$
   $\therefore F \supset N$

9. $A \lor (B \cdot G)$
$(A \lor C) \lor (D \lor E)$
$D \equiv E$
$(C \supset \sim D) \cdot (\sim C \supset \sim F)$
$G \supset (\sim F \supset \sim G)$
$(A \lor D) \cdot (C \lor H)$
$E \equiv A$
$\overline{\therefore G \cdot H}$

10. $(E \supset A) \cdot (B \supset F)$
$A \supset (\sim C \supset B)$
$\sim (C \cdot D)$
$(G \cdot \sim D) \lor (D \cdot \sim G)$
$(H \supset I) \cdot (G \supset J)$
$\sim J \lor \sim H$
$(H \lor D) \cdot (H \lor C)$
$\overline{\therefore E \equiv F}$

III. INCONSISTENCY

If no truth value assignment can be given to the constituent simple statements of an argument which makes its premisses true and its conclusion false, then the argument must be *valid*. Although this follows from the definition of "validity," it has a curious consequence. Consider the following argument, whose premisses appear to be utterly irrelevant to its conclusion:

If the airplane had engine trouble it would have landed at Bridge-port.
If the airplane did not have engine trouble it would have landed at Cleveland.
The airplane did not land at either Bridgeport or Cleveland.
Therefore the airplane must have landed in Denver.

and its symbolic translation:

$$A \supset B$$
$$\sim A \supset C$$
$$\sim (B \lor C)$$
$$\overline{\therefore D}$$

Any attempt to assign truth values to its constituent statements so as to make the conclusion false and the premisses all true is doomed to failure. If we ignore the conclusion and concentrate our attention upon the other objective, that of making all the premisses true by an assignment of truth values to their constituent simple statements, we are bound to fail even here, in this apparently less ambitious project.

The reason the premisses cannot be made true and the conclusion false is that the premises cannot possibly be made true *in any case* by *any* truth value assignment. No truth value assignment can make the premises true because they are *inconsistent with each other.* Their conjunction is *self-contradictory,* being a substitution instance of a self-contradictory statement form. Were we to construct a truth table for the given argument we should find that in every row at least one of the premises is false. There is no row in which the premises are all true, hence there is no row in which the premises are all true *and* the conclusion false. Hence the truth table for this argument would establish its *validity.* Its validity can also be established by the following formal proof:

1. $A \supset B$
2. $\sim A \supset C$
3. $\sim (B \vee C)/\therefore D$
4. $\sim B \cdot \sim C$ 3, De M.
5. $\sim B$ 4, Simp.
6. $\sim A$ 1,5, M.T.
7. C 2,6, M.P.
8. $\sim C \cdot \sim B$ 4, Com.
9. $\sim C$ 8, Simp.
10. $C \vee D$ 7, Add.
11. D 10,9, D.S.

In this proof the steps up through 9 are devoted to making explicit the inconsistency which was implicitly contained in the premisses. That inconsistency emerges in steps 7 and 9, which assert C and $\sim C$, respectively. Once this explicit contradiction is achieved, the conclusion follows swiftly by the Principle of Addition and the Disjunctive Syllogism.

Thus we see that if a set of premisses is inconsistent, those premisses will validly yield *any* conclusion, no matter how irrelevant. The essence of the matter is more simply shown in the case of the following argument, whose openly inconsistent premisses allow us validly to infer an irrelevant and fantastic conclusion.

Today is Sunday. Today is not Sunday.
Therefore the moon is made of green cheese.

In symbols, we have:

1. S
2. $\sim S /\mathrel{\therefore} M$

The formal proof of its validity is almost immediately obvious:

3. $S \vee M$ 1, Add.
4. M 3,2, D.S.

What is wrong here? How can such meager and even inconsistent premises make any argument in which they occur valid? It should be noted first that if an argument is valid because of an inconsistency in its premises, *it cannot possibly be a sound argument.* If they are inconsistent with each other, the premisses cannot possibly all be *true.* No conclusion can be *established as true* by an argument with inconsistent premisses, since its premises are of necessity false themselves.

The present situation is closely related to the so-called "paradox of material implication." In discussing the latter, we observed that the statement form $\sim p \supset (p \supset q)$ is a tautology, having all its substitution instances true. Its formulation in English asserts that *a false statement materially implies any statement whatever,* which is easily proved by means of truth tables. What has been established in the present discussion is that the argument form $p, \sim p \mathrel{\therefore} q$ is *valid.* Its formulation in English asserts that *any argument with inconsistent premises is valid, regardless of what its conclusion may be.* It may be established either by a truth table or by the kind of formal proof given above.

The premises of a *valid* argument imply its conclusion not merely in the sense of "material" implication, but *logically* or "strictly." In a valid argument, it is logically impossible for the premises to be true when the conclusion is false. And this situation obtains whenever it is logically impossible for the premises to be true, even when the question of the truth or falsehood of the conclusion is ignored. Its analogy with the corresponding property of material implication has led some writers on logic to call this a "paradox of *strict* implication." In view of the normal definition of "validity," however, it does not seem to be especially "paradoxical." The alleged paradox arises primarily from treating a technical term as if it were a term of ordinary everyday language.

The foregoing discussion helps to explain why consistency is so highly prized. One reason, of course, is that inconsistent statements cannot both be true. This fact underlies the strategy of cross-examination, where an attorney may seek to maneuver a hostile witness into contradicting himself. If testimony contains incompatible or inconsistent assertions, it cannot all be true, and the witness's credibility is destroyed—or at least shaken. But another reason why inconsistency is so repugnant is that any and every conclusion *follows logically* from inconsistent statements taken as premises. Inconsistent statements are not "meaningless," their trouble is just the opposite. They mean too much—they mean everything, in the sense of implying everything. And if *everything* is asserted, half of what is asserted is surely *false,* since every statement has a denial.

The preceding discussion incidentally provides us with an answer to the old riddle: What happens when an irresistible force meets an immovable object? The description involves a contradiction. For an irresistible force to meet an immovable object, both must exist. There must be an irresistible force and there must be an immovable object. But if there is an irresistible force there can be no immovable object. Here is the contradiction made explicit: there is an immovable object, and there is no immovable object. Given these inconsistent premises, *any* conclusion may validly be inferred. So the correct answer to the question

What happens when an irresistible force meets an immovable object?

is

Everything!

EXERCISES

For each of the following, decide whether or not the indicated conclusion follows validly from the stated premises. If it does, construct
a formal proof of validity; if not, prove invalidity by the method of
assigning truth values to the simple statements involved.

1. If the linguistics investigators are correct, then if more than one
   dialect was present in Ancient Greece then different tribes came
   down at different times from the North. If different tribes came
   down at different times from the North they must have
   come from the Danube River valley. But archeological excavations would have revealed traces of different tribes there if different tribes had come down at different times from the North,
   and archeological excavations have revealed no such traces there.
   Hence if more than one dialect was present in Ancient Greece
   then the linguistics investigators are not correct. (*C, M, D, V, A*)
2. If there are the ordinary symptoms of a cold and the patient has
   a high temperature, then if there are tiny spots on his skin, he
   has measles. Of course the patient cannot have measles if his
   record shows that he has had them before. The patient does
   have a high temperature, and his record shows that he has had
   measles before. Besides the ordinary symptoms of a cold there
   are tiny spots on his skin. I conclude that the patient has a virus
   infection. (*O, T, S, M, R, V*)
3. If God were willing to prevent evil, but unable to do so, he
   would be impotent; if he were able to prevent evil, but unwilling
   to do so, he would be malevolent. Evil can exist only if God is
   either unwilling or unable to prevent it. There is evil. If God
   exists, he is neither impotent nor malevolent. Therefore God
   does not exist. (*W, A, I, M, E, G*)
4. If I buy a new car this spring or have my old car fixed, then I'll
   get up to Canada this summer and stop off in Duluth. I'll visit
   my parents if I stop of in Duluth. If I visit my parents they'll
   insist upon my spending the summer with them. If they insist
   upon my spending the summer with them I'll be there till
   autumn. But if I stay there till autumn, then I won't get to
   Canada after all! So I won't have my old car fixed. (*N, F, C, D,
   V, I, A*)

5. If Smith is intelligent and studies hard then he will get good grades and pass his courses. If Smith studies hard but lacks intelligence then his efforts will be appreciated, and if his efforts are appreciated then he will pass his courses. If Smith is intelligent then he studies hard. Therefore Smith will pass his courses. (*I, S, G, P, A*)

6. If there is a single norm for greatness of poetry, then Milton and Edgar Guest cannot both be great poets. If either Pope or Dryden is regarded as a great poet, then Wordsworth is certainly no great poet; but if Wordsworth is no great poet, then neither is Keats or Shelley. But after all, even though Edgar Guest is not, Dryden and Keats are both great poets. Hence there is no single norm for greatness of poetry. (*N, M, G, P, D, W, K, S*)

7. If the butler was present he would have been seen, and if he was seen he would have been questioned. If he had been questioned he would have replied, and if he had replied he would have been heard. But the butler was not heard. If the butler was neither seen nor heard then he must have been on duty, and if he was on duty he must have been present. Therefore the butler was questioned. (*P, S, Q, R, H, D*)

8. If the butler told the truth then the window was closed when he entered the room; and if the gardener told the truth then the automatic sprinkler system was not operating on the evening of the murder. If the butler and the gardener are both lying, then a conspiracy must exist to protect someone in the house and there would have been a little pool of water on the floor just inside the window. We know that the window could not have been closed when the butler entered the room. There was a little pool of water on the floor just inside the window. So if there is a conspiracy to protect someone in the house then the gardener did not tell the truth. (*B, W, G, S, C, P*)

9. Their chief would leave the country if he feared capture, and he would not leave the country unless he feared capture. If he feared capture and left the country, the enemy's espionage network would be demoralized and powerless to harm us. If he did not fear capture and remained in the country it would mean that he was ignorant of our own agents' work. If he is really ignorant of our agents' work, then our agents can consolidate their positions within the enemy's organization; and if our agents can

consolidate their positions there they will render the enemy's espionage network powerless to harm us. Therefore the enemy's espionage network will be powerless to harm us. (*L, F, D, P, I, C*)

10. If the investigators of extra-sensory perception are regarded as honest, then considerable evidence for extra-sensory perception must be admitted; and the doctrine of clairvoyance must be considered seriously if extra-sensory perception is tentatively accepted as a fact. If considerable evidence for extra-sensory perception is admitted, then it must be tentatively accepted as a fact and an effort must be made to explain it. The doctrine of clairvoyance must be considered seriously if we are prepared to take seriously that class of phenomena called "occult"; and if we are prepared to take seriously that class of phenomena called "occult," a new respect must be paid to mediums. If we pursue the matter further, then if a new respect must be paid to mediums, we must take seriously their claims to communicate with the dead. We do pursue the matter further, but still we are practically committed to believing in ghosts if we take seriously the mediums' claims to communicate with the dead. Hence if the investigators of extra-sensory perception are regarded as honest, we are practically committed to believing in ghosts. (*H, A, C, F, E, O, M, P, D, G*)

CHAPTER TEN

Propositional Functions

I. SINGULAR PROPOSITIONS

The logical techniques presented in the two preceding chapters permit us to discriminate between valid and invalid arguments of one certain type. Arguments of that type are roughly characterized as those whose validity depends upon the ways in which the simple statements they contain are truth-functionally combined into compound statements. There are, however, *other* types of arguments to which the validity criteria of the two preceding chapters do not apply. An example of a different type is the following obviously valid argument:

> All humans are mortal.
> Socrates is human.
> _____
> Therefore Socrates is mortal.

Were we to apply to this argument the evaluation methods previously introduced, we would symbolize it as:

$$M$$
$$S$$
$$\therefore H$$

But in this notation it appears to be invalid. The techniques of symbolic logic presented thus far cannot be applied to arguments of this new type. The validity of the given argument *does not depend* upon the way in which simple statements are compounded, for no compound statements occur in it. Its validity depends rather upon the inner logical structure of the noncompound statements involved. To formulate methods for testing the validity of arguments of this new sort, techniques for describing and symbolizing non-compound statements by reference to their inner logical structure must be devised.*

The simplest kind of non-compound statement is illustrated by the second premiss of the preceding argument, "Socrates is human." Statements of this kind have traditionally been called *singular propositions*. An (affirmative) singular proposition asserts that a particular individual possesses a specified property. In the case of the present example, ordinary grammar and traditional logic would agree in classifying "Socrates" as the *subject* term and "human" as the *predicate* term. The subject term denotes a particular individual and the predicate term designates some property which the individual is asserted to have.

It is clear that one and the same subject term can occur in different singular propositions. Thus we have the term "Socrates" as subject term in each of the following: "Socrates is mortal," "Socrates is female," "Socrates is wise," and "Socrates is beautiful." Of these, some are true (the first and third) and some are false (the second and fourth).† It is also clear that one and the same predicate term can occur in a number of singular propositions. Thus we have the term "human" as predicate term in each of the following: "Aristotle is human," "Brazil is human," "Chicago is human," and "Diogenes is hu-

---

* It was to arguments of this type that the classical or Aristotelian logic was primarily devoted, as described in Chapters Five and Six. The older methods, however, do not possess the generality or power of the newer symbolic logic and cannot be extended to cover asyllogistic inference.

† We shall follow the custom of ignoring the time factor, and will use the verb "is" in the tenseless sense of "is, will be, or has been." Where considerations of time change are crucial, the somewhat more complicated methods of the logic of relations are needed for an adequate treatment.

man." Of these, some are true (the first and fourth) and some are false (the second and third).

It should be clear from the foregoing that the word "individual" is used to refer not only to persons, but to any *thing* —such as a country, a city, or in fact to anything of which a property can be meaningfully predicated. In all the examples given thus far the predicate term has been an *adjective*. From the point of view of grammar the distinction between adjective and noun is of considerable importance, but it is without significance from the point of view of logic. Thus there is logically no difference between "Socrates is mortal," and "Socrates is a mortal." Nor is there any difference between "Socrates is wise," and "Socrates is a wise individual." A predicate may be either an adjective or a noun, or even a verb, as in "Aristotle writes," which can alternatively be expressed as "Aristotle is a writer."

Assuming that we know the difference between individuals which have properties and the properties they may have, we can introduce and use two different kinds of symbols for referring to these two different types of entities. In the following discussion we shall use small or lower case letters from *"a"* through *"w"* to denote particular individuals. It will usually be convenient to denote an individual by the first letter of its (or his) name. Thus in the present context we should use the letters *"s," "a," "b," "c," "d,"* to denote the individuals Socrates, Aristotle, Brazil, Chicago, and Diogenes, respectively. We shall use capital letters to symbolize properties, and it will be convenient to use the same guiding principle here, using the letters *"H," "M," "F," "W," "B,"* to symbolize the properties of being human, of being mortal, of being female, of being wise, and of being beautiful, respectively.

Having two groups of symbols, one for individuals and one for properties of individuals, we can adopt the convention that writing a property symbol immediately to the left of an individual symbol will constitute the symbolic translation of the singular proposition which asserts that the particular individual named has the property specified. Thus the singular proposition "Socrates is human," will be symbolized as *"Hs."* The other singular propositions mentioned involving the predicate "human" are symbolized as *"Ha," "Hb," "Hc,"* and *"Hd."* All of these, it will be observed, have a certain common pattern, not to be symbolized as *"H"* by itself, but rather as *"H —"* where the *"—"* indicates that to the right of the predicate symbol another symbol—an individual symbol—occurs. Instead of using the dash symbol (*"—"*) as a place marker, it is customary to use the letter *"x"* (which is available since only the letters *"a"* through *"w"* are used to denote particular individuals) . We use the symbol *"Hx"* (sometimes written *"H(x)"*) to symbolize the common pattern of all singular propositions which assert that particular individuals have the property of being human. The letter *"x"*—called an "individual variable"—is a mere *place marker,* serving only to indicate where the various letters *"a"* through *"w"*—called "individual constants"—may be written for singular propositions to result.

The various singular propositions *"Ha," "Hb," "Hc," "Hd,"* are either true or false; but *"Hx"* is neither true nor false, not being a statement or proposition at all. The expression *"Hx"* is called a "propositional function," and for our present purpose may be given an overly-simplified explanation, being temporarily defined as an expression which contains an individual variable and which becomes a singular proposition when the individual variable is replaced by an individual constant.* Individual constants, as has been implied, are to be thought of as proper names of particular individuals. Any singular proposition may thus be regarded as a *substitution instance* of a propositional function, that is, as the result of replacing the propositional function's individual variable by that individual constant which is the subject term of the singular proposition. Ordinarily, a propositional function will have some true substitution instances and some false substitution instances. The propo-

---

* Some writers have regarded "propositional functions" as the *meanings* of such expressions, but here we define them to be the expressions themselves.

sitional functions considered thus far, that is, *"Hx,"* *"Mx,"* *"Fx,"* and *"Wx"* are all of this kind.

II. QUANTIFICATION

The substitution of individual constants for their individual variables is not the only way in which propositions can be obtained from propositional functions. Propositions may also be obtained by the process called "generalization" or "quantification." Predicate terms occur frequently in propositions other than singular ones. Thus the propositions "Everything is mortal," and "Something is beautiful," contain predicate terms, but are not singular propositions since they do not contain the names of any particular individuals. Indeed, they do not refer specifically to *any* particular individuals, being *general* propositions.

The first of these may be expressed in various ways which are logically equivalent: either as "All things are mortal," or as

> Given any thing in the universe, it is mortal.

In the latter formulation, the word "it" is a relative pronoun, referring back to the word "thing" which precedes it in the statement. Using the letter *"x,"* our individual variable, in place of the pronoun "it" and its antecedent, we may rewrite the first general proposition as:

> Given any *x* in the universe, *x* is mortal.

Or, using the notation introduced in the preceding section, we may write:

> Given any *x* in the universe, *Mx.*

Although the propositional function *"Mx"* is not a proposition, here we have an expression *containing* it which *is* a proposition. The phrase "Given any *x* in the universe" is customarily symbolized by " *(x)* " and is called the "universal quantifier." Our first general proposition may be completely symbolized as:

> *(x)Mx.*

The second general proposition, "Something is beautiful," may also be expressed as:

There exists at least one thing which is beautiful.

In the latter formulation, the word "which" is a relative pronoun referring back to the word "thing." Using our individual variable "x" in place of both the pronoun "which" and its antecedent, we may rewrite the second general proposition as:

There exists at least one x such that x is beautiful.

Or, using the notation at hand, we may write:

There exists at least one x such that Bx.

Just as before, although "Bx" is only a propositional function, we have here an expression containing it which is a proposition. The phrase "there exists at least one x such that" is customarily symbolized by " $(\exists x)$ " and is called the "existential quantifier." The second general proposition may be completely symbolized as:

$$(\exists x)\, Bx$$

Thus we see that propositions may be formed from propositional functions either by *instantiation,* that is, by substituting an individual constant for its individual variable, or by *generalization,* that is, by placing a universal or existential quantifier before it. It is clear that the universal quantification of a propositional function is true if and only if all of its substitution instances are true, and that the existential quantification of a propositional function is true if and only if it has at least one true substitution instance. If we grant that there is at least one individual in the universe, so that every propositional function has at least one substitution instance, then for any propositional function, if its universal quantification is true then its existential quantification is true also.

All the propositional functions which have been specifically mentioned thus far have had only affirmative singular propositions as substitution instances. But not all propositions are affirmative. The denial of the affirmative singular proposition "Socrates is mortal," is the *negative* singular proposition "Socrates is not mortal." In symbols we have *"Ms"* and *"$\sim Ms$."* The first is a substitution instance of the propositional function *"Mx."* The second can with equal propriety be regarded as a substitution instance of the propositional function *"$\sim Mx$."* Here we enlarge our notion of propositional functions to permit them to contain the negation symbol *"$\sim$."*

Now the further connections between universal and existential quantification can be illustrated. The (universal) general proposition "Everything is mortal" is denied by the (existential) general proposition "Something is not mortal." These are symbolized as *"$(x)Mx$"* and *"$(\exists x) \sim Mx$"* respectively. Since one is the denial of the other, the equivalences:

$$[\sim(x)Mx] \equiv [(\exists x)\sim Mx] \quad \text{and} \quad [(x)Mx] \equiv [\sim(\exists x)\sim Mx]$$

are logically true. Similarly, the (universal) general proposition "Nothing is mortal" is denied by the (existential) general proposition "Something is mortal." These are symbolized as *"$(x)\sim Mx$"* and *"$(\exists x)Mx$"* respectively. Since one is the denial of the other, the further equivalences:

$$[\sim(x)\sim Mx] \equiv [(\exists x)Mx] \quad \text{and} \quad [(x)\sim Mx] \equiv [\sim(\exists x)Mx]$$

are logically true also. Where we use the Greek letter *phi* to represent any predicate whatsoever, the general connections between universal and existential quantification can be set down as follows:

$$[(x)\ \phi x] \equiv [\sim (\exists x) \sim \phi x]$$
$$[(\exists x)\ \phi x] \equiv [\sim (x) \sim \phi x]$$
$$[(x) \sim \phi x] \equiv [\sim (\exists x) \phi x]$$
$$[(\exists x) \sim \phi x] \equiv [\sim (x) \phi x]$$

III. TRADITIONAL SUBJECT–PREDICATE PROPOSITIONS

The four types of general propositions traditionally emphasized in the study of logic are illustrated by the following:

All humans are mortal.
No humans are mortal.
Some humans are mortal.
Some humans are not mortal.

These have been classified as "universal affirmative," "universal negative," "particular affirmative," and "particular negative," respectively, and their types abbreviated as *"A," "E," "I,"* and *"O,"* again respectively.*

In symbolizing these propositions by means of quantifiers we shall be led to a further enlargement of our notion of a propositional function. Turning first to the *A* proposition, we proceed by means of successive paraphrasings, beginning with:

Given any thing in the universe, if it is human then it is mortal.

The two instances of the relative pronoun "it" clearly refer back to their common antecedent, the word "thing." As in the early part of the preceding section, since the three words have the same (indefinite) reference, they can be replaced by the letter *"x,"* and the proposition rewritten as:

Given any x in the universe, if x is human then x is mortal.

Now using our previously introduced notation for "if-then," we can rewrite the preceding as:

Given any x in the universe, x is human $\supset$ x is mortal.

Finally, using our now familiar notation for propositional functions and quantifiers, the original *A* proposition is expressed as:

$$(x)[Hx \supset Mx].$$

Our symbolic translation of the *A* proposition appears as the universal quantification of a new kind of propositional function. The expression *"Hx $\supset$ Mx"* is a propositional function which has as its substitution instances neither affirmative nor negative singular propositions, but hypothetical statements whose antecedents and consequents are singular propositions

* An account of their traditional analysis and nomenclature is presented in Chapter Five.

having the same subject term. Among the substitution instances of the propositional function *"Hx ⊃ Mx"* are the hypothetical statements *"Ha ⊃ Ma," "Hb ⊃ Mb," "Hc ⊃ Mc," "Hd ⊃ Md,"* and so on. There are also propositional functions whose substitution instances are conjunctions of singular propositions having the same subject terms. Thus the conjunctions *"Ha · Ma," "Hb · Mb," "Hc · Mc, "Hd · Md,"* and so on, are substitution instances of the propositional function *"Hx · Mx."* There are also propositional functions such as *"Wx v Bx,"* whoe substitution instances are disjunctions such as *"Wa v Ba,"* and *"Wb v Bb."* In fact, any truth-functionally compound statement whose ultimate simple constituent statements are singular propositions all having the same subject term can be regarded as a substitution instance of a propositional function containing some or all of the various truth functional connectives dot, wedge, horseshoe, three-bar equivalence, and curl. In our translation of the *A* proposition as " *(x)* [*Hx ⊃ Mx*]" the square brackets serve as punctuation marks. They indicate that the universal quantifier " *(x)* " *applies to* or *has within its scope* the entire propositional function *"Hx ⊃ Mx."*

Before going on to discuss the other traditional forms of categorical propositions, it should be observed that our symbolic formula " *(x)* [*Hx ⊃ Mx*]" translates correctly not only the standard form proposition "All *H*'s are *M*'s," but any other English statement *having the same meaning*. There are many ways in English of saying the same thing—a partial list of them may be set down as: *"H*'s are *M*'s," "An *H* is an *M*," "Every *H* is *M*," "Each *H* is *M*," "Any *H* is *M*," "No *H*'s are not *M*," "Everything which is *H* is *M*," "Anything which is *H* is *M*," "If anything is *H* it is *M*," "If something is *H* it is *M*," "Whatever is *H* is *M*," "H*'s are all *M*'s," "Only *M*'s are *H*'s," "None but *M*'s are *H*'s," "Nothing is an *H* unless it is an *M*," and "Nothing is an *H* but not an *M*."* Some English idioms are a little misleading in using a temporal term when no reference to time is intended. Thus the proposition *"H*'s are always *M*'s" is properly understood as meaning simply that *all H*'s are *M*'s.

Again, the same meaning may be expressed by the use of abstract nouns: "Humanity implies mortality" is correctly symbolized as an **A** proposition. That the language of symbolic logic has a single expression for the common meaning of a considerable number of English sentences may be regarded as an advantage of symbolic logic over English for cognitive or informative purposes—although admittedly a disadvantage from the point of view of rhetorical power or poetic expressiveness.

The **E** proposition "No humans are mortal," may be successively paraphrased as:

Given any thing in the universe, if it is human then it is not mortal.
Given any x in the universe, if x is human then x is not mortal.
Given any x in the universe, x is human $\supset$ x is not mortal.

and finally as:

$$(x)[Hx \supset \sim Mx].$$

The preceding symbolic translation expresses not only the traditional **E** form in English but also such diverse ways of saying the same thing as: "There are no H's which are M," "Nothing is both an H and an M," "H's are never M," and so on.

Similarly, the **I** proposition "Some humans are mortals," may be successively paraphrased as:

There exists at least one thing which is human and mortal.
There exists at least one x such that x is human and x is mortal.
There exists at least one x such that x is human $\cdot$ x is mortal.

and then as:

$$(\exists x) [Hx \cdot Mx].$$

Finally, the **O** proposition "Some humans are not mortal" is successively paraphrased as:

There exists at least one thing which is human but not mortal.
There exists at least one x such that x is human and x is not mortal.
There exists at least one x such that x is human $\cdot \sim x$ is mortal.

and completely symbolized as:

$$(\exists x) [Hx \cdot \sim Mx].$$

Where the Greek letters *phi* and *psi* are used to represent any predicates whatever, the four general subject-predicate propositions of traditional logic may be represented in a square array as:

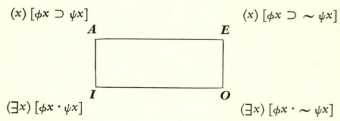

$(x) [\phi x \supset \psi x]$ $(x) [\phi x \supset \sim \psi x]$

A E

I O

$(\exists x) [\phi x \cdot \psi x]$ $(\exists x) [\phi x \cdot \sim \psi x]$

Of these, the *A* and the *O* are "contradictories," each being the denial of the other; *E* and *I* are also contradictories.

It might be thought that an *I* proposition follows from its corresponding *A* proposition, and an *O* from its corresponding *E;* but this is not so. An *A* proposition may very well be true while its corresponding *I* proposition is false. Where "ϕx" is a propositional function which has no true substitution instances, then no matter what kinds of substitution instances the propositional function "ψx" may have, the universal quantification of the (complex) propositional function "$\phi x \supset \psi x$" will be true. For example, consider the propositional function "*x* is a centaur," which we abbreviate as "*Cx*." Since there are no centaurs, every substitution instance of "*Cx*" is false, that is, "*Ca*," "*Cb*," "*Cc*," . . . are all false. Hence every substitution instance of the complex propositional function "*Cx* ⊃ *Bx*" will be a hypothetical statement whose antecedent is false. The substitution instances "*Ca* ⊃ *Ba*," "*Cb* ⊃ *Bb*," "*Cc* ⊃ *Bc*," . . . are all *true,* since any hypothetical statement asserting a material implication must be true if its antecedent is false. Since all its substitution instances are true, the universal quantification of the propositional function "*Cx* ⊃ *Bx*," which is our *A* proposition " (*x*) [*Cx* ⊃ *Bx*]," is true. But the corresponding *I* proposition " (∃*x*) [*Cx* · *Bx*]" is false, since the propositional function "*Cx* · *Bx*" has no true substitution instances. That "*Cx* · *Bx*" has no true substitution instances follows from the fact that "*Cx*" has no true substitution instances. The various substitution instances of "$Cx \cdot Bx$" are: "$Ca \cdot Ba$," "$Cb \cdot Bb$," "$Cc \cdot Bc$," . . . each of which is a conjunction one of whose conjuncts is false, since "Ca," "Cb," "Cc," . . . are all false. Since all its substitution instances are false, the existential quantification of the propositional function "$Cx \cdot Bx$," which is our *I* proposition "$(\exists x)[Cx \cdot Bx]$," is false. Hence an *A* proposition may be true while its corresponding *I* proposition is false. If the propositional function "Bx" is replaced by the propositional function "$\sim Bx$" in the preceding discussion, it will then establish that an *E* proposition may be true while its corresponding *O* proposition is false.

If we make the general assumption that there exists at least one individual in the universe, then "$(x)[Cx \supset Bx]$" does imply "$(\exists x)[Cx \supset Bx]$." But the latter is not an *I* proposition. The *I* proposition "Some centaurs are beautiful" is symbolized as "$(\exists x)[Cx \cdot Bx]$," which asserts that there is at least one centaur. But what is symbolized as "$(\exists x)[Cx \supset Bx]$" can be rendered in English as *there exists at least one thing such that if it is a centaur then it is beautiful*. It does not assert that there is a centaur, but only that there is an individual which is either not a centaur or is beautiful. And this proposition would be false in only two possible cases: first, if there were no individuals at all; and second, if all individuals were centaurs and none of them were beautiful. We rule out the first case by making the explicit (and obviously true) assumption that there is at least one individual in the universe. And the second case is so extremely unplausible that any proposition of the form $(\exists x)[\phi x \supset \psi x]$ is bound to be quite trivial—in contrast to the significant *I* form $(\exists x)[\phi x \cdot \psi x]$.

The foregoing should make clear that although in English the *A* and *I* propositions "All humans are mortal" and "Some humans are mortal" differ only in their initial words "all" and "some," their difference in meaning is not confined to the matter of universal versus existential quantification, but goes deeper than that. The propositional functions quantified to yield *A* and *I* propositions are not just differently quantified, they are different functions, one containing "⊃", the other "·". In other words, *A* and *I* propositions are not so much alike as they appear in English. Their differences are brought out very clearly in the new notation of propositional functions and quantifiers.

Before turning to the topic of inferences involving non-compound statements, the reader should acquire some practice in translating non-compound statements from English into our logical symbolism. The English language has so many irregular or idiomatic constructions that there can be no simple rules for translating an English sentence into logical notation. What is required in each case is that the *meaning* of the sentence be understood and then re-expressed in terms of propositional functions and quantifiers.

EXERCISES

Translate each of the following into the logical notation of propositional functions and quantifiers, in each case using the abbreviations suggested:

1. Nothing worth having can be obtained easily. (*Wx*—*x* is worth having; *Ox*—*x* can be obtained easily.)
2. He prayeth well who loveth well. (*Px*—*x* prayeth well; *Lx*—*x* loveth well.)
3. Race horses are all thoroughbreds. (*Rx*—*x* is a race horse; *Tx*—*x* is a thoroughbred.)
4. Only members are admitted. (*Mx*—*x* is a member; *Ax*—*x* is admitted.)
5. To know her is to love her. (*Kx*—*x* knows her; *Lx*—*x* loves her.)
6. Only employees may use the service elevators. (*Ex*—*x* is an employee; *Ux*—*x* may use the service elevators.)
7. Employees may use only the service elevators. (*Ex*—*x* is an elevator that employees may use; *Sx*—*x* is a service elevator.)
8. Lions are carnivorous. (*Lx*—*x* is a lion; *Cx*—*x* is carnivorous.)
9. Children are present. (*Cx*—*x* is a child; *Px*—*x* is present.)
10. None but the brave deserve the fair. (*Bx*—*x* is brave; *Dx*—*x* deserves the fair.)
11. No passengers survived. (*Px*—*x* is a passenger; *Sx*—*x* survived.)

12. Snakes are never found in the Arctic. (*Sx*—*x* is a snake; *Ax*—*x* is found in the Arctic.)
13. The whale is a mammal. (*Wx*—*x* is a whale; *Mx*—*x* is a mammal.)
14. A bat is not a bird. (*Bx*—*x* is a bat; *Rx*—*x* is a bird.)
15. Everyone that asketh receiveth. (*Ax*—*x* asketh; *Rx*—*x* receiveth.)
16. An elephant is a pachyderm. (*Ex*—*x* is an elephant; *Px*—*x* is a pachyderm.)
17. An elephant appeared. (*Ex*—*x* is an elephant; *Ax*—*x* appeared.)
18. He jests at scars that never felt a wound. (*Jx*—*x* jests at scars; *Nx*—*x* never felt a wound.)
19. All that glitters is not gold. (*Gx*—*x* glitters; *Ax*—*x* is gold.)
20. None think the great unhappy but the great. (*Tx*—*x* thinks the great unhappy; *Gx*—*x* is great.)

IV. PROVING VALIDITY

If we wish to construct formal proofs of validity for arguments whose validity turns upon the inner structures of non-compound statements occurring in them, we must expand our list of elementary valid argument forms. Only four additional elementary valid argument forms are required, and these will be introduced in connection with arguments for which they are needed. Let us consider the first argument cited in the present chapter: *All humans are mortal; Socrates is human; Therefore Socrates is mortal.* This is symbolized as:

$$(x)[Hx \supset Mx]$$
$$Hs$$
$$\overline{}$$
$$\therefore Ms$$

The first premiss affirms the truth of the universal quantification of the propositional function "*Hx* ⊃ *Mx*." Since the universal quantification of a propositional function is true if and only if all of its substitution instances are true, from the first premiss we can infer any desired substitution instance of the propositional function "*Hx* ⊃ *Mx*." In particular we can infer the substitution instance "*Hs* ⊃ *Ms*." And from this and the second premiss "*Hs*" the conclusion "*Ms*" follows directly by *modus ponens*.

If we add to our list of elementary valid argument forms the principle that any substitution instance of a propositional function can validly be inferred from its universal quantification, then we can give a formal proof of the validity of the given argument by reference to the expanded list of elementary valid argument forms. This new elementary valid argument form may be written as:

$$\frac{(x)\,\phi\,x}{\therefore\,\phi\,z}$$ where "z" is any individual symbol;

and referred to as "**UI**" (the principle of Universal Instantiation.) * A formal proof of validity may now be written as:

1. $(x)[Hx \supset Mx]$
2. Hs $/\therefore Ms$
3. $Hs \supset Ms$ 1, **UI**
4. Ms 3,2, M.P.

The addition of **UI** strengthens our proof apparatus considerably, but more is required. The need for additional rules governing quantification arises in connection with arguments like: "All humans are mortal; All Greeks are human; Therefore all Greeks are mortal." The symbolic translation of this argument is

$$(x)[Hx \supset Mx]$$
$$(x)[Gx \supset Hx]$$
$$\overline{\therefore (x)[Gx \supset Mx]}$$

Here both premises and conclusion are general propositions rather than singular ones, universal quantifications of propositional functions rather than substitution instances of them. From the two premises, by **UI**, we may validly infer the following pairs of hypothetical statements:

$$\begin{cases} Ha \supset Ma \\ Ga \supset Ha \end{cases}, \begin{cases} Hb \supset Mb \\ Gb \supset Hb \end{cases}, \begin{cases} Hc \supset Mc \\ Gc \supset Hc \end{cases}, \begin{cases} Hd \supset Md \\ Gd \supset Hd \end{cases} \cdots$$

---

* This rule and the three which follow are variants of rules for "natural deduction" which were devised independently by Gerhard Gentzen and Stanislaw Jaskowski in 1934.

and by successive uses of the principle of the Hypothetical Syllogism we may validly infer the conclusions:

$$Ga \supset Ma, Gb \supset Mb, Gc \supset Mc, Gd \supset Md, \ldots$$

Granted that $a, b, c, d, \ldots$ are all the individuals in the universe, it follows that from the truth of the premises one can validly infer the truth of all substitution instances of the propositional function "$Gx \supset Mx$." Since the universal quantification of a propositional function is true if and only if all of its substitution instances are true, from the above we can infer the truth of "$(x)[Gx \supset Mx]$," which is the conclusion of the given argument.

The preceding paragraph may be thought of as containing an *informal* proof of the validity of the given argument, in which the principle of the Hypothetical Syllogism and *two* principles governing quantification are appealed to. But it describes two indefinitely long sequences of statements, one the list of all pairs of substitution instances of the two propositional functions which were quantified universally in the premises, the other the list of all substitution instances of the propositional function whose universal quantification is the conclusion. A *formal* proof cannot contain such indefinitely, perhaps even infinitely long sequences of statements, so some method must be sought for expressing those indefinitely long sequences in some finite, definite fashion.

A method for doing this is suggested by a common technique of elementary mathematics. A geometer, seeking to prove that *all* triangles possess a certain property, may begin with the words: "Let ABC be any arbitrarily selected triangle." Then the geometer begins to reason about the triangle ABC, and establishes that it has the property in question. From this he concludes that *all* triangles have that property. Now what justifies his final conclusion? Granted of *the* triangle ABC that *it* has the property, why does it follow that *all* triangles do? The answer to this question is easily given. If no assumption other than its triangularity is made about the triangle ABC, then the symbol "ABC"

can be taken as denoting any triangle you please. Then the
geometer's argument establishes that *any* triangle has the property in question, and if *any* triangle has it then *all* triangles do.
We wish now to introduce a notation analogous to the geometer's in talking about "any arbitrarily selected triangle *ABC*."
This will avoid the pretense of listing an indefinite or infinite
number of substitution instances of a propositional function,
for instead we shall talk about *any* substitution instance of the
propositional function.

We shall use the (hitherto unused) small letter "*y*" to denote
any arbitrarily selected individual. We shall use it in a way
similar to that in which the geometer used the letters "*ABC*."
Since the truth of *any* substitution instance of a propositional
function follows from its universal quantification, we can infer
the substitution instance which results from replacing "*x*" by
"*y*," where "*y*" denotes *any arbitrarily selected* individual. Thus
we may begin our formal proof of the validity of the given argument as follows:

1. $(x)[Hx \supset Mx]$
2. $(x)[Gx \supset Hx]/\therefore (x)[Gx \supset Mx]$
3. $Hy \supset My$ 1, **UI**
4. $Gy \supset Hy$ 2, **UI**
5. $Gy \supset My$ 4,3, H.S.

From the premises we have deduced the statement "$Gy \supset My$,"
which in effect, since "*y*" denotes *any arbitrarily selected* individual, asserts the truth of *any* substitution instance of the
propositional function "$Gx \supset Mx$." Since *any* substitution instance is true, all substitution instances must be true, and hence
the universal quantification of that propositional function is
true also. We may add this Principle to our list of elementary
valid argument forms, stating it as: From the substitution instance of a propositional function with respect to the name of
any arbitrarily selected individual one can validly infer the universal quantification of that propositional function. This new
elementary valid argument form may be written as:

$$\frac{\phi y}{\therefore (x)\phi x}$$ (where "*y*" denotes *any arbitrarily selected individual*)

Since this new principle permits us to *generalize,* that is, to go from a (particular kind of) substitution instance to a generalized or universally quantified expression, we may refer to it as **"UG"** (the principle of Universal Generalization). The sixth and final step of the formal proof already begun may be written (and justified) as:

6. $(x)[Gx \supset Mx]$ 5, **UG**

Another argument the demonstration of whose validity requires the use of **UG** as well as **UI** is: *No humans are perfect; All Greeks are human; Therefore no Greeks are perfect.* The formal proof of its validity is:

1. $(x)[Hx \supset \sim Px]$
2. $(x)[Gx \supset Hx] / \therefore (x)[Gx \supset \sim Px]$
3. $Hy \supset \sim Py$ 1, **UI**
4. $Gy \supset Hy$ 2, **UI**
5. $Gy \supset \sim Py$ 4,3, H.S.
6. $(x)[Gx \supset \sim Px]$ 5, **UG**

There may seem to be some artificiality about the foregoing. It may be urged that distinguishing carefully between "$(x) \phi x$" and "ϕy," so that they are not identified but must be inferred from each other by **UI** and **UG,** is to insist upon a distinction without a difference. But there is certainly a formal difference between them. The statement "$(x) [Hx \supset Mx]$" is a noncompound statement, while "$Hy \supset My$" is compound, being a hypothetical. From the two non-compound statements "$(x) [Gx \supset Hx]$" and "$(x) [Hx \supset Mx]$" no inference can be drawn by means of the original list of nineteen elementary valid argument forms. But from the compound statements "$Gy \supset Hy$" and "$Hy \supset My$" the indicated conclusion "$Gy \supset My$" follows by a Hypothetical Syllogism. The principle of **UI** is used to get from non-compound statements to which our earlier forms of inference do not apply to compound statements to which they can be applied. The quantification principles thus serve to augment our logical apparatus so that it becomes capable of validating arguments essentially involving non-compound (generalized) propositions as well as the other (simpler) kind of argument discussed in our earlier chapters. On the other hand, in spite of this formal difference, there must be a logical equivalence between "$(x)\ \phi x$" and "ϕy" or the rules **UI** and **UG** would not be valid. Both the difference and the equivalence are important for our purpose of validating arguments by reference to a list of elementary valid argument forms. The addition of **UI** and **UG** to our list strengthens it considerably.

The list must be further expanded when we turn to arguments involving existential general propositions. A convenient example with which to begin is: *All criminals are vicious; Some humans are criminals; Therefore some humans are vicious;* which is symbolized as:

$$(x)\ [Cx \supset Vx]$$
$$\underline{(\exists x)\ [Hx \cdot Cx]}$$
$$\therefore (\exists x)\ [Hx \cdot Vx]$$

The existential quantification of a propositional function is true if and only if it has at least one true substitution instance. Hence, whatever property may be designated by "ϕ," "$(\exists x)\ \phi x$" asserts that there is at least one individual in the universe which has the property ϕ. If an individual constant, say "w," is used nowhere earlier in the context, we may use it to denote either the individual which has the property ϕ or some one of the individuals which have ϕ. Knowing that there is such an individual, and having agreed to denote it by "w," we know that "ϕw" is a true substitution instance of the propositional function "ϕx." Hence we add to our list of elementary valid argument forms the principle that from the existential quantification of a propositional function we may infer the truth of its substitution instance with respect to an individual constant which occurs nowhere earlier in that context. The new argument form may be written as:

$$\frac{(\exists x)\ \phi x}{\therefore\ \phi z}$$ (where "*z*" is any individual constant having no previous occurrence in the context)

and referred to as "**EI**" (the principle of Existential Instantiation).

Granted the additional valid argument form **EI**, we may begin a demonstration of the validity of the stated argument:

1. $(x)\ [Cx \supset Vx]$
2. $(\exists x)\ [Hx \cdot Cx]\ /\ \therefore\ (\exists x)\ [Hx \cdot Vx]$
3. $Hw \cdot Cw$ 2, **EI**
4. $Cw \supset Vw$ 1, **UI**
5. $Cw \cdot Hw$ 3, Com.
6. Cw 5, Simp.
7. Vw 4,6, M.P.
8. Hw 3, Simp.
9. $Hw \cdot Vw$ 8,7, Conj.

Thus far we have deduced "$Hw \cdot Vw$," which is a substitution instance of the propositional function whose existential quantification is asserted by the conclusion. Since the existential quantification of a propositional function is true if and only if it has at least one true substitution instance, from any true substitution instance of a propositional function we may validly infer its existential quantification. We add as our fourth quantification rule the valid argument form:

$$\frac{\phi z}{\therefore\ (\exists x)\ \phi x}$$ (where "*z*" is any individual symbol)

which will be referred to as "**EG**" (the principle of Existential Generalization). The tenth and final step of the demonstration already begun may now be written (and justified) as:

10. $(\exists x)[Hx \cdot Vx]$ 9, **EG**

The need for the indicated restriction on the use of **EI** can be seen by considering the obviously invalid argument: *Some alligators are kept in captivity; some birds are kept in captivity; therefore some alligators are birds.* If we failed to heed the restriction on **EI** that the substitution instance inferred by it from an existential quantification can contain only an individual symbol which has no previous occurrence in the context, then we might proceed to construct a "proof" of validity for this invalid argument. Such an erroneous "proof" might proceed:

1. $(\exists x) [Ax \cdot Cx]$
2. $(\exists x) [Bx \cdot Cx] / \therefore (\exists x) [Ax \cdot Bx]$
3. $Aw \cdot Cw$ 1, **EI**
4. $Bw \cdot Cw$ 2, **EI** (erroneous)
5. Aw 3, Simp.
6. Bw 4, Simp.
7. $Aw \cdot Bw$ 5,6, Conj.
8. $(\exists x) [Ax \cdot Bx]$ 7, **EG**

The error in this "proof" occurs at step 4. From the second premiss " $(\exists x) [Bx \cdot Cx]$ " we know that there is at least one thing which is both a bird and kept in captivity. *If* we were free to assign it the name *"w"* we could, of course, assert *"Bw · Cw."* But we are not free to make any such assignment of *"w,"* for it has already been preëmpted in step 3 to serve as a name for an *alligator* which is kept in captivity. To avoid errors of this sort, we must obey the indicated restriction whenever we use **EI**. The preceding discussion should make clear that in any demonstration requiring the use of both **EI** and **UI**, **EI** should always be used *first*.

For more complicated modes of argumentation, especially those which involve relations, certain additional restrictions must be placed on our four quantification rules. But for arguments of the present sort, traditionally called Categorical Syllogisms, the present restrictions are sufficient to prevent erroneous inferences.

EXERCISES

Construct formal proofs of validity for the arguments numbered 1, 3, 4, 6, 9 in the Exercises on pages 161–2, for the arguments numbered 1, 2, 4, 5, 6, 8 in the Exercises on pages 190–1, and for the arguments numbered 1, 2, 5 in the Exercises on page 210.

V. PROVING INVALIDITY

To prove the invalidity of an argument involving quantifiers, we can use the method of refutation by logical analogy. For example, the argument "All communists are opponents of the Administration; some delegates are opponents of the Administration; therefore some delegates are communists" is proved invalid by the analogy "All cats are animals; some dogs are animals; therefore some dogs are cats"; which is obviously invalid since its premisses are true and its conclusion false. But such analogies are not always easy to devise. Some more nearly effective method of proving invalidity is desirable.

In the preceding chapter we developed a method of proving invalidity for arguments involving compound statements. That method consisted of making truth value assignments to the simple constituent statements of arguments in such a way as to make their premisses true and their conclusions false. That method can be adapted for arguments involving quantifiers. The adaptation involves our general assumption that there exists at least one individual in the universe. For an argument involving quantifiers to be valid it must be impossible for its premisses to be true and its conclusion false as long as at least one individual exists.

The general assumption that at least one individual exists is satisfied if exactly one individual exists, or exactly two individuals exist, or exactly three individuals exist, or etc. If any of these assumptions about the exact number of individuals existing is made, there is an equivalence between general propositions and truth functional compounds of singular propositions. If there is exactly one individual in the universe, say a, then:

$$(x) \, \phi x \equiv \phi a \equiv (\exists x) \, \phi x$$

If there are exactly two individuals in the universe, say a and b, then:

$$(x) \, \phi x \equiv [\phi a \cdot \phi b] \text{ and } (\exists x) \, \phi x \equiv [\phi a \, \text{v} \, \phi b]$$

If there are exactly three individuals, say a, b, and c, then:

$$(x) \, \phi x \equiv [\phi a \cdot \phi b \cdot \phi c] \text{ and } (\exists x) \, \phi x \equiv [\phi a \, \text{v} \, \phi b \, \text{v} \, \phi c]$$

In general, if there are exactly n individuals, say $a, b, c, \ldots n,$ then:

$$(x)\ \phi x \equiv [\phi a \cdot \phi b \cdot \phi c \ldots \phi n] \text{ and } (\exists x)\ \phi x \equiv [\phi a \lor \phi b \lor \phi c \lor \ldots \lor \phi n]$$

An argument involving quantifiers is valid *if* it is valid no matter how many individuals there are in the universe, provided there is at least one. So an argument involving quantifiers is proved invalid if there is a possible universe containing at least one individual such that the argument's premises are true and its conclusion false *of that universe*. Consider the argument: "All mercenaries are undependable; no guerrillas are mercenaries; therefore no guerrillas are undependable." It may be symbolized as:

$$(x)\ [Mx \supset Ux]$$
$$(x)\ [Gx \supset\ \sim Mx]$$
$$\therefore (x)\ [Gx \supset\ \sim Ux]$$

If there is exactly one individual in the universe, say a, this argument is logically equivalent to:

$$Ma \supset Ua$$
$$Ga \supset\ \sim Ma$$
$$\therefore Ga \supset\ \sim Ua$$

The latter can be proved invalid by assigning the truth value *true* to "Ga" and "Ua" and *false* to "Ma." Hence the original argument is not valid for a universe which contains exactly one individual, and is therefore *invalid*. Similarly, we can prove the invalidity of the first argument mentioned in this section by describing a universe containing exactly one individual a such that "Aa" and "Da" are assigned *truth* and "Ca" is assigned *falsehood*.

Some arguments may be valid for any universe in which there is exactly one individual, but invalid for a universe containing two or more individuals. Such arguments are to be counted as invalid also. An example of such an argument is: "Some animals are cats; some animals are dogs; therefore some dogs are cats." Its symbolic translation is:

$$(\exists x)\,[Ax \cdot Cx]$$
$$(\exists x)\,[Ax \cdot Dx]$$
$$\therefore (\exists x)\,[Dx \cdot Cx]$$

For a universe containing exactly one individual *a* it is logically equivalent to:

$$Aa \cdot Ca$$
$$Aa \cdot Da$$
$$\therefore Da \cdot Ca$$

which is valid. But for a universe containing two individuals *a* and *b* it is equivalent to:

$$(Aa \cdot Ca) \,\text{v}\, (Ab \cdot Cb)$$
$$(Aa \cdot Da) \,\text{v}\, (Ab \cdot Db)$$
$$\therefore (Da \cdot Ca) \,\text{v}\, (Db \cdot Cb)$$

which is proved invalid by assigning *truth* to "*Aa*," "*Ab*," "*Ca*," "*Db*," and *falsehood* to "*Da*" and "*Cb*." Hence the original argument is not valid for a universe containing exactly two individuals, and is therefore *invalid*. For any invalid argument of this general type it is possible to describe a universe containing some definite number of individuals for which its equivalent truth-functional argument can be proved invalid by the method of assigning truth values.

EXERCISES

1. Prove the invalidity of the arguments numbered 2, 5, 7, 8, 10 in the Exercises on pages 161–2, of the arguments numbered 3, 7, 9, in the Exercises on pages 190–1, and of the argument numbered 4 in the Exercises on page 210.
2. Evaluate each of the arguments in the Exercises on pages 176–7: if the argument is valid, construct a formal proof of its validity; if it is invalid, prove its invalidity.

VI. ASYLLOGISTIC INFERENCE

All of the arguments considered in the preceding two sections were of the form traditionally called "Categorical Syllogisms." These consist of two premisses and a conclusion, each of which is analyzable either as a singular proposition or as one of the *A*, *E*, *I*, or *O* varieties. We turn now to the problem of evaluating somewhat more complicated arguments. These require no greater logical apparatus than has already been developed. Yet they are *asyllogistic* arguments and require a more powerful logic than was *traditionally* used in testing categorical syllogisms.

In this section we are still concerned with arguments which involve those general propositions which arise from quantifying propositional functions containing only a single individual variable. In the categorical syllogism, the only kinds of propositional functions quantified were of the forms "$\phi x \supset \psi x$," "$\phi x \supset \sim \psi x$," "$\phi x \cdot \psi x$," and "$\phi x \cdot \sim \psi x$." But now we shall be quantifying propositional functions which have more complicated internal structures. An example will help make this clear. Consider the argument:

Hotels are both expensive and depressing.
Some hotels are shabby.
Therefore some expensive things are shabby.

This argument, for all its obvious validity, is not amenable to the traditional sort of analysis. True enough, it can be expressed in terms of *A* and *I* propositions by using the symbols "Hx," "Bx," "Sx," and "Ex" to abbreviate the propositional functions "x is a hotel," "x is both expensive and depressing," "x is shabby," and "x is expensive," respectively. Using these abbreviations, the argument can be symbolized as:

$$(x) [Hx \supset Bx]$$
$$(\exists x) [Hx \cdot Sx]$$
$$\therefore (\exists x) [Ex \cdot Sx]$$

But forcing the argument into the strait jacket of the traditional *A* and *I* forms in this way obscures its validity. The argument in symbols is invalid, although the original argument is perfectly valid. The notation here obscures the logical connection between "Bx" and "Ex." A more adequate analysis is obtained by using only "Hx," "Sx," and "Ex," as explained above, plus "Dx"

as an abbreviation for "*x* is depressing." Using these symbols, the original argument can be translated as:

1. (*x*) [*Hx* ⊃ (*Ex* · *Dx*)]
2. (∃*x*) [*Hx* · *Sx*] / ∴ (∃*x*) [*Ex* · *Sx*]

So formulated, a demonstration of its validity is easily constructed. One such demonstration proceeds:

3. *Hw* · *Sw*	2, **EI**
4. *Hw* ⊃ (*Ew* · *Dw*)	1, **UI**
5. *Hw*	3, Simp.
6. *Ew* · *Dw*	4,5, M.P.
7. *Ew*	6, Simp.
8. *Sw* · *Hw*	3, Com.
9. *Sw*	8, Simp.
10. *Ew* · *Sw*	7,9, Conj.
11. (∃*x*) [*Ex* · *Sx*]	10, **EG**

In symbolizing general propositions which result from quantifying more complicated propositional functions, care must be taken not to be misled by the deceptiveness of ordinary English. One cannot translate from English into our logical notation by following any formal or mechanical rules. In every case one must *understand the meaning* of the English sentence, and then *reëxpress* that meaning in terms of propositional functions and quantifiers. Three locutions of ordinary English which are sometimes troublesome to students will be discussed briefly at this time.

First it should be observed that a statement like "All university students are either graduates or undergraduates," is *not* a disjunction, although it contains the connective "or." It definitely does *not* have the same meaning as "Either all university students are graduates or all university students are undergraduates." The former is properly symbolized—using obvious abbreviations, as:

$$(x) [Sx \supset (Gx \vee Ux)]$$

while the latter is to be symbolized as:

$$\{(x) [Sx \supset Gx]\} \vee \{(x) [Sx \supset Ux]\}$$

Second, it should be observed that a statement like "Oysters and clams are delicious," while it *can* be expressed as the conjunction of two general propositions, "Oysters are delicious and clams are delicious," can also be expressed as a single non-compound general proposition, in which case the word "and" is more properly symbolized by the "v" than by the " · ". The stated proposition is symbolized as:

$$(x) \, [(Ox \text{ v } Cx) \supset Dx]$$

not as:

$$(x) \, [(Ox \cdot Cx) \supset Dx]$$

For to say that oysters and clams are delicious is to say that anything is delicious which is *either* an oyster *or* a clam, *not* to say that anything is delicious which is *both* an oyster *and* a clam!

Third, alternative ways of symbolizing *exceptive* propositions should be noted.* Such propositions as: "All except previous winners are eligible," "All but previous winners are eligible," "Previous winners alone are not eligible," are traditionally called *exceptive* propositions. Any proposition of this form may be translated as a conjunction of two general propositions, as for example:

$$\{(x) \, [Px \supset \sim Ex]\} \cdot \{(x) \, [\sim Px \supset Ex]\}$$

It may also be translated as a non-compound general proposition which is the universal quantification of a propositional function containing the equivalence symbol "$\equiv$". For the present example we have the translation:

$$(x) \, [Ex \equiv \sim Px]$$

which can alternatively be rendered in English as: "Anyone is eligible if and only if he is not a previous winner." In general, exceptive propositions are most conveniently regarded as quantified equivalences.

We have seen that the expanded list of elementary valid

---

* Cf. the earlier discussion of exceptive propositions on pages 195–7.

argument forms which enabled us to demonstrate the validity of valid categorical syllogisms also suffice for the validation of asyllogistic arguments of the type described above. The same method of describing possible non-empty universes which was used to prove the invalidity of incorrect syllogisms also suffices to prove the invalidity of asyllogistic arguments of the present type. The following asyllogistic argument:

Foremen and superintendents are either competent men or relatives of the owner.
Anyone who dares to complain must be either a superintendent or a relative of the owner.
Foremen alone are competent men.
Someone did dare to complain.
Therefore some superintendent is a relative of the owner.

may be symbolized as:

$$(x) [(Fx \text{ v } Sx) \supset (Cx \text{ v } Rx)]$$
$$(x) [Dx \supset (Sx \text{ v } Rx)]$$
$$(x) [Fx \equiv Cx]$$
$$(\exists x) [Dx]$$
$$\therefore (\exists x) [Sx \cdot Rx]$$

and we can prove it invalid by describing a (non-empty) universe containing the single individual *a* and assigning the truth value *true* to "*Ca*," "*Da*," "*Fa*," "*Ra*," and the truth value *false* to "*Sa*."

EXERCISES

I. Evaluate each of the arguments in the Exercise set on pages 202–4: if the argument is valid construct a formal proof of its validity; if it is invalid, prove its invalidity.

II. Do the same for each of the following, in each case using the notation suggested:

1. All citizens who are not traitors are present. All officials are citizens. Some officials are not present. Therefore there are traitors. (*Cx, Tx, Px, Ox*)

2. Doctors and lawyers are professional men. Professional men and executives are respected. Therefore doctors are respected. (*Dx, Lx, Px, Ex, Rx*)

3. Only lawyers and politicians are members. Some members are not college graduates. Therefore some lawyers are not college graduates. (*Lx, Px, Mx, Cx*)

4. All cut-rate items are either shopworn or out of date. Nothing shopworn is worth buying. Some cut-rate items are worth buying. Therefore some cut-rate items are out of date. (*Cx, Sx, Ox, Wx*)

5. Some diamonds are used for adornment. Only things worn as jewels or applied as cosmetics are used for adornment. Diamonds are never applied as cosmetics. Nothing worn as a jewel is properly used if it has an industrial application. Some diamonds have industrial applications. Therefore some diamonds are not properly used. (*Dx, Ax, Jx, Cx, Px, Ix*)

6. No candidate who is either endorsed by labor or opposed by the Tribune can carry the farm vote. No one can be elected who does not carry the farm vote. Therefore no candidate endorsed by labor can be elected. (*Cx, Lx, Ox, Fx, Ex*)

7. No metal is friable that has been properly tempered. No brass is properly tempered unless it is given an oil immersion. Some of the ash trays on the shelf are brass. Everything on the shelf is friable. Brass is a metal. Therefore some of the ash trays were not given an oil immersion. (*Mx-x* is metal; *Fx-x* is friable; *Tx-x* is properly tempered; *Bx-x* is brass; *Ox-x* is given an oil immersion; *Ax-x* is an ash tray; *Sx-x* is on the shelf).

8. Anyone on the committee who knew the nominee would vote for him if we were free to do so. Everyone on the committee was free to vote for the nominee except those who were either instructed not to by the party caucus or had pledged support to someone else. Everyone on the committee knew the nominee. No one who knew the nominee had pledged support to anyone else. Not everyone on the committee voted for the nominee. Therefore the party caucus had instructed some members of the committee not to vote for the nominee. (*Cx-x* is on the committee; *Kx-x* knows the nominee; *Vx-x* votes for the nominee; *Fx-x* is free to vote for the nominee; *Ix-x* is instructed by the party caucus not to vote for the nominee; *Px-x* had pledged support to someone else.)

9. All the members of Beta Omicron are good dancers and please their dates. To please his date one must buy her a corsage if he takes her dancing or some ice cream if he takes her to a movie. No good dancer takes his date to a movie if he can afford to take her dancing. Some members of Beta Omicron buy their dates ice cream instead of corsages. Therefore not all the members of Beta Omicron can afford to take their dates dancing. (*Bx-x* is a member of Beta Omicron; *Gx-x* is a good dancer; *Px-x* pleases his date; *Cx-x* buys his date a corsage; *Dx-x* takes his date dancing; *Ix-x* buys his date ice cream; *Mx-x* takes his date to a movie; *Ax-x* can afford to take his date dancing.)

10. Some criminal robbed the Russell mansion. Whoever robbed the Russell mansion either had an accomplice among the servants or had to break in. To break in one would have to either smash the door or pick the lock. Only an expert locksmith could have picked the lock. Had anyone smashed the door he would have been heard. Nobody was heard. If the criminal who robbed the Russell mansion managed to fool the guard he must have been a convincing actor. No one could rob the Russell mansion unless he fooled the guard. No criminal could be both an expert locksmith and a convincing actor. Therefore some criminal had an accomplice among the servants. (*Cx-x* is a criminal; *Rx-x* robbed the Russell mansion; *Sx-x* had an accomplice among the servants; *Bx-x* broke in; *Dx-x* smashed the door; *Px-x* picked the lock; *Lx-x* is an expert locksmith; *Hx-x* was heard; *Fx-x* fooled the guard; *Ax-x* is a convincing actor.)

PART THREE

Induction

CHAPTER ELEVEN

Analogy and Probable Inference

1. ARGUMENT BY ANALOGY

The preceding chapters have dealt with deductive arguments, which are valid if their premisses establish their conclusions demonstratively, but invalid otherwise. Not all arguments are intended to be deductive, however. A great many arguments do not pretend to *demonstrate* the truth of their conclusions as following *necessarily* from their premisses, but merely to establish them as *probable,* or *probably true.* Arguments of this latter kind are generally called *inductive,* and are radically different from the deductive variety. Of these non-deductive or inductive arguments, perhaps the type most commonly used is the "argument by analogy." Two examples of analogical argument are these:

1. . . . the first industrial revolution, the revolution of the "dark satanic mills," was the devaluation of the human arm by the competition of machinery. There is no rate of pay at which a United States pick-and-shovel laborer can live which is low enough to compete

with the work of a steam shovel as an excavator. The modern industrial revolution [high speed electronic computers, so-called "thinking machines"] is similarly bound to devalue the human brain at least in its simpler and more routine decisions. Of course, just as the skilled carpenter, the skilled mechanic, the skilled dressmaker have in some degree survived the first industrial revolution, so the skilled scientist and the skilled administrator may survive the second.*

2. We may observe a very great similitude between this earth which we inhabit, and the other planets, Saturn, Jupiter, Mars, Venus, and Mercury. They all revolve round the sun, as the earth does, although at different distances and in different periods. They borrow all their light from the sun, as the earth does. Several of them are known to revolve round their axis like the earth, and, by that means, must have a like succession of day and night. Some of them have moons, that serve to give them light in the absence of the sun, as our moon does to us. They are all, in their motions, subject to the same law of gravitation, as the earth is. From all this similitude, it is not unreasonable to think, that those planets may, like our earth, be the habitation of various order of living creatures. There is some probability in this conclusion from analogy.†

Most of our own everyday inferences are by analogy. Thus I infer that a new pair of shoes will wear well on the grounds that I got good wear from other shoes previously purchased from the same store. If a new book by a certain author is called to my attention, I infer that I will enjoy reading it on the basis of having read and enjoyed other books by that author. Analogy is at the basis of most of our ordinary reasonings from past experience to what the future will hold. Not an explicitly formulated argument, of course, but something very much like analogical inference is presumably involved in the conduct of the burnt child who shuns the fire.

None of these arguments is *certain*, or demonstratively valid. None of their conclusions follow with "logical necessity" from

---

* Reprinted by permission from *Cybernetics* by N. Wiener, published jointly by The Technology Press, John Wiley & Sons, Inc., and Hermann et Cie, 1948.

† *Essays on the Intellectual Powers of Man*, by Thomas Reid. (Essay I, Chapter 4.)

their premisses. It is logically possible that what happened to skilled manual workers may not happen to skilled brain workers, that earth may be the only inhabited planet, that the new shoes may not wear well at all, and that I may find my favorite author's latest book to be intolerably dull. It is even *logically* possible that one fire may burn but not another. But then, no argument by analogy is *intended* to be mathematically certain. Analogical arguments are not to be classified as either "valid" or "invalid." Probability is all that is claimed for them.

In addition to their frequent use in arguments, analogies are very often used non-argumentatively, and these different uses should not be confused. Since earliest times writers have made use of analogy for the purpose of lively description. The literary uses of analogy in metaphor and simile are tremendously helpful to the writer who strives to create a vivid picture in the reader's mind. Analogy is also used in explanation, where something unfamiliar is made intelligible through being compared to something else, presumably more familiar, to which it has certain similarities. The use of analogies in description and explanation should not be confused with their use in argument.

Whether used argumentatively or otherwise, "analogy" is not difficult to define. To draw an analogy between two or more entities is to indicate one or more respects in which they are similar. This explains what an *analogy* is, but there is still the problem of characterizing an *argument by analogy*. We may approach this problem by examining a particular analogical argument and analyzing its structure. Let us take the simplest of the examples cited thus far, the argument that my new pair of shoes will wear well because my old shoes, which were purchased from the same store, have worn well. The two things said to be similar are the two pairs of shoes. There are three points of analogy involved: the respects in which the two entities are said to resemble each other are *first,* in being shoes; *second,* in being purchased from the same store; and *third,* in wearing well. The three points of analogy do not play identical roles in the argument, however. The first two occur in the premises, while the third is asserted by the conclusion. In quite general terms, then, the given argument may be described as having premises which assert the similarity of two things in two respects and a conclusion which asserts that they are similar in a third respect.

Not every analogical argument need concern exactly two things or exactly three different respects, of course. Thus the argument quoted from Reid draws analogies among six things (the then known planets) in some eight respects. Apart from these numerical differences, however, all analogical arguments have the same general structure or pattern. Every analogical inference proceeds from the similarity of two or more things in one or more respects to the similarity of those things in some further respect. Schematically, where a, b, c, and d are any entities, and P, Q, and R are any properties or "respects," an analogical argument may be represented as having the form

> a, b, c, d all have the properties P and Q.
> a, b, c all have the property R.
> _____
> Therefore d has the property R.

EXERCISES

All of the following passages contain analogies. Distinguish those which contain analogical arguments from those which make non-argumentative uses of analogy:

1. Metchnikoff bounced into the austere Pasteur Institute and started a circus there which lasted for twenty years; it was as if a skilled proprietor of a medicine show had become pastor of a congregation of sober Quakers.*

2. . . . and one day to his disgust, Pasteur observed that a bottle of boiled urine in which he had planted anthrax bacilli was swarming with unbidden guests, contaminating microbes of the air that had sneaked in. The following morning he observed that there were no anthrax germs left at all; they had been completely choked out by the bacilli from the air.

* Reprinted from *Microbe Hunters* by Paul de Kruif. Copyright, 1926, by Harcourt, Brace and Company, Inc.

At once Pasteur jumped to a fine idea: "If the harmless bugs from the air choke out the anthrax bacilli in the bottle, they will do it in the body too! It is a kind of dog-eat-dog!" *

3. There is nothing which for my part I like better, Cephalus, than conversing with aged men; for I regard them as travellers who have gone a journey which I too may have to go, and of whom I ought to enquire, whether the way is smooth and easy, or rugged and difficult. And this is a question which I should like to ask of you who have arrived at that time which the poets call the 'threshold of old age'—Is life harder towards the end, or what report do you give of it?

(Plato, *Republic*, Book I)

4. I am a lover of knowledge, and the men who dwell in the city are my teachers, and not the trees or the country. Though I do indeed believe that you have found a spell with which to draw me out of the city into the country, like a hungry cow before whom a bough or a bunch of fruit is waved. For only hold up before me in like manner a book, and you may lead me all round Attica, and over the wide world.

(Plato, *Phaedrus*)

5. The name "synchrotron" is suggested by the analogy with a synchronous motor: a phonograph turntable, for instance, will settle down to a speed determined only by the frequency of the voltage supply, no matter how it is pushed or held back during starting. If the frequency of the line voltage wavers while the turntable is running, it will slow down or speed up accordingly.

All the big postwar cyclotrons operate on this principle. The magnetic field is kept constant, but as the protons gain in energy the period of the accelerating field is slowly lengthened. By such modification cyclotrons have been boosted to an energy of about 450 Mev.†

6. One of the few relatively effective means the physicist has found for feeling his way into the nucleus is to whip some of the simpler nuclei up to high speeds, throw them at various materials and observe what, if anything, happens. His position is precisely that of a blind man who finds a pile of strong boxes and wants to know what is in them. The scheme of investigation

* *Ibid.*

† Reprinted from "The Bevatron" by Lloyd Smith, in *Scientific American,* Vol. 184, No. 2, February 1951.

he has hit upon, in effect, is to set a ladder in the center of the pile, climb up with one of the boxes, drop it on the others and come down to grope for something that feels different, in the hope that one of the boxes has split open. Just as a box-dropper's chance of smashing a box gets better as he climbs higher, so the physicist's chance is improved if he puts more energy into his projectiles.*

7. And he said, How shall we liken the kingdom of God? or in what parable shall we set it forth? It is like a grain of mustard seed, which, when it is sown upon the earth, though it be less than all the seeds that are upon the earth, yet when it is sown, groweth up, and becometh greater than all the herbs, and putteth out great branches; so that the birds of the heaven can lodge under the shadow thereof.

(Mark 4:30–32)

8. And David said unto Saul, Thy servant was keeping his father's sheep; and when there came a lion, or a bear, and took a lamb out of the flock, I went out after him, and smote him, and delivered it out of his mouth; and when he arose against me, I caught him by his beard, and smote him, and slew him. Thy servant smote both the lion and the bear: and this uncircumcised Philistine shall be as one of them, seeing he hath defied the armies of the living God.

(I Samuel 17:34–36)

9. Any critic who goes to the trouble of explaining laboriously why a piece of out-and-out tripe is out-and-out tripe is not a critic so much as he is a pretentious and imbecile space-filler. All the constructive criticism this side of Beverly Hills, California, that concerned itself with "The Blue Ghost," "Oh, Professor," "House Afire" and a hundred other such doses of claptrap would not be of half the critical service and merit that the single exclamation "Junk!" is. When a house has smallpox in it, the best and most sufficient thing to do is to tack a card on it reading *Smallpox*. There is little sense or need to put up a three-sheet explaining in detail what smallpox is, its contagious quality, the desirability of everyone keeping at a safe distance, how the disease can be cured, the diet of the patient, the grief

---

* Reprinted from "The Bevatron" by Lloyd Smith, in *Scientific American,* Vol. 184, No. 2, February 1951.

of the latter's parents, the name of the doctor's second cousin, and the number of times a day the nurse (duly stated to be a blonde of petting tendencies or a dark hussy given to gin) has to change the sheets.*

10. Two-thirds of the professors in our colleges are simply cans full of undigested knowledge, mechanically acquired; they cannot utilize it; they cannot think. We are cursed likewise with hordes of lawyers who would be happier and more useful driving trucks, and hordes of doctors who would be strained even as druggists. So in the realm of beautiful letters. Poetry has become a recreation among us for the intellectually unemployed and unemployable: persons who, a few generations ago, would have taken it out on china-painting. The writing of novels is undertaken by thousands who lack the skill to describe a dog-fight.†

II. APPRAISING ANALOGICAL ARGUMENTS

Although no argument by analogy is ever "valid," in the sense of having its conclusion follow from its premises with logical necessity, some are more cogent than others. Analogical arguments may be appraised as establishing their conclusions as more or less probable. In this section we shall discuss some of the criteria which are applied to arguments of this type.

The first criterion relevant to the appraisal of an analogical argument is the number of entities between which the analogies are said to hold. This principle is deeply rooted in common sense. If I advise you not to send your shirts to such and such a laundry because I sent one there once and it came back ruined, you might caution me against "jumping to conclusions," and urge that they ought perhaps to be given another chance. On the other hand, if I give you the same advice and justify it by recounting four different occasions on which unsatisfactory work was done by them on my clothing, and report further that our mutual friends Jones and Smith have

---

* Reprinted from *Testament of a Critic* by George Jean Nathan. Copyright, 1931, by George Jean Nathan. Published by Alfred A. Knopf.

† Reprinted from *Selected Prejudices* by H. L. Mencken. Copyright, 1927, by Alfred A. Knopf.

also patronized them repeatedly with unhappy results, these premisses serve to establish the conclusion with a great deal higher probability than did the first argument which cited only a single instance. It should not be thought, however, that there is any simple numerical ratio between the number of instances and the probability of the conclusion. If I have known only one chow dog, and that one was ill-tempered, this gives some probability to the conclusion that the next one I meet will be ill-tempered also. On the other hand, if I have known ten chow dogs, all of them ill-tempered, this gives considerably higher probability to the conclusion that the next one will also be ill-tempered. But it by no means follows that the second argument's conclusion is *exactly ten times* as probable.

A second criterion for appraising analogical arguments is the number of respects in which the things involved are said to be analogous. Take the example of the shoes again. That a new pair of shoes was purchased at the same store as an old pair that gave good wear is certainly a premiss from which it follows that the new shoes will probably give good wear also. But that same conclusion follows with greater probability if the premisses assert not only that the shoes were purchased from the same store, but that they were manufactured by the same company, that they sold for the same price, that they are the same style, and that I plan to wear them in the same circumstances and activities. Again, it should not be thought that there is any simple numerical ratio between the number of points of resemblance asserted in the premisses and the probability of the conclusion.

A third criterion by which analogical arguments may be judged is the strength of their conclusions relative to their premisses. If Jones has a new car and gets twenty-three miles to the gallon, from this Smith can infer with some probability that his new car, of the same make and model as Jones', will also give good mileage. Smith can construct alternative arguments here, with the same premisses but different conclusions. If he draws the conclusion that his car will go over twenty miles to the gallon, that is very probable. If he infers that his car will go over twenty-one miles to the gallon, his argument is not so strong; that is, there is less likelihood or probability of his conclusion being true. If he concludes, however, that his own car will give *exactly* twenty-three miles to the gallon, he has a very much weaker argument.

A fourth criterion used in appraising analogical arguments has to do with the number of *disanalogies* or points of difference between the instances mentioned in the premises and the instance with which the conclusion is concerned. The conclusion of the preceding argument is made very doubtful if it is pointed out that Jones drives his car for the most part at a steady pace of about twenty-five miles per hour, while Smith habitually drives at speeds in excess of eighty miles per hour. This disanalogy between the instance in the premiss and that of the conclusion weakens the argument, and greatly reduces the probability of its conclusion.

Of course the larger the number of instances appealed to in the premises, the less likely it is that they will *all* be disanalogous to the instance mentioned in the conclusion. To minimize disanalogies between the instances of the premises and the instance of the conclusion, however, we need not enumerate more and more instances in the premises. The same end can be achieved by taking instances in our premisses which are dissimilar to each other. The less similar the instances of the premises are to each other, the less likely it is for *all* of them to be dissimilar to the conclusion's instance. Our fifth criterion for appraising arguments by analogy, then, is that the more dissimilar the instances mentioned in its premisses, the stronger is the argument.

This principle is just as often appealed to and just as commonly accepted as any of the others that have been mentioned. The conclusion that Johnny Jones, an entering freshman at State, will successfully finish his college education and receive a degree, can be established as highly probable on the grounds that ten other students who graduated from the same high

school as Johnny Jones, and received grades there very similar
to his, have entered State as freshmen and have successfully
finished their college educations and received degrees. The
argument is appreciably stronger if the ten other students mentioned in the premisses do not resemble each other too closely.
The argument is strengthened by pointing out that those ten
other students did not all come from the same economic back-
grounds, that they differ from each other in racial stock, in religious affiliation, and so on. Incidentally, the fifth criterion explains the importance of the first. The greater the number of
instances appealed to, the greater the number of disanalogies
which can probably be pointed out among them. None of these
five criteria are new or in any way startling. They are con-
stantly used by us in appraising analogical arguments.

There is just one criterion for arguments by analogy that remains to be discussed. Although last, it is definitely not least,
being the most important of them all. The examples presented
thus far have all been fairly good arguments, because their
analogies have all been *relevant*. Thus in support of the conclusion that Smith's new car will give good mileage, we adduced as evidence the fact that Jones' new car, which is known
to give good mileage, is the same model; that is, it has the
same number of cylinders, the same body weight, and the
same horsepower as Smith's. These are all *relevant* considerations. Contrast this argument with one which draws the same
conclusion from different premisses, from premisses which assert nothing about cylinders, body weight, or horsepower, but
affirm instead that the two cars have the same color, the same
number of gauges on their dashboards, and the same style of
upholstery in their interiors. The latter is a much weaker argument. But it cannot be judged so by any of the first five criteria
mentioned. The two arguments appeal to the same number of
instances and the same number of analogies. The reason why
the first is a good argument and the second ridiculously bad
is that the factors in the first are relevant to mileage, while
those of the second are completely irrelevant.

The question of relevance is all important. An argument based on a single *relevant* analogy connected with a single instance will be more cogent than one which points out a dozen *irrelevant* points of resemblance between its conclusion's instance and over a score of instances enumerated in its premises. Thus a doctor's inference is sound when he reasons that Mr. Black will be helped by a specific drug on the grounds that Mr. White was helped by it when a blood test showed exactly the same type of germs in his system that are now in Mr. Black's. But it would be fantastic for him to draw the same conclusion from premises which assert that Smith, Jones, and Robinson were all helped by it, and that they and Black all patronize the same tailor, drive the same make and model car, have the same number of children, had similar educations, and were all born under the same sign of the zodiac. The reason for the weakness of the second argument is that the points of resemblance cited are strictly irrelevant to the matter with which the conclusion is concerned.

Although there may be disagreement about what analogies are relevant for certain conclusions, that is, what properties are relevant for proving the presence of certain other properties in a given instance, it is doubtful that there is any disagreement about the *meaning* of "relevance." An illustration given by Professor J. H. Wigmore in one of his important legal treatises is the following:

To show that a certain boiler was not dangerously likely to explode at a certain pressure of steam, other instances of non-explosion of boilers at the same pressure would be relevant, provided the other boilers were substantially similar in type, age, and other circumstances affecting strength.*

Here we are given a criterion for relevance itself. An analogy is *relevant* to establishing the presence of a given property (strength, in Wigmore's illustration) provided it is drawn

* Reprinted from *Wigmore's Code of the Rules of Evidence in Trials at Law* by John H. Wigmore. Copyright, 1910, 1915, 1935, 1938, 1942 by John H. Wigmore. Published by Little, Brown and Company.

with respect to *other circumstances affecting it.* One property
or circumstance is relevant to another, for purposes of analogical argument, if the first *affects* the second, that is, if it has a
causal or determining effect on that other.

The factor of relevance is to be explained in terms of causal-
ity. In an argument by analogy, the relevant analogies are
those which deal with causally related properties or circumstances. If my neighbor has his house insulated and his fuel
bill goes down, then if I have my own house insulated I can
confidently expect my own fuel bill to decrease. The analogy
is a good one, because insulation is relevant to the size of fuel
bills, being causally connected with fuel consumption. Analogical arguments are highly probable whether they go from
cause to effect, or from effect to cause. They are even probable
when the property in the premiss is neither cause nor effect
of the conclusion's property, provided that both are effects of
the *same* cause. Thus from the presence of some symptoms
of a given disease a doctor can predict other symptoms—not
that either symptom is the cause of the other, but because they
are jointly caused by one and the same malady.

To evaluate analogical arguments, then, requires some knowledge of causal connections. These are discovered only empirically, by observation and experiment. The theory of empirical investigation is the central concern of inductive logic,
and to this topic we turn in the following chapters.

EXERCISES

I. Each of the following arguments by analogy has six additional
premises suggested for it. For each of these alternative premises
decide whether its addition would make the resulting argument
more or less probable.

1. A traveling salesman spends one day in Peoria, Illinois every
   month, and for the past ten months has always eaten his lunch at
   Mom's Diner in that city. In every case he has enjoyed his meal.
   On his present visit he decides to eat there again, reasoning that
   he will probably enjoy his lunch there again.

(a) Suppose he had eaten lunch there once every week instead of once every month for the past ten months?

(b) Suppose he has always ordered ham and eggs before, and plans to order ham and eggs today too?

(c) Suppose that he had not merely enjoyed his previous meals there, but had found them delicious beyond all powers of description?

(d) Suppose he suddenly learns that a new chef had been installed yesterday?

(e) Suppose instead that there has been a continual change of personnel at Mom's Diner, with a new chef having been installed every month for the past year?

(f) Suppose he sees that the cashier's desk has been switched from the left side of the entrance to the right hand side?

2. A devotee of the sport of kings bets his money on Whirligig, who has won his last six races.

(a) Suppose he bets Whirligig to show rather than to win?

(b) Suppose the last six races have been over distances of less than a mile, while the present race is a mile and a quarter?

(c) Suppose instead that two of the six races were steeplechases, and the remaining four were on tracks of varying lengths, from the shortest to the longest, and exactly three have been on muddy tracks?

(d) Suppose that Whirligig had won his last sixteen races instead of only his last six?

(e) Suppose the same jockey had ridden Whirligig in his last six races that is riding him today?

(f) Suppose the bettor dreamed of finding a horseshoe for the first time on the night before the present race?

3. The Republocrats have elected Winnemac's governor in every election during the past eight years, and it is confidently expected that they will carry the gubernatorial contest this year too.

(a) Suppose that during the past six years the Governorship was the *only* state office to be occupied by a Republocrat?

(b) Suppose that all of the previous Republocrat candidates have been farmers, while this year they are supporting a college professor?

(c) Suppose that the Republocrats are supporting the present incumbent for reelection?

(d) Suppose that Winnemac has always elected a Republocrat governor ever since the time of the Civil War?

(e) Suppose Winnemac has elected Republocrats to every state, national, and local office during the past eight years?

(f) Suppose the previous Republocrat candidates have included a farmer, a businessman, a doctor, and a lawyer?

II. Analyze the structures of the analogical arguments in the following passages, and evaluate them in terms of the six criteria that have been explained:

1. There is not the least inherent improbability, as it seems to me, in virtuous tendencies being more or less strongly inherited; for, not to mention the various dispositions and habits transmitted by many of our domestic animals to their offspring, I have heard of authentic cases in which a desire to steal and a tendency to lie appeared to run in families of the upper ranks; and as stealing is a rare crime in the wealthy classes, we can hardly account by accidental coincidence for the tendency occurring in two or three members of the same family. If bad tendencies are transmitted, it is probable that good ones are likewise transmitted.

(Charles Darwin, *Descent of Man,* Ch. 4)

2. And it came to pass, that he went through the corn fields on the sabbath day; and his disciples began, as they went, to pluck the ears of corn.

And the Pharisees said unto him, Behold, why do they on the sabbath day that which is not lawful?

And he said unto them, Have ye never read what David did, when he had need, and was an hungred, he, and they that were with him?

How he went into the house of God in the days of Abiathar the high priest, and did eat the shewbread, which is not lawful to eat but for the priests, and gave also to them which were with him?

(Mark 2:23–26)

3. What I mean may be put into the form of a question, I said: Are dogs divided into hes and shes, or do they both share equally in hunting and in keeping watch and in the other duties of dogs? or do we entrust to the males the entire and exclusive care of the

flocks, while we leave the females at home, under the idea that
the bearing and suckling their puppies is labour enough for them?

No, he said, they share alike; the only difference between them
is that the males are stronger and the females weaker.

But can you use different animals for the same purpose, unless
they are bred and fed in the same way?

You cannot.

Then, if women are to have the same duties as man, they must
have the same nurture and education?

Yes.

The education which was assigned to the men was music and
gymnastic.

Yes.

Then women must be taught music and gymnastic and also the
art of war, which they must practice like the men?

That is the inference, I suppose.

(Plato, Republic, Book 5)

4. "But I'm *not* a serpent, I tell you!" said Alice. "I'm a—I'm a—"

"Well! *What* are you?" said the Pigeon. "I can see you're trying
to invent something!"

"I—I'm a little girl," said Alice, rather doubtfully, as she remembered the number of changes she had gone through, that day.

"A likely story indeed!" said the Pigeon, in a tone of the deepest
contempt. "I've seen a good many little girls in my time, but never
one with such a neck as that! No, no! You're a serpent; and there's
no use denying it. I suppose you'll be telling me next that you
never tasted an egg!"

"I *have* tasted eggs, certainly," said Alice, who was a very truth-
ful child; "but little girls eat eggs quite as much as serpents do,
you know."

"I don't believe it," said the Pigeon; "but if they do, then
they're a kind of serpent: that's all I can say."

(Lewis Carroll, Alice's Adventures in Wonderland)

5. Look around the world: Contemplate the whole and every part
of it: You will find it to be nothing but one great machine, sub-
divided into an infinite number of lesser machines, which again
admit of subdivisions, to a degree beyond what human senses and
faculties can trace and explain. All these various machines, and

even their most minute parts, are adjusted to each other with an accuracy, which ravishes into admiration all men, who have ever contemplated them. The curious adapting of means to ends, throughout all nature, resembles exactly, though it much exceeds, the productions of human contrivance; of human design, thought, wisdom, and intelligence. Since therefore the effects resemble each other, we are led to infer, by all the rules of analogy, that the causes also resemble; and that the Author of nature is somewhat similar to the mind of man; though possessed of much larger faculties, proportioned to the grandeur of the work, which he has executed. By this argument *a posteriori* and by this argument alone, we do prove at once the existence of a Deity, and his similarity to human mind and intelligence.

(David Hume, *Dialogues Concerning Natural Religion*, Part 2)

6. . . . a man who intends keeping pointers naturally tries to get as good dogs as he can, and afterwards breeds from his own best dogs, but he has no wish or expectation of permanently altering the breed. Nevertheless we may infer that this process, continued during centuries, would improve and modify any breed, in the same way as Bakewell, Collins, &c., by this very same process, only carried on more methodically, did greatly modify, even during their lifetimes, the forms and qualities of their cattle.

(Charles Darwin, *The Origin of Species,* Ch. 1)

CHAPTER TWELVE

Causal Connections: Mill's Methods of Experimental Inquiry

I. THE MEANING OF "CAUSE"

To exercise any measure of control over our environment we must have some knowledge of causal connections. For a physician to cure an illness he must know what *causes* it, and he must understand the *effects* of the drugs he administers. Since there are several different meanings of the word "cause," we must make clear the sense in which we intend to use it in the present chapter.

It is a fundamental axiom in the study of nature that events do not just "happen," but occur only under certain conditions. It is customary to distinguish between "necessary" and "sufficient" conditions for the occurrence of an event. A *necessary* condition for the occurrence of a specified event is a circumstance in whose *absence* the event *cannot* occur. For example, the presence of oxygen is a necessary condition for combustion

327

to occur: if combustion occurs then oxygen must have been present, for in the absence of oxygen there can be no combustion.

Although it is a necessary condition, the presence of oxygen is not a *sufficient* condition for combustion to occur. A *sufficient* condition for the occurrence of an event is a circumstance in whose *presence* the event *must* occur. The presence of oxygen is not a sufficient condition for combustion because oxygen *can* be present without combustion occurring. On the other hand, for almost any substance there is some degree of temperature such that *being above that temperature in the presence of oxygen* is a sufficient condition for combustion of that substance. It is obvious that there may be several *necessary* conditions for the occurrence of an event, and that they must all be included in the *sufficient* condition.

The word "cause" is sometimes used in the sense of necessary condition and sometimes in the sense of sufficient condition. It is most often used in the sense of necessary condition when the problem at hand is the elimination of some undesirable phenomenon. To eliminate it, one need only find some condition which is necessary to its existence, and then eliminate that condition. Thus a physician seeks to discover what kind of germ is the "cause" of a certain illness in order to cure the illness by prescribing a drug which will destroy those germs. The germs are said to be the "cause" of the disease in the sense of a necessary condition for it, since in their absence the disease cannot occur.

The word "cause" is used in the sense of sufficient condition when we are interested not in the elimination of something undesirable but rather in the production of something desirable. Thus a metallurgist seeks to discover the "cause" of strength in alloys in order to be able to produce stronger metals. The process of mixing and heating and cooling is said to be the "cause" of the strengthening in the sense of a sufficient condition, since such processing suffices to produce a stronger alloy.

In certain practical situations, the word *cause* is used in still a different sense. An insurance company might send an investigator to determine the cause of a mysterious fire. If the investigator sent back a report that the fire was caused by the presence of oxygen in the atmosphere, he would not keep his job very long. And yet he would be right—in the sense of necessary condition—for had there been no oxygen present, there would have been no fire. But the insurance company did not have *that* sense of "cause" in mind when they sent him to investigate. Nor is the company interested in the sufficient condition. If after several weeks the investigator reported that although he had proof that the fire was deliberately ignited by the policyholder, he hadn't as yet been able to learn *all* the necessary conditions, and so hadn't been able to determine the cause (in the sense of sufficient condition), the company would recall the investigator and tell him to stop wasting his time and their money. The insurance company was using the word "cause" in another sense—what they wanted to find out was the incident or action which, in the presence of those conditions which are ordinarily present, made the difference between the occurrence or non-occurrence of the event.

We may distinguish between two different subdivisions of this third sense of cause. These are traditionally characterized as the "remote" and the "proximate" causes. In this case the *proximate* cause was the policyholder's lighting the fire. But his action, and thus the fire, may have been caused by his wife's nagging him for more money, and her nagging may have been caused by a neighbor's wife getting a new fur coat, which may have been caused by the neighbor's grain speculations turning out well because of rising food prices which were caused by a Canadian crop failure. The crop failure was a *remote* cause of the fire, but the insurance company would not have been interested in hearing that the mysterious fire was caused by a Canadian crop failure.

There are several different senses of the term "cause," as we have seen. We can legitimately infer cause *from* effect only in the sense of necessary condition. And inference from cause *to* effect is legitimate only in the sense of sufficient condition. Since we wish to count as legitimate all inferences from causes to their effects as well as from effects to their causes, we shall find it most convenient to use the term "cause" in the sense of *necessary and sufficient condition*. This sense is the one most often used in writings on logic.

The notion of cause as used in everyday life and in science involves or presupposes the doctrine that cause and effect are *uniformly* connected. We admit that a particular circumstance caused a particular effect only if we agree that any other circumstance *of that type* will—if the attendant circumstances are sufficiently similar—cause another effect *of the same kind as the first*. In other words, similar causes produce similar effects. Part of the very meaning of the word "cause" as used today is that every occurrence of a cause producing an effect is an *instance* or *example* of the general causal law that such circumstances are *always* accompanied by such phenomena. Thus we are willing to relinquish a belief that circumstance *C* was the cause of effect *E* in one particular case if it can be shown that the same (type of) circumstance was present in another situation which was the same as the first except that the effect *E did not occur* in the latter.

One further point should be noted. Common sense is of the opinion that a given phenomenon may have been the result of many different causes. If a man's death occurs, it may have been caused by heart failure, or by poisoning, by a bullet, by a traffic accident, or by any of the hundreds of other circumstances which are capable, as we say, of causing death. But the view that there may be a "plurality of causes" of a single kind of effect conflicts with the notion that a cause is a *necessary* and sufficient condition for its effect. If there can be a plurality of causes, then inferences from effects to their causes are not possible. The doctrine of plurality of causes is very widely accepted indeed. A crop failure may be caused either by drouth or by excessive rainfall, or by grasshoppers.

It should not be concluded, however, that interpreting cause as necessary and sufficient condition is mistaken and unfruitful. Any farmer would agree that there are different kinds of crop failures, and the kind produced by drouth could not possibly have been caused by excessive rainfall or grasshoppers. If an effect is specified with sufficient precision, the apparent plurality of causes disappears. True enough, "death-in-general" may be caused by a plurality of alternative circumstances, but a specific kind of death, that induced, say, by strychnine poisoning, could not possibly have resulted from a coronary thrombosis. The unique cause of death is frequently discovered by post mortem examinations, where an autopsy reveals the particular kind of death with enough specificity to permit an inference that *the* cause of the death in question was one thing rather than any other. The doctrine of plurality of causes may be rejected, then, for in every case in which it is thought that alternative circumstances may have caused a given phenomenon, it is probable that a further specification or more precise description of that phenomenon would make the apparent plurality of causes disappear.

We need not rule out plurality of causes in an *a priori* fashion. We may regard the doctrine of uniqueness of cause as itself the result of an inductive generalization. In every case of alleged plurality of causes encountered thus far, the apparent plurality vanishes when the effect in question is more precisely specified. From this fact we can conclude with probability that in every case a more precise specification of the effect will decrease the number of alternative circumstances which might have caused that effect. And so we can accept, not as necessarily true *a priori*, but as highly probable on the evidence, the working hypothesis that every effect of a specific kind has a single and unique kind of cause.

An even stronger case can be made against the doctrine of plurality of causes. We may quote in this connection William James's dictum that *every difference must make a difference.* If two circumstances can result in the *same* kinds of effects, it is proper to regard them as being themselves of the same kind. If their effects are no different, then they are not really different from each other. Ordinarily we pay attention only to those differences which are important to us and ignore those in which we have no interest. Certainly their *effects* are of greatest moment in distinguishing circumstances as being of the same or of different kinds. If all their effects are the same —that is, do not differ in any "important" respects—then two circumstances are also "the same," whereas if their effects are significantly different, this difference is the basis on which we distinguish them as *different* circumstances. If we agree that *every difference must make a difference,* then we shall reject the doctrine of plurality of causes.

Since a general causal law is implied by every assertion that a particular circumstance was the cause of a particular phenomenon, there is an element of generality in every such assertion. A causal law—as we shall use the term—is an assertion that such and such a circumstance is invariably attended by such and such a phenomenon, no matter when or where it occurs. Now how do we come to know such general truths? The causal relation is not a purely logical or deductive relationship; it cannot be discovered by any *a priori* reasoning. Causal laws can be discovered only *empirically,* by an appeal to experience. But our experiences are always of particular circumstances, particular phenomena, and particular sequences of them. We may observe several instances of a certain kind of circumstance (say C), and every instance *that we observe* may be accompanied by an instance of a certain kind of phenomenon (say P). These observations show us, of course, only that *some* cases of C are cases of P. How are we to get from this evidence to the general proposition that *all* cases of C are cases of P, which is involved in saying that C *causes P?*

The method of arriving at general or universal propositions from the particular facts of experience is called "inductive generalization." From premises which assert that three particular pieces of blue litmus paper turned red when dipped in acid, we may draw either a particular conclusion about what will happen to a particular fourth piece of blue litmus paper if it is dipped in acid, or a general conclusion about what happens to *all* blue litmus paper dipped in acid. If we draw the first, we have an argument by analogy; the second is an *inductive generalization*. The structure of these two types of arguments may be analyzed as follows. The premisses report a number of instances in which two properties (or circumstances or phenomena) occur together. By analogy we may infer that a different particular instance of one property will also exhibit the other property. By inductive generalization we may infer that *all* instances of the one property will also be instances of the other. An inductive generalization of the form:

Instance 1 of phenomenon E is accompanied by circumstance C.
Instance 2 of phenomenon E is accompanied by circumstance C.
Instance 3 of phenomenon E is accompanied by circumstance C.

....

Therefore all instances of phenomenon E are accompanied by circumstance C.

is an induction by *simple enumeration*. An induction by simple enumeration is very similar to argument by analogy, differing only in having a general rather than a particular conclusion.

Simple enumeration is often used in establishing causal connections. Where a number of instances of a phenomenon are invariably accompanied by a certain type of circumstance, it is only natural to infer the existence of a causal relationship between them. Since the circumstance of dipping blue litmus paper in acid is accompanied in all observed instances by the phenomenon of the paper's turning red, we conclude that dipping blue litmus paper in acid is the *cause* of its turning red. Similarly, from the fact that a number of men have contracted yellow fever after being bitten by mosquitoes which had previously fed on yellow fever patients, we may infer by simple enumeration that the bite of such a mosquito *causes* yellow fever infection. The analogical character of such arguments is very apparent.

Because of the great similarity between argument by simple enumeration and argument by analogy, it should be clear that the same types of criteria apply to both. Some arguments by simple enumeration may establish their conclusions with a higher degree of probability than others. The greater the number of instances appealed to, the higher the probability of the conclusion. The various instances or cases of phenomenon *E* accompanied by circumstance *C* are often called *confirming instances* of the causal law which asserts that *C* causes *E*. The greater the number of confirming instances, the higher the probability of the causal law—other things being equal. Thus the first criterion for analogical arguments applies directly to arguments by simple enumeration also.

Inductions by simple enumeration are very frequently made, and despite their weaknesses, are often very valuable and suggestive. But they are not very trustworthy. For example, consider the following argument:

Tom broke a mirror and cut his hand, which was bad luck.
Dick broke a mirror and then sprained his ankle, which was bad luck.
Harry broke a mirror and then lost his wallet, which was bad luck.

Therefore breaking a mirror *causes* bad luck.

Most of us would be inclined to put very little trust in such an argument. Yet it is an argument by simple enumeration, appealing to three "confirming instances." Nevertheless, we should probably say that the three instances reported were coincidences rather than cases of a causal law. This is the chief weakness of arguments by simple enumeration. Their very nature prevents them from distinguishing between confirming instances of genuine causal laws, on the one hand, and mere accidents or coincidences, on the other.

Our criticism of the method of simple enumeration can be put in this way. A single negative or disconfirming instance will overthrow an alleged causal law (any exception obviously *disproves* a rule), while the method of simple enumeration takes no account of such exceptions. For an exception or negative instance is either one where *C* is present without *E,* or where *E* is present without *C;* but the only legitimate premisses in an argument by simple enumeration are reports of instances in which both *C* and *E* are present. In other words, if we were to confine ourselves to simple enumeration arguments exclusively, we should look only for confirming instances and would tend to *ignore* any negative or disconfirming instances that might otherwise be found. For this reason, despite their fruitfulness and value in *suggesting* causal laws, inductions by simple enumeration are not at all suitable for *testing* causal laws. For the testing of causal laws, other types of inductive arguments have been devised, and to these we now turn.

II. MILL'S METHODS

His criticisms of induction by simple enumeration led the British philosopher Sir Francis Bacon (1561–1626) to recommend other types of inductive procedure. These were given their classic formulation by another British philosopher, John Stuart Mill (1806–1873), and have come to be called "Mill's Methods" of inductive inference. Mill formulated five of these "canons," as he called them, and they are known as the *Method of Agreement,* the *Method of Difference,* the *Joint Method of Agreement and Difference,* the *Method of Residues,* and the *Method of Concomitant Variation.* They will be presented here in that order.

1. **Method of Agreement.** The Method of Agreement is best introduced by way of an example. Suppose that some of the residents of a certain dormitory have become violently ill, suffering stomach distress and nausea, and it is desired to determine the cause of this illness. Half a dozen of the affected students are interviewed to find out what they ate the day on which the illness began. The first student ate soup, bread and butter, salad, vegetables, and canned pears; the second student ate soup, bread

and butter, vegetables, and canned pears; the third student ate
soup, a pork sandwich, salad, and canned pears; the fourth
student ate bread and butter, salad, a pork sandwich, vegetables,
and canned pears; the fifth student ate soup, salad, vegetables,
and canned pears; and the sixth student ate bread and butter,
vegetables, and canned pears. To make this information more
readily available, we can set it down in the form of a table, using
the capital letters "A," "B," "C," "D," "E," "F" to denote the
presence of the "antecedent circumstances" of having eaten soup,
bread and butter, salad, pork sandwich, vegetables, and canned
pears, respectively, and using the small letter "s" to denote the
presence of the phenomenon of being sick. Where the six students are the six "instances" examined, our information can be
represented as:

instance	*antecedent*		*circumstances*				*phenomenon*
1	A	B	C		E	F	s
2	A	B			E	F	s
3	A		C	D		F	s
4		B	C	D	E	F	s
5	A		C		E	F	s
6		B			E	F	s

From this data we should naturally infer that the circumstance
F was the cause of the phenomenon *s*, that is, that the illness
was due to eating the particular canned pears served in the dormitory. As in any other inductive argument, these premisses do
not *prove* the conclusion, but they do establish it as probable.
Any inference of this type is characterized as using the Method
of Agreement. Mill's general formulation is this:

*If two or more instances of the phenomenon under investigation
have only one circumstance in common, the circumstance in which
alone all the instances agree, is the cause (or effect) of the given
phenomenon.*

Schematically, the Method of Agreement may be represented
as follows, where capital letters represent circumstances, and
small letters denote phenomena:

A B C D occur together with *a b c d*.
A E F G occur together with *a e f g*.

Therefore *A* is the cause (or the effect) of *a*.

Another illustration of the use of the Method of Agreement can be drawn from a fairly recent innovation in dental hygiene. It was observed that the inhabitants of several cities enjoyed a much lower rate of dental decay than the national average, and some thought was given to discovering the cause of this happy phenomenon. It was found that the circumstances of these cities differed in many ways; in latitude and longitude, in elevation, in their types of economy, etc. But one circumstance was common to all of them. This common circumstance was the presence of an unusually high percentage of fluorine in their water supplies, which meant that the diet of the inhabitants of these cities included an unusually large quantity of fluorine. It was inferred that the use of fluorine can cause a decrease in the incidence of dental decay, and acceptance of this conclusion has led to the adoption of fluorine treatments for this purpose in many other localities. Whenever we have found a single circumstance common to all instances of a given phenomenon, we believe ourselves to have discovered its cause.

A word should be said here about the limitations of the Method of Agreement. The available data in our first illustration of that method was remarkably well suited to the application of that method. But such convenient data may not always be available. For example, it might have been the case that all of the stricken students had eaten *both* salad and canned pears. In that case the Method of Agreement would have *eliminated* the soup, the bread and butter, the pork sandwiches, and the vegetables as possible causes of the illness, but would have left open the question as to whether it was the salad, the canned pears, or the combination of them which was responsible for the students' sickness. A different inductive method is required to establish the cause here, and it is provided by the second of Mill's Methods.

EXERCISES

Analyze each of the following arguments in terms of "circumstances" and "phenomena" to show that they follow the pattern of the Method of Agreement:

1. Chloromycetin for Whooping Cough

    The antibiotic, chloromycetin, has been found highly effective as a rapid treatment of whooping cough, a disease which causes more deaths among children less than two years old than polio and scarlet fever combined.

    Parke, Davis & Co., maker of the drug, reported that 62 patients seriously ill in Cochabamba, Bolivia, had shown marked improvement and regained normal temperatures only one to three days after starting chloromycetin treatments.

    The patients were symptom-free in three and a half to six days, and no remaining infection was found one week after treatment.

    In another study, five infants 8 to 26 weeks old and severely ill with whooping cough showed "immediate improvement in general condition in all the cases, followed by rapid recovery." Four of the children improved within 12 hours and the fifth, in 24 hours.*

2. Over in Denmark Johannes Fibiger, a pathologist of the University of Copenhagen, had been working thirteen years on the problem of tuberculosis among laboratory animals. During a series of postmortem examinations of tubercular rats, he found three had suffered from stomach cancers. Fibiger knew enough about cancer to realize that he had come across a singular phenomenon. Rats rarely suffered from tumors of the stomach.

    Fibiger made a visit to the dealer who had been supplying him with these rats, and on questioning found that those sent to his laboratory had all come from a sugar refinery. Was there anything peculiar about this refinery which could account for the unusually large percentage of stomach-cancerous mice from this spot? He investigated the place and found nothing unusual except a high infestation with cockroaches, which formed a fairly

* Reprinted from "The Progress of Medicine," in *Science Digest,* Vol. 29, No. 6, June 1951.

large part of the diet of its rats. Could he find some connection between roaches, rats, and cancer? Cancer as a disease of filth had been spoken about for years, and vermin were said to be responsible for the so-called "cancer houses," private homes from which emerged many a human cancer victim of the same family.

Fibiger planned a controlled experiment. He collected thousands of the refinery roaches and fed them to rats from another breeding establishment. The rats enjoyed this strange treatment, and for three years—that was the normal life span of his rodents —Fibiger remained skeptical. Then they died, and one by one he opened them up. To his astonishment, he found many stomach cancers. Fibiger made a careful microscopic study of the growths. He discovered that in every case they had formed around a parasitic worm, the same worm to which the roach had been host before it was fed to the rat. The larva of the worm coiled up in the muscles of the rat, later developing into an adult worm in the animal's stomach. Around this the tumorous growth had appeared. Fibiger had actually for the first time produced artificial cancer in a laboratory animal.*

3. Dr. P. Potts in 1775 had called attention to the frequent occurrence of cancer of the scrotum among chimney sweeps, and thought it might be in some way connected with soot. Coal tar and paraffin shale workers were also known to be subject to warts, which often became cancerous. Two Japanese, a century and a half later, decided to test out the relation of tar and cancer. Yamagiwa and Ichikawa used rabbits. At regular intervals they painted the ears of their rabbits with tar and actually witnessed the appearance of tumorous growths at the points of irritation. Then these tumors were transplanted by other scientists to normal rabbits, and the grafts took. This was a startling piece of scientific news. Here was another form of experimental cancer in animals which could be studied under controlled laboratory conditions.*

2. Method of Difference. The Method of Difference is often applicable to such cases as those described in our first illustration of the Method of Agreement, even where the data will not

---

* *Outposts of Science* by Bernard Jaffe. Copyright, 1935, by Bernard Jaffe. Reprinted by permission of Simon and Schuster, Publishers.

permit the use of the Method of Agreement. If on further investigation in the dormitory we found a student who, on the day that many had become ill, had eaten soup, bread and butter, salad, and vegetables only, and had *not* become ill, we could profitably compare his case with that of the first student described. Denoting this last student as "instance *n*," and using the same abbreviations as in our first table, we can set down a new table as:

instance	antecedent circumstances	phenomenon
1	A B C E F	s
n	A B C E –	–

From this new data we should again naturally infer that the circumstance *F* was the cause of the phenomenon *s;* that is, the illness was due to eating the canned pears. Of course, the conclusion follows with probability rather than with certainty, but this is merely to say that the inference is inductive rather than deductive. Any inference of this type uses the Method of Difference, which was formulated by Mill in these words:

If an instance in which the phenomenon under investigation occurs, and an instance in which it does not occur, have every circumstance in common save one, that one occurring only in the former; the circumstance in which alone the two instances differ, is the effect, or the cause, or an indispensable part of the cause, of the phenomenon.

Schematically, the Method of Difference may be represented as follows, where again capital letters represent circumstances, and small letters denote phenomena:

A B C D occur together with *a b c d;*
B C D occur together with *b c d;*

Therefore *A* is the cause, or the effect, or an indispensable part of the cause, of *a.*

Strictly speaking, we should have inferred not that eating the canned pears was *the* cause of sickness, but that eating the canned pears was "an indispensable part of the cause" of the sickness. This distinction is perhaps brought out more clearly in the case of a simpler example. We might have two cigarette lighters in exactly the same condition except that the flint has been removed from one but not the other. The presence of the flint is the only circumstance in which they differ, and the phenomenon of lighting occurs in the one instance but not in the other, yet we should not say that the presence of flint was *the* cause, but rather *an indispensable part of the cause* of the light. Where it is known that the phenomenon occurs later in time than the circumstance, as when eating the canned pears was an *antecedent* circumstance, there need be no doubt as to which is cause and which effect, for an effect can never precede its cause.

A more serious illustration of the Method of Difference is provided by the following:

Experiments were devised to show that yellow fever was transmitted by the mosquito alone, all other reasonable opportunities for being infected being excluded. A small building was erected, all windows and doors and every other possible opening being absolutely mosquito-proof. A wire mosquito screen divided the room into two spaces. In one of these spaces fifteen mosquitoes, which had fed on yellow fever patients, were liberated. A non-immune volunteer entered the room with the mosquitoes and was bitten by seven mosquitoes. Four days later, he suffered an attack of yellow fever. Two other non-immune men slept for thirteen nights in the mosquito-free room without disturbances of any sort.

To show that the disease was transmitted by the mosquito and not through the excreta of yellow fever patients or anything which had come in contact with them, another house was constructed and made mosquito-proof. For 20 days, this house was occupied by three non-immunes, after the clothing, bedding and eating utensils and other vessels soiled with the discharge, blood and vomitus of yellow fever patients had been placed in it. The bed clothing which they used had been brought from the beds of the patients who had died of yellow fever, without being subjected to washing or any other treatment to remove anything with which it might have been soiled. The experiment was twice repeated by other non-immune volunteers. During the entire period all the men who occupied the house were strictly quarantined and protected from mosquitoes. None of those exposed to these experiments contracted yellow fever. That they were not immune was subsequently shown, since four of them became infected either by mosquito bites or the injection of blood from yellow fever patients.*

The preceding account contains three distinct uses of the Method of Difference. In the first paragraph, the reasoning involved may be schematized as follows, where "*A*" denotes the circumstance of being bitten by an infected mosquito, "*a*" denotes the phenomenon of suffering an attack of yellow fever, "*B*," "*C*," "*D*," denote the circumstances of living in the small building described, and "*b*," "*c*," "*d*," denote phenomena common to *all* the volunteers referred to:

$A\ B\ C\ D$——$a\ b\ c\ d$	first non-immune man
$B\ C\ D$——$b\ c\ d$	second non-immune man
$B\ C\ D$——$b\ c\ d$	third non-immune man

Therefore A is the cause of a.

The second paragraph involves a refinement on the preceding, for the infected mosquitoes, presumably, did not merely bite the first non-immune man but in lighting on him deposited some matter which they had picked up from the yellow fever patients on whom they had previously fed. That it was the *bite* of the mosquito (A) which caused infection (a), rather than the circumstance (M) of coming into contact with matter which had been in contact with a yellow fever patient, is established by the following pattern of argument:

$B\ C\ D\ M$——$b\ c\ d\ m$	non-immune men in house
$A\ B\ C\ D\ M$——$a\ b\ c\ d\ m$	same non-immune man when subsequently bitten.

Therefore A (rather than M) is the cause of a.

The third pattern of argument found in the preceding account emerges when the first and second paragraphs are considered to-

---

gether. Here we focus our attention on two instances: first, the non-immune man who was both bitten by a mosquito *and* thus brought into contact with matter from a yellow fever patient, and second, the non-immune man who was not bitten but was nevertheless brought into contact with matter from a patient. Here the pattern emerges as:

$$A\ M\text{-----}a\ m$$
$$M\text{-----}m$$

Therefore A is the cause of a.

All these patterns exemplify the Method of Difference, which is thus seen to be a very pervasive type of experimental inference.

It frequently happens that the available data will not permit either the Method of Agreement or the Method of Difference to be applied separately. In some such cases a third pattern of inductive inference is available; this is the third of Mill's Methods, to which we next turn.

EXERCISES

Analyze each of the following arguments in terms of "circumstances" and "phenomena" to show that they follow the pattern of the Method of Difference:

1. What Makes Gobies Jump?

Gobies are tropical shore fish about an inch and a half long. As they swim about near the shore they sometimes get trapped by a low tide in shallow land-locked pools. When a goby finds itself in such a fix, it may leap out of the pool and over rocks toward deep water, sometimes clearing nine inches in a jump. And the most remarkable thing about it is that the fish always knows which way to jump. If it leaped onto shore instead of into the ocean, it would be a dead goby; but the canny animal never guesses wrong.

How does the goby know which way to jump?

This problem in fish psychology was tackled by Lester R. Aronson of the American Museum of Natural History. After watching a great many gobies jump about in the waters near

Bimini, British West Indies, he began to have a suspicion of the answer. To test his theory he put some gobies in a tank containing four separate pools. Most of the fish stayed in their own pools; the few that ventured to jump jumped wrong—into a part of the tank without water. Then Dr. Aronson flooded the tank. The gobies had a chance to swim over the bottom and learn its topography. When he lowered the water level to separate the pools once more, the gobies now happily jumped from one pool to another, never making a mistake.

Dr. Aronson's conclusion: the gobies remember the terrain they swim over, and when trapped, jump from memory. He thinks they can remember for as long as two weeks.*

2. Eijkman fed a group of chickens exclusively on white rice. They all developed polyneuritis and died. He fed another group of fowl unpolished rice. Not a single one of them contracted the disease. Then he gathered up the polishings from rice and fed them to other polyneuritic chickens, and in a short time the birds recovered. He had accurately traced the cause of polyneuritis to a faulty diet. For the first time in history, he had produced a food deficiency disease experimentally, and had actually cured it. It was a fine piece of work and resulted in some immediate remedial measures. Eijkman was later recalled to Holland to a professorship at the University of Utrecht.†

3. The flowers of many fruit plants often are killed by late spring frosts, resulting in enormous losses to the industry. If flowering could be delayed 10 days or more in many instances the danger of frost would be past . . . Two-year-old vigorous Bristol black raspberries afforded the best example of the effects of maleic hydrazide in delaying blossoming. Leaflets were expanded to about 1 cm and side branches were just beginning to appear on April 27, when plants were sprayed. The treated plants blossomed 24 to 38 days later than check plants, and matured their fruit 16 to 23 days later than check plants. Fruit set was good and no difference in size or flavor of the berries was apparent. Vegetative development was temporarily inhibited and although new canes

---

* Reprinted from "Science and the Citizen" in *Scientific American*, Vol. 184, No. 4, April 1951.

† *Outposts of Science* by Bernard Jaffe. Copyright, 1935, by Bernard Jaffe. Reprinted by permission of Simon and Schuster, Publishers.

appeared late they grew rapidly and by midsummer no vegetative differences were apparent.*

3. Joint Method of Agreement and Difference. The Joint Method of Agreement and Difference is frequently regarded as merely the joint use of the methods of Agreement and Difference, so that it can be applied only where the first two Methods can be applied separately. But Mill's own statement of the Method does not support this interpretation, for his formulation is:

If two or more instances in which the phenomenon occurs have only one circumstance in common, while two or more instances in which it does not occur have nothing in common save the absence of that circumstance, the circumstance in which alone the two sets of instances differ, is the effect, or the cause, or an indispensable part of the cause, of the phenomenon.

Mill's words here suggest that the pattern of the Joint Method should be:

$A\ B\ C$———$a\ b\ c$ $X\ Y$———$x\ y$
$A\ D\ E$———$a\ d\ e$ $U\ V$———$u\ v$

Therefore A is the effect, or the cause, or an indispensable part of the cause, of a.

As stated, it would seem to be merely a double use of the Method of Agreement: only that method is involved in the left hand set of premises, while the right hand set can be seen in this light more clearly if we symbolize the *absence* of circumstance A by "$\bar{A}$" and the *absence* of phenomenon a by "$\bar{a}$," writing:

$\bar{A}\ X\ Y$———$\bar{a}\ x\ y$
$\bar{A}\ U\ V$———$\bar{a}\ u\ v$

From the latter we infer the causal connection of $\bar{A}$ and $\bar{a}$ by the Method of Agreement, and of course for $\bar{A}$ and $\bar{a}$ to be causally connected, A and a must be causally connected.

* Reprinted from "Blossoming of Fruits Delayed by Maleic Hydrazide" by D. G. White, in *Science,* Vol. 111, No. 2882, March 24, 1950.

A more common interpretation of the Joint Method is to regard its pattern as:

$A\ B\ C\text{———}a\ b\ c$	$A\ B\ C\text{———}a\ b\ c$
$A\ D\ E\text{———}a\ d\ e$	$B\ C\text{———}b\ c$

Therefore A is the effect, or the cause, or an indispensable part of the cause, of a.

Here it appears explicitly as the separate employments of the first two Methods, that of Agreement and that of Difference. Since each Method, used separately, affords some probability to the conclusion, their joint use as illustrated above affords a higher probability to the conclusion. Although this interpretation would scarcely fit in with the view that the Joint Method is an additional and separate Method, it does reveal it as an extremely powerful pattern of inductive inference. Its use, in this form, is illustrated in Zeeman's report of his discovery of what has come to be known as the "Zeeman Effect":

In consequence of my measurements of Kerr's magneto-optical phenomena, the thought occurred to me whether the period of the light emitted by a flame might be altered when the flame was acted upon by magnetic force. It has turned out that such an action really occurs. I introduced into an oxyhydrogen flame, placed between the poles of a Ruhmkorff's electromagnet, a filament of asbestos soaked in common salt. The light of the flame was examined with a Rowland's grating. Whenever the circuit was closed both D lines were seen to widen.

Since one might attribute the widening to the known effects of the magnetic field upon the flame, which would cause an alteration in the density and temperature of the sodium vapour, I had resort to a method of experimentation which is much more free from objection.

Sodium was strongly heated in a tube of biscuit porcelain, such as Pringsheim used in his interesting investigations upon the radiation of gases. The tube was closed at both ends by plane parallel glass plates, whose effective area was 1 cm. The tube was placed horizontally between the poles, at right angles to the lines of force. The light of an arc lamp was sent through. The absorption spectrum showed both *D* lines. The tube was continuously rotated round its axis to avoid temperature variations. Excitation of the magnet caused immediate widening of the lines. It thus appears very probable that the period of sodium light is altered in the magnetic field.*

The pattern of Zeeman's inference may be schematized by using the following symbols: "*A*" denotes the presence of a magnetic field, "*B*" denotes the presence of an open oxyhydrogen flame, "*C*" denotes the arc lamp illumination described, "*a*" denotes the widening of the *D* lines of the sodium spectrum, "*b*" denotes the usual effects of an open oxyhydrogen flame, and "*c*" denotes the usual effects of arc lamp illumination. The inference is now symbolized as:

$$
\begin{array}{ccc}
A\ B \text{——} a\ b & A\ B \text{——} a\ b & A\ C \text{——} a\ c \\
A\ C \text{——} a\ c & B \text{——} b & C \text{——} c \\
\hline
\end{array}
$$

Therefore *A* is the cause, or an indispensable part of the cause, of *a*.

Here the left hand pair of premises yields the conclusion by the Method of Agreement, while the middle and right hand pairs yield the conclusion by the Method of Difference, so that the whole argument proceeds by the Joint Method, according to our second interpretation of that Method.

There is a third interpretation of the Joint Method which makes it a considerably more powerful tool for induction. To illustrate it we revert to our earlier problem of finding the cause of widespread digestive disturbances in a dormitory. If we have *only* the facts that for six students the circumstances and phenomena are these:

$$
\begin{array}{l}
A\ B\ C\ D\ E \text{——} a\ b\ c\ d\ e \\
A\ F\ G\ H\ E \text{——} a\ f\ g\ h\ e \\
A\ I\ J\ K\ E \text{——} a\ i\ j\ k\ e \\
B\ G\ K\ E \text{——} b\ g\ k\ e \\
C\ H\ I\ E \text{——} c\ h\ i\ e \\
D\ F\ J\ E \text{——} d\ f\ j\ e
\end{array}
$$

---

* By permission from *A Source Book in Physics*, by William Francis Magie. Copyright, 1935, by the McGraw-Hill Book Company, Inc.

where *a* is the phenomenon whose cause we are interested in discovering, it is clear that neither the Method of Agreement nor the Method of Difference can be directly applied. Every instance in which the phenomenon *a* occurs has *both* circumstances *A* and *E* present also, so by the Method of Agreement we can narrow the cause of *a* down to either *A* or *E* or the combination of them, but we can go no further by this Method. The Method of Difference is not directly applicable either, for given any instance in which *a* occurs and any instance in whch *a* does not occur, the two of them do *not* "have every circumstance in common save one." However, if we first apply the Method of Agreement to the first three instances and draw the inference that either *A* alone, or *E* alone, or the combination of *A* with *E,* is the cause of *a,* then we can ignore the other circumstances *B, C, D, F, G, H, I, J, K,* and apply the Method of Difference to narrow the range of possible causes down still further. With the eliminated factors not even mentioned, the first and fourth instances above can be represented as:

$$A \, E \text{------} a \, e$$
$$E \text{------} e$$

and from this we can infer, by the Method of Difference, that *A* is either the cause, or an indispensable part of the cause, of *a.* It may be that *E* also is an indispensable part of the cause of *a,* but we have eliminated the possibility of *E*'s being the whole cause, which was one of the possibilities allowed in the first conclusion arrived at by the Method of Agreement.

It cannot be emphasized too strongly that the availability of more evidence, that is, the addition of further premises to an inductive argument, can change the conclusion arrived at. Thus if we had a further instance, representable as:

$$A \, B \, H \, J \text{---} b \, h \, j$$

This would permit the further inference that *A* is not *the* cause of *a,* but at most an indispensable part of the cause, and it would also permit the inference that *E* *is* an indispensable part of the cause. Simply omitting mention of those circumstances already inferred to be irrelevant, we can take the first instance together with the additional one mentioned above, represented now as:

$$A\ E\text{---}a$$
$$A\ \ \text{---}\overline{a}$$

and by the Method of Difference we can infer that E too is an indispensable part of the cause of a. In the presence, then, of the last additional piece of information, we would be justified in concluding that the combination of A with E is the cause of a, both A and E being indispensable parts of the cause of a.

The conclusion that circumstance A is the effect, or the cause, or an indispensable part of the cause, of phenomenon a, can be inferred with probability from any of these three different sets of premisses: first,

$$A\ B\ C\text{------}a\ b\ c \qquad\qquad X\ Y\text{------}x\ y$$
$$A\ D\ E\text{------}a\ d\ e \qquad\qquad U\ V\text{------}u\ v$$

second,

$$A\ B\ C\text{------}a\ b\ c \qquad\qquad A\ B\ C\text{------}a\ b\ c$$
$$A\ D\ E\text{------}a\ d\ e \qquad\qquad B\ C\text{------}b\ c$$

and third,

$$A\ B\ C\text{------}a\ b\ c \qquad\qquad A\ B\ C\text{------}a\ b\ c$$
$$A\ B\ D\text{------}a\ b\ d \qquad\qquad B\text{------}b$$

In classifying inductive inferences, those falling under any of the three patterns described above are generally regarded as examples of the Joint Method of Agreement and Difference. This classification is standard even though the first pattern has nothing to do with the Method of Difference, being rather a double application of the Method of Agreement, and despite the fact that the second pattern consists of separate applications of the first two methods, so that it scarcely merits the status of a separate and distinct method.

EXERCISES

Analyze each of the following arguments in terms of "circumstances" and "phenomena" to show that they follow the pattern of the Joint Method of Agreement and Difference:

1. . . . McLarty had reasoned that these physiological disorders were most probably caused by some mineral deficiency or mineral unbalance within the trees. Following up this line of reasoning, he injected severely affected apple trees with some thirty different chemicals. In these experiments, the dry test material was packed in holes drilled into the trunks of the trees. The holes were about one-half inch in diameter and two inches deep. After having been filled the holes were sealed with a commercial grafting compound. The dry materials were used because of the convenience of handling and also because greater amounts could be used without injury to the foliage. The following year the crop of two of the injected trees was practically free of the disorders, and it was noted that one of these trees had been injected with boric acid and the other with manganese borate. The trees injected with manganese compounds, other than the borate, showed no change. Following up this lead, forty trees were injected with either boric acid or borax in the fall of 1934. In the summer of 1935 every tree that had been injected the previous fall showed none of the diseases or a very low incidence of them. Because of the great economic losses which many of the growers were suffering that year, the committee decided that it was well worth-while to make an immediate recommendation that all affected trees be injected with boric acid crystals . . .*

2. So Metchnikoff, with Roux always being careful and insisting upon good check experiments—so Metchnikoff, after all of his theorizing about why we are immune, performed one of the most profoundly practical of all the experiments of microbe hunting. He sat himself down and invented the famous calomel ointment— that now is chasing syphilis out of armies and navies the world over. He took two apes, inoculated them with the syphilitic virus fresh from a man, and then, one hour later, he rubbed the grayish

---

* Reprinted from "The Role of Boron in the Agricultural Regions of the Pacific Northwest" by C. G. Woodbridge, in *The Scientific Monthly*, Vol. LXX, No. 2, February 1950.

ointment into that scratched spot on one of his apes. He watched the horrid signs of the disease appear on the unanointed beast, and saw all signs of the disease stay away from the one that had got the calomel.

Then for the last time Metchnikoff's strange insanity got hold of him. He forgot his vows and induced a young medical student, Maisonneuve, to volunteer to be scratched with syphilis from an infected man. Before a committee of the most distinguished medical men of France, this brave Maisonneuve stood up, and into six long scratches he watched the dangerous virus go. It was a more severe inoculation than any man would ever get in nature. The results of it might make him a thing for loathing, might send him, insane, to his death. . . . For one hour Maisonneuve waited, then Metchnikoff, full of confidence, rubbed the calomel ointment into the wounds—but not into those which had been made at the same time on a chimpanzee and a monkey. It was a superb success, for Maisonneuve showed never a sign of the ugly ulcer, while the simians, thirty days afterwards, developed the disease—there was no doubt about it.*

3. The discovery was made in this way. I had dissected and prepared a frog . . . and while I was attending to something else, I laid it on a table on which stood an electrical machine at some distance from its conductor and separated from it by a considerable space. Now when one of the persons who were present touched accidentally and lightly the inner crural nerves of the frog with the point of a scalpel all the muscles of the legs seemed to contract again and again as if they were affected by powerful cramps. Another one who was there, who was helping us in electrical researches, thought that he had noticed that the action was excited when a spark was discharged from the conductor of the machine. Being astonished by this new phenomenon he called my attention to it, who at that time had something else in mind and was deep in thought. Whereupon I was inflamed with an incredible zeal and eagerness to test the same and to bring to light what was concealed in it. I therefore myself touched one or the other nerve with the point of the knife and at the same time one of those present drew a spark. The phenomenon was always the same. Without fail there

* Reprinted from *Microbe Hunters* by Paul de Kruif. Copyright, 1926, by Harcourt, Brace and Company, Inc.

occurred lively contractions in every muscle of the leg at the same instant as that in which the spark jumped, as if the prepared animal was affected by tetanus.

With the thought that these motions might arise from the contact with the point of the knife, which perhaps caused the excited condition, rather than by the spark, I touched the same nerves again in the same way in other frogs with the point of the knife, and indeed with greater pressure, yet so that no one during this time drew off a spark. Now no motions could be detected. I therefore came to the conclusion that perhaps to excite the phenomenon there were needed both the contact of a body and the electric spark.*

4. Method of Residues.   In his statement of the Method of Residues, Mill varies his terminology slightly, referring not to *circumstances* and phenomena but to *antecedents* and phenomena. Of course what he means is *antecedent circumstances.* Mill's formulation is:

Subduct from any phenomenon such part as is known by previous inductions to be the effect of certain antecedents, and the residue of the phenomenon is the effect of the remaining antecedents.

An illustration of this method is provided by the discovery of the planet Neptune.

In 1821, Bouvard of Paris published tables of the motions of a number of planets, including Uranus. In preparing the latter he had found great difficulty in making an orbit calculated on the basis of positions obtained in the years after 1800 agree with one calculated from observations taken in the years immediately following discovery. He finally disregarded the older observations entirely and based his tables on the newer observations. In a few years, however, the positions calculated from the tables disagreed with the observed positions of the planet and by 1844 the discrepancy amounted to 2 minutes of arc. Since all the other known planets agreed in their motions with those calculated for them, the discrepancy in the case of Uranus aroused much discussion.

In 1845, Leverrier, then a young man, attacked the problem. He

* By permission from *A Source Book in Physics*, by William Francis Magie. Copyright, 1935, by the McGraw-Hill Book Company, Inc.

checked Bouvard's calculations and found them essentially correct. Thereupon he felt that the only satisfactory explanation of the trouble lay in the presence of a planet somewhere beyond Uranus which was disturbing its motion. By the middle of 1846 he had finished his calculations. In September he wrote to Galle at Berlin and requested the latter to look for a new planet in a certain region of the sky for which some new star charts had just been prepared in Germany but of which Leverrier apparently had not as yet obtained copies. On the twenty-third of September Galle started the search and in less than an hour he found an object which was not on the chart. By the next night it had moved appreciably and the new planet, subsequently named Neptune, was discovered within 1° of the predicted place. This discovery ranks among the greatest achievements of mathematical astronomy.*

Here the phenomenon being investigated was the movement of Uranus. The part of the phenomenon known by previous inductions to be the effect of certain antecedents was a certain calculated orbit known to be the effect of the gravitational influence of the sun and the interior planets. The residue of the phenomenon was the perturbation in the calculated orbit. The remaining antecedent was the (hypothesized) planet Neptune, which was inferred to be the *cause* of the residue of the phenomenon by the Method of Residues.

Schematically, the Method of Residues can be represented as follows:

$$A\ B\ C\text{——}a\ b\ c$$

B is known to be the cause of b.
C is known to be the cause of c.

Therefore A is the cause of a.

A simpler illustration of the use of this method is in the weighing of various types of cargo, especially that of trucks. The truck is weighed when empty, and then weighed again when it has been loaded. The total phenomenon is the passage of the scale's pointer past the various numerals on its dial. The antecedents here are two: the truck and its cargo. The part of the

* By permission from *The Elements of Astronomy* by Edward Arthur Fath. Copyright, 1926, 1928, 1934, by the McGraw-Hill Book Company, Inc.

phenomenon which consists of the scale's pointer moving up to the numeral which corresponds with the weight of the empty truck is known to be due to the truck alone. Then the residue of the phenomenon, the amount by which the scale's pointer moves beyond the numeral corresponding to the weight of the empty truck, is concluded to be the effect of the cargo, and therefore a measure of its weight.

The Method of Residues is sometimes said to be a strictly deductive pattern of inference and not inductive at all. It must be admitted that there are certainly differences between the other Methods and the Method of Residues. Each of the other Methods requires the examination of at least two instances, while the Method of Residues can be used with the examination of only one case. And none of the other Methods, as formulated by Mill, requires an appeal to any antecedently established causal laws, while the Method of Residues definitely does depend upon antecedently established causal laws. These differences are present, but they do not spell the difference between induction and deduction. For despite the presence of premises which state causal laws, a conclusion inferred by the Method of Residues is only probable, and cannot be *validly deduced* from its premises. Of course an additional premiss or two might serve to transform an inference by the Method of Residues into a valid deductive argument, but the same can be said for the other Methods as well. There seems to be no basis for the claim that the Method of Residues is deductive rather than inductive.

EXERCISES

Analyze each of the following arguments in terms of "antecedents" and "phenomena" to show that they follow the pattern of the Method of Residues:

1. Hoarders
   Is avarice a natural tendency or an acquired habit? Two Harvard psychologists have been investigating this question with rats.

Louise C. Licklider and J. C. R. Licklider provided six rats with all the food they could eat and more. Their food after weaning consisted of pellets of Purina Laboratory Chow. Although none of the rats had ever experienced a food shortage, all immediately started hoarding pellets. Even after they had accumulated a hoard and the food-supply bin was empty, they kept coming back to hunt for more.

This behavior confirmed what previous investigators had found. But the Lickliders refined the experiment to try to unearth the rats' motives for hoarding. They covered half of the pellets with aluminum foil, thus eliminating their value as food. The experimenters discovered that four of the six avaricious rats actually preferred the worthless, inedible pellets in hoarding.

The rats were then put on short rations for six days. After this "deprivation period" they hoarded even more greedily and showed more interest in the plain food pellets, but some still hoarded foilwrapped pellets and continued to prefer them.

The Lickliders conclude, in a report to the *Journal of Comparative and Clinical Psychology:* "The factors that lead to hoarding and that determine what is hoarded are by no means entirely alimentary. The initiation of hoarding seems to be for the rat, as for the human being, a complex motivational problem to which sensory and perceptual factors, rather than blood chemistry, hold the key." *

2. The radioactivity of every pure uranium compound is proportional to its uranium content. The ores are, however, relatively four times as active. This fact led M. and Mme. Curie, just after 1896, to the discovery that the pitchblende residues, from which practically all of the uranium had been extracted, exhibited nevertheless considerable radioactivity. About a ton of the very complex residues having been separated laboriously into the components, it was found that a large part of the radioactivity remained with the sulphate of barium. From this a product free from barium, and at least one million times more active than uranium, was finally secured in the form of the bromide. The nature of the spectrum and the chemical relations of the element, now named radium, placed it with the metals of the alkaline

earths. The ratio by weight of chlorine to radium in the chloride is 35.46 : 113, so that, on the assumption that the element is bivalent, its chloride is $RaCl_2$ and its atomic weight is 226. With this value it occupies a place formerly vacant in the periodic table.[*]

3. In H. Davies' experiments on the decomposition of water by galvanism, it was found that besides the two components of water, oxygen and hydrogen, an acid and an alkali were developed at opposite poles of the machine. Since the theory of the analysis of water did not give reason to expect these products, their presence constituted a problem. Some chemists thought that electricity had the power of producing these substances of itself. Davies conjectured that there might be some hidden cause for this part of the effect—the glass might suffer decomposition, or some foreign matter might be in the water. He then proceeded to investigate whether or not the diminution or total elimination of possible causes would change or eliminate the effect in question. Substituting gold vessels for glass ones, he found no change in the effect and concluded that glass was not the cause. Using distilled water, he found a decrease in the quantity of acid and alkali involved, yet enough remained to show that the cause was still in operation. He inferred that impurity of the water was not the sole cause, but was a concurrent cause. He then suspected that perspiration from the hands might be the cause, as it would contain salt which would decompose into acid and alkali under electricity. By avoiding such contact, he reduced the quantity of the effect still further, till only slight traces remained. These might be due to some impurity of the atmosphere decomposed by the electricity. An experiment determined this. The machine was put under an exhausted receiver and when it was thus secured from atmospheric influences, no acid or alkali was produced.[†]

5. **Method of Concomitant Variation.** At this point we may observe the common pattern which runs through all of the first four of Mill's Methods. In the Method of Agreement we eliminate as possible causes of a given phenomenon all those cir-

---

[*] Reprinted from *Smith's College Chemistry* by James Kendall. Copyright, 1905, 1906, 1908, 1916, 1923, 1929, by Appleton-Century-Crofts, Inc.

[†] Adapted from *The Art of Scientific Discovery* by G. Gore. Longmans, Green, and Company, 1878.

cumstances in whose absence the phenomenon can nevertheless occur, and the remaining circumstance is then inferred to be its cause. The essential character of that Method is thus seen to be eliminative. In the Method of Difference we exclude one of the circumstances which accompany a given phenomenon, while leaving the other circumstances the same. If the phenomenon is also removed thereby, we infer that the remaining circumstances can be eliminated as possible causes. Here we conclude that the one circumstance whose absence prevents the occurrence of the phenomenon in question is the cause of that phenomenon. The second Method also proceeds by elimination. The Joint Method, on any of its three interpretations, is easily shown to be essentially eliminative also, while the Method of Residues proceeds by eliminating as possible causes those antecedent circumstances whose effects have already been established by previous inductions.

There are situations, however, in which certain circumstances cannot possibly be eliminated, so that none of the first four methods is applicable. One of Mill's own examples in discussing this problem concerns the cause of the phenomenon of the tides. We know that it is the gravitational attraction of the moon which causes the rise and fall of the tides, but this could not have been established by any of the first four Methods. The proximity of the moon at high tide is not the *only* circumstance present in all cases of high tide, for the fixed stars are also present, and cannot be eliminated. Nor can the moon be removed from the heavens for the sake of applying the Method of Difference. The Joint Method is inapplicable, as is the Method of Residues also. Of such situations, Mill writes:

But we have still a resource. Though we can not exclude an antecedent altogether, we may be able to produce, or nature may produce for us some modification in it. By a modification is here meant, a change in it not amounting to its total removal. . . . We can not try an experiment in the absence of the moon, so as to observe what terrestrial phenomena her annihilation would put an end to; but when we find that all the variations in the *position* of the moon are

followed by corresponding variations in the time and place of high
water, the place being always either the part of the earth which is
nearest to, or that which is most remote from, the moon, we have
ample evidence that the moon is, wholly or partially, the cause which
determines the tides.*

The argument here proceeds according to what Mill named
the Method of Concomitant Variation. The general statement
of this Method is:

*Whatever phenomenon varies in any manner whenever another
phenomenon varies in some particular manner, is either a cause or
an effect of that phenomenon, or is connected with it through some
fact of causation.*

If we use plus and minus signs to indicate the greater or lesser
degree to which a varying phenomenon is present in a given
situation, the Method of Concomitant Variation can be schematized as follows:

$$A \quad B\ C \text{——} a \quad b\ c$$
$$A + B\ D \text{——} a + b\ d$$
$$A - B\ C \text{——} a - b\ c$$

Therefore *A* and *a* are causally connected.

This method is very widely used. A farmer establishes that there
is a causal connection between the application of fertilizer to
his ground and the size of his crop by applying different
amounts to different parts of his field and noting that the parts
to which more fertilizer has been applied yield a more abundant harvest. A business man verifies the efficacy of advertising
by running larger and smaller advertisements at different intervals and noting that his business activity is increased during
a period of intensive advertising. Here the phenomena are seen
to vary *directly* with each other, that is, when one increases,
the other increases also. However, the statement of the Method
speaks of variation "in any manner," and in fact we infer a

---

* *A System of Logic,* by John Stuart Mill. Book III, Chapter 8, § 6.

causal connection between phenomena which vary *inversely,* that is, phenomena such that when one increases the other *decreases*. Schematically, the Method of Concomitant Variation can also be represented as:

$$A \quad B\ C \text{———} a \quad b\ c$$
$$A + B\ C \text{———} a - b\ d$$
$$A - E\ C \text{———} a + e\ c$$

Therefore A and a are causally connected.

An example to illustrate this inverse variation is provided by economic phenomena: if the demand for a given type of goods remains constant, then any *increase* in the supply of those goods will be accompanied by a *decrease* in the price commanded by them. This concomitant variation is certainly part of the evidence for a causal connection between the supply and the price of a given commodity.

Mill's discussion of his own example is not altogether satisfactory. It may be objected that it is not the moon which is the cause of the tides, but the relative *position* of the moon. The moon itself is a circumstance which is never absent, but its occupation of this or that particular position is present only once every twenty-four hours, absent the rest of the time. Hence the Joint Method of Agreement and Difference is applicable to the situation and can perfectly well suffice to establish the causal connection between the position of the moon and the flow of the tides. The Method of Concomitant Variation is a new and important method, but its value was not adequately explained by Mill.

The other methods have an "all or nothing" character. Their use involves only the presence or absence of a given circumstance, the occurrence or non-occurrence of a given phenomenon. Thus the first four methods permit only a limited kind of evidence to be adduced in favor of causal laws. The Method of Concomitant Variation utilizes our ability to observe changes in the degree to which circumstances and phenomena are present and admits a vastly greater amount of data as evidence for the presence of causal connections. Its chief virtue lies in admitting more evidence, for thereby the new method widens the range of inductive inference.

The Method of Concomitant Variation is important as the first *quantitative* method of inductive inference, the preceding ones having all been qualitative. Its use, therefore, presupposes the existence of some method of measuring or estimating—even if only roughly—the degrees to which phenomena vary.

EXERCISES

Analyze each of the following arguments in terms of the variation of "phenomena" to show that they follow the pattern of the Method of Concomitant Variation:

1. Effect of Moonlight on Insect Activity

It has been known to entomologists for many years that if a bright light is used for attracting insects at night, the catches are considerably higher near the period of new moon than near full moon. One of us (C. B. W.) showed that in three successive years, between May and October, the catches in a light trap, both of Lepidoptera alone and of all insects together (chiefly Diptera), reached a peak at, or shortly after, new moon, when the geometric mean catches were three to four times as great as those at full moon.

In spite of the fact that it is generally believed that other methods of catching are also poor at full moon, in the absence of any real evidence for this there was a distinct probability that the low catches in a light trap might be due to a lowered relative luminosity and hence a lowered attractiveness of the trap at full moon.

During the summer of 1950, we carried out continuous trapping of insects at night by means of a "suction-trap" which draws in the insects by a strong electric fan, and thus is in no way dependent on reaction to light. The insects so caught are mostly Diptera; but many other orders are present.

An analysis of five complete lunar cycles between July and November 1950 shows that the geometric mean catches in the four weeks, that is, three days on either side of (1) full moon,

(2) last quarter, (3) new moon and (4) first quarter, were as follows:

204; 589; 1,259 and 562.

Each of these figures is the mean of thirty-five nights.

These results are slightly affected by accidental differences in temperature and wind on the different nights, and when a correction is made for these, the figures become:

240; 490; 1,175 and 589.

Thus the geometric mean catch in the new moon week is nearly five times that in the full moon week. As the records include nights with cloud as well as clear nights, the effect of full moon on a clear night must be greater than this.

Mr. Healy, of the Statistical Department at this station, informs me that the differences between full and new moon are significant at the 2 per cent level.

It appears, therefore, that the moonlight must have a definite effect on nocturnal insects, and that the low catches in a light trap at full moon are not merely due to a physical reduction of the efficiency of the trap.

Further repetition and analysis will be carried out during the present year. In the meantime, we would be glad of any other evidence on this problem, particularly long series of night catches of insects by any technique not depending on attraction to light.

C. B. WILLIAMS
B. P. SINGH

Department of Entomology,
Rothamsted Experimental Station,
Harpenden.
Jan. 22.*

2. Even as Banting was slaying dogs to save men, Evans was achieving a startling discovery in this field with another mysterious gland, *hypophysis cerebri,* commonly called the *pituitary.* This is a bit of an organ safely housed in a small pocket of bone attached to the base of the brain. Both Galen and Vesalius knew of this gland and thought it supplied the body with spit (in Latin, *sputus*). It is one of the most inaccessible glands in the living body. For many years, there appeared to be some connection be-

* Reprinted from *Nature,* Vol. 167, No. 4256, May 26, 1951.

tween body growth and the functioning of this gland. In 1783 John Hunter had bargained with an undertaker for the body of an Irish giant of eight feet, four inches—Charles O'Brien, who had died at the age of twenty-two. The physician finally bought the body for twenty-five hundred dollars, and found a pituitary almost as large as a hen's egg. That of a normal adult man weighs hardly more than half a gram. A century later, *acromegaly,* an enlargement of the hands, feet, nose, lips, and jaw, was declared to be due to a tumor of the pituitary. The pituitary glands of dwarfs, some of them only eighteen inches high, all showed relatively small development or partial atrophy.*

3. First Douglass attempted to get records of rainfall of this district as far back as possible, to test the correlation of moisture and the thickness of tree rings. Fortunately, temperature and rainfall measurements had been made and recorded at Whipple Barracks to the south of Flagstaff since 1867, and they were made available for his study. Then, in January, 1904, he visited the lumber yards of the Arizona Lumber and Timber Company and spent hours in the snow measuring the rings of many of their oldest trees. The president of the company became interested in the singular pastime of this strange hybrid of astronomer and politician, and had sections cut from the ends of scores of logs and stumps sent to Douglass for analysis. These pieces were carefully scraped with razor blades and brushed with kerosene for examination under the microscope. Every ring from the center of the tree to its bark was scrupulously scrutinized. To facilitate the dating of the rings, Douglass would make one pin prick to mark the last year of each decade, two to mark the middle year of each century, and three for the century year. Those cross sections which contained more than a thousand rings had an additional four pin pricks at the thousand-year tree-ring position. Douglass made tens of thousands of measurements, tabulated the data, drew curves and graphs, and as the average age of his trees was 348 years, he was able to draw conclusions regarding the rainfall and tree-ring appearance of periods hundreds of years back.

Douglass found a striking correlation between tree growth and the recorded rainfall of the region. So accurate were his

---

* *Outposts of Science* by Bernard Jaffe. Copyright, 1935, by Bernard Jaffe. Reprinted by permission of Simon and Schuster, Publishers.

measurements and so apparently reliable his method that any marked peculiarity of any year could be identified with surprising ease and clarity in trees which often had grown more than four hundred miles apart. For example, the yellow pine ring of 1851 is small in trees which grew in regions between Santa Fe and Fresno because it represents a drought year. He could illustrate the accuracy of his technique in another way. He would pick out an old pine stump, study its rings, and then declare in what year the tree had been felled, much to the surprise of the owner of the land on which the tree had been cut. His tree time or "dendrochronology" was uncannily accurate.*

III. CRITICISMS OF MILL'S METHODS

There are two general types of criticism that can be made of Mill's Methods. The first is that the Methods fail to fulfill the claims made for them by Bacon and Mill; the second is that the five Methods, as stated, do not constitute an adequate or complete account of scientific method. We shall discuss these criticisms separately. Before we can state and evaluate the first criticism, we must report the claims that have been made for these methods and explain the motivations for those claims.

It is a truism today that knowledge is power, that an understanding of natural laws and causal connections is needed for man to cope with his frequently hostile environment. Such understanding is not given to all men in the same degree. Beyond the more elementary cause and effect relations, such as those between fire and pain, or rainfall and harvest, the discovery of causal connections requires a rare and genuine insight. It is a sad truth, and like most sad truths, has often been denied. Devices have been sought which would permit *anyone* to discover causal connections, regardless of his natural aptitudes or lack of them. These Methods have been hailed as just such a device; Bacon himself wrote that:

Our method of discovering the sciences is such as to leave little to the acuteness and strength of wit, and indeed rather to level wit and

---

* *Ibid.*

intellect. For as in the drawing of a straight line, or accurate circle by the hand, much depends on its steadiness and practice, but if a ruler or compass be employed there is little occasion for either; so it is with our method.

(*Novum Organum,* Vol. I, Section 61)

This claim has certainly not been fulfilled. Scores of competent scientists have been working for decades to discover the cause of cancer (or the causes of the various types of cancer), and Bacon's "method"—Mill's Methods—have been used, but so far without success. There is no simple device or mechanical method for achieving scientific knowledge. In fact, the advance of empirical science has pushed the frontiers back so far that only those with the highest degree of "acuteness and strength of wit" can master enough of any field to approach the point from which new results can be obtained. Bacon's claim must be rejected as extravagant: his method simply cannot do what it is supposed to.

Mill himself made similar claims, regarding his Methods as adequate to serve two distinct functions. According to Mill they are methods of *discovering* causal connections and also methods of *proving* or *demonstrating* the existence of particular causal connections. Mill's insistence upon the use of his Methods in discovering causal connections brought him into a long controversy with another nineteenth century British philosopher, Dr. William Whewell, who minimized the value of Mill's Methods as instruments for discovery. In arguing against Whewell, Mill stated his view with great vigor, writing:

. . . Dr. Whewell's argument, if good at all, is good against all inferences from experience. In saying that no discoveries were ever made by the . . . Methods, he affirms that none were ever made by observation and experiment; for assuredly if any were, it was by processes reducible to one or other of those methods.*

Mill was convinced further that his Methods permitted the *demonstration* of causal connections, writing that:

* *A System of Logic,* by John Stuart Mill, Book III, Chapter 9, § 6.

The business of Inductive Logic is to provide rules and models (such as the Syllogism and its rules are for ratiocination) to which if inductive arguments conform, those arguments are conclusive, and not otherwise. This is what the . . . Methods profess to be . . .*

These are Mill's claims for his Methods: They are instruments for *discovery,* and they are rules for *proof.*

Let us examine first the doctrine that the Methods are instruments for discovery. We may begin with an example or two in which the scrupulous use of the Methods results in a more or less conspicuous failure to discover the cause of a given phenomenon. A favorite example used by critics of the Method of Agreement is the case of the Scientific Drinker, who was extremely fond of liquor, and got drunk every night of the week. He was ruining his career and his health, and his few remaining friends pleaded with him to stop. Realizing himself that he could not go on, he resolved to conduct a careful experiment to discover the exact cause of his frequent inebriations. For five nights in a row he collected instances of the given phenomenon, the antecedent circumstances being respectively scotch and soda, bourbon and soda, brandy and soda, rum and soda, and gin and soda. Then using the Method of Agreement, he swore a solemn oath never to touch soda again!

Here is a case where the use of Mill's Method results in an abysmal failure. The trouble here is not that the Method was not followed, for it was followed explicitly. The error, as we all can see, lies in a faulty analysis of the antecedent circumstances. Had the various liquors not been treated as so many different single circumstances but analyzed into their alcoholic contents plus their various other constituents, the Method of Agreement would have revealed, of course, that besides the soda, the alcohol too was a common circumstance, and then the Method of Difference would have sufficed to eliminate the soda and reveal the true cause. But how is one to know what kind of analysis to make of the antecedent circumstances? To make a correct anal-

---

* *Ibid.*

ysis requires previous knowledge of causal laws, which must
have been discovered by means other than Mill's Methods.
Mill's Methods are not *sufficient* instruments for discovery, because their successful use requires a proper analysis of the factors of the antecedent circumstances, and the Methods themselves do not tell how to distinguish between a proper and an
improper analysis.

Another objection to the use of Mill's Methods as sufficient
instruments for discovery is illustrated by the following comment on an experiment which was interpreted as showing two
things:

(a) frustration leads to aggression and (b) aggression which arises
in a group with strong in-group feeling will be expressed against
an out-group.

Thirty-one young men between the ages of eighteen and twenty
years who worked in a camp were the subjects of this experiment.
These young men looked forward to attending Bank Night in the
theater in a nearby town, an event which was considered by them
to be the most interesting one in the week. Interest in Bank Night
was especially keen since one of the men had won $200 the previous
week. The conditions of the experiment were such, however, that
the men missed this event. This then formed the frustrating circumstance. Instead of Bank Night there was "suddenly substituted" a
"regime of testing." The tests were long and difficult.

The 31 young men were called to the auditorium of the camp on
the night in question. Without any forewarning as to what was in
store for them, they were given a check list of twenty items pertaining to desirable and undesirable characteristics of two outgroups—
Japanese and Mexicans. Half of the men rated the Japanese, the
other half rated the Mexicans. The men were then given a series of
tests which caused them to miss the truck to town. After the testing
program, the half that rated the Japanese initially now rated the
Mexicans, and likewise for the other half.

The authors of the experiment concluded that the hypothesis
that frustration leads to aggression was confirmed, because the young
men became angry at the camp officials who ordered the tests and at
the experimenters. With regard to the second hypothesis—that be-

cause of this aggression the men would rate the Japanese and Mexicans more unfavorably—the authors claim that the evidence pointed in the direction of confirming the hypothesis.

From the point of view of the young men, the procedure of suddenly giving a series of long, difficult, and boring examinations when it was probably well known that the night in question was one of significance to them must have seemed unjust. Why not some other time? Do not their rights merit consideration by the camp officials in setting plans? The aggressiveness of these young men probably represents a reaction to an unfair situation rather than to the mere fact of a frustrating circumstance. In this case, aggression serves to maintain a sense of dignity or individuality.*

The structure of the argument criticized in the preceding passage is clearly that of the Method of Difference.† There are thirty-one instances *after* the truck to town had been missed, in which the antecedent circumstance was frustration and the phenomena were aggression and more unfavorable ratings given the out-groups. And there are thirty-one instances *before* the truck had left, in which the antecedent circumstances did not include frustration and the phenomena included neither agression nor so unfavorable a rating for the out-groups. Schematically, with the letter "*A*" denoting frustration, "*B*" denoting the presence of the thirty-one men taking the tests, "*a*" denoting the phenomena of aggression and more unfavorable ratings for the outgroup, and "*b*" denoting the usual phenomena arising when such tests are administered, the experiment can be represented as:

$$A\ B \text{———} a\ b$$
$$B \text{———} b$$

Therefore A causes a.

The criticism of this argument (regardless of whether one agrees or disagrees with the general point of view expressed) is

* Reprinted from "A Neglected Factor in the Frustration-Aggression Hypothesis: A Comment" by Nicholas Pastore, in *The Journal of Psychology*, Volume 29 Second Half, April 1950.

† A more subtle analysis would show the Method of Concomitant Variation to be exemplified here also, but is not necessary for our purpose in this discussion.

perfectly straightforward. The preceding inference is unsound, according to the critic, because *a relevant factor was ignored.* The relevant factor which the experimenters ignored is characterized by their critic as *unfairness* or *injustice.* The suggestion seems implicit here that had the frustration been produced by natural or inevitable causes with which no human unfairness or injustice could be associated, neither aggression nor any lower ratings of out-groups would have occurred. Regardless of our own thoughts about the particular point at issue here, we should be able to see that, formally, the criticism is well taken. If a relevant circumstance is ignored, the Method of Difference is not properly applied, for according to its statement that Method requires that the two or more instances "have every circumstance in common save one."

It should be realized that this criticism is different from the one levelled at the Method of Agreement. There the problem was the correct analysis of the instances into a proper set of distinct circumstances. Here the criticism turns on relevant factors or circumstances being *omitted* rather than improperly analyzed. The problem of relevance, to which our discussion of analogical argument had previously led, arises once again. The Methods cannot be used unless all relevant circumstances are taken into account. But circumstances do not come wearing neat little tags marked "relevant" and "irrelevant." Questions of relevance are questions about *causal connectedness,* and at least some of these must be answered *before* Mill's Methods can be used. Hence Mill's Methods cannot be *the* methods for discovering causal connections, for some causal connections must be known prior to any application of those Methods.

It may be objected that what Mill's Methods call for is a consideration of *all* circumstances, rather than just the relevant ones, so that questions of relevance need not arise in the use of the Methods. True enough, Mill's statements of his Methods read *"all"* rather than *"all relevant"* circumstances. But if Mill is taken quite literally here, the situation is made worse instead of better as far as the use of his Methods is concerned. Consider the Method of Agreement. In its application we must verify that two or more instances of a phenomenon have only *one* circumstance in common. But the number of circumstances common to any two physical objects is probably unlimited, no matter how different they may appear. In our earlier example, in which the instances were two students living in the same dormitory who suffered digestive disturbances on the same day, what circumstances might be common here? Presumably they both are students, each has two legs, both are over ten years old, each has a nose, both are over three feet tall, each weighs less than 400 pounds, and so on and on and on. It would be an unimaginative reasoner indeed who could ever stop and say that he had enumerated *all* common circumstances.

In the Method of Difference, two instances must "have every circumstance in common save one." Here the situation is even more hopeless, for it is extremely doubtful that *any* two things could differ in only one circumstance. Even of two peas in a pod, one must of necessity be either to the north or to the east or higher than the other, one must be closer to the stem, and it is extremely doubtful that microscopic and chemical analysis would not reveal any number of differences between them. More devastating still is the fact that *all possible* circumstances in which they *might* differ must be examined to make sure that they do not differ in more than one of them before the Method of Difference can legitimately be applied. No, to interpret Mill literally here would make the Methods hopelessly inapplicable. The Methods must be understood as referring to *relevant* circumstances alone. When so understood, the previous criticism is inescapable, and we must conclude that Mill's Methods are not *the* methods for *discovering* causal laws.

So much for Mill's claim that the Methods are instruments for scientific discovery. Of his Methods Mill wrote:

. . . but even if they were not methods of discovery, it would not be the less true that they are the sole methods of Proof . . .*

* *Loc. cit.*

Let us see whether or not this second claim is true. There are two reasons for denying that the Methods are *demonstrative*. In the first place, all of the Methods proceed on the basis of antecedent hypotheses about which circumstances are causally relevant to the phenomenon under investigation. Since not all circumstances can be considered, attention must be confined to those believed to be possible causes. This prior judgment is liable to error, and if it *is* mistaken, the conclusion inferred by Mill's Methods will be infected by the same mistake. A variant of this same criticism has to do with the different ways in which even the relevant circumstances may be analyzed into separate factors. That analysis must be "correct" if the kind of mistake made by the Scientific Drinker is not to pervade all uses of Mill's Methods. Such an analysis *must* be made prior to the use of the Methods, but since the analysis may be incorrect the conclusion inferred may be incorrect also. This first criticism provides a strong reason for rejecting the claim that Mill's Methods are methods of Proof or Demonstration.

The second criticism is even more damaging. It applies most obviously, perhaps, to the Method of Concomitant Variation. It may well be the case that in a number—even a very large number—of observed instances of two phenomena they are seen to vary concomitantly. It might be the case, for example, that for a year or more the daily wind velocity in Chicago was found to vary with the birth rate in India. Such a correlation would generally be regarded as a mere coincidence rather than evidence of any causal connection between the two phenomena. Correlations, despite the great dependence of some of the social sciences upon them, are very often misleading. The danger of deception is attested by the common saying that there are three kinds of liars: liars, damn liars, and statistics! An observed correlation between two phenomena may be either a chance property peculiar to the *observed* instances, or it may be a regular, that is, lawful property of *all* instances of those phenomena. The greater the number of observed instances (and the greater the number of disanalogies among those instances), the higher the probability that the correlation is lawful rather than fortuitous. But no matter how great the number of observed instances, any inference from their properties to the properties of as yet unobserved instances will never be *certain*. It must be repeated that inductive inferences are never demonstrative.

This criticism applies with equal force to all of Mill's Methods. In the Method of Agreement, of all the circumstances explicitly taken into account, only one may accompany all of the observed instances of the phenomenon under investigation. But the very next instance examined might *not* be accompanied by that circumstance. The greater the number of instances examined, the lower the probability of finding an exception; but so long as there are any unobserved instances, there is always the possibility of the inductive conclusion's being shown to be false by later investigation. The same remarks may be made of the Method of Difference, the Joint Method, and the Method of Residues. Moreover, since we rejected the possibility of a plurality of causes on the basis of an argument which was admitted to be at best merely probable, there is always the logical possibility that any particular phenomenon being investigated may have more than a single cause; if it has, none of the Methods will work. The plain fact is that there *is* a difference between deduction and induction. A valid deductive argument constitutes a proof or demonstration, but an inductive argument is at best highly probable. Therefore Mill's claim that his Methods are "methods of Proof" must be rejected along with his claim that they are "*the* methods of Discovery."

IV. VINDICATION OF MILL'S METHODS

The preceding criticisms are harsh; however, they were not directed against the Methods themselves, but rather against the too extravagant claims made for them. Mill's Methods are more limited instruments than Bacon and Mill conceived them to be, but within those limits they are indispensable. Their indispensability is shown by the following considerations.

Since it is absolutely impossible to take *all* circumstances into account, Mill's Methods can be used only in conjunction with the *hypothesis* that the circumstances mentioned are the only relevant ones. Such a hypothesis amounts to saying that the only possible causes are the circumstances listed. Every experimental investigation of the cause of a phenomenon must start with some such hypothesis. If we are investigating the cause of phenomenon *a*, we may begin with the hypothesis that either *A* or *B* or *C* or *D* or *E* or *F* or *G* is the cause of *a*. Then the following two instances:

$$A \ B \ C \ D \text{———} a \ b \ c \ d$$
$$A \ E \ F \ G \text{———} a \ e \ f \ g$$

which by the Method of Agreement yield the inductive conclusion that *A* is the cause of *a*, yield that conclusion *deductively*, that is, *validly, in the presence of the stated hypothesis as an additional premiss*. The way in which the deduction proceeds is very simple. If *G* is the cause of *a*, then *a* cannot occur in the absence of *G*. But the first instance is a case in which *a* does occur in the absence of *G*. Therefore *G* is not the cause of *a*. The first instance also shows that neither *E* nor *F* is the cause of *a*, while the second instance shows that neither *B* nor *C* nor *D* is the cause of *a*. From the two instances, then, we can infer that neither *B* nor *C* nor *D* nor *E* nor *F* nor *G* is the cause of *a*, and from this conclusion together with the original hypothesis, it follows validly that *A* is the cause of *a*. Although the Method of Agreement cannot be used without a hypothesis of the type indicated, in the presence of that hypothesis it provides us with a valid deductive argument.

Exactly similar remarks can be made with respect to the other Methods. If we are attempting to determine the cause of phenomenon *a* by the Method of Difference, we may begin with the hypothesis that either *A* or *B* is the cause of *a*. Our instances here may be:

$$A \ B \text{———} a \ b$$
$$B \text{———} b$$

from which the conclusion that *A* is the cause of *a* follows inductively by the Method of Difference. In the second instance circumstance *B* occurs without phenomenon *a* being present, which shows that *B* is not the cause of *a*. But by hypothesis, either *A* is the cause of *a* or *B* is the cause of *a*, so it follows validly that *A* is the cause of *a*. In every case, Mill's Methods cannot be used unless some hypothesis is made about possible causes. But in every such case, where the hypothesis is explicitly added as a premiss, the use of the Methods provides a deductive, rather than a merely inductive, argument. The conclusion, however, is deduced not from the particular facts or instances alone but depends upon that additional premiss whose status is merely *hypothetical*. To gain a clearer insight into the type of argument which emerges here, we must examine the nature of these additional hypothetical premisses.

What was referred to in the preceding paragraph as *the* hypothesis that either *A* or *B* is the cause of *a* may with advantage be divided into *two* hypotheses: one, that *A* is the cause of *a*, the other, that *B* is the cause of *a*. Then we can apply the Method of Difference by setting up a situation in which circumstance *B* is present but not *A*. If the phenomenon *a* does not appear when this is done, we have refuted the second of the two hypotheses, and only the first remains. In Section II of the present chapter it was observed that Mill's Methods are essentially eliminative, for their applications serve in each case to show that some particular circumstance is *not* the cause of a given phenomenon. We can rephrase this account in terms of alternative hypotheses, where each hypothesis states that some different circumstance is the cause of the phenomenon under investigation. Mill's Methods now appear as instruments for testing hypotheses. Their statements describe the method of *controlled experiment,* which is an absolutely indispensable weapon in the arsenal of modern science. An example or two should suffice to make this fact clear.

In a famous experiment conducted in the spring of 1881, Pasteur put to the test his hypothesis that anthrax vaccination produces immunity to the disease. That hypothesis had been ridiculed by the veterinarians, and the experiment was performed publicly under the auspices of the Agricultural Society of Melun.* At the farm of Pouilly-le-Fort, twenty-four sheep, one goat, and several cattle were given Pasteur's vaccination against anthrax, while twenty-four other sheep, one goat, and several other cattle were left unvaccinated. These unvaccinated animals constituted the "control group," being instances which were assumed to differ from the first group in only the one circumstance V (vaccination). After the vaccinations had been properly administered,

. . . on the fateful thirty-first of May all of the forty-eight sheep, two goats, and several cattle—those that were vaccinated and those to which nothing whatever had been done—all of these received a surely fatal dose of virulent anthrax bugs.†

Then on the second day of June, at two o'clock, when Pasteur and his assistants came to inspect the animals, they found that:

Not one of the twenty-four vaccinated sheep—though two days before millions of deadly germs had taken residence under their hides —not one of these sheep . . . had so much as a trace of fever. They ate and frisked about as if they had never been within a thousand miles of an anthrax bacillus.

But the unprotected, the not vaccinated beasts—alas—there they lay in a tragic row, twenty-two out of twenty-four of them; and the remaining two were staggering about, at grips with that last inexorable, always victorious enemy of all living things. Ominous black blood oozed from their mouths and noses.

"See! There goes another one of those sheep that Pasteur did not vaccinate!" shouted an awed horse doctor.‡

The pattern of Pasteur's experiment is the Joint Method of Agreement and Difference, and may be analyzed as follows. Where the phenomenon in question is immunity to anthrax, the vaccinated animals constitute some thirty instances which agree

---

* As recounted by Paul de Kruif in *Microbe Hunters*. Copyright, 1926, by Harcourt, Brace and Company, Inc.

† *Ibid.*, p. 161.

‡ *Ibid.*, p. 162.

in only the one relevant circumstance of having been vaccinated, although they all exhibit the phenomenon of immunity. From a consideration of these instances, the inference can be drawn that vaccination causes immunity, and this follows by the pattern of the Method of Agreement. The Method of Difference is also exemplified here. The infected animals which sickened and died constituted thirty-odd instances in which the phenomenon of immunity did *not* occur; the one respect in which they differed from the equal number of immune animals was the vaccination administered to the others but not to them. From these facts, by the Method of Difference, the conclusion follows that Pasteur's vaccination does cause immunity. This account should make it clear that Mill's Methods do describe the general pattern of the modern scientific method of controlled experimentation.

It is obvious that the experiment *confirms* Pasteur's hypothesis. The newspaper reporter who was observing the experiment telegraphed his paper, the London *Times,* that, "The experiment at Pouilly-le-Fort is a perfect, an unprecedented success." * The language used in his report was not too strong, considering the epoch-making nature of the event, but it is dangerously liable to misinterpretation. It must not be thought that the experiment was a "proof" or "demonstration" of the truth of Pasteur's hypothesis, in the sense of a valid deductive argument. It rendered it highly probable, but there still remains a possibility that what happened was fortuitous rather than a genuine instance of the causal law stated by Pasteur. This type of possibility is illustrated by another, somewhat simpler experiment in which Pasteur participated.

Several years prior to the experiment reported above, there had been

. . . a great to-do about a cure for anthrax, invented by the horse doctor, Louvrier, in the Jura mountains in the east of France. Louvrier had cured hundreds of cows who were at death's door, said the influential men of the district: it was time that this treatment received scientific approval. . . .

* *Ibid.,* p. 164.

Pasteur arrived there, escorted by his young assistants, and found that this miraculous cure consisted first, in having several farm hands rub the sick cow violently to make her as hot as possible; then long gashes were cut in the poor beast's skin and into these cuts Louvrier poured turpentine; finally the now bellowing and deplorably maltreated cow was covered—excepting her face!—with an inch thick layer of unmentionable stuff soaked in hot vinegar. This ointment was kept on the animal—who now doubtless wished she were dead—by a cloth that covered her entire body.

Pasteur said to Louvrier: "Let us make an experiment. All cows attacked by anthrax do not die, some of them just get better by themselves; there is only one way to find out, Doctor Louvrier, whether or no it is your treatment that saves them."

So four good healthy cows were brought, and Pasteur in the presence of Louvrier and a solemn commission of farmers, shot a powerful dose of virulent anthrax microbes into the shoulder of each one of these beasts: this stuff would have surely killed a sheep, it was enough to do to death a few dozen guinea-pigs. The next day Pasteur and the commission and Louvrier returned, and all the cows had large feverish swellings on their shoulders, their breath came in snorts—they were in a bad way, that was very evident.

"Now, Doctor," said Pasteur, "choose two of these sick cows—we'll call them A and B. Give them your new cure, and we'll leave cows C and D without any treatment at all." So Louvrier assaulted poor A and B with his villainous treatment. The result was a terrible blow to the sincere would-be curer of cows, for one of the cows that Louvrier treated got better—but the other perished; and one of the creatures that had got no treatment at all, died—but the other got better.

"Even this experiment might have tricked us, Doctor," said Pasteur. "If you had given your treatment to cows A and D instead of A and B—we all would have thought you had really found a sovereign remedy for anthrax." *

This experiment involving four cows, two being given the alleged cure, the other two constituting the control group, served to refute the hypothesis that the horse doctor's treatment was a cure for anthrax. But Pasteur was right in remarking that had

* *Ibid.,* pp. 149–150.

the cows been grouped differently the experiment's results would have been deceptive. This remark emphasizes that the results of an experiment, even one which is carefully controlled and accords perfectly with Mill's Methods, are never demonstrative. A successful experiment (like Pasteur's own) *confirms* the hypothesis being tested, rendering it more probable, but never establishes its conclusion with *certainty*. Such qualifications are not intended to minimize the value of experimental investigation, but only to emphasize that its nature is inductive rather than deductive.

In concluding this chapter, we may summarize our discussion of Mill's Methods in these terms. Our need to control and understand the world in which we live leads us to search for causal connections between its various parts or aspects. Any assertion of a particular causal connection involves an element of generality, for to say that *C* is the cause of *E* is to say that *whenever* circumstance *C* occurs, *E* is sure to follow. Causal laws or general propositions are never *discovered* by Mill's Methods, nor are they ever established *demonstratively* by them. However, those Methods constitute the basic patterns for any attempt to confirm or disconfirm, by observation or experiment, a hypothesis asserting a causal connection. Experimental investigations cannot proceed without hypotheses, which are thus seen to play an all-important role in inductive logic. So important is the role of hypothesis in systematic empirical investigation that the formulation and testing of hypotheses can be regarded as *the* method of science. It is with science and hypothesis that our next chapter is concerned.

EXERCISES

Analyze each of the following arguments in terms of "circumstances" or "antecedents" and "phenomena," and indicate which of Mill's Methods are being used in each of them:

1. On August 23, 1948, individual tagged fruits of Rome Beauty apples and adjacent spur leaves were sprayed at the Plant In-

dustry Station, Beltsville, Maryland, with aqueous solutions of 2, 4, 5–T at 10-, 100-, and 200-ppm concentrations. Fruits that received either the 100- or the 200-ppm spray concentration developed red coloration and were maturing rapidly by September 13. This same stage of maturity on unsprayed fruits was not attained until one month later, October 12, the usual harvest date for this variety. At 10-ppm concentration, the spray had no observable effect. Measurements on fruit softening were made on September 27 with the aid of a fruit pressure tester. At this time the untreated fruits showed an average pressure reading of 25.9 lb., whereas the fruits sprayed with 10-, 100-, and 200-ppm concentrations of 2, 4, 5–T tested 24.8, 19.8, and 18.9 lb., respectively.*

2. In the Spring of 1922, while the downy green of spring masked the discouragement of those Terra Ceia lands, Howell laid out his test plots: some with no tons of limestone; some with two tons to the acre; others with four; yet others with six—exactly as Hoffer had said. But he did more, did this Farmer Howell. Other little plots he laid out, with all the different amounts of limestone—from no tons to six tons per acre. But to each of *these* plots he added phosphate.

And to another set of little oblongs of ground, exactly like the first two, with more and more limestone, Howell added potash, crude sulphate of potash. . . .

Into all of them he sowed good seed of maize.

"I am testing the relative value of different fertilizer elements, both individually and collectively, in connection with lime and no lime," wrote Howell to Hoffer. Both individually and collectively—there he was at the very guts of science. . . .

Carefully Howell plowed each of these dozens of little plots of corn, the right number of times he cultivated them like the efficient farmer that he was; then he laid them by, and waited.

By late July he had the answer to his needs, the cure of the troubles of the tired Terra Ceia land. On the phosphate plats, and on the plats that had got phosphate and limestone, and on the land that had got limestone alone—even six tons to the acre of it!—there was sadness, there were broken-stalked, droop-

* Reprinted from "Effect of 2,4,5-Trichlorophenoxyacetic Acid on Ripening of Apples and Peaches" by P. C. Marth, C. P. Harley, and A. L. Havis, in *Science,* Vol. 111, No. 2883, March 31, 1950.

shanked plants of maize with ears hanging down, chaffy, dejected.

But on every little plat where he'd put the potash, the corn trees shot up straight and strong. It was wonderful. Nearly as good these plants grew as if they were on the best black Iowa loam. It was potash that turned the trick—oh, no doubt of it. That stuck out like a sore thumb. "It has increased our yield from two hundred to three hundred percent," wrote Howell to Hoffer, in jubilation.*

3. About three years ago in the Carnegie Institution Laboratory at Cold Spring Harbor, N. Y., we were irradiating bacteria and the group of soil microorganisms known as the actinomycetes with ultraviolet light and X-rays. The purpose was to produce mutants with antibiotic activity. The radiation dose necessary to induce maximal mutation killed most of the cells (mutants were found among the few survivors). We noticed that when a culture of the actinomycete *Streptomyces griseus* was stored in the icebox for a few days after being irradiated with ultraviolet, the number of survivors would increase, sometimes as much as 10-fold. Some of the cells that had been thought "killed" had recovered.

Now a phenomenon similar to this had been observed a number of years before by Alexander Hollaender and Chester W. Emmons at the National Institute of Health. They had noticed that fungus spores irradiated with ultraviolet recovered after being stored in salt solution for several days. It was also known that X-rayed organisms sometimes partially recovered from radiation injury when they were kept cold after irradiation. It seemed to us that the phenomenon was eminently worth studying, because it might tell us something about the lethal and genetic effects of ultraviolet.

We set out to investigate more closely the possible role of temperature in the recovery of damaged cells. In an early experiment in this test we compared the survival rates of organisms (actinomycete spores) at icebox temperature and at room temperatures. After irradiation with large doses of ultraviolet, some suspensions of the spores were stored in the icebox at 5 degrees Centigrade and some in a glass bottle on a shelf in the laboratory. This produced a surprising result. While the organisms in the icebox

---

* Reprinted from *Hunger Fighters* by Paul de Kruif. Copyright, 1928, by Harcourt, Brace and Company, Inc.

showed the usual slight recovery (a 2- to 10-fold increase in survival), the survival rate of those stored at room temperatures increased 10,000 times!

Obviously cold *per se* had nothing to do with recovery. Indeed, it was a handicap. We began a systematic study of survival rates at various temperatures. There was considerable variation in the results of these experiments, even at the same temperature. We had stored some of the irradiated organisms in a thermostatically controlled water bath on a table in front of a window. The organisms in this bath consistently showed high recovery rates. After a systematic study of various environmental factors that might be influencing recovery, we came to the conclusion that the recovery factor must be the light coming in the windows. We tested the light hypothesis by storing some irradiated spores in darkness and some in light. The result was clear-cut and conclusive. In the light there was a 10,000-fold increase in survival; in the dark there was none. The reason for the original observations —the recovery of organisms that had been stored in iceboxes or other places—was now plain: because of the extra handling they received, stored samples were generally exposed to more light than would otherwise have been the case.*

4. M. Arago, having suspended a magnetic needle by a silk thread, and set it in vibration, observed, that it came much sooner to a state of rest when suspended over a plate of copper, than when no such plate was beneath it. Now, in both cases there were two *verae causae* (antecedents known to exist) why it *should* come at length to rest, viz., the resistance of the air, which opposes, and at length destroys, all motions performed in it; and the want of perfect mobility in the silk thread. But the effect of these causes being exactly known by the observation made in the absence of the copper, and being thus allowed for and subducted, a residual phenomenon appeared, in the fact that a retarding influence was exerted by the copper itself; and this fact, once ascertained, speedily led to the knowledge of an entirely new and unexpected class of relations.†

* Reprinted from "Revival by Light" by Albert Kelner in *Scientific American*, Vol. 184, No. 5, May 1951.
† Reprinted from *A System of Logic* by John Stuart Mill, Book III, Chapter IX, § 5.

5. On the 31st of August, 1909, Paul Ehrlich and Hata stood before a cage in which sat an excellent buck rabbit. Flourishing in every way was this rabbit, excepting for the tender skin of his scrotum, which was disfigured with two terrible ulcers, each bigger than a twenty-five-cent piece. These sores were caused by the gnawing of the pale spirochete of the disease that is the reward of sin. They had been put under the skin of that rabbit by S. Hata a month before. Under the microscope—it was a special one built for spying just such a thin rogue as that pale microbe—under this lens Hata put a wee drop of the fluid from these ugly sores. Against the blackness of the dark field of this special microscope, gleaming in a powerful beam of light that hit them sidewise, shooting backwards and forwards like ten thousand silver drills and augers, played myriads of these pale spirochetes. It was a pretty picture, to hold you there for hours, but it was sinister—for what living things can bring worse plague and sorrow to men?

Hata leaned aside. Paul Ehrlich looked down the shiny tube. Then he looked at Hata, and then at the rabbit.

"Make the injection," said Paul Ehrlich. And into the ear-vein of that rabbit went the clear yellow fluid of the solution of 606, for the first time to do battle with the disease of the loathsome name.

Next day there was not one of those spiral devils to be found in the scrotum of that rabbit. His ulcers? They were drying already! Good clean scabs were forming on them. In less than a month there was nothing to be seen but tiny scabs—it was like a cure of Bible times—no less! And a little while after that Paul Ehrlich could write:

"It is evident from these experiments that, if a large enough dose is given, the spirochetes can be destroyed *absolutely and immediately with a single injection!*" *

* Reprinted from *Microbe Hunters* by Paul de Kruif. Copyright, 1926, by Harcourt, Brace and Company, Inc.

CHAPTER THIRTEEN

Science and Hypothesis

I. THE VALUES OF SCIENCE

Although modern science has been in existence for only a few hundred years, there is scarcely a single aspect of daily life in the Western world that has not been profoundly changed by it. Improvements in farming and manufacturing, in communication and transportation, in health and hygiene, and in our standards of living generally, have all resulted from the application of scientific knowledge. The harnessing of steam and water power to run our machinery and the diverting of waterways to turn deserts into vineyards are but two examples of the beneficent uses of science as an instrument for ameliorating a hostile environment.

Some of the practical results of science, of course, are not so cheerful. The tremendous increase in the destructive power of weapons has made the threat of modern warfare a menace to civilization itself. Yet, despite these unhappy aspects of scientific achievement, on the whole the development of science and its applications have benefited mankind. Terrible as the ravages of atomic explosions are, their toll of human life would seem to be considerably less than that of the great plagues which formerly swept over Europe, decimating the population. And those plagues have been almost completely wiped out by modern medical science. The *practical* value of science lies in the easier and more abundant life made possible by technological advances based on scientific knowledge.

The practical is not the only value of science, however. Science is knowledge and thus an end in itself. The laws and principles discovered in scientific investigation have a value apart from any narrow utility they may possess. This intrinsic value is the satisfaction of curiosity, the fulfillment of the desire to know. That human beings have such a desire has long been recognized. Aristotle wrote long ago that: ". . . to be learning something is the greatest of pleasures not only to the philosopher but also to the rest of mankind, however small their capacity for it . . ." * If we consult one of the most distinguished of contemporary scientists, Albert Einstein, we are told that: "There exists a passion for comprehension, just as there exists a passion for music. That passion is rather common in children, but gets lost in most people later on. Without this passion, there would be neither mathematics nor natural science." † Scientific knowledge does not merely give its possessor power to satisfy his various practical needs; it is itself a direct satisfaction of a particular desire, the desire to know.

Some philosophers, to be sure, have denied the second of these values, claiming that there is no such thing as a purely disinterested desire for knowledge. Men have only practical wants, it is said, and science is simply an instrument to be used for the control of nature. There can be no doubt that its utility has provided great stimulation for the development of science generally. But when the great contributors to scientific progress are consulted about their own motives for research, their answers seldom mention this pragmatic or engineering aspect.

---

* *Poetics*, 1448^b 14.

† Reprinted from "On the Generalized Theory of Gravitation" by Albert Einstein, in *Scientific American*, Vol. 182, No. 4, April 1950.

Most answers to such questions are like that of Einstein: "What, then, impels us to devise theory after theory? Why do we devise theories at all? The answer to the latter question is simply: because we enjoy 'comprehending,' *i.e.* reducing phenomena by the process of logic to something already known or (apparently) evident." * These remarks of Einstein suggest a very fruitful conception of the nature of science.

The job of science, we all know, is to discover facts; but a haphazard collection of facts cannot be said to constitute a science. To be sure, some parts of science may focus on this or that particular fact. A geographer, for example, may be interested in describing the exact configuration of a particular coastline, or a geologist in the precise nature of rock strata in a particular locality. But in the more advanced sciences, bare descriptive knowledge of this or that particular fact is of little importance. The scientist is eager to search out more general truths, of which particular facts are instances and for which they constitute evidence. Isolated particular facts may be known—in a sense—by direct observation. That a particular released object falls, that this ball moves more slowly down an inclined plane than it did when dropped directly downwards, that the tides ebb and flow, all these are matters of fact open to direct inspection. But the scientist seeks more than a mere record of such phenomena; he strives to *understand* them. To this end he seeks to formulate general laws which state the patterns of all such occurrences and the systematic relationships between them. The scientist is engaged in a search for the natural laws according to which all particular events occur and the fundamental principles which underlie them.

This preliminary exposition of the theoretical aims of science can perhaps be made clearer by means of an example. By careful observation, and the application of geometrical reasoning to the data thus collected, the Italian physicist and astronomer Galileo (1564–1642) succeeded in formulating the laws of falling bodies, which gave a very general description of the behavior of bodies

* *Loc. cit.*

at the surface of the earth. At about the same time the great German astronomer Kepler (1571–1630), basing his reasonings very largely on the astronomical data collected by Tycho Brahe (1546–1601), formulated the laws of planetary motion, which gave an accurate description of the elliptical orbits traveled by the planets round the sun. Each of these two great scientists succeeded in unifying the various phenomena in his own field of investigation by formulating the interrelations between them: Kepler in celestial mechanics, Galileo in terrestrial mechanics. Their discoveries were great achievements, but they were, after all, separate and apart. Just as isolated particular facts challenge the scientist to unify and explain them by discovering their lawful connections, so a plurality of general laws challenges the scientist to unify and explain them by discovering a still more general principle which subsumes the several laws as special cases. In the case of Kepler's and Galileo's laws, this challenge was met by one of the greatest scientific geniuses of all time, Sir Isaac Newton (1642–1727). By means of his Theory of Gravitation, together with his three Laws of Motion, Newton unified and explained celestial and terrestrial mechanics by showing them both to be deducible within the framework of a single more fundamental *theory*. The scientist seeks not merely to know what the facts are, but to explain them, and to this end he devises *theories*. To understand exactly what is involved here, we must consider the general nature of explanation itself.

II. EXPLANATIONS: SCIENTIFIC AND UNSCIENTIFIC

In everyday life it is the unusual or startling for which we demand explanations. An office boy may arrive at work on time every morning for ever so long, and no curiosity will be aroused. But let him come an hour late one day, and his employer will demand an *explanation*. What is it that is wanted when an explanation for something is requested? An example will help to answer this question. The office boy might reply that he had taken the seven-thirty bus to work as usual, but the bus had been involved in a traffic accident which had entailed considerable delay. In the absence of any other transportation, the boy had had to wait for the bus to be repaired, and that had taken a full hour. This account would probably be accepted as a satisfactory explanation. It can be so regarded because from the statements which constitute the explanation the fact to be explained follows logically and no longer appears puzzling. An explanation is a group of statements or a story from which the thing to be explained can logically be inferred and whose assumption removes or diminishes its problematic or puzzling character. Of course the inference of the fact as conclusion from the explanation as premiss may be enthymematic, where the "understood" additional premisses may be generally accepted causal laws,* or the conclusion may follow with probability rather than deductively. It thus appears that explanation and inference are very closely related. They are, in fact, the same process regarded from opposite points of view. Given certain premisses, any conclusion which can logically be inferred from them is regarded as being explained by them. And given a fact to be explained, we say that we have found an explanation for it when we have found a set of premisses from which it can logically be inferred.

Of course some proposed explanations are better than others. The chief criterion for evaluating explanations is *relevance*. If the tardy office boy had offered as explanation for his late arrival the fact that there is a war in China or a famine in India, that would properly be regarded as a very poor explanation, or rather as "no explanation at all." Such a story would have "nothing to do with the case"; it would be *irrelevant*, because from it the fact to be explained can *not* be inferred. The relevance of a proposed explanation, then, corresponds exactly to the cogency of the argument by which the fact to be explained is inferred from the proposed explanation. Any acceptable explanation must be relevant, but not all stories which are relevant in this sense are acceptable explanations. There are other cri-

---

* This complication will be considered further in Section VI, but for the present it can be ignored.

teria for deciding the worth or acceptability of proposed explanations.

The most obvious requirement to propose is that the explanation be *true*. In the example of the office boy's lateness, the crucial part of his explanation was a particular fact, the traffic accident, of which he was (presumably) an eye witness. But the explanations of science are for the most part *general* rather than particular. The keystone of Newtonian Mechanics is the Law of Universal Gravitation, whose statement is:

Every particle of matter in the universe attracts every other particle with a force which is directly proportional to the product of the masses of the particles and inversely proportional to the square of the distance between them.

Newton's law is not directly verifiable in the same way that a bus accident is at the time it occurs. There is simply no way in which we can inspect *all* particles of matter in the universe and see that they do attract each other in precisely the way that Newton's law asserts. Few propositions of science are *directly* verifiable as true. In fact, none of the important ones are. For the most part they concern *unobservable* entities, such as molecules and atoms, electrons and protons, and the like. Hence the proposed requirement of truth is not *directly* applicable to most scientific explanations. Before considering more useful criteria for evaluating scientific theories, it will be helpful to compare scientific with unscientific explanations.

Science is supposed to be concerned with facts, and yet in its further reaches we find it apparently committed to highly speculative notions which are far removed from the possibility of direct experience. How then are scientific explanations to be distinguished from those which are frankly mythological or superstitious? An unscientific "explanation" of the regular motions of the planets was the doctrine that each heavenly body was the abode of an "Intelligence" or "Spirit" which controlled its movement. A certain humorous currency was achieved during World War II by the unscientific explanation of certain aircraft failures as being due to "gremlins," which were said to be invisible but mischievous little men who played pranks on aviators. The point to note here is that from the point of view of observability and direct verifiability, there is no great difference between modern scientific theories and the unscientific doctrines of mythology or theology. One can no more see or touch a Newtonian "particle," an atom, or electron, than an "Intelligence" or a "gremlin." What then are the differences between scientific and unscientific explanations?

There are two important and closely related differences between the kind of explanation sought by science and the kind provided by superstitions of various sorts. The first significant difference lies in the attitudes taken towards the explanations in question. The typical attitude of one who really *accepts* an unscientific explanation is *dogmatic*. What he accepts is regarded as being absolutely true and beyond all possibility of improvement or correction. During the Middle Ages and the early modern period the word of Aristotle was the ultimate authority to which scholars appealed for deciding questions of fact. However empirically and open-mindedly Aristotle himself may have arrived at his views, they were accepted by the non-scientific schoolmen in a completely different and unscientific spirit. One of the schoolmen to whom Galileo offered his telescope to view the newly discovered moons of Jupiter declined to look, being convinced that none could possibly be seen because no mention of them could be found in Aristotle's treatise on astronomy! Because unscientific beliefs are absolute, ultimate, and final, within the framework of any such doctrine or dogma there can be no rational method of ever considering the question of its truth. The scientist's attitude towards his explanations is altogether different. Every explanation in science is put forward tentatively and provisionally. Any proposed explanation is regarded as a mere hypothesis, more or less probable on the basis of the available facts or relevant evidence. It must be admitted that the scientist's vocabulary is a little misleading on this point. When what was first suggested as a "hypothesis" becomes well confirmed, it is frequently elevated to the position of a "theory." And when, on the basic of a great mass of evidence, it achieves well nigh universal acceptance, it is promoted to the lofty status of a "law." This terminology is not always strictly adhered to: Newton's discovery is still called the "Law of Gravitation," while Einstein's contribution, which supersedes or at least improves on Newton's, is referred to as the "Theory of Relativity." The vocabulary of "hypothesis," "theory," and "law" is unfortunate, since it obscures the important fact that *all* of the general propositions of science are regarded as hypotheses, never as dogmas.

Closely allied with the difference in the way they are regarded is the second and more fundamental difference between scientific and unscientific explanations or theories. This second difference lies in the basis for accepting or rejecting the view in question. Many unscientific views are mere prejudices, which their adherents could scarcely give any reason for holding. Since they are regarded as "certain," however, any challenge or question is likely to be regarded as an affront and met with abuse. If one who accepts an unscientific explanation *can* be persuaded to discuss the basis for its acceptance, there are only a few grounds on which he will attempt to "defend" it. It is true because "we've always believed it," or because "everyone knows it." These all too familiar phrases express appeals to tradition or popularity rather than evidence. Or a questioned dogma may be defended on the grounds of revelation or authority. The absolute truth of their religious creeds and the absolute falsehood of all others have been revealed from on high, at various times, to Moses, to Paul, to Mohammed, to Joseph Smith, and to many others. That there are rival traditions, conflicting authorities, and revelations which contradict one another does not seem disturbing to those who have embraced an absolute creed. In general, unscientific beliefs are held independently of anything we should regard as *evidence* in their favor. Because they are *absolute,* questions of evidence are regarded as having little or no importance.

The case is quite different in the realm of science. Since every scientific explanation is regarded as a hypothesis, it is regarded as worthy of acceptance only to the extent that there is *evidence* for it. As a hypothesis, the question of its truth or falsehood is *open,* and there is continual search for more and more evidence to decide that question. The term "evidence" as used here refers ultimately to experience; *sensible* evidence is the ultimate court of appeal in verifying scientific propositions. Science is *empirical* in holding that sense experience is the *test of truth* for all its pronouncements. Consequently, it is of the essence of a *scientific* proposition that it be capable of being tested by observation.

Some propositions can be tested *directly.* To decide the truth or falsehood of the proposition which asserts that it is now raining outside, we need only look out the window. To tell whether a traffic light shows green or red, all we have to do is to look at it. But the propositions which scientists usually offer as explanatory hypotheses are not of this type. Such general propositions as Newton's Laws or Einstein's Theory are not *directly testable* in this fashion. They can, however, be tested *indirectly.* The *indirect method* of testing the truth of a proposition is familiar to all of us, though we may not be familiar with this name for it. For example, if his employer had been suspicious of the office boy's explanation of his tardiness, he might have checked up on it by telephoning the bus company to find out whether an accident had really happened to the seven-thirty bus. If the bus company's report checked with the boy's story, this would serve to dispel the employer's suspicions; whereas if the bus company denied that an accident had occurred, it would probably convince the employer that his office boy's story was false. This inquiry would constitute an *indirect test* of the office boy's explanation.

The pattern of *indirect testing* or *indirect verification* consists of two parts. First one deduces from the proposition to be tested one or more other propositions which *are* capable of being tested *directly.* Then these consequences are tested and found to be either true or false. If the consequences are false, any proposition which implies them must be false also. On the other hand, if the consequences are true, they are evidence for the truth of the proposition being tested, which is thus confirmed *indirectly*.

It should be noted that indirect testing is never demonstrative or certain. To deduce directly testable conclusions from a proposition usually requires additional premisses. The conclusion that the bus company will *reply* that the seven-thirty bus had an accident this morning does not follow validly from the proposition that the seven-thirty bus *did* have an accident. Additional premisses are needed, for example, that all accidents are reported to the company's office, that the reports are not mislaid or forgotten, and the company does not make a policy of denying its accidents. So the bus company's denying that an accident occurred would not demonstrate the office boy's story to be false, for the discrepancy might be due to the falsehood of one of the other premisses mentioned. Those others, however, ordinarily have such a high degree of probability that a negative reply on the part of the bus company would render the office boy's story very doubtful indeed.

Similarly, establishing the truth of a conclusion does not demonstrate the truth of the premisses from which it was deduced. We know very well that a valid argument may have a true conclusion even though its premisses are not all true. In the present example, the bus company might affirm that an accident occurred to the seven-thirty bus because of some mistake in their records, even though no accident had occurred. So the inferred consequent *might* be true even though the *premisses* from which it was deduced were not. In the usual case, though, that is highly unlikely; so that a successful or affirmative direct testing of a conclusion serves to render probable the premisses from which it was deduced.

It must be admitted that every proposition, scientific or unscientific, which is a relevant explanation for any observable fact, has *some* evidence in its favor, namely the fact to which it is relevant. Thus the regular motions of the planets must be conceded to constitute evidence for the (unscientific) theory that the planets are inhabited by "Intelligences" which cause them to move in just the orbits which are observed. The motions themselves are as much evidence for that myth as they are for Newton's or Einstein's theories. The difference lies in the fact that that is the *only* evidence for the unscientific hypothesis. Absolutely no other *directly* testable propositions can be deduced from the myth. On the other hand, a very large number of directly testable propositions can be deduced from the scientific explanations mentioned. Here, then, is *the* difference between scientific and unscientific explanations. A scientific explanation for a given fact will have directly testable propositions deducible from it other than the one asserting the fact to be explained. But an unscientific explanation will have no other directly testable propositions deducible from it. It is of the essence of a scientific proposition to be empirically verifiable.

It is clear that we have been using the term "scientific explanation" in a quite general sense. As here defined, an explanation may be scientific even though it is not a part of one of the various special sciences like physics or psychology. Thus the office boy's explanation of his tardiness would be classified as a *scientific* one, for it is testable, even if only indirectly. But had he offered as explanation the proposition that *God willed him to be late that morning, and God is omnipotent,* the explanation would have been unscientific. For although his being late that morning is deducible from the proffered explanation, no other directly testable proposition is, and so the explanation is not even indirectly testable, and hence is unscientific.

III. EVALUATING SCIENTIFIC EXPLANATIONS

The question naturally arises as to how scientific explanations are to be evaluated, that is, judged as good or bad, or at least as better or worse. This question is especially important because there is usually more than a single scientific explanation for one and the same fact. A man's abrupt behavior may be explained either by the hypothesis that he is shy or by the hypothesis that he is unfriendly. In a criminal investigation two different and incompatible hypotheses about the identity of the criminal may equally well account for the known facts. In the realm of science proper, that an object expands when heated is explained by both the caloric theory of heat and the kinetic theory. The caloric theory regarded heat as an invisible weightless fluid called "caloric," with the power of penetrating, expanding, and dissolving bodies, or dissipating them in vapor. The kinetic theory, on the other hand, regards the heat of a body as consisting of random motions of the molecules of which the body is composed. These are *alternative* scientific explanations which serve equally well to explain some of the phenomena of thermal expansion. They cannot both be true, however, and the problem is to evaluate or choose between them.

What is wanted here is a list of conditions which a good hypothesis can be expected to fulfill. It must not be thought that such a list of conditions can constitute a *recipe* by whose means anyone at all can construct good hypotheses. No one has ever pretended to lay down a set of rules for the invention or discovery of hypotheses. It is likely that none could ever be laid down, for that is the *creative* side of the scientific enterprise. Ability to create is a function of a person's imagination and talent and cannot be reduced to a mechanical process. A great scientific hypothesis, with wide explanatory powers like those of Newton's or Einstein's, is as much the product of genius as a great work of art. There is no formula for discovering new hypotheses, but there are certain rules to which acceptable hypotheses can be expected to conform. These can be regarded as the criteria for evaluating hypotheses.

There are five criteria which are used in judging the worth or acceptability of hypotheses. They may be listed as (1) relevance, (2) testability, (3) compatibility with previously well established hypotheses, (4) predictive or explanatory power, and (5) simplicity. The first two have already been discussed, but we shall review them briefly here.

1. Relevance. No hypothesis is ever proposed for its own sake but is always intended as an explanation of some fact or other. Therefore it must be *relevant* to the fact which it is intended to explain, that is, the fact in question must be *deducible* from the proposed hypothesis—either from the hypothesis alone or from it together with certain causal laws which may be presumed to have already been established as highly probable, or from these together with certain assumptions about particular initial conditions. A hypothesis which is not relevant to the fact it is intended to explain simply fails to explain it and can only be regarded as having failed to fulfill its intended function. A good hypothesis must be *relevant*.

2. Testability. The chief distinguishing characteristic of scientific hypotheses (as contrasted with unscientific ones) is that they are testable. That is, there must be the possibility of making observations which tend to confirm or disprove any scientific hypothesis. It need not be *directly* testable, of course. As has already been observed, most of the really important scientific hypotheses are formulated in terms of such unobservable entities as electrons or electromagnetic waves. As one contemporary research scientist has written: "A physicist of this century, interested in the basic structure of matter, deals with radiation he cannot see, forces he cannot feel, particles he cannot touch.* But there must be some way of getting from statements about such unobservables to statements about directly observable entities such as tables and chairs, or pointer readings, or lines on a photographic plate. In other words, there must be some connection between any scientific hypothesis and empirical data or facts of experience.

3. Compatibility with Previously Well Established Hypotheses. The requirement that an acceptable hypothesis must be compatible or consistent with other hypotheses which have al-

* Reprinted from "The Bevatron" by Lloyd Smith in *Scientific American*, Vol. 184, No. 2, February 1951.

ready been well confirmed is an eminently reasonable one. Science, in seeking to encompass more and more facts, aims at achieving a *system* of explanatory hypotheses. Of course such a system must be self-consistent, for no self-contradictory set of propositions could possibly be true—or even intelligible. Ideally, the way in which scientists hope to make progress is by gradually expanding their hypotheses to comprehend more and more facts. For such progress to be made each new hypothesis must be consistent with those already confirmed. Thus Leverrier's hypothesis that there was an additional but not yet charted planet beyond the orbit of Uranus was perfectly consistent with the main body of accepted astronomical theory. A new theory must *fit in* with older theories if there is to be orderly progress in scientific inquiry.

It is possible, of course, to overestimate the importance of the third criterion. Although the ideal of science may be the gradual growth of theoretical knowledge by the addition of one new hypothesis after another, the actual history of scientific progress has not always followed that pattern. Many of the most important of new hypotheses have been inconsistent with older theories and have in fact replaced them rather than fitted in with them. Einstein's Relativity Theory was of that sort, shattering many of the preconceptions of the older Newtonian theory. The phenomenon of radioactivity, first observed during the last decade of the Nineteenth Century, led to the overthrow—or at least the modification—of many cherished theories which had almost achieved the status of absolutes. One of these was the principle of the Conservation of Matter, which asserted that matter could neither be created nor destroyed. The hypothesis that radium atoms undergo spontaneous disintegration was inconsistent with that old established principle—but it was the principle which was relinquished in favor of the newer hypothesis.

The foregoing is not intended to give the impression that scientific progress is a helter-skelter process in which theories are abandoned right and left in favor of newer and shinier ones. Older theories are not so much abandoned as corrected. Einstein himself has always insisted that his own work is a modification rather than a rejection of Newton's. The principle of the Conservation of Matter was modified by being absorbed into the more comprehensive principle of the Conservation of Mass-Energy. Every established theory has been established through having proved adequate to explain a considerable mass of data, of observed facts. And it cannot be dethroned or discredited by any new hypothesis unless that new hypothesis can account for the same facts as well or even better. There is nothing capricious about the development of science. Every change represents an improvement, a more comprehensive and thus more adequate explanation of the way in which the world manifests itself in experience. Where inconsistencies occur between hypotheses, the greater age of one does not automatically prove it to be correct and the newer one wrong. The *presumption* is in favor of the older one if it has already been extensively confirmed. But if the new one in conflict with it *also* receives extensive confirmation, considerations of age or priority are definitely irrelevant. Where there is a conflict between two hypotheses, we must turn to the observable facts to decide between them. Ultimately, our last court of appeal in deciding between rival hypotheses is experience. What our third criterion, compatibility with previously well established hypotheses, comes to is this: the totality of hypotheses accepted at any time should be consistent with each other,* and—other things being equal—of two new hypotheses, the one which fits in better with the accepted body of scientific theory is to be preferred. The question of what is involved in "other things being equal" takes us directly to our fourth criterion.

4. Predictive or Explanatory Power. By the predictive or explanatory power of a hypothesis is meant the range of observable facts that can be deduced from it. This criterion is re-

---

* Scientists may, however, consider and even use inconsistent hypotheses for years while awaiting the resolution of that inconsistency. This situation obtains today with respect to the wave and the corpuscular theories of light.

lated to, but different from, that of testability. A hypothesis is testable if *some* observable fact is deducible from it. If one of two testable hypotheses has a greater number of observable facts deducible from it than from the other, then it is said to have greater predictive or explanatory power. For example, Newton's hypothesis of universal gravitation together with his three laws of motion had greater predictive power than either Kepler's or Galileo's hypotheses, because all observable consequences of the latter two were also consequences of the former, and the former had many more besides. An observable fact which can be deduced from a given hypothesis is said to be explained by it and also can be said to be *predicted* by it. The greater the predictive power of a hypothesis, the more it explains, and the better it contributes to our understanding of the phenomena with which it is concerned.

Our fourth criterion has a negative side which is of crucial importance. If a hypothesis is inconsistent with any well attested fact of observation, the hypothesis is false and must be rejected. Where two different hypotheses are both relevant to explaining some set of facts and both are testable, and both are compatible with the whole body of already established scientific theory, it may be possible to choose between them by deducing incompatible propositions from them which are directly testable. If H_1 and H_2, two different hypotheses, entail incompatible consequences, it may be possible to set up a *crucial experiment* to decide between them. Thus if H_1 entails that under circumstance C phenomenon P will occur, while H_2 entails that under circumstance C phenomenon P will *not* occur, then all we need do to decide between H_1 and H_2 is to realize circumstance C and observe the presence or absence of phenomenon P. If P occurs, this is evidence *for* H_1 and *against* H_2, while if P does not occur, this is evidence *against* H_1 and *for* H_2.

This kind of crucial experiment to decide between rival hypotheses may not always be easy to carry out, for the required circumstance C may be difficult or impossible to realize. Thus the decision between Newtonian Theory and Einstein's

General Theory of Relativity had to await a total eclipse of the sun—a situation or circumstance which it is clearly beyond the present powers of man to produce. In other cases the crucial experiment may have to await the development of new instruments, either for the production of the required *circumstances,* or for the observation or measurement of the predicted phenomenon. The proponents of rival astronomical hypotheses must frequently mark time while awaiting the construction of new and more powerful telescopes, for example. The topic of crucial experiments will be discussed further in Section VI.

5. Simplicity. It sometimes happens that two rival hypotheses satisfy the first four criteria equally well. Historically the most important pair of such hypotheses were those of Ptolemy (fl. 127–151) and Copernicus (1473–1543). Both were intended to explain all of the then known data of astronomy. According to the Ptolemaic theory, the earth is the center of the universe, and the heavenly bodies move about it in orbits which require a very complicated geometry of epicycles to describe. Ptolemy's theory was relevant, testable, and compatible with previously well established hypotheses, satisfying the first three criteria perfectly. According to the Copernican theory, the sun rather than the earth is at the center, and the earth itself moves around the sun along with the other planets. Copernicus' theory too satisfied the first three criteria perfectly. And with respect to the fourth criterion, the two theories were almost exactly on a par. (True enough, the Copernican theory seemed to predict a stellar parallax which could not be observed, but this failure was easily accounted for by the auxiliary hypothesis that the fixed stars were too far away for any parallax to be noticed.) To all intents and purposes, the Ptolemaic and Copernican theories were of equal predictive or explanatory power. There was only one significant difference between the two rival hypotheses. Although both required the clumsy method of epicycles to account for the observed positions of the various heavenly bodies, *fewer* such epicycles were required within the Copernican theory. The Copernican system was therefore *simpler,* and on this basis it was accepted by all later astronomers, despite the greater age and equal predictive power of the Ptolemaic system, and in the teeth of persecution by the Medieval Church!

The criterion of simplicity is a perfectly natural one to invoke. In ordinary life as well as in science, the simplest theory which fits all the available facts is the one we tend to accept. In court trials of criminal cases the prosecution attempts to develop a hypothesis which includes the guilt of the accused and fits in with all the available evidence. Opposing him, the defense attorney seeks to set up a hypothesis which includes the innocence of the accused and also fits all the available evidence. Often both sides succeed, and then the case is usually decided —or *ought* to be decided—in favor of that hypothesis which is simpler or more "natural." Simplicity, however, is a very difficult term to define. Not all controversies are as straight-forward as the Ptolemaic-Copernican one, in which the latter's greater simplicity consisted merely in requiring a smaller number of epicycles. And of course "naturalness" is an almost hopelessly deceptive term—for it seems much more "natural" to believe that the earth is still while the apparently moving sun really does move. The fifth and last criterion, simplicity, is an important and frequently decisive one, but it is vague and not always easy to apply.

IV. THE DETECTIVE AS SCIENTIST

Now that we have formulated and explained the criteria by which hypotheses are evaluated, we are in a position to describe the general pattern of scientific research. Before doing so, however, it will be instructive to examine an illustration of that method. A perennial favorite in this connection is the detective, whose problem is not quite the same as that of the pure scientist, but whose approach and technique illustrate the method of science very clearly. The classical example of the astute detective who can solve even the most baffling mystery is A. Conan Doyle's immortal creation, Sherlock Holmes.

Holmes, his stature undiminished by the passage of time, will
be our hero in the following account.

1. **The Problem.** Some of our most vivid pictures of Holmes
are those in which he is busy with magnifying glass and tape
measure, searching out and finding essential clues which had
escaped the attention of those stupid bunglers, the "experts" of
Scotland Yard. Or those of us who are by temperament less
vigorous may think back more fondly on Holmes the thinker,
". . . who, when he had an unsolved problem upon his mind,
would go for days, and even for a week, without rest, turning
it over, rearranging his facts, looking at it from every point of
view until he had either fathomed it or convinced himself that
his data were insufficient." * At one such time, according to
Dr. Watson:

He took off his coat and waistcoat, put on a large blue dressing-
gown, and then wandered about the room collecting pillows from
his bed and cushions from the sofa and armchairs. With these he
constructed a sort of Eastern divan, upon which he perched himself cross-legged, with an ounce of shag tobacco and a box of matches
laid out in front of him. In the dim light of the lamp I saw him
sitting there, an old briar pipe between his lips, his eyes fixed
vacantly upon the corner of the ceiling, the blue smoke curling up
from him, silent, motionless, with the light shining upon his strong-
set aquiline features. So he sat as I dropped off to sleep, and so he
sat when a sudden ejaculation caused me to wake up, and I found
the summer sun shining into the apartment. The pipe was still
between his lips, the smoke still curled upward, and the room was
full of a dense tobacco haze, but nothing remained of the heap of
shag which I had seen upon the previous night.*

But such memories are incomplete. Holmes was not always
searching for clues or pondering over solutions. We all remember those dark periods—especially in the earlier stories—when,
much to the good Watson's annoyance, Holmes would drug
himself with morphine or cocaine. That would happen, of
course, *between* cases. For when there is no mystery to be un-

* "The Man with the Twisted Lip."

raveled, no man in his right mind would go out to look for clues. Clues, after all, must be *clues for* something. Nor could Holmes, or anyone else, for that matter, engage in profound thought unless he had something to think *about*. Sherlock Holmes was a genius at solving problems, but even a genius must *have* a problem before he can solve it. All reflective thinking, and this term includes criminal investigation as well as scientific research, is a problem-solving activity, as John Dewey and other pragmatists have rightly insisted. There must be a problem felt before either the detective or the scientist can go to work.

Of course the active mind sees problems where the dullard sees only familiar objects. One Christmas season Dr. Watson visited Holmes to find that the latter had been using a lens and forceps to examine ". . . a very seedy and disreputable hard-felt hat, much the worse for wear, and cracked in several places." * After they had greeted each other, Holmes said of it to Watson, "I beg that you will look upon it not as a battered billycock but as an intellectual problem." * It so happened that the hat led them into one of their most interesting adventures, but it could not have done so had Holmes not seen a problem in it from the start. A problem may be characterized as a fact or group of facts for which we have no acceptable explanation, which seem unusual, or which fail to fit in with our expectations or preconceptions. It should be obvious that *some* prior beliefs are required if anything is to appear problematic. If there are no expectations, there can be no surprises.

Sometimes, of course, problems came to Holmes already labeled. The very first adventure recounted by Dr. Watson began with the following message from Gregson of Scotland Yard:

My Dear Mr. Sherlock Holmes:

There has been a bad business during the night at 3, Lauriston Gardens, off the Brixton Road. Our man on the beat saw a light there about two in the morning, and as the house was an empty

---

* "The Adventure of the Blue Carbuncle."

one, suspected that something was amiss. He found the door open,
and in the front room, which is bare of furniture, discovered the
body of a gentleman, well dressed, and having cards in his pocket
bearing the name of 'Enoch J. Drebber, Cleveland, Ohio, U.S.A.'
There had been no robbery, nor is there any evidence as to how the
man met his death. There are marks of blood in the room, but
there is no wound upon his person. We are at a loss as to how
he came into the empty house; indeed, the whole affair is a puzzler.
If you can come round to the house any time before twelve, you
will find me there. I have left everything in statu quo until I hear
from you. If you are unable to come, I shall give you fuller details,
and would esteem it a great kindness if you would favour me with
your opinion.

Yours faithfully,

TOBIAS GREGSON.*

Here was a problem indeed. A few minutes after receiving
the message, Sherlock Holmes and Dr. Watson "were both in
a hansom, driving furiously for the Brixton Road."

2. **Preliminary Hypotheses.**   On their ride out Brixton way,
Holmes "prattled away about Cremona fiddles and the difference between a Stradivarius and an Amati." Dr. Watson chided
Holmes for not giving much thought to the matter at hand, and
Holmes replied: "No data yet . . . It is a capital mistake to
theorize before you have all the evidence. It biases the judgment." * This point of view was expressed by Holmes again and
again. On one occasion he admonished a younger detective that
"The temptation to form premature theories upon insufficient
data is the bane of our profession." † Yet for all of his confidence about the matter, on this one issue Holmes was completely mistaken. Of course one should not reach a *final judgment* until a great deal of evidence has been considered, but this
procedure is quite different from *not theorizing.* As a matter
of fact, it is strictly impossible to make any serious attempt to
collect evidence unless one *has* theorized beforehand. As

* *A Study in Scarlet.*
† *The Valley of Fear.*

Charles Darwin, the great biologist and author of the modern theory of evolution, observed: ". . . all observation must be for or against some view, if it is to be of any service." The point is that there are too many particular facts, too many data in the world, for anyone to try to become acquainted with them all. Everyone, even the most patient and thorough investigator, must pick and choose, deciding which facts to study and which to pass over. He must have some working hypothesis for or against which to collect relevant data. It need not be a *complete* theory, but at least the rough outline must be there. Otherwise how could one decide what facts to select for consideration out of the totality of all facts, which is too vast even to begin to sift?

Holmes' actions were wiser than his words in this connection. After all, the words were spoken in a hansom speeding towards the scene of the crime. If Holmes really had no theory about the matter, why go to Brixton Road? If facts and data were all that he wanted, any old facts and any old data, with no hypotheses to guide him in their selection, why should he have left Baker Street at all? There were plenty of facts in the rooms at 221-B, Baker Street. Holmes might just as well have spent his time counting all the words on all the pages of all the books there, or perhaps making very accurate measurements of the distances between each separate pair of articles of furniture in the house. He could have gathered data to his heart's content and saved himself cab fare into the bargain!

It may be objected that the facts to be gathered at Baker Street have nothing to do with the case, whereas those which awaited Holmes at the scene of the crime were valuable clues for solving the problem. It was, of course, just this consideration which led Holmes to ignore the "data" at Baker Street and hurry away to collect those off Brixton Road. It must be insisted, however, that the greater relevance of the latter could not be *known* before hand but only conjectured on the basis of previous experience with crimes and clues. It was in fact a *hypothesis* which led Holmes to look in one place rather than another for his facts, the hypothesis that there was a murder, that the crime was committed at the place where the body was found, and that the murderer had left some trace or clue which could lead to his discovery. Some such hypothesis is always required to guide the investigator in his search for relevant data, for in the absence of any preliminary hypothesis there are simply too many facts in this world to examine. The preliminary hypothesis ought to be highly tentative, and it must be based on previous knowledge. But a preliminary hypothesis is as necessary as the existence of a problem for any serious inquiry to be begun.

It must be emphasized that a preliminary hypothesis, as here conceived, need not be a *complete* solution to the problem. The hypothesis that the man was murdered by someone who had left some clues to his identity on or near the body of his victim was what led Holmes to Brixton Road. This hypothesis is clearly incomplete: it does not say *who* committed the crime, or *how* it was done, or *why*. Such a preliminary hypothesis may be *very* different from the final solution to the problem. It will never be complete: it may be a tentative explanation of only *part* of the problem. But however partial and however tentative, a preliminary hypothesis is required for any investigation to proceed.

3. **Collecting Additional Facts.** Every serious investigation begins with some fact or group of facts which strike the detective or the scientist as problematic and which initiate the whole process of inquiry. The initial facts which constitute the problem are usually too meager to suggest a wholly satisfactory explanation for themselves, but they will suggest—to the competent investigator—some preliminary hypotheses which lead him to search out additional facts. These additional facts, it is hoped, will serve as clues to the final solution. The inexperienced or bungling investigator will overlook or ignore all but the most obvious of them; but the careful worker will aim at completeness in his examination of the additional facts to

which his preliminary hypotheses lead him. Holmes, of course, was the most careful and painstaking of investigators.

Holmes insisted on dismounting from the hansom a hundred yards or so from their destination and approached the house on foot, looking carefully at its surroundings and especially at the pathway leading up to it. When Holmes and Watson entered the house, they were shown the body by the two Scotland Yard operatives, Gregson and Lestrade. ("There is no clue," said Gregson. "None at all," chimed in Lestrade.) But Holmes had already started his own search for additional facts, looking first at the body:

. . . his nimble fingers were flying here, there, and everywhere, feeling, pressing, unbuttoning, examining . . . So swiftly was the examination made, that one would hardly have guessed the minuteness with which it was conducted. Finally, he sniffed the dead man's lips, and then glanced at the soles of his patent leather boots.*

Then turning his attention to the room itself,

. . . he whipped a tape measure and a large round magnifying glass from his pocket. With these two implements he trotted noiselessly about the room, sometimes stopping, occasionally kneeling, and once lying flat upon his face. So engrossed was he with his occupation that he appeared to have forgotten our presence, for he chattered away to himself under his breath the whole time, keeping up a running fire of exclamations, groans, whistles, and little cries suggestive of encouragement and of hope. As I watched him I was irresistibly reminded of a pure-blooded, well-trained foxhound as it dashes backward and forward through the covert, whining in its eagerness, until it comes across the lost scent. For twenty minutes or more he continued his researches, measuring with the most exact care the distance between marks which were entirely invisible to me, and occasionally applying his tape to the walls in an equally incomprehensible manner. In one place he gathered up very carefully a little pile of gray dust from the floor and packed it away in an envelope. Finally he examined with his glass the word upon the wall, going over every letter of it with the most minute exactness.

* *A Study in Scarlet.*

This done, he appeared to be satisfied, for he replaced his tape and his glass in his pocket.

"They say that genius is an infinite capacity for taking pains," he remarked with a smile. "It's a very bad definition, but it does apply to detective work." *

One matter deserves to be emphasized very strongly. Steps (2) and (3) are not completely separable but are usually very intimately connected and interdependent. True enough, we require a preliminary hypothesis to begin any intelligent examination of facts, but the additional facts may themselves suggest new hypotheses, which may lead to new facts, which suggest still other hypotheses, which lead to still other additional facts, and so on. Thus having made his careful examination of the facts available in the house off Brixton Road, Holmes was led to formulate a further hypothesis which required the taking of testimony from the constable who found the body. The man was off duty at the moment, and Lestrade gave Holmes the constable's name and address.

Holmes took a note of the address.

"Come along, Doctor," he said: "we shall go and look him up. I'll tell you one thing which may help you in the case," he continued, turning to the two detectives. "There has been murder done, and the murderer was a man. He was more than six feet high, was in the prime of life, had small feet for his height, wore coarse, square-toed boots and smoked a Trichinopoly cigar. He came here with his victim in a four-wheeled cab, which was drawn by a horse with three old shoes and one new one on his off fore-leg. In all probability the murderer had a florid face, and the fingernails of his right hand were remarkably long. These are only a few indications, but they may assist you."

Lestrade and Gregson glanced at each other with an incredulous smile.

"If this man was murdered, how was it done?" asked the former.

"Poison," said Sherlock Holmes curtly, and strode off.*

* *Ibid.*

4. Formulating the Hypothesis. At some stage or other of his investigation, any man—whether detective, scientist, or ordinary mortal—will get the feeling that he has all the facts needed for his solution. He has his "2 and 2," so to speak, but the task still remains of "putting them together." At such a time Sherlock Holmes might sit up all night, consuming pipe after pipe of tobacco, trying to think things through. The result or end product of such thinking, if it is successful, is a hypothesis which accounts for all the data, both the original set of facts which constituted the problem, and the additional facts to which the preliminary hypotheses pointed. The actual discovery of such an explanatory hypothesis is a process of creation, in which imagination as well as knowledge is involved. Logic has nothing to say about the *discovery* of hypotheses; this process is more properly to be investigated by psychologists. Holmes, who was a genius at inventing hypotheses, described the process as reasoning "backwards." As he put it,

Most people, if you describe a train of events to them, will tell you what the result would be. They can put those events together in their minds, and argue from them that something will come to pass. There are few people, however, who, if you told them a result, would be able to evolve from their own inner consciousness what the steps were which led up to that result.*

Here is Holmes' description of the process of formulating an explanatory hypothesis. When a hypothesis has been proposed, however, its evaluation must be along the lines that were sketched in Section III. Granted its relevance and testability, and its compatibility with other well attested beliefs, the ultimate criterion for evaluating a hypothesis is its predictive power.

5. Deducing Further Consequences. A really fruitful hypothesis will not only explain the facts which originally inspired it but will explain many others in addition. A good hypothesis will point beyond the initial facts in the direction of others

* *Ibid.*

whose existence might otherwise not have been suspected. And of course the verification of those further consequences will tend to confirm the hypothesis which led to them. Holmes' hypothesis that the murdered man had been poisoned was soon put to such a test. A few days later the murdered man's secretary and traveling companion was also found murdered. Holmes asked Lestrade, who had discovered the second body, whether he had found anything in the room which could furnish a clue to the murderer. Lestrade answered "Nothing," and went on to mention a few quite ordinary effects. Holmes was not satisfied and pressed him, asking "And was there nothing else?" Lestrade answered, "Nothing of any importance," and named a few more details, the last of which was "a small chip ointment box containing a couple of pills." At this information,

Sherlock Holmes sprang from his chair with an exclamation of delight.

"The last link," he cried, exultantly. "My case is complete."

The two detectives stared at him in amazement.

"I have now in my hands," my companion said, confidently, "all the threads which have formed such a tangle. . . . I will give you a proof of my knowledge. Could you lay your hands upon those pills?"

"I have them," said Lestrade, producing a small white box . . .*

On the basis of his hypothesis about the original crime, Holmes was able to predict that the pills found at the scene of the second crime must contain poison. Here deduction has an essential role in the process of any scientific or inductive inquiry. The ultimate value of any hypothesis lies in its predictive or explanatory power, which means that additional facts must be deducible from an adequate hypothesis. From his theory that the first man was poisoned and that the second victim met his death at the hands of the same murderer, Holmes inferred that the pills found by Lestrade must be poison. His theory, however sure he may have felt about it, was only a theory and

* *Ibid.*

needed further confirmation. He obtained that confirmation by testing the consequences deduced from the hypothesis and finding them to be true. Having used deduction to make a prediction, his next step was to test it.

6. Testing the Consequences.   The consequences of a hypothesis, that is, the predictions made on the basis of that hypothesis, may require different means for their testing. Some require only observation. In some cases, Holmes needed only to watch and wait—for the bank robbers to break into the vault, in the "Adventure of the Red-headed League," or for Dr. Roylott to slip a venomous snake through a dummy ventilator, in the "Adventure of the Speckled Band." In the present case, however, an *experiment* had to be performed.

Holmes asked Dr. Watson to fetch the landlady's old and ailing terrier, which she had asked to have put out of its misery the day before. Holmes then cut one of the pills in two, dissolved it in a wineglass of water, added some milk, and

. . . turned the contents of the wineglass into a saucer and placed it in front of the terrier, who speedily licked it dry. Sherlock Holmes's earnest demeanour had so far convinced us that we all sat in silence, watching the animal intently, and expecting some startling effect. None such appeared, however. The dog continued to lie stretched upon the cushion, breathing in a laboured way, but apparently neither the better nor the worse for its draught.

Holmes had taken out his watch, and as minute followed minute without result, an expression of the utmost chagrin and disappointment appeared upon his features. He gnawed his lip, drummed his fingers upon the table, and showed every other symptom of acute impatience. So great was his emotion that I felt sincerely sorry for him, while the two detectives smiled derisively, by no means displeased at this check which he had met.

"It can't be a coincidence," he cried, at last springing from his chair and pacing wildly up and down the room: "it is impossible that it should be a mere coincidence. The very pills which I suspected in the case of Drebber are actually found after the death of Stangerson. And yet they are inert. What can it mean? Surely my whole chain of reasoning cannot have been false. It is impossible!

And yet this wretched dog is none the worse. Ah, I have it! I have it!" With a perfect shriek of delight he rushed to the box, cut the other pill in two, dissolved it, added milk, and presented it to the terrier. The unfortunate creature's tongue seemed hardly to have been moistened in it before it gave a convulsive shiver in every limb, and lay as rigid and lifeless as if it had been struck by lightning.

Sherlock Holmes drew a long breath, and wiped the perspiration from his forehead.*

By the favorable outcome of his experiment, Holmes' hypothesis had received dramatic and convincing confirmation.

7. **Application.**　The detective's concern, after all, is a practical one. Given a crime to solve, he has not merely to explain the facts but to apprehend and arrest the criminal. The latter involves making *application* of his theory, using it to predict where the criminal can be found and how he may be caught. He must deduce still further consequences from the hypothesis, not for the sake of additional confirmation but for practical purposes. From his general hypothesis Holmes was able to infer that the murderer was acting the role of a cabman. We have already seen that Holmes had formed a pretty clear description of the man's appearance, and he had sent out his army of "Baker Street Irregulars," street urchins of the neighborhood, to search out and summon the cab driven by just that man. The successful "application" of this hypothesis can be described again in Dr. Watson's words. A few minutes after the terrier's death,

. . . there was a tap at the door, and the spokesman of the street Arabs, young Wiggins, introduced his insignificant and unsavoury person.

"Please, sir," he said, touching his forelock, "I have the cab downstairs."

"Good boy," said Holmes, blandly. "Why don't you introduce this pattern at Scotland Yard?" he continued, taking a pair of steel handcuffs from a drawer. "See how beautifully the spring works. They fasten in an instant."

* *Ibid.*

"The old pattern is good enough," remarked Lestrade, "if we can only find the man to put them on."

"Very good, very good," said Holmes, smiling. "The cabman may as well help me with my boxes. Just ask him to step up, Wiggins."

I was surprised to find my companion speaking as though he were about to set out on a journey, since he had not said anything to me about it. There was a small portmanteau in the room, and this he pulled out and began to strap. He was busily engaged at it when the cabman entered the room.

"Just give me a help with this buckle, cabman," he said, kneeling over his task, and never turning his head.

The fellow came forward with a somewhat sullen, defiant air, and put down his hands to assist. At that instant there was a sharp click, the jangling of metal, and Sherlock Holmes sprang to his feet again.

"Gentlemen," he cried, with flashing eyes, "let me introduce you to Mr. Jefferson Hope, the murderer of Enoch Drebber and of Joseph Stangerson." *

Here we have a picture of the detective as scientist, reasoning from observed facts to a testable hypothesis which not only explains the facts but permits of practical application.

V. SCIENTISTS IN ACTION: THE PATTERN OF SCIENTIFIC INVESTIGATION

As the term "scientific" is generally used today it refers to any reasoning which seeks to proceed from observable facts of experience to reasonable (that is, relevant and testable) explanations for those facts. The scientific method is not confined to professional scientists: anyone can be said to be proceeding scientifically who follows the general pattern of reasoning from evidence to conclusions which can be tested by experience. The skilled detective is a scientist in this sense, as are most of us—in our more rational moments, at least. The pervasive pattern of all scientific inquiry is expressible in terms of the steps illustrated in the preceding section.

* *Ibid.*

Those seven steps will be explained further by analyzing an important example of scientific research.* During the Eighteenth Century, the caloric theory of heat became very widely accepted. Heat was believed to be a subtle, highly elastic fluid which could be added to or extracted from a body, thereby causing temperature changes in it. The hypothesized heat fluid was supposed to be indestructible; its particles were thought to be self-repellent but attracted by ordinary matter; and it was alleged to be all-pervading. The caloric theory of heat had considerable explanatory power. The expansion of bodies when heated was explained as the natural result of "swelling" due to the heat fluid being forced into its pores. The production of heat by pounding on a body was explained as being due to the releasing or "jarring loose" of some of the caloric which had been condensed in the body, so that pounding increased the amount of free caloric or heat in it. Even the conversion of fuel to power in the early steam engine could be explained on the caloric theory: a given quantity of caloric "falling" from a higher to a lower temperature was analogous to a given quantity of water falling from a higher to a lower level—each was capable of producing mechanical power. By the end of the Eighteenth Century the caloric theory of heat as a material substance was universally accepted.

It was against this background of accepted theory that Count Rumford (1753–1814) encountered the problem which guided much of his subsequent research. Rumford described the beginning in these words:

Being engaged, lately, in superintending the boring of cannon, in the workshops of the military arsenal at Munich, I was struck with the very considerable degree of heat which a brass gun acquires, in a short time, in being bored; and with the still more intense heat (much greater than that of boiling water, as I found by experiment) of the metallic chips separated from it by the borer.

* The following account is freely adapted from *Introduction to Modern Physics*, by F. K. Richtmyer. Copyright, 1928, 1934, by the McGraw-Hill Book Company, Inc.

The more I meditated on these phaenomena, the more they appeared to me to be curious and interesting.*

Here we have the first step in any inquiry: a problem is felt. It should be noted that in this case the felt problem arose from an apparent conflict between the data of experience and accepted scientific theories. The relevant theories were two: first, the caloric theory which asserted heat to be a material substance, and second, the principle of the conservation of matter, which asserted that material substance could neither be created nor destroyed. The observed fact, on the other hand, was that considerable amounts of heat were produced—without any apparent decrease in the amounts of any other material substances. The production of *as much* heat as Rumford observed was inexplicable on the basis of the science of his day. The situation was problematic, and demanded a solution. It should be clear that the problem would not be felt by anyone who was ignorant of the accepted theories. Nor would it be felt by an unobservant individual who took no notice of the facts before him. Finally, it would not be felt by anyone whose mind was not disturbed by gaps or inconsistencies between theory and practice. It may be remarked, then, that the requisite qualities a person must have to initiate any fruitful inquiry are three: one must be familiar with current theories, observant of new facts, and uncomfortable in the presence of any conflict or gap between fact and theory.

Judging by the various experiments he was subsequently led to perform, it seems reasonable to suppose that Count Rumford's preliminary hypothesis was something like the following. Since considerable heat was generated without appreciable diminution of any other material substances present, it might be possible to obtain an unlimited amount of heat without exhausting the supply of matter at hand. This conjecture was certainly suggested by the original data which posed the problem. Helpful in setting up an experiment to test this hypothesis, or to collect data suggested by it, was Rumford's previous knowledge that boring with dull tools generates more heat than is obtained using sharp ones.

On the basis of this knowledge, and being guided by the preliminary hypothesis mentioned, Rumford went about collecting some additional relevant data, which he procured by the following experimental setup. He caused a blunt steel boring tool to rotate, under great pressure, against a piece of brass, while both were immersed in water. The apparatus was powered by two horses. In just two and one half hours the water actually boiled, a process that continued as long as the horses kept the machinery in motion. Rumford thus arrived at the additional fact that there was no limit to the amount of heat which could be produced without any decrease in the amount of material substance in the vicinity. This fact was clearly incompatible with the caloric theory of heat, according to which there can be only a finite or limited amount of the heat fluid in any body.

Having gathered this additional data, Count Rumford addressed himself to the task of formulating a hypothesis which should explain all the facts encountered. It was with some reluctance that he abandoned the popular caloric theory. But the facts were stubborn, and not to be got round. Rumford wrote:

. . . anything which any isolated body, or system of bodies, can continue to furnish without limitation cannot possibly be a material substance; and it appears to me to be extremely difficult, if not quite impossible, to form any distinct idea of anything capable of being excited and communicated in the manner heat was excited and communicated in these experiments, except it be motion.*

Rumford's hypothesis that heat is a form of motion has come to be called the *mechanical* or *kinetic* theory of heat. On the

---

* By permission from *Introduction to Modern Physics* by F. K. Richtmyer. Copyright, 1928, 1934, by the McGraw-Hill Book Company, Inc.

basis of the facts at his disposal he rejected the *materialistic* or *caloric* theory.

But in science, as elsewhere, progress must struggle against inertia. The caloric theory had been accepted for a very long time, and Rumford's hypothesis was so revolutionary that its acceptance was very slow in coming. (Actually, it had been anticipated by Sir Isaac Newton in Query 18 of his *Opticks* almost one hundred years earlier, but Newton's authority had not been established in this field.) Before the kinetic theory could be widely accepted, further confirmation was necessary. That confirmation was supplied by other scientists.

Here we come to a very important aspect of scientific thought. Science is *social,* an activity of the group rather than an isolated individual enterprise. A scientific structure can be built or created by many investigators, and the extensively developed branches of science are all joint enterprises. The cooperative nature of scientific research accounts for the "objectivity" of science. The data with which scientists deal are public data, available to any qualified investigator who makes the appropriate observations. Scientists, in reporting their experiments, include a wealth of detail, not for its own intrinsic interest but to enable any other investigator to *duplicate* the experimental setup and thus see for himself whether the reported result really does occur. There are many cases in which individuals are mistaken in what they *think* they see. In a court of law witnesses will swear to conflicting versions of events at which both were present, with no intentional perjury on the part of either. Many times men will see what they *expect,* or what they *want* to see, rather than what actually occurs. Although the facts of experience are the ultimate court of appeal for scientists, they must be *public* facts which *everyone* can experience under appropriate conditions. When elaborate experiments are repeated by various different scientists again and again, it does not token suspicion or distrust of the other man's results, but universal agreement that to be decisive facts must be public and repeatable. Repetition and careful checking by qualified observers minimizes the intrusion of subjective factors and helps maintain the objectivity of science.

Sir Humphry Davy (1778–1829) was the next scientist of importance to interest himself in the kinetic theory of heat. From the two theories Davy deduced testable consequences which were strictly incompatible with each other. He argued that *if* the caloric theory were true, then two pieces of ice which were initially below the melting point and were kept in a vacuum would not be melted by any amount of friction that could be produced between them.* On the other hand, with the kinetic theory of heat as premiss he deduced the conclusion that two pieces of ice which were rubbed together would melt no matter what their initial temperatures and regardless of whether or not the operation was performed in a vacuum. These deductions pointed the way to further experimentation.

The crucial experiment made possible by these deductions was then performed by Davy, who reported his procedures in great detail, specifying that he used "two parallelopipedons of ice, of the temperature of 29°, six inches long, two wide, and two-thirds of an inch thick . . ." † It was experimentally verified that under the described conditions the ice *did melt.* That result convinced Sir Humphry Davy of the correctness of the kinetic theory of heat and of the untenability of the caloric theory. In Davy's own words:

It has . . . been experimentally demonstrated that caloric, or the matter of heat, does not exist. . . . Since bodies become expanded by friction, it is evident that their corpuscles must move or separate from each other. Now a motion or vibration of the corpuscles of bodies must be necessarily generated by friction and percussion. Therefore we may reasonably conclude that this motion or vibration is heat, or the repulsive power.

Heat, then, or that power which prevents the actual contact of

---

* His actual deduction involved considerations having to do with the theory of "heat capacity" and the phenomenon of oxidation and is too complex to reproduce here in detail. It can be found on pages 161–165 of W. F. Magie's *Source Book in Physics.*

† *Ibid.*

the corpuscles of bodies, and which is the cause of our peculiar sensations of heat and cold, may be defined as a peculiar motion, probably a vibration, of the corpuscles of bodies, tending to separate them.*

Davy's experimental testing of his predictions resulted in the confirmation of Rumford's hypothesis. Perhaps more decisive even than Davy's experiments were those of the British physicist James Prescott Joule (1818–1889) who made the kinetic theory *quantitative* by experimentally establishing the mechanical equivalent of heat.

Especially in its quantitative form, the kinetic theory of heat has many applications. Some of these are theoretical: especially in connection with the kinetic theory of gases it serves to unify mechanics with the theory of heat phenomena. The almost independent science of thermodynamics has been one result of this unification. As for *practical* applications of the kinetic theory of heat, the most obvious is in the field of artificial refrigeration, which is only one of the technological results made possible by that theory.

EXERCISES

1. Take some detective story and analyze its structure in terms of the seven steps discussed in the preceding sections.
2. Find an account of some specific line of research in a popular or semi-popular book on science, and analyze its structure in terms of the seven steps discussed in the preceding sections.

VI. CRUCIAL EXPERIMENTS AND AD HOC HYPOTHESES

From the foregoing account, a reader might form the opinion that scientific progress is ridiculously easy to make. It might appear that, given any problem, all one needs to do is set down all relevant hypotheses and then perform a series of

---

* By permission from *A Source Book in Physics,* by William Francis Magie. Copyright, 1935, by the McGraw-Hill Book Company, Inc.

crucial experiments to eliminate all but one of them. The surviving hypothesis is then "the answer," and we are ready to go on to the next problem. But no opinion could possibly be more mistaken.

It has already been insisted that formulating or discovering relevant hypotheses is not a mechanical process but a creative one, some hypotheses requiring genius for their discovery. It has been observed further that crucial experiments may not always be possible, either because no different observable consequences are deducible from the alternative hypotheses, or because we lack the power to arrange the experimental circumstances in which different consequences would manifest themselves. We wish at this time to point out a more pervasive theoretical difficulty with the program of deciding between rival hypotheses by means of crucial experiments. It may be well to illustrate our discussion by means of a fairly simple example. One that is familiar to all of us concerns the shape of the earth.

During the Middle Ages and the Renaissance the prevailing opinion was that the earth was flat. Most readers will remember that Christopher Columbus was looked upon as a madman for his belief that the earth is round—or rather, spherical. One of Columbus' arguments was that as a ship sails away from shore, the upper portions of it remain visible to a watcher on land long after its lower parts have disappeared from view. A slightly different version of the same argument was included by Nikolaus Copernicus in his epoch-making treatise *On the Revolutions of the Heavenly Spheres*. In Section II of Book I of that work, entitled "That the Earth also is Spherical," he presented a number of arguments intended to establish the truth of that view. Of the many found there we quote the following:

That the seas take a spherical form is perceived by navigators. For when land is still not discernible from a vessel's deck, it is from the masthead. And if, when a ship sails from land, a torch be fastened from the masthead, it appears to watchers on the land to go downward little by little until it entirely disappears, like a heavenly body setting.*

As between these two rival hypotheses about the earth's shape, we might regard the foregoing as a description of a crucial experiment. The general pattern is clear. From the hypothesis that the earth is flat, H_f, it follows that if a ship gradually recedes from view, then neither its masthead nor its decks should remain visible after the other has vanished. On the other hand, from the hypothesis that the earth is spherical, H_s, it follows that if a ship gradually recedes from view, its masthead should remain visible after its decks have vanished from sight. The rationale involved here is nicely represented by a diagram.

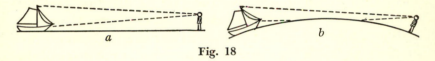

a　b

Fig. 18

In the figure, a represents the situation which would obtain if H_f were true. It is clear that *if* the earth is flat there is no reason why any one portion of the ship should disappear from sight before any other portion. The figure b represents the situation corresponding to H_s. As the ship recedes, the curvature of the earth rises between the observor and the ship, blocking out his view of the decks while the masthead still remains visible. In each case the rays of light passing from ship to observer are represented by dotted lines. Now the experiment is performed, a receding ship is watched attentively, and the masthead *does* remain visible after the decks have disappeared. Our experiment may not have demonstrated the truth of H_s, it can be admitted, but surely it has established the falsehood of H_f. It is as clear an example of a crucial experiment as it is possible to obtain.

* Reprinted from *On the Revolutions of the Heavenly Spheres* by Nikolaus Copernicus, as contained in *Masterworks of Science, Digests of 13 Great Classics,* edited by John Warren Knedler, Jr. Copyright, 1947, by Doubleday & Company, Inc.

But the experiment described is *not* crucial. It is entirely possible to accept the observed facts and still maintain that the earth is flat. The experiment has considerable value as evidence, but it is not decisive. It is not crucial because the various testable predictions were not inferred from the stated hypotheses H_f and H_s alone, but from them *plus* the additional hypothesis that *light travels in straight lines*. The diagrams show clearly that this additional assumption is essential to the argument. That the decks disappear before the masthead does is not deducible from H_s alone but requires the additional premiss that light rays follow a rectilinear path (H_r). And that the decks do *not* disappear before the masthead does is not deducible from H_f alone but requires the same additional premiss: that light rays follow a rectilinear path (H_r). The latter argument may be formulated as:

The earth is flat (H_f)
Light rays follow a rectilinear path (H_r).
Therefore the decks of a receding ship will *not* disappear from view
   before the masthead.

Here is a perfectly good argument whose conclusion is observed to be false. Its premisses can not both be true; at least one of them must be false. But which one? We can maintain the truth of the first premiss, H_f, if we are willing to reject the second premiss, H_r. The second premiss, after all, is not a truth of logic but a contingent statement which is easily conceived to be false. If we adopt the contrary hypothesis that light rays follow a *curved* path, concave upwards, (H_c), what follows as conclusion now? Here we can infer the *denial* of the conclusion of the former argument. From H_f and H_c it follows that the decks of a receding ship *will* disappear before its masthead does. Figure 19 explains the reasoning involved here.

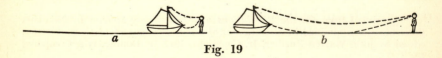

Fig. 19

In this figure, *a* represents the situation when the ship is near the shore, while *b* shows that as the ship recedes, the earth (even though flat) blocks out the view of the decks while the masthead still remains visible. The light rays in this diagram too are represented by dotted lines, but in this case curved rather than rectilinear. The same experiment is performed, the decks *do* disappear before the masthead, and the observed fact is perfectly compatible with this group of hypotheses which includes H_f, the claim that the earth is flat. The experiment, therefore, is not *crucial* with respect to H_f, for that hypothesis can be maintained as true regardless of the experiment's outcome.*

The point is that where hypotheses of a fairly high level of abstractness or generality are involved, no observable or directly testable prediction can be deduced from just a single one of them. A whole group of hypotheses must be used as premisses, and if the observed facts are other than those predicted, *at least one* of the hypotheses in the group is false. But we have not established which one is in error. An experiment *can* be crucial in showing the untenability of a *group* of hypotheses. But such a group will usually contain a considerable number of separate hypotheses, the truth of any one of which can be maintained in the teeth of *any* experimental result, however "unfavorable," by the simple expedient of rejecting some *other* hypothesis of the group. The conclusion to be drawn from these considerations is that no individual hypothesis can ever be subjected to a crucial experiment.

The preceding discussion may be objected to strenuously. It may be urged that the experiment in question "really does" refute the hypothesis that the earth is flat. It may be charged that the argument to the contrary is guilty of making an *ad hoc* hypothesis to obscure and get around the plain facts of the case. It may be felt that only the invention of *ad hoc* hypotheses right and left can prevent some experiments from being crucial

* This illustration was first suggested to me by my colleague, Professor C. L. Stevenson.

and decisively refuting single hypotheses. This reaction is perfectly natural and deserves careful attention.

The crux of the objection would seem to lie in the phrase *"ad hoc,"* which is a highly charged term of abuse. Of its emotive significance there can be little doubt, but its literal meaning is somewhat ambiguous. There are three different senses in which the term *"ad hoc"* is often used. Its first and etymological meaning would seem to be that an *ad hoc* hypothesis is one which is specially made up to account for some fact *after* that fact had been established. In this sense, however, *all* hypotheses are *ad hoc*, since it makes no sense to speak of a hypothesis which has not been devised to account for *some* antecedently established fact or other. Hence the first sense does not fit in very well with the derogatory emotive significance of the term. We must consider its other meanings.

The term *"ad hoc"* is often used to characterize a hypothesis which accounts *only* for the particular fact or facts it was invented to explain and has no other explanatory power, that is, no other testable consequences. No *scientific* hypothesis is *ad hoc* in this second sense of the term, although *every* hypothesis is *ad hoc* in the first sense explained. An hypothesis which is *ad hoc* in the second sense is unscientific; since it is not testable it has no place in the structure of science. The second sense of *ad hoc* fits in perfectly with the derogatory emotive meaning of the term. But it should be realized that the auxiliary hypothesis about light rays traveling in curved paths, which was sufficient to save the hypothesis that the earth is flat from being definitely refuted by the experiment described, is *ad hoc* only in the first sense, not the second. For it does have a considerable number of empirically testable consequences.

There is a third sense of the term *"ad hoc,"* in which it is used to denote a mere descriptive generalization. Such a descriptive hypothesis will assert only that all facts of a particular sort occur in just some particular kinds of circumstances and will have no explanatory power or theoretical scope. For example, limiting their diet to polished rice was found by Eijkman to cause polyneuritis in the small group of chickens with which he was working (as described in Exercise 2 under the Method of Difference in the preceding chapter). Eijkman's hypothesis to account for this fact was *ad hoc* in the third sense: he simply drew the generalization that a diet limited to polished rice will cause polyneuritis in *any* group of chickens. His hypothesis accounts for more than just the particular facts observed; it is testable by controlling the diets of *other* groups of chickens. But it is descriptive rather than explanatory, *merely* empirical rather than theoretical. The science of nutrition has come a long way since Eijkman's contribution. The identification of vitamins and their analysis are required for a more adequate account of the facts first observed by Eijkman. Science seeks to explain rather than merely to describe, and hypotheses which consist of bare generalizations of the facts observed are said to be *ad hoc*.

The classical example of an *ad hoc* hypothesis, in this third sense, is the Fitzgerald Contraction Effect introduced to account for the results of the Michelson-Morley experiment on the velocity of light. By affirming that bodies moving at extremely high velocities contract, Fitzgerald accounted for the given data; his account was testable by repetitions of the experiment. But it was generally held to be *ad hoc* rather than explanatory, and not until Einstein's Special Theory of Relativity were the anomalous results of the Michelson-Morley experiment given an adequate, that is, a theoretical explanation. It should be noted that the auxiliary hypothesis about the curved path of light rays is not *ad hoc* in this third sense either, since it is not a mere generalization of observed facts. (It is, in fact, an essential ingredient in the General Theory of Relativity.)

The general situation seems to be that it is not necessary to invoke *ad hoc* hypotheses—in either the second or third senses of the term, which are the derogatory ones—to prevent experiments from being crucial. Even if we confine our attention to theoretically significant hypotheses, and never invoke any *ad hoc* hypotheses whatsoever, since hypotheses are testable only in groups, no experiments are ever crucial for individual hypotheses. Our limitation here serves to illuminate again the *systematic* character of science. Scientific progress consists in building ever more adequate theories to account for the facts of experience. True enough, it is of value to collect or verify isolated particular facts, for the ultimate basis of science is factual. But the theoretical structure of science grows in a more organic fashion. In the realm of theory, piecemeal progress, one step at a time advances, *can* be accomplished, but only *within* the framework of a generally accepted body of scientific theory. The notion that scientific hypotheses, theories, or laws are wholly discrete and independent is a naive and outdated view.

The term "crucial experiment" is not a useless one, however. Within the framework of accepted scientific theory which we are not concerned to question, a hypothesis *can* be subjected to a crucial experiment. If a negative result is obtained, that is, if some phenomenon fails to occur which had been predicted on the basis of the single dubious hypothesis together with accepted parts of scientific theory, then the experiment is crucial and the hypothesis is rejected. But there is nothing absolute about such a procedure, for even well-accepted scientific theories tend to be changed in the face of new and contrary evidence. Science is not monolithic, either in its practices or in its aims.

Perhaps the most significant lesson to be learned from the preceding discussion is the importance to scientific progress of dragging "hidden assumptions" into the open. That light travels in straight lines was assumed in the arguments of Columbus and Copernicus, but it was a hidden assumption. Because they are hidden, there is no chance to examine such assumptions critically and to decide intelligently whether they are true or false. Progress is often achieved by formulating explicitly an assumption which had previously been hidden and then scrutinizing and rejecting it. An important and dramatic instance of this occurred when Einstein challenged the universally accepted assumption that it always makes sense to say of two events that they occurred *at the same time*. In considering how an observer could discover whether or not two distant events occurred "at the same time," Einstein was led to the conclusion that two events could be simultaneous for one observer but not for another, depending upon their locations and velocities relative to the events in question. Rejecting the assumption led to the Special Theory of Relativity, which constituted a tremendous step forward in explaining such phenomena as those revealed by the Michelson-Morley experiment. It is clear that an assumption must be *recognized* before it can be challenged, and this fact indicates the importance to scientific progress of formulating explicitly all relevant assumptions in any hypothesis, allowing none of them to remain hidden.

VII. CLASSIFICATION AS HYPOTHESIS

It might be objected that hypotheses play important roles only in the more advanced sciences, not in those which are relatively less advanced. It may be urged that although explanatory hypotheses may be central to such sciences as physics and chemistry, they play no such role—at least not yet—in the biological or social sciences. The latter are still in their descriptive phases, and it may be felt that the method of hypothesis is not relevant to the so-called descriptive sciences, such as botany or history. This objection is easily answered. An examination of the nature of description will show that description itself is based on or embodies hypotheses. Hypotheses are as basic to the various systems of taxonomy or classification in biology as they are in history or any of the other social sciences.

The importance of hypothesis in the science of history is easily shown and will be discussed first. Some historians believe that the study of history will reveal the existence of a single cosmic purpose or pattern, either religious or naturalistic, which accounts for or explains the entire course of recorded history. Others deny the existence of any such cosmic design but insist that the study of history will reveal certain historical *laws* which explain the actual sequence of past events and can be used to predict the future. On either of these views, explanations are to be sought by the historian which must account for and be confirmed by the recorded events of the past. On either of these views, therefore, history is a theoretical rather than a merely descriptive science, and the role of hypothesis must be admitted as central in the historian's enterprise.

There is, however, a third group of historians who set themselves what is apparently a more modest goal. According to them, the task of the historian is simply to chronicle the past, to set forth a bare description of past events in their chronological order. On this view, it might seem, the "scientific" historian has no need of hypotheses, since his concern is with the facts themselves, not with any theories about them.

But past events are not so easily chronicled as this view implies. The past itself is simply not available for this kind of description. What *is* available are present records and traces of the past. These range all the way from official government archives of the recent past to epic poems celebrating the exploits of half-legendary heroes and from the writings of older historians to artifacts of bygone eras unearthed in the excavations of archaeologists. *These* are the only facts available to the historian, and from them he must *infer* the nature of those past events it is his purpose to describe. Not *all* hypotheses are general; some are particular. The historian's description of the past is a particular hypothesis which is intended to account for his present data, and for which his present data constitute evidence.

The historian is a detective on a grand scale. Their methods are the same, and their difficulties too. The evidence is scanty, and much of it has been destroyed—if not by the bungling local constabulary, then by intervening wars and natural disasters. And just as the criminal may have left false or misleading clues to throw his pursuer off the scent, so many present "records" are falsifications of the past they purport to describe, either intentional, as in the case of such forged historical documents as the "Donation of Constantine," or unintentional, as in the writings of early uncritical historians. Just as the detective must use the method of science in formulating and testing his hypotheses, so the historian must make hypotheses too. Even those historians who seek to limit themselves to bare descriptions of past events must work with hypotheses: they are theorists in spite of themselves.

The biologist is in a somewhat more favorable position. The facts with which he deals are present and available for inspection. To describe the flora and fauna of a given region he need not make elaborate inferences of the sort to which the historian is condemned. The data can be perceived directly. His description of these items is not casual, of course, but systematic. He is usually said to *classify* plants and animals, rather than merely to describe them. But classification and description are really the same process. To describe a given animal as carnivorous is to classify it as a carnivore; to classify it as a reptile is to describe it as reptilian. To describe any object as having a certain property is to classify it as a member of the class of objects having that property.

Classification, as generally understood, involves not merely a single division of objects into separate groups but further subdivision of each group into subgroups or subclasses, and so on. This pattern is familiar to most of us, if not from our various studies in school, then certainly from playing the old game of "Animal, Vegetable, or Mineral?" or its more modern version, "Twenty Questions." Apart from such games, there are many motives that have led men to classify objects. For primitive man to live, he was required to classify roots and berries as edible or poisonous, animals as dangerous or harmless, and other men as friend or foe. People tend to draw distinctions which are of practical importance to them and to neglect those that play a less immediate role in their affairs. A farmer will classify grains and vegetables carefully and in detail but may call all flowers "posies"; whereas a florist will classify his merchandise with the greatest of care but may lump all of the farmer's crops together as "produce." There are several motives that may lead us to classify things. One is practical, another theoretical. If one had only three or four books, he could know them all well and could easily take them all in at a glance, so that there would be no need for classifying them. But in a public or college library containing many thousands of volumes, the situation is different. If the books there were not classified, the librarian could not find the books that might be wanted, and the collection would be practically useless. The larger the number of objects, the greater is the need for classifying them. A practical purpose of classification is to make large collections accessible. This is especially apparent in the case of libraries, museums, and public records of one sort or another.

In considering the *theoretical* purpose of classification we must realize that the adoption of this or that alternative classification scheme is not anything which can be true or false. Objects can be described in different ways, from different points of view. The scheme of classification adopted depends upon the purpose or interest of the classifier. Books, for example, would be classified differently by a librarian, a bookbinder, and a bibliophile. The librarian would classify them according to their contents or subject matter, the bookbinder according to their bindings, and a bibliophile according to their date of printing or perhaps their relative rarity. The possibilities are not thereby exhausted, of course: a book packer would divide books according to their shapes and sizes, and persons with still other interests will classify them differently in the light of those different interests.

Now what special interest or purpose does the scientist have which can lead him to prefer one scheme of classification to another? The scientist's aim is knowledge, not merely of this or that particular fact for its own sake, but knowledge of the general laws to which they conform and the causal interrelationships among them. One classification scheme is better than another, from the scientist's point of view, to the extent that it is more fruitful in suggesting scientific laws and more helpful in the formulation of explanatory hypotheses.

The theoretical or scientific motive for classifying objects is the desire to increase our knowledge of them. Increased knowledge of things is further insight into their properties, their similarities and differences, and their interrelations. A classification scheme made for narrowly practical purposes may tend to obscure important similarities and differences. Thus a division of animals into dangerous and harmless will assign the wild boar and the rattlesnake to one class and the domestic pig and the grass snake to the other; calling attention away from what we should today regard as more profound similarities in order to emphasize superficial resemblances. A scientifically fruitful classification of objects requires considerable knowledge about them. A slight acquaintance with their more obvious properties would lead one to classify the bat with birds, as flying creatures, and the whale with fishes, as creatures that live in the sea. But a more extensive knowledge would lead us to classify both bats and whales as mammals, since being warm-blooded, bearing their young alive, and suckling them are more important characteristics on which to base a classificatory scheme.

A characteristic is important when it serves as a clue to the presence of other characteristics. An *important* characteristic, from the point of view of science, is one which is causally connected with many other characteristics, and hence relevant to the framing of a maximum number of causal laws and the formulation of very general explanatory hypotheses. That classification scheme is best, then, which is based on the most important characteristics of the objects to be classified. But we do not know in advance what causal laws obtain, and causal laws themselves partake of the nature of hypotheses, as was emphasized in the preceding chapter. Therefore any decision as to which classification scheme to adopt is itself a hypothesis, which subsequent investigations may lead us to reject. If later investigations revealed *other* characteristics to be more important, that is, involved in a greater number of causal laws and explanatory hypotheses, it would be reasonable to expect the earlier classification scheme to be rejected in favor of a newer one based upon the more important characteristics.

This view of classification schemes as hypotheses is borne out by the actual role such schemes play in the sciences. Thus taxonomy is a legitimate, important, and growing branch of biology, in which some classification schemes, like that of Linnaeus, have been adopted, used, and subsequently abandoned in favor of better ones, which are themselves in turn subject to modification in the light of new data. Classification is generally most important in the early or less developed stages of a science. It need not always diminish in importance as the science develops, however. For example, the standard classification scheme for the elements, as set forth in Mendeleeff's Table, is still an important tool for the investigator in the relatively far advanced science of chemistry.

In the light of the foregoing discussion, a further remark can be made on the role of hypothesis in the science of history. It has already been remarked that the historian's descriptions of past events are themselves hypotheses based on present data. There is an additional, equally significant role which hypotheses play in the descriptive historian's enterprise. It is obvious that no historical era or event of any magnitude can be described in *complete detail*. Even if all its details could be known, no historian could possibly include them all in his narrative. Life is too short to permit an *exhaustive* description of *anything*. The historian must therefore describe the past selectively, recording only some of its aspects. Upon what basis shall he make his selection? Clearly, the historian wants to include what is significant or important in his descriptions, and to ignore what is insignificant or trivial. The subjective bias of this or that historian may lead him to lay undue stress on the religious, the economic, the personal, or some other aspect of the historic process. But to the extent that he can make an objective or scientific appraisal, the historian will regard those aspects as important which enter into the formulation of causal laws and general explanatory hypotheses. Such appraisals are, of course, subject to correction in the light of further research.

The first Western historian, Herodotus, described a great many aspects of the events he chronicled, personal and cultural as well as political and military. The so-called first "scientific" historian, Thucydides, restricted himself much more to the political and the military. For a long period of time most historians followed Thucydides, but now the pendulum is swinging in another direction, and the economic and cultural aspects of the past are being given increased emphasis. Just as the biologist's classification scheme embodies his hypothesis as to which characteristics of living things are involved in a maximum number of causal laws, so the historian's decision to describe past events in terms of one rather than another set of properties embodies his hypothesis as to which properties are causally related to a maximum number of others. Some such hypothesis is required before the historian can even begin any systematic description of the past. It is this hypothetical character of classification and description, whether biological or historical, which leads us to regard hypothesis as the all-pervasive method of scientific inquiry.

EXERCISES

In each of the following passages:
  (a) What data are to be explained?
  (b) What hypotheses are proposed to explain them?
  (c) Evaluate the hypotheses in terms of the criteria presented in Section III.

1. On the 7th of January 1610, at one o'clock in the morning, when he directed his telescope to Jupiter, he observed three stars near the body of the planet, two being to the east and one to the west of him. They were all in a straight line, and parallel to the ecliptic, and they appeared brighter than other stars of the same magnitude. Believing them to be fixed stars, he paid no great attention to their distances from Jupiter and from one another. On the 8th of January, however, when, from some cause or other, he had been led to observe the stars again, he found a very different arrangement of them: all the three were on the west side of Jupiter, *nearer one another than before,* and almost at equal distances. Though he had not turned his attention to the extraordinary fact of the mutual approach of the stars, yet he

began to consider how Jupiter could be found to the east of the three stars, when but the day before he had been to the west of two of them. The only explanation which he could give of this fact was, that the motion of Jupiter was *direct,* contrary to astronomical calculations, and that he had got before these two stars by his own motion.

In this dilemma between the testimony of his senses and the results of calculation, he waited for the following night with the utmost anxiety; but his hopes were disappointed, for the heavens were wholly veiled in clouds. On the 10th, two only of the stars appeared, and both on the east of the planet. As it was obviously impossible that Jupiter could have advanced from west to east on the 8th of January, and from east to west on the 10th, Galileo was forced to conclude that the phenomenon which he had observed arose from the motion of the stars, and he set himself to observe diligently their change of place. On the 11th, there were still only two stars, and both to the east of Jupiter; but the more eastern star was now *twice as large as the other one,* though on the preceding night they had been perfectly equal. This fact threw a new light upon Galileo's difficulties, and he immediately drew the conclusion, which he considered to be indubitable, '*that there were in the heaven three stars which revolved round Jupiter, in the same manner as Venus and Mercury revolved round the sun.*' On the 12th of January, he again observed them in new positions, and of different magnitudes; and, on the 13th, he discovered a fourth star, which completed the *four* secondary planets with which Jupiter is surrounded.*

2. Again however solid things are thought to be, you may yet learn from this that they are of rare body: in rocks and caverns the moisture of water oozes through and all things weep with abundant drops; food distributes itself through the whole body of living things; trees grow and yield fruit in season, because food is diffused through the whole from the very roots over the stem and all the boughs. Voices pass through walls and fly through houses shut, stiffening frost pierces to the bones. Now if there are no void parts, by what way can the bodies severally pass? You would see it to be quite impossible. Once more, why do we see one thing surpass another in weight though not larger in size? For if there

* Reprinted from *The Martyrs of Science* by Sir David Brewster.

is just as much body in a ball of wool as there is in a lump of lead, it is natural it should weigh the same, since the property of body is to weigh all things downwards, while on the contrary the nature of void is ever without weight. Therefore when a thing is just as large, yet is found to be lighter, it proves sure enough that it has more of void in it; while on the other hand that which is heavier shows that there is in it more of body and that it contains within it much less of void. Therefore that which we are seeking with keen reason exists sure enough, mixed up in things; and we call it void.*

3. Alice took up the fan and gloves, and, as the hall was very hot, she kept fanning herself all the time she went on talking. "Dear, dear! How queer everything is today! And yesterday things went on just as usual. I wonder if I've changed in the night? Let me think: *was* I the same when I got up this morning? I almost think I can remember feeling a little different. But if I'm not the same, the next question is 'Who in the world am I?' Ah, *that's* the great puzzle!" And she began thinking over all the children she knew that were of the same age as herself, to see if she could have been changed for any of them.

"I'm sure I'm not Ada," she said, "for her hair goes in such long ringlets, and mine doesn't go in ringlets at all; and I'm sure I can't be Mabel, for I know all sorts of things, and she, oh, she knows such a very little! Besides, *she's* she, and *I'm* I, and—oh dear, how puzzling it all is! I'll try if I know all the things I used to know. Let me see: four times five is twelve, and four times six is thirteen, and four times seven is—oh dear! I shall never get to twenty at that rate! However, the Multiplication-Table doesn't signify: let's try Geography. London is the capital of Paris, and Paris is the capital of Rome, and Rome—no *that's* all wrong, I'm certain! I must have been changed for Mabel!" †

4. For several years a lively controversy has been going on among chemists concerning an eerie apparent phenomenon known as "long-range forces." It was started by certain observations of Alexandre Rothen of the Rockefeller Institute for Medical Research. He found that some molecules seemed to have the power to react chemically with one another at relatively great distances, even

* From Book I, *On the Nature of Things* by Lucretius.
† Reprinted from *Alice in Wonderland* by Lewis Carroll.

though they were separated by a plastic barrier (*Scientific American,* October, 1948). Since this finding was in defiance of all chemical theory, which assumes that molecules can interact only when they are in contact, chemists were both mystified and skeptical. Many tried to disprove or explain Rothen's results. Two investigators now report that they have found an orthodox explanation of his findings.

In a typical experiment Rothen covered a layer of albumin 50 Angstroms thick (one Angstrom is about 1/40,000,000-inch) with a 200-Angstrom layer of inert plastic. On top of the plastic he placed a film of antibody proteins which combine specifically with albumin. Despite the plastic barrier the antibody on top reacted with the albumin underneath.

Chemists who questioned the theory that the reaction was effected by long-range forces decided that the plastic must be less impervious than it seemed. Somehow the molecules must have migrated through the plastic, either through accidental cracks in it or through some unknown opening. Hans. J. Trurnit of the Army Chemical Center in Maryland now reports that he has established how the molecules get through. The plastic "barrier," he says, is actually a fine mesh screen with holes due to its natural physical structure. The antibodies Rothen studied are normally suspended in a phosphate salt solution. Trurnit deposited pure phosphate solution, completely free of antibodies, on top of plastic-albumin preparations. After 10 minutes, he found some of the underlying albumin in the phosphate solution. His observation indicated that the solution seeped through holes in the plastic and made contact with the bottom layer. Some of the albumin molecules then dissolved and "floated" to the upper surface of the plastic screen.

Further proof that the plastic has holes in it will be published shortly by S. J. Singer of the California Institute of Technology, and Rothen himself has found similar evidence. Rothen still believes, however, that the new facts do not explain all his experiments and long-range forces may act in certain cases.*

5. Crustacea, like many invertebrates, have organs called otocysts. These are small sacs each containing a tuft of hairs which are

* Reprinted from "Science and the Citizen" in *Scientific American,* Vol. 182, No. 3, March 1950.

connected to nerve endings at their base. On top of this tuft reposes a mass of stony material called an otolith. In most crustaceans the otocysts are completely enclosed, but in one genus of prawn, Palaemon, they are open, being pockets in the shell of the animal. No otoliths are secreted by Palaemon but it stirs up sand at the bottom of the water and stuffs grains into the openings of the otocysts. When this has been done, the opening to the otocyst is closed. Since like all crustaceans it sheds its shell periodically, Palaemon must repeat this process after each moulting.

The function of otocysts remained in doubt till the end of the nineteenth century. There was some reason to consider them organs of balance since if the animal moved so as to make the pressure of the otoliths on the hairs as great as possible, it would automatically stay right side up. No conclusive proof was given, however, that this was the function.

In 1893, Kriedl placed a newly moulted Palaemon in an aquarium whose bottom was covered with iron filings in place of sand. For want of sand, the prawn stuffed some filings into its otocysts after which Kriedl placed a powerful electromagnet next to the animal. It turned, tilting its back at an angle away from the magnet. Kriedl reasoned that, because of the pull of the magnet on the filings in the otocysts, the prawn was moving so as to keep the pressure on the hairs at a maximum. This was in accord with the theory which he therefore considered established.

The experiment has been repeated several times, notably by Prentiss, with the same result.*

6. While walking one night with Dr. Frink, we accidentally met a colleague, Dr. P., whom I had not seen for years, and of whose private life I knew nothing. We were naturally very pleased to meet again, and on my invitation, he accompanied us to a cafe, where we spent about two hours in pleasant conversation. To my question as to whether he was married, he gave a negative answer, and added, 'Why should a man like me marry?'

On leaving the cafe, he suddenly turned to me and said: 'I should like to know what you would do in a case like this: I know a nurse who was named as co-respondent in a divorce case. The

---

* Reprinted from *Exercises in Elementary Logic* by Paul Henle and W. K. Frankena. Copyright, 1940, by Paul Henle and W. K. Frankena.

wife sued the husband for divorce and named her as co-respondent, and *he* got the divorce.' I interrupted him saying, 'You mean
she got the divorce.' He immediately corrected himself, saying,
'Yes, she got the divorce,' and continued to tell how the excite-
ment of the trial had affected this nurse to such an extent that
she became nervous and took to drink. He wanted me to advise
him how to treat her.

As soon as I had corrected his mistake, I asked him to explain
it, but, as is usually the case, he was surprised at my question.
He wanted to know whether a person had no right to make mistakes in talking. I explained to him that there is a reason for
every mistake, and that if he had not told me that he was unmarried, I should say that he was the hero of the divorce case in
question, and that the mistake showed that he wished he had
obtained the divorce instead of his wife, so as not to be obliged
to pay alimony and to be permitted to marry again in New York
State.

He stoutly denied my interpretation, but his emotional agita-
tion, followed by loud laughter, only strengthened my suspicions.
To my appeal that he should tell the truth 'for science' sake,' he
said, 'Unless you wish me to lie, you must believe that I was
never married, and hence, your psychoanalytic interpretation is
all wrong.' He, however, added that it was dangerous to be with
a person who paid attention to such little things. Then he suddenly remembered that he had another appointment and left us.

Both Dr. Frink and I were convinced that my interpretation
of his *lapsus linguae* was correct, and I decided to corroborate
or disprove it by further investigation. The next day, I found
a neighbor and old friend of Dr. P., who confirmed my interpretation in every particular. The divorce was granted to Dr. P.'s wife
a few weeks before, and a nurse was named as co-respondent. A
few weeks later, I met Dr. P., and he told me that he was thor-
oughly convinced of the Freudian mechanisms.*

* Reprinted from *Psychoanalysis: Its Theories and Practical Applications* by
A. A. Brill. Copyright, 1921, by W. B. Saunders Co.

CHAPTER FOURTEEN

Probability

I. ALTERNATIVE CONCEPTIONS OF PROBABILITY

The words "probable" and "probability" have been frequently used thus far in our discussion of inductive logic and scientific method. Even a hypothesis which fits all the available facts is not thereby established conclusively, it was said, but only *with probability*. And the most protracted and careful uses of Mill's Methods of experimental inquiry do not *demonstrate* the laws to which they lead as being certain, but only tend to confirm them as being highly *probable*. Even the best inductive arguments fall short of that certainty which attaches to valid deductive arguments.

The words "probable" and "probability" are used in various different ways. We say, for example, that the probability of a tossed coin showing *heads* is $\frac{1}{2}$; that the probability of a twenty-five year old man surviving his twenty-sixth birthday is .963; and that on the present evidence, it is highly probable that Einstein's unified field theory is correct. There are other contexts in which the words "probable" and "probability" are used, as in speaking of "probable errors" of measurement, and so on.

But the first three may be taken as the most important and typical uses of the terms. The third is the most significant for scientific hypotheses. It differs from the first two in not assigning any numerical coefficient of probability. *Degrees* of probability are assigned to scientific hypotheses only in terms of more and less. Thus the Darwinian theory is regarded as more probable than the account of creation given in the Book of Genesis, and the atomic theory has a higher degree of probability than any of the recent highly speculative hypotheses concerning the inner structures of nuclei.

The first two of our three examples assign numbers as measures of the probabilities they assert. The sources of these numbers seem fairly clear. Coins have two sides, heads and tails, and when they fall, one side or the other must face upwards. One chance out of two will place heads up, and so the probability ½ is assigned to heads. To arrive at the probability coefficient mentioned in the second example, mortality statistics must be gathered and compared. Of perhaps one thousand men who had celebrated their twenty-fifth birthday, it was found that nine hundred sixty-three of them lived at least one additional year, and on the basis of these findings the figure .963 was assigned to the probability of a twenty-five year old man's surviving his twenty-sixth birthday. Such probability measurements as these are utilized by life insurance companies in fixing the size of premiums to be charged for their policies.

As the first two examples may suggest, studies of probability are bound up with gambling and mortality statistics; in fact, the modern study of probability had its beginnings in these two fields. The theory of probability is commonly regarded as having begun with the correspondence between Blaise Pascal (1623–1662) and Pierre de Fermat (1608–1665) over the proper division of the stakes in an interrupted game of chance. Another version has it that it began with Pascal's advice to the Chevalier de Méré, a notorious Seventeenth-Century gambler, on how to wager in throwing dice. In connection with the study of mortality, in 1662 Captain John Graunt published a discussion of the mortality records which had been kept in London since 1592. Presumably as a consequence of its mixed ancestry, probability has been given two different interpretations.

The classical theory of the nature of probability, as formulated by Laplace, De Morgan, Keynes, and others, regards it as measuring degree of rational belief. When we are completely convinced of something, the measure of our belief may have the number *one* assigned it. And when we are utterly certain that a specified event cannot possibly happen, our belief that it *will* happen can be assigned the number *zero*. Thus a rational man's belief that a tossed coin will *either* show heads or not show heads is 1, and his belief that it will *both* show heads and not show heads is 0. Where he is not sure, the degree of his reasonable belief will fall somewhere between 0 and 1. Probability is predicated of an event according to the degree to which one rationally believes that it will occur. Or probability may be predicated of a statement or proposition according to the degree to which a completely rational man will believe that it is true.

On the classical view, probability is always a result of partial knowledge and partial ignorance. If the exact motion of one's fingers in flipping a coin were known, together with the initial position, dimensions, and weight distribution of the coin, one could predict its trajectory and final resting position with complete confidence. But such complete information is not available. Only some information is known: that the coin has only two sides, that it will fall, and so on. Consequently our belief that it will show heads is measured by a consideration of the various possibilities, which are 2, of which heads is only 1. Therefore the probability ½ is assigned to the event of the coin showing heads. Similarly, when a deck of cards is about to be dealt, the cards are in just the order that they are, and will come off the deck, in an honest deal, in exactly the sequence of spades and hearts and diamonds and clubs, aces and kings and queens and jacks, that is determined by their arrangement in the deck. But we do not know that arrangement. We know only that there are thirteen spades, out of fifty-two cards altogether, so the probability that the first card dealt will be a spade is exactly $^{13}\!/_{52}$ or $\frac{1}{4}$.

This view is known as the *a priori* theory of probability. It is so called because no trials need be run before the probability is assigned, no sample deals need be examined. All that is required is a knowledge of the antecedent conditions: that there are four aces only in the deck, that there are fifty-two cards altogether, and that it is an honest deal, so that one card has as much chance as any other of being dealt first. On the *a priori* view, all that we need do to compute the probability of an event's occurring in given circumstances is to divide the number of ways in which it can occur by the total number of possible outcomes of those circumstances, provided there is no reason to believe that any one of those possible outcomes is more likely than any other.

An alternative to the *a priori* view is the theory which regards probability as a measure of "relative frequency." The relative frequency theory seems especially suited to take account of probability judgments arising out of statistical investigations. Thus an actuary observes a number of men in order to determine what mortality rate they exhibit. Here we have a class and a property, the class being that of twenty-five year old men, the property that of surviving their twenty-sixth birthdays. The probability assigned is the measure of the relative frequency with which the members of the class exhibit the property in question. Of a thousand twenty-five year old men, if nine hundred sixty-three exhibit the property of surviving at least one additional year, the number .963 is assigned as the probability coefficient for the occurrence of this property in any such class. On the relative frequency theory of probability, then, probability is not defined in terms of rational belief. Probability is defined as the relative frequency with which members of a class exhibit a specified property.

The relative frequency theory, as its name implies, regards probability as relative. Thus if the question is raised as to the probability with which blondness of hair occurs, this varies with respect to the different reference classes relative to which the property may occur. For example, the probability of blondness is higher relative to the class of Scandinavians than it is relative to the total population of the world.

The *a priori* theory also regards probability as relative. In the language of the classical *a priori* theory, no event has any *intrinsic* probability. It can be assigned a probability only on the basis of the evidence available to the person making the assignment. This relativity is to be expected on a view which regards probability as a measure of rational belief, for the reasonable man's beliefs change according to the state of his knowledge. Suppose, for example, that two people are watching a deck of cards being shuffled. When the shuffle is finished, the dealer accidentally "flashes" the top card. One observer sees that the card is black, although he is not able to observe whether it is a spade or a club. But the second observer notices nothing. If the two observers are asked to estimate the probability of the first card's being a spade, the first observer will assign the probability ½, since there are only twenty-six black cards, of which half are spades. But the second observer will assign the probability ¼, since he knows only that there are thirteen spades in the deck of fifty-two cards. The two observers thus assign different probabilities to the same event. Has one of them made a mistake? Certainly not: each has assigned the correct probability *relative to the evidence at his disposal.* Both estimates are correct—even if the card turns out to be a club. No event has any probability *by itself,* which means that any prediction will have different probabilities in different contexts, that is, relative to different sets of evidence. It is important to notice that although the event has different probabilities relative to different amounts of evidence, it would be a mistake for anyone to use less than the total evidence available to him in judging probabilities.

Because of their agreement upon the relative nature of probability, adherents of both theories agree on the acceptability and utility of the probability calculus, of which an elementary presentation will be made in the following section.

II. THE PROBABILITY CALCULUS

The probability calculus is a branch of pure mathematics which can be used in computing the probabilities of complex events from the probabilities of their component events. A complex event can be regarded as a whole of which its component events are parts. For example, the complex event of drawing two spades from a deck of playing cards is a whole of which the two parts are the event of drawing the first spade and the event of subsequently drawing another spade. Again, the complex event of a bride and groom living to celebrate their golden wedding is a whole of which the parts are the event of the bride's living an additional fifty years, the groom's living an additional fifty years, and no separation taking place. When it is known how the component events are related to each other, the probability of the complex event can be *calculated* from the probabilities of its components. Although the probability calculus has a much wider range of applications, it is most easily explained in terms of games of chance, so that most of our examples and illustrations in this section will be drawn from the sphere of gambling. And the *a priori* theory will be used here, though it should be emphasized that all our results, with a minimum of reinterpretation, can be expressed and justified in terms of the frequency theory.

1. **Joint Occurrences.** Let us first turn our attention to complex events which have as their component parts events which are *independent*. Two events are said to be *independent* if the occurrence or non-occurrence of either of them has absolutely no effect on the occurrence or non-occurrence of the other. For example, if two coins are tossed, whether one comes down heads or tails has no effect upon whether the other shows heads or tails. Let us pose as our first problem: what is the probability of getting two heads in tossing two coins? There are three possible outcomes to tossing two coins: we may get two heads,

or we may get two tails, or we may get one head and one tail. *But these are not equipossible alternatives,* for there are *two* ways of getting one head and one tail, as contrasted with only one way of getting two heads. The first coin may be heads and the second tails, or the first coin may be tails and the second one heads; these are two distinct cases. There are *four* distinct possible events which may occur when two coins are tossed; they may be listed as follows:

First Coin	Second Coin
H	H
H	T
T	H
T	T

There is no reason for expecting any one of these cases to occur rather than any other, so we regard them as equipossible. The *favorable* case, that of getting two heads, is only one of four equipossible events, so· the probability of getting two heads in tossing two coins is $\frac{1}{4}$. The probability for this complex event may be calculated from the probabilities of its two independent component events. The complex event of getting two heads is constituted by the *joint* occurrence of the event of getting a head on the first *and* the event of getting a head on the second. The probability of getting a head on the first is $\frac{1}{2}$, and the probability of getting a head on the second is also $\frac{1}{2}$. The events are presumed to be independent, so that the *product theorem* of the probability calculus can be used to compute the probability of their joint occurrence. The *product theorem* for independent events asserts that the probability of the joint occurrence of two independent events is equal to the product of their separate probabilities. The general formula may be written:

$$P(a \text{ and } b) = P(a) \times P(b)$$

where "*a*" and "*b*" designate the two independent events, "*P(a)*" and "*P(b)*" designate their separate probabilities, and "*P(a* and *b)*" designates the probability of their joint occurrence. In the present case, since *a* is the event of the first coin falling heads, and *b* is the event of the second coin falling heads, $P(a) = \frac{1}{2}$ and $P(b) = \frac{1}{2}$, so that $P(a \text{ and } b) = \frac{1}{2} \times \frac{1}{2} = \frac{1}{4}$.

Let us consider a second problem of the same sort. What is the probability of getting a twelve in rolling two dice? Two dice will show twelve points only if each of them shows six points. Each die has six sides, any one of which is as likely to be face up after a roll as any other. Where *a* is the event of the first die showing a six, $P(a) = \frac{1}{6}$. And where *b* is the event of the second die showing a six, $P(b) = \frac{1}{6}$. The complex event of the two dice showing a twelve is constituted by the joint occurrence of *a* and *b*. By the product theorem, then $P(a \text{ and } b) = \frac{1}{6} \times \frac{1}{6} = \frac{1}{36}$, which is the probability of getting a twelve on one roll of two dice. We can arrive at the same result by taking the trouble to enumerate all the possible events which may occur when two dice are rolled. There are thirty-six equipossible events, which may be listed as follows, where of each pair of numbers the first stands for the number on the top face of the first die, the second for the number showing on the second one:

1–1	2–1	3–1	4–1	5–1	6–1
1–2	2–2	3–2	4–2	5–2	6–2
1–3	2–3	3–3	4–3	5–3	6–3
1–4	2–4	3–4	4–4	5–4	6–4
1–5	2–5	3–5	4–5	5–5	6–5
1–6	2–6	3–6	4–6	5–6	6–6

Of these thirty-six equipossible cases, only one is favorable (to getting a twelve), so that the probability is thus seen directly to be $\frac{1}{36}$.

The product theorem may be *generalized* to cover the joint occurrence of any number of independent events. Thus if we draw a card from a deck, replace it and draw again, and replace it and draw once more, the event of drawing three spades is the joint occurrence of the event of getting a spade on the first draw, the event of getting a spade on the second draw, and the event of getting a spade on the third draw. Where these three events are designated by "*a*," "*b*," and "*c*," their joint probability P (*a* and *b* and *c*) is equal to the product of the separate probabilities of the three events: $P(a) \times P(b) \times P(c)$. The probability is easily computed. A deck of cards contains fifty-two different cards of which thirteen are spades. There are fifty-two equipossible drawings, of which thirteen are favorable to the event of drawing a spade. The probability of getting a spade is $\frac{13}{52}$ or $\frac{1}{4}$. Since the card drawn is replaced before drawing again, the initial conditions for the second drawing are the same, and so $P(a)$, $P(b)$, and $P(c)$ are all equal to $\frac{1}{4}$. Their joint occurrence has the probability P (*a* and *b* and *c*) $= \frac{1}{4} \times \frac{1}{4} \times \frac{1}{4} = \frac{1}{64}$. The *general product theorem* allows us to compute the probability of the joint occurrence of any number of independent events. Next we turn to events which are *not* independent.

It is frequently possible to compute the probability of the joint occurrence of several events even when they are not completely independent. In the previous example, if the card drawn is *not* replaced in the deck before the next drawing, the outcome of the earlier drawings *does* have an effect on the outcome of the later drawings. If the first card drawn is a spade, then for the second draw there are only twelve spades left among a total of fifty-one cards, whereas if the first card is *not* a spade, then there are thirteen spades left among fifty-one cards. Where *a* is the event of drawing a spade from the deck and not replacing it, and *b* is the event of drawing a spade from among the remaining cards, then the probability of *b*, P (*b* if *a*), is $\frac{12}{51}$ or $\frac{4}{17}$. And if both *a* and *b* occur, the third draw will be made from a deck of fifty cards containing only eleven spades. If *c* is this last event, then P (*c* if *a* and *b*) is $\frac{11}{50}$. Thus the probability that all three are spades if three cards are drawn from a deck and not replaced is, according to the product theorem, $\frac{13}{52} \times \frac{12}{51} \times \frac{11}{50}$, or $\frac{11}{850}$. This is *less* than the probability of getting three spades in three draws when the cards drawn are replaced before drawing again, which was to be expected, since replacing a spade enhances the probability of getting a spade on the next draw.

Another example of the joint probability of dependent events may help make the method clearer. Suppose we have an urn which contains two white balls and one black ball. If two balls are drawn in succession, the first one *not* being replaced before drawing the second, what is the probability that both balls drawn will be white? Let a be the event of drawing a white ball on the first draw. There are three equipossible draws, one for each ball. Of these, two are favorable, since two of the balls are white. The probability of getting a white ball on the first draw, $P(a)$, is therefore $\frac{2}{3}$. If a occurs, then there remain only two balls in the urn, one white and one black. The probability of getting a white ball on the second draw, which event we may call "b," is clearly $\frac{1}{2}$; that is, $P(b \text{ if } a) = \frac{1}{2}$. Now by the general product theorem, the probability of getting two white balls is the probability of the joint occurrence of a and b if a, and this is the product of the probabilities of their separate occurrences, $\frac{2}{3} \times \frac{1}{2} = \frac{1}{3}$. The general formula here is

$$P(a \text{ and } b) = P(a) \times P(b \text{ if } a).$$

The probability of getting two white balls in two such successive draws can be reached, in this simple situation, by considering all possible cases. Where one white ball is designated by "W_1" and the other white ball by "W_2" and the black ball by "B," the following equipossible pairs of draws may be listed:

First Draw	Second Draw
W_1	W_2
W_1	B
W_2	W_1
W_2	B
B	W_1
B	W_2

Of these six equipossible events, two are favorable (the first and third); this gives $\frac{1}{3}$ directly as the probability of getting two white balls in two successive draws with no replacement made.

EXERCISES

1. What is the probability of getting tails every time in three tosses of a coin?
2. What is the probability of getting three aces in three successive draws from a deck of cards: (a) if the card drawn is replaced before making the next drawing; (b) if the cards drawn are not replaced?
3. An urn contains twenty-seven white balls and forty black balls. What is the probability of getting four black balls in four successive drawings: (a) if each ball drawn is replaced before making the next drawing; (b) if the balls are not replaced?
4. What is the probability of rolling three dice so that the total number of points which appear on their top faces is three, three times in a row?
5. Four men whose houses are built around a square spend an evening celebrating in the center of the square. At the end of the celebration each staggers off to one of the houses, no two going to the same house. What is the probability that each one reached his own house?
6. A dentist has his office in a building with five entrances, all equally accessible. Three patients arrive at his office at the same time. What is the probability that they all entered the building by the same door?
7. Suppose that the probability that a man of twenty-five will survive his fiftieth birthday is .742, and that the probability that a woman of twenty-two will survive her forty-seventh birthday is .801. Suppose further that the probability that a marriage contracted by such a couple will not end in divorce is .902. What is the probability that such a couple will live to celebrate their silver wedding?
8. In each of two closets there are three cartons. Five of the cartons contain canned vegetables. The other carton contains canned fruits: ten cans of pears, eight cans of peaches, and six cans of fruit cocktail. Each can of fruit cocktail contains three hundred chunks of fruit of approximately equal size, of which three are cherries. If a child goes into one of the closets, unpacks one of the cartons, opens a can and eats two pieces of its contents, what is the probability that he will enjoy two cherries?

9. A player at draw poker holds the seven of spades and the eight, nine, ten, and ace of diamonds. Aware that all the other players are drawing three cards, he figures that any hand he could win with a flush he could also win with a straight. For which should he draw?

10. How would you distribute fifty white balls and fifty black balls in two urns so as to maximize the probability that a random drawing of one ball from each urn would yield two white balls?

2. **Alternative Occurrences.** The preceding discussion dealt with complex events constituted by the joint occurrence of two or more component events. Some events whose probability it may be desired to compute are of a different sort. These may be constituted by the occurrence of one or more of several alternative events. For example, in tossing two coins, we may be interested not in the event of getting two heads but in the event of getting *either* two heads or two tails. These component events, one of getting two heads, the other of getting two tails, are *exclusive* events, that is, they cannot both occur. The formula for computing the probability of a complex event which is said to occur when either of two *mutually exclusive* events occurs is:

$$P(a \text{ or } b) = P(a) + P(b)$$

That is, the probability that at least one of two mutually exclusive events occurs is the *sum* of their separate probabilities. Since the probability of getting two heads is ¼ and the probability of getting two tails is ¼, and since these are exclusive possibilities, the probability of getting *either* two heads or two tails is ¼ + ¼ = ½. This result may also be obtained, in this simple case, by considering that the four equipossible events which could occur when two coins are tossed are *H–H, H–T, T–H, T–T,* of which two, the first and fourth, are favorable to the event of getting either two heads or two tails. Here direct inspection shows the probability to be ½.

The *addition theorem* stated in the preceding paragraph obviously generalizes to the case of any number of exclusive alternative events. The product theorem and the addition theorem may be used together to compute the probabilities of complex events. Consider the problem of computing the probability of being dealt a flush in a poker game (a *flush* consists of five cards all of the same suit). There are four exclusive alternatives here: the event of getting five spades, the event of getting five hearts, the event of getting five diamonds, the event of getting five clubs. The probability of getting five spades, according to the product theorem for dependent probabilities, is $^{13}\!/_{52} \times {}^{12}\!/_{51} \times {}^{11}\!/_{50} \times {}^{10}\!/_{49} \times {}^{9}\!/_{48} = {}^{33}\!/_{66,640}$. Each of the other exclusive alternatives has the same probability, so the probability of getting a flush is ${}^{33}\!/_{66,640} + {}^{33}\!/_{66,640} + {}^{33}\!/_{66,640} + {}^{33}\!/_{66,640} = {}^{33}\!/_{16,660}$.

One more example will be considered. In drawing one ball from each of two urns, one containing two white balls and four black balls, the other containing three white balls and nine black balls, what is the probability of getting two balls of the same color? The event in whose probability we are interested is the alternative occurrence of two mutually exclusive events, one that of getting two white balls, the other that of getting two black balls. Their probabilities are to be computed separately and then added. The probability of getting two white balls is $^{2}\!/_{6} \times {}^{3}\!/_{12} = {}^{1}\!/_{12}$. And the probability of getting two black balls is $^{4}\!/_{6} \times {}^{9}\!/_{12} = {}^{1}\!/_{2}$. So the probability of getting two balls of the same color is $^{1}\!/_{12} + {}^{1}\!/_{2} = {}^{7}\!/_{12}$.

The addition theorem applies only when the alternative events are mutually exclusive. It may, however, be required to compute the probabilities of complex events which are constituted by the occurrence of at least one of two or more alternatives which are *not* mutually exclusive. For example, what is the probability of getting at least one head on two tosses of a coin? Here we know that the probability of getting a head on the first toss is $^{1}\!/_{2}$, and the probability of getting a head on the second toss is also $^{1}\!/_{2}$; but the sum of these probabilities is 1, or certainty, and it is *not* certain that at least one toss will yield a head, since both may yield tails. The point here is that the two events are *not exclusive;* both may occur. In computing the probability of the alternative occurrence of non-exclusive events, the addition theorem is *not directly applicable.* There are, however, two methods that can be used in computing probabilities of this type.

The first method of computing the probability that at least one of two non-exclusive events will occur requires that we break down or analyze the favorable cases into exclusive events. In the problem of finding the probability that at least one head will appear in two tosses of a coin, the equipossible cases are *H–H, H–T, T–H, T–T.* These are all mutually exclusive, and each of them has the probability $\frac{1}{4}$. The first three are favorable, that is, if any one of the first three occurs it will be true that at least one head appears in the two tosses. Hence the probability of getting at least one head is equal to the sum of the separate probabilities of all of the mutually exclusive favorable cases, which is $\frac{1}{4} + \frac{1}{4} + \frac{1}{4} = \frac{3}{4}$.

The other method of computing the probability that at least one of two non-exclusive events will occur depends upon the fact that *no case can be both favorable and unfavorable,* and the fact that *every case must be either favorable or unfavorable.* If "*a*" designates an event, say the event of getting at least one head on two tosses of a coin, then we shall use the notation "*ā*" to designate the event *unfavorable* to *a,* that is, the event of not getting any head at all on two tosses of the coin. Since no case can be both favorable and unfavorable, *a* and *ā* are *mutually exclusive,* that is, *a* and *ā* cannot possibly both occur. And since every case must be either favorable or unfavorable, it is certain that either *a* or *ā* must occur. Since zero is the probability coefficient we assign to an event which we believe to be impossible, and one is the probability coefficient assigned to an event which is certain to occur, the following two equations are true:

$$P(a \text{ and } \bar{a}) = 0;$$
$$P(a \text{ or } \bar{a}) = 1;$$

where P (a and $\bar{a}$) is the probability that a and $\bar{a}$ will both occur, and P (a or $\bar{a}$) is the probability that either a or $\bar{a}$ will occur. Since a and $\bar{a}$ are mutually exclusive, the addition theorem is applicable, and we have

$$P(a \text{ or } \bar{a}) = P(a) + P(\bar{a})$$

The last two equations combine to give

$$P(a) + P(\bar{a}) = 1$$

which yields

$$P(a) = 1 - P(\bar{a}).$$

Hence we can compute the probability of an event's occurrence by computing the probability that the event will *not* occur and subtracting that figure from 1. Applied to the event of tossing at least one head in two tosses of a coin, we can easily see that the only case in which the event does *not* occur is when both tosses result in tails. This is the unfavorable case, and by the product theorem, its probability is $\frac{1}{2} \times \frac{1}{2} = \frac{1}{4}$, whence the probability that the event of getting at least one head in two tosses *does* occur is $1 - \frac{1}{4} = \frac{3}{4}$.

Another illustration of an event which is composed of alternative but non-exclusive occurrences is this. If one ball is drawn from each of two urns, the first containing two white balls and four black balls, the second containing three white balls and nine black balls, what is the probability of getting at least one white ball? This problem can be solved in either of the two ways discussed in the two previous paragraphs. We can divide the favorable cases into mutually exclusive alternatives. These are: a white ball from the first urn and a black ball from the second, a black ball from the first urn and a white ball from the second, and a white ball from both urns. The respective probabilities of these three are: $\frac{2}{6} \times \frac{9}{12} = \frac{1}{4}$, $\frac{4}{6} \times \frac{3}{12} = \frac{1}{6}$, and $\frac{2}{6} \times \frac{3}{12} = \frac{1}{12}$. Then the addition theorem for exclusive alternatives gives us $\frac{1}{4} + \frac{1}{6} + \frac{1}{12} = \frac{1}{2}$ as the probability of getting at least one white ball. The other method is somewhat

simpler. The unfavorable case in which the draw does not result in at least one white ball is the event of getting two black
balls. The probability of getting two black balls is $\frac{4}{6} \times \frac{9}{12} =$
$\frac{1}{2}$, so the probability of getting at least one white ball is $1 - \frac{1}{2}$
$= \frac{1}{2}$.

Let us now attempt to work out a moderately complicated
problem in probability. The game of craps is played with two
dice. The *shooter,* who rolls the dice, wins if a seven or an
eleven turns up on his first roll, but loses if a two, or three, or
twelve turn up on his first roll. If one of the remaining numbers,
four, five, six, eight, nine, or ten turns up on his first roll, the
shooter continues to roll the dice until either that same number
turns up again, in which case he wins, or a seven appears, in
which case he loses. The problem can be posed: What is the
probability that the shooter will win? First of all, let us obtain
the probabilities that the various numbers will occur. There are
thirty-six different equipossible ways for two dice to fall. Only
one of these ways will show a two, so the probability here is
$\frac{1}{36}$. Only one of these ways will show a twelve, so here the probability is also $\frac{1}{36}$. There are two ways to throw a three, 1–2 and
2–1, so the probability of a three is $\frac{2}{36}$. Similarly, the probability of getting an eleven is $\frac{2}{36}$. There are three ways to throw a
four: 1–3, 2–2, and 3–1, so the probability of a four is $\frac{3}{36}$.
Similarly, the probability of getting a ten is $\frac{3}{36}$. Since there are
four ways to roll a five: 1–4, 2–3, 3–2, and 4–1, its probability is
$\frac{4}{36}$, and this is also the probability of getting a nine. A six can
be obtained in any one of five ways: 1–5, 2–4, 3–3, 4–2, and 5–1,
so the probability of getting a six is $\frac{5}{36}$; and the same probability exists for an eight. There are six different combinations that
yield seven: 1–6, 2–5, 3–4, 4–3, 5–2, and 6–1, so the probability
of rolling a seven is $\frac{6}{36}$.

The probability that the shooter will win on his first roll is
the sum of the probability that he gets a seven and the prob-
ability that he gets an eleven, which is $\frac{6}{36} + \frac{2}{36} = \frac{8}{36}$ or $\frac{2}{9}$.
The probability that he will lose on his first roll is the sum
of the probabilities of getting a two, a three, and a twelve,

which is $\frac{1}{36} + \frac{2}{36} + \frac{1}{36} = \frac{4}{36}$ or $\frac{1}{9}$. The shooter is twice as likely to *win on his first roll* as to *lose on his first roll;* however, he is most likely not to do either on his first roll, but to get a four, five, six, eight, nine, or ten. If he throws one of these six numbers, he is obliged to continue rolling the dice until he gets that number again, in which case he wins, or until he gets a seven, in which case he loses. Those cases in which neither the number first thrown nor a seven occurs can be ignored, for they are not decisive. Suppose the shooter gets a four on his first roll. The next *decisive* roll will show either a four or a seven. In a decisive roll, the equipossible cases are the three combinations that make up a four (1–3, 2–2, 3–1) and the six combinations that make up a seven. The probability of throwing a second four is therefore $\frac{3}{9}$. The probability of getting a four on his first roll was $\frac{3}{36}$, so the probability of winning by throwing a four on the first roll and then getting another four before a seven occurs is $\frac{3}{36} \times \frac{3}{9} = \frac{1}{36}$. Similarly, the probability of the shooter winning by throwing a ten on his first roll and then getting another ten before a seven occurs is also $\frac{3}{36} \times \frac{3}{9} = \frac{1}{36}$.

By the same line of reasoning, we can find the probability of the shooter winning by throwing a five on his first roll and then getting another before getting a seven. In this case, there are ten equipossible cases for the decisive roll: the four ways to make a five (1–4, 2–3, 3–2, 4–1), and the six ways to make a seven. The probability of winning with a five is therefore $\frac{4}{36} \times \frac{4}{10} = \frac{2}{45}$. The probability of winning with a nine is also $\frac{2}{45}$. The number six is still more likely to occur on the first roll, its probability being $\frac{5}{36}$. And it is more likely than the others mentioned to occur a second time before a seven appears, the probability here being $\frac{5}{11}$. So the probability of winning with a six is $\frac{5}{36} \times \frac{5}{11} = \frac{25}{396}$. And again similarly, the probability of winning with an eight is $\frac{25}{396}$.

There are eight different ways for the shooter to win. If he throws a seven or eleven on his first roll he wins. If he throws one of the six numbers four, five, six, eight, nine, or ten on his first roll *and* throws it again before getting a seven, then he wins also. These ways are all exclusive; so the total probability of the shooter's winning is the sum of the probabilities of the alternative ways in which he can win, and this is $\frac{6}{36} + \frac{2}{36} + \frac{1}{36} + \frac{2}{45} + \frac{25}{396} + \frac{25}{396} + \frac{2}{45} + \frac{1}{36} = \frac{244}{495}$. Expressed as a decimal fraction, this is .493 —, which shows that in a crap game the shooter has less than an even chance of winning—only slightly less, to be sure, but still less than .500.

EXERCISES

1. Calculate the shooter's chances of winning in a crap game by the second method, that is, compute the chances of his losing, and subtract it from 1.

2. In drawing three cards in succession from a standard deck, what is the probability of getting at least one spade: (a) if each card is replaced before making the next drawing; (b) if the cards drawn are not replaced?

3. What is the probability of getting at least one head in three tosses of a coin?

4. If three balls are selected at random from an urn containing five red, ten white, and fifteen blue balls, what is the probability that they will all be the same color: (a) if each ball is replaced before the next one is withdrawn; (b) if the balls selected are not replaced?

5. If someone offers to bet you even money that you will not throw an ace on any one of three successive throws of a die, should you accept the bet?

6. From a piggy bank containing three quarters, two dimes, five nickels, and eleven pennies, two coins are shaken out. What is the probability that their total value amounts to exactly:

   (a) 50¢? (b) 35¢? (c) 30¢? (d) 26¢? (e) 20¢?
   (f) 15¢? (g) 11¢? (h) 10¢? (i) 6¢?   (j) only 2¢?

7. If the probability that a man of twenty-five will survive his fiftieth birthday is .742, and the probability that a woman of twenty-two will survive her forty-seventh birthday is .801, and such a man and woman marry, what is the probability: (a) that at least one of them lives at least another twenty-five years;

(b) that only one of them lives at least another twenty-five years?

8. One partly filled case contains two bottles of root beer, four bottles of coke, and four bottles of beer; another partly filled case contains three bottles of root beer, seven cokes, and two beers. A case is opened at random and a bottle selected at random from it. What is the probability that it contains a soft drink? Had all the bottles been in one case, what is the probability that a bottle selected at random from it would contain a soft drink?

9. A player in a draw poker game is dealt three jacks and two small odd cards. He discards the latter and draws two cards. What is the probability that he improves his hand on the draw?

10. Remove all cards except aces and kings from a deck, so that only eight cards remain, of which four are aces and four are kings. From this abbreviated deck, deal two cards to a friend. If he looks at his cards and announces (truthfully) that his hand contains an ace, what is the probability that both his cards are aces? If he announces instead that one of his cards is the ace of spades, what is the probability then that both his cards are aces? (These two probabilities are *not* the same!)

3. Expectation or Expected Value. In placing bets or in making investments, it is important to consider not only the probability of winning or receiving a return, but *how much* can be won on the bet or returned on the investment. The *safest* investment is not always the best one to make, nor is the one which promises the greatest return *if* it succeeds. In order to compare bets or investments, the notion of *expectation* or *expected value* has been introduced. An example or two will serve to illustrate how these terms are used.

If a coin is tossed and an even money bet of, say, one dollar is placed on heads, the dollar wagered may be thought of as a purchase price. What it purchases is a certain *expectation*, or *expected value*. If heads appears, then the bettor receives two dollars (one is his own, the other is his winnings). If tails appears, then the bettor receives no return, or a return of zero dollars. The two events (heads appearing, tails appearing) are the only two possible outcomes, and there is a certain *return*

associated with each. The probability that heads will appear is
$\frac{1}{2}$, and there is the same probability of $\frac{1}{2}$ that tails will appear. If we multiply the return yielded on each possible outcome by the probability that that possible outcome will be realized, the sum of all such products is the expectation or expected value of the bet or investment. The expected value of a dollar bet that heads will appear when a coin is tossed is thus equal to $(\frac{1}{2} \times \$2) + (\frac{1}{2} \times \$0)$ which is one dollar. In this case, as is well known, the odds are even, which means that the expected value of the purchase is equal to the purchase price.

The game of chuck-a-luck, often called "crown and anchor," is a good illustration of the disparity between the price and the expected value of most purchases made in gambling casinos. The patron makes his bet by placing his money on one or more of six squares which are numbered "1" through "6." Three dice are tossed—usually inside an hour-glass shaped cage—and the "house" pays off each bet according to how many dice show the number on which the bet was made. If all three dice show the number 4, then a dollar bet on 4 would win three dollars; if only two showed 4, a dollar on 4 would win two dollars; if only one of the dice showed 4, a dollar on 4 would win one dollar; while if none of the dice showed a 4, the dollar bet on 4 would be lost. These are the returns associated with each outcome. A dollar bet on any single number is the purchase price of the expectation described. What is that expectation worth? There are four different possible outcomes, but they have very different probabilities. For definiteness, let us say that one dollar is bet on 4. The probability that all three dice show the number 4 is $\frac{1}{6} \times \frac{1}{6} \times \frac{1}{6} = \frac{1}{216}$. The probability that exactly two dice show the number 4 is $(\frac{1}{6} \times \frac{1}{6} \times \frac{5}{6}) + (\frac{1}{6} \times \frac{5}{6} \times \frac{1}{6}) + (\frac{5}{6} \times \frac{1}{6} \times \frac{1}{6}) = \frac{15}{216}$. The probability that just a single one of the dice will show a 4 is $(\frac{1}{6} \times \frac{5}{6} \times \frac{5}{6}) + (\frac{5}{6} \times \frac{1}{6} \times \frac{5}{6}) + (\frac{5}{6} \times \frac{5}{6} \times \frac{1}{6}) = \frac{75}{216}$. The probability that none of the dice will show a 4 is $\frac{5}{6} \times \frac{5}{6} \times \frac{5}{6} = \frac{125}{216}$. The returns to the bettor on each of these outcomes are \$4, \$3, \$2, and \$0, respectively. The expected vaue of his bet is then equal to the sum of the products of the return on each possible outcome and the probability of that outcome; in this case it is $(\frac{1}{216} \times \$4) + (\frac{15}{216} \times \$3) + (\frac{75}{216} \times \$2) + (\frac{125}{216} \times \$0) = \$^{199}\!/_{216}$ or approximately 92 cents. This means that of every such dollar bet, almost 8 cents is a gift to the "house."

Some gamblers, in playing chuck-a-luck, try to beat the game by placing bets on more than one number, in the belief that this increases their chances of winning. Suppose you break your dollar and bet fifty cents each on the numbers 3 and 4. The greatest possible return is obtained when the dice show either two 3's and a 4 or two 4's and a 3; in either case you receive $2.50—which includes your own dollar, of course. Each of these two cases has a probability of $\frac{3}{216}$. If all three dice show 4's, the return is only $2, since the 50¢ bet on 3 is lost. The probability here is also $\frac{1}{216}$, as it is for three 3's, which yields the same return. Curiously enough, an equal return is obtained when one of the dice shows 3, a second shows 4, and the third some other number. The probability here is easily verified to be $\frac{24}{216}$. If exactly two of the dice show 3 and the other one some number other than 4, the return is $1.50; the probability that this will happen is $\frac{12}{216}$. The same return and the same probability attach to the event of two of the dice showing 4 and the other some number other than 3. If a single 4 turns up, and no 3 at all, the return is $1; the probability that this happens is $\frac{48}{216}$. The same return and the same probability attach to the event of a single 3 turning up, and no 4 at all. Since any other possible outcome results in a zero return, we need not bother to compute the probability here. What is the expectation purchased for a dollar spent on two fifty cent bets on different numbers at chuck-a-luck? It is the sum of the following products: $(\frac{3}{216} \times \$2.50) + (\frac{3}{216} \times \$2.50) + (\frac{1}{216} \times \$2.00) + (\frac{1}{216} \times \$2.00) + (\frac{24}{216} \times \$2.00) + (\frac{12}{216} \times \$1.50) + (\frac{12}{216} \times \$1.50) + (\frac{48}{216} \times \$1.00) + (\frac{48}{216} \times \$1.00) = \$^{199}\!/_{216}$ or again approximately 92¢. True enough, there are more chances of winning by dividing a dollar bet between two numbers, but the *amounts* which can be won are sufficiently smaller to keep the

expectation constant. In either case the expected value is almost
8¢ less than the purchase price, the difference being the patron's
contribution to the casino's overhead—and profit.

It is sometimes argued that in a game in which there are even
money stakes to be awarded on the basis of approximately equi-
probable alternatives, such as tossing a coin or betting black
versus red on a roulette wheel, one can be *sure to win* by
making the same bet consistently—always heads, or always
black, say—and doubling the amount of money wagered after
each loss. Thus if I bet one dollar on heads, and tails show,
then I should bet heads again to the tune of two dollars. If tails
show again, my next bet—also on heads—should be four dollars, and so on. One cannot fail to win by following this procedure, because extended runs are highly improbable; the longest run must *sometimes* end—and when it does, the man who
has pyramided or continued to double his bets will be money
ahead!

What is wrong with this theory? Why need anyone work for
a living, when we can all adopt this foolproof system of winning
at the gaming table? We can ignore the fact that the usual gaming house has an upper limit on the size of the wager it will accept, and focus our attention on the real fallacy contained in the
prescription. Although a long run of tails, say, is almost certain
to end sooner or later, it may end later rather than sooner. An
adverse run *may* last long enough to exhaust any finite amount
of money the bettor may have to play. To be certain of being
able to continue doubling his bet each time, no matter how
long the adverse run may continue, the bettor would have to
begin with an infinite amount of money. But of course a player
with an infinite amount of money could not possibly win—in
the sense of increasing his wealth. Such a case is too fanciful,
anyway; let us confine our discussion to a player who has only
a fixed, finite amount of money to lose. For definiteness, we
may suppose that he has decided in advance how long he will
play: if he is resolved to play until all his money is gone, then
he is bound to lose all his money, sooner or later (provided that

the house has sufficient funds to cover all of his bets, of course) ; while if he is resolved to play until he wins some antecedently specified amount, the game might go on forever with the player never either reaching his goal or going broke.

For the sake of simplicity, suppose a player begins with just $3, so that he is prepared to sustain just one loss: two in a row would wipe him out. Let him decide to bet just twice, and consider the different possible outcomes. The $3 is his purchase price; what is the expectation purchased? If two heads come up in a row, the player, winning $1 on each, will get a return of $5. If there is a head first and then a tail, the return will be just $3. If there is a tail first and then a head, having lost $1 on the first toss and having bet $2 on the second, which won, the player's return will be $4. Finally, two tails will wipe him out, yielding a return of $0. Each of these events has a probability of ¼, so the expected value is (¼ × $5) + (¼ × $3) + (¼ × $4) = $3. The player's expectation is no greater when he uses the doubling technique than when he risks his entire capital on one toss of a coin.

Let us make a different supposition, that the same player decides to play three times (if his money holds out) so that with luck he can double his money. The eight possible outcomes can be listed in the form of a table:

First toss	Second toss	Third toss	Return	Probability
H	H	H	$6	⅛
H	H	T	$4	⅛
H	T	H	$5	⅛
H	T	T	$1	⅛
T	H	H	$5	⅛
T	H	T	$3	⅛
T	T	H	$0	⅛
T	T	T	$0	⅛

The expectation on this new strategy remains the same, still $3.

Let us consider just one more aspect of the doubling technique. Suppose the same man wants to win just a single dollar, which means that he will play until he wins just once or else goes broke. With this more modest aim, what is the probable value of his investment? If heads appears on the first toss, the return is $4 (the $1 won and the original stake of $3) and having won his dollar, the man stops playing. If tails appears on the first toss, $2 is bet on the second. If heads appears, the return is $4, and the player quits with his winnings. If tails appears, the return is $0, and the player quits because he has lost all his money. There are only these three possible outcomes, the first of which has a probability of ½, the second ¼, and the third ¼. Such a player, following such a strategy, is three times as likely to win as to lose. But of course he can lose three times as much as he can win by this method. The expected value is: (½ × $4) + (¼ × $4) + (¼ × $0) = $3. The expectation is not increased at all by following the doubling technique. The *chances of winning* are increased, just as by betting on more numbers at chuck-a-luck or roulette, but the *amount* which can be won decreases rapidly enough to keep the *expected value constant*.

EXERCISES

1. What is the expected value of a wager which consists of betting one dollar each on the numbers 1, 2, and 3 at chuck-a-luck?
2. What is the expected value of a wager which consists of betting one dollar on all six numbers at chuck-a-luck?
3. At most crap tables in gambling houses, the house will give odds of six to one against rolling a 4 the "hard way," that is, with a pair of 2's as contrasted with a 3 and a 1, which is the "easy way." A bet made on a "hard way" 4 wins if a pair of 2's show before either a 7 is rolled or a 4 is made the "easy way," otherwise it loses. What is the expectation purchased by a dollar bet on a "hard way" 4?
4. If the odds are eight to one against rolling an 8 the "hard way" (that is, with two 4's), what is the expectation purchased by a dollar bet on a "hard way" 8?
5. What expectation does a man with $15 have who bets on heads,

beginning with a $1 bet, and uses the doubling technique, if he resolves to play just four times and quit?

6. On the basis of past performance, the probability that the favorite will win the Bellevue Handicap is .46, while there is a probability of only .1 that a certain dark horse will win. If the favorite pays even money and the odds offered are eight to one against the dark horse, which is the better bet?

7. If one hundred dollars invested in the preferred stock of a certain company will yield a return of one hundred ten dollars with a probability of .85, while the probability is only .67 that the same amount invested in common stock will yield a return of one hundred forty dollars, which is the better investment?

8. A punchboard has a thousand holes, one containing a number which pays five dollars, five containing numbers which pay two dollars each, and ten containing numbers which pay one dollar each. What is the expected value of a punch which costs five cents?

9. An investor satisfies himself that a certain region contains radio-active deposits, which may be either plutonium or uranium. For five hundred dollars he can obtain an option which will permit him to determine which element is present and to enjoy the proceeds from its extraction and sale. If only plutonium is present he will lose four-fifths of his option money, while if uranium is present he will enjoy a return of forty thousand dollars. If there is only one chance in a hundred that uranium is present, what is the expected value of the option?

10. Before the last card is dealt in a stud poker game, a man who has the ace and king of spades and the six of diamonds showing bets the limit of two dollars. You are certain that he has an ace or a king in the hole, while your hand consists of the three and five of hearts and the four and six of clubs. No other player calls. If you are certain that your opponent will check and call a two dollar bet after the last card is dealt, how much money must there be in the pot for your call to be worth two dollars?

Special Symbols

Index